Also by Stanley Edgar Hyman

ESSAYS

AND

REVIEWS

1942-1962

The

KENT. *Is this the promised end?*
EDGAR. *Or image of that horror?*

Promised End

814

by STANLEY EDGAR HYMAN

CLEVELAND AND NEW YORK

THE WORLD PUBLISHING COMPANY

"The Dialectic of Christianity" first appeared in *Culture in History*, edited by Stanley Diamond, which was published by Columbia University Press in 1961, and is reprinted with their permission.

"The Symbols of Folk Culture" is reprinted with the permission of the copyright holder, The Conference on Science, Philosophy and Religion in Their Relation to the Democratic Way of Life, Incorporated, and was written for its thirteenth symposium volume, *Symbols and Values: An Initial Study*, published in New York City, in 1954.

Acknowledgment is made to the American Folklore Society, Inc., for permission to reprint from the *Journal of American Folklore* a review of the *Standard Dictionary of Folklore*, July-September 1951; "The Ritual View of Myth and the Mythic," October-December 1955; a review of two books on the Dead Sea Scrolls, October-December 1956; and "The Child Ballad in America: Some Aesthetic Criteria," July-September 1957. Copyright 1951, 1955, 1956, 1957 by the American Folklore Society, Inc.

"Some Trends in the Novel" appeared in the October, 1958, *College English*. Copyright, 1958, by the National Council of Teachers of English and reprinted with permission.

Published by The World Publishing Company
2231 West 110th Street, Cleveland 2, Ohio

Published simultaneously in Canada by
Nelson, Foster & Scott Ltd.

Library of Congress Catalog Card Number: 63-18586

FIRST EDITION

HC963

TO KENNETH BURKE

Contents

Preface

THESE TWENTY-ODD essays and reviews, all of which appeared in magazines between 1942 and 1962, are the record of a self-education. Rereading one's scattered and occasional writings can be a chastening experience, and deciding what to reprint and what to omit requires a degree of objectivity from the critic that he is more likely to demonstrate on the work of others than on his own tender sprouts. I have included only those essays that seem to me to retain their interest today, and only those reviews that discuss important general issues transcending the books involved.

Rereading my work with that hard objective eye, as though it were the work of someone else, I can now see that too much of what I have had to say over the years has been tied to reviews, sometimes of the most trivial books, and that quite a lot of it has been put negatively. A review-essay form that I used frequently now seems to me to have been a very roundabout way of operating. Its first section would publicly execute a dozen worthless books; its second section would generalize the sad state of affairs in that area; and its third section would propose my beautiful alternative. I have not included these review-essays, except to reprint the third sections in two cases.

The arrangement here is chronological only within groupings by topic, which tends to obscure the shift in my ambitions and preoccupations over the years. The essays of the forties are concerned with American literature and civilization; in the early fifties, the focus is on folk literature; then psychology, anthropology, even theology are raided; finally there is a more general and better-informed interest in the relationship of literature to the culture. A stridency or shrillness of tone reaches a height in 1949, as though the author of those pieces (I can hardly recognize him as myself) really despaired of it all; after that the tone grows more genial, and may now even seem benign.

What unity these essays have is the unity of my own sensibility, as it performs the varied acts of criticism. Beyond that the essays have a few common themes that never disappear: the ritual origins of myth; the importance of a true folk tradition for art; the tragic vision; literature as secular salvation and redemption; the painful difficulty of being a writer in America. Because of these changeless concerns, the book is often repetitive, with the same slogans and examples recurring in a variety of contexts. All that an author can do in such a case is hope that he has at least achieved repetition with variation, which ought to be as legitimate a form in literary criticism as in music.

It is disappointing to realize how few of these essays are about great literature. There are a number of reasons for this: an early preoccupation with the American and the contemporary; an inadequate command of foreign languages; an uneasy feeling that there is little new to say about the great works, or that one cannot compete with the specialists in them. Nevertheless, huff and puff as I may, I am now teaching Homer and Virgil, Greek tragedy and the Bible, Shakespeare and Milton. The next collection of essays may look quite different.

In selecting and editing these pieces I have been primarily concerned with producing a book, not a scrapbook. The field with which I have been most engaged in other books, the criticism of literary criticism, is not represented here. It seems to me that those essays and reviews have a specialized context, and someday they may go into a revision of *The Armed Vision* or a sequel to it. None of my *New Leader* reviews has been included, in the hope that they too will eventually make a book of their own.

In editing I have corrected errors of fact and style, where I can recognize them. I have not corrected opinions, even when they are manifestly absurd, like the 1946 statement that Henry Thoreau and perhaps Abraham Lincoln were the only first-rate American prose stylists. I have added a few 1963 afternotes, recording the occasion of writing, or controversy produced by a piece, or my present disagreements with it. In a few cases I have changed titles that appeared in magazines, or added material written at the time that for one reason or another was not printed then. I have as much as possible refrained from giving any piece a 1963 look, but it is my hope that the book as a whole, as an outspoken and honest record of discovery and self-discovery, has its justification in 1963.

These essays and reviews have appeared in *Accent, The American Scholar, The Atlantic Monthly, College English, Commentary, Harper's, The Hudson Review, The Journal of American Folklore, The Kenyon Review, The Massachusetts Review, New Mexico Quarterly, The New Republic, Partisan Review, The Saturday Evening Post*, and *The Western Review*. Others have appeared in symposia: *Culture for the Millions?, Culture in History: Essays in Honor of Paul Radin*, and *Symbols and Values: An Initial Study*. All are reprinted here through the kindness of the editors.

My personal indebtedness to friends, colleagues, and students who have educated me over two decades, and advised on many of these pieces when they were written, cannot be individually acknowledged. It is here collectively acknowledged with gratitude. One of the greatest of my debts is inadequately repaid in the dedication. Aaron Asher and the staff at The World Publishing Company have been enormously helpful and encouraging. Barbara Karmiller assisted in the selection, and generously copyread the entire manuscript. Once again my beloved wife, Shirley Jackson, has helped beyond the possibilities of acknowledgment.

STANLEY EDGAR HYMAN

North Bennington, Vermont
June 1963

Images of
the American
Writer

John Steinbeck:
Of Invertebrates
and Men

[1942]

WHEN ONE OF AMERICA's foremost novelists, a man whose last novel was a whopping success in terms of laurel as well as gravy, sits down to collaborate with the director of the Pacific Biological Laboratories on a semiscientific account of a trip studying the marine fauna in the Gulf of California,[1] something is cooking. The two unavoidable questions for a reviewer are, Why did he write it? and What good is it? and both answers turn out more complicated than you might think.

There have been many guesses as to why Steinbeck wrote it, ranging from his desperate search for a new form for every work (this is the one that appealed to the reviewers) to any writer's normal desire to convert a vacation trip that cost him money into a few bucks in royalties (this is the one the reviewers never mention). But the principal reason for the book may be stated in a sentence, and it is the key to much of Steinbeck's work. John Steinbeck, simply enough, dislikes literature and feels the breathless veneration for science of a small boy peeking in through a laboratory window. The contempt that writers express for their own trade is not a new thing, and the pages of literature are full of bitter and

[1] *Sea of Cortez,* by John Steinbeck and Edward F. Ricketts.

17

distorted self-portraits: Shakespeare's Iago, who moved men with the dramatist's weapons; Mann's long series of literary men, sick with the cancer and perversion of art and humble before any burgher; Hemingway's pale-pink novelists with their whirling catheters. In Shakespeare's case the dichotomy was artist (remember, the playwright in his day classed with mountebanks and vagrants) versus respectable member of society, in Mann's case the same, in Hemingway's case artist versus man of action, and in Steinbeck's case, artist versus scientist.

Steinbeck's work, going as far back as his earliest books, is loaded with symbolic attacks on writers and writing. In his short story "The Snake," a woman comes into a scientist's laboratory and, by her morbid romanticization of a snake's eating a rat, horrifies the scientist who had always seen it as a perfectly natural biologic process. An earlier story in *The Pastures of Heaven* is a rephrasing of the same conflict, so that Raymond Banks's clinical interest in an execution is spoiled for him by Bert Monroe's fictive imagination. Of numerous other examples, the clearest is the story "Johnny Bear," about a character who should rank with Iago in the great gallery of libels on the artist. Johnny Bear is an idiot monster, almost unable to speak, with one remarkable talent: he can reproduce any conversation he hears with phonographic accuracy, in the exact words and voice of the speaker. The rustics use his gift for entertainment, and buy him whiskies for any particularly juicy monologue he brings to the saloon (a lovely picture of the artist and his relation to society!). "He hasn't brains enough to make anything up," someone says of Johnny, "so you know that what he says is what he heard."

What good this book is has thus been partially answered. For Steinbeck, it canalized something that has been bothering him for a long time. For the lay reader, its chief value lies in giving the most elaborate statement so far of Steinbeck's beliefs and ideas, and it is thus an invaluable key to much that was obscure and misinterpreted in his earlier work. Steinbeck has had a paucity of serious critical study anyway. Kenneth Burke has done a masterful analysis of *The Grapes of Wrath*; Edmund Wilson has set up certain ideas that have been generally accepted as The Slant on Steinbeck; and there has been little else.

Wilson's theories are worth discussion, because *Sea of Cortez* might seem to be a complete confirmation of them. Wilson's principal theory is that Steinbeck presents life in animal terms, that his characters are all animals or rudimentary humans: the *paisanos* in *Tortilla Flat* are "amusing guinea pigs or rabbits," the *Grapes of Wrath* people are "lemmings," the people in the stories identify themselves with horses, snakes, and white quail. This is like saying, after reading Caroline Spurgeon's *Shakespeare's Imagery*, that because Shakespeare packed *Hamlet* with images of disease and decay, he thought of all people as diseased. Steinbeck does tend to present life in animal terms, but the animal symbols and images have a very real function that is made clear in *Sea of Cortez*. They are just the simplest examples, not of man, but of the problem that concerns the author most, the problem of ecology, in which man is only a more complex example.

Steinbeck is an ecologist; to use his own definition, "a student of the mutual relationship between organism and environment." Not only is *Sea of Cortez* the record of an ecological study of marine fauna, but all Steinbeck's books are now revealed as ecological studies. *The Grapes of Wrath* was a textbook in ecology, from the dust storms that forced the Okies off their land (unscientific farming and inadequate conservation were a crime against ecology, and dust and drought were the punishment) to the crimes against human ecology that the Associated Farmers sprang on the Joads in California. George in *Of Mice and Men*, in trying to preserve Lennie and hold him to a socially useful pattern, violated ecology (as much as Candy would have had he insisted on saving his useless old dog from being shot) and the punishment was inevitable. Henry Morgan in *The Cup of Gold* violated ecology and was punished, and so on all through the other books and stories. If you disturb the balance you will be destroyed, Steinbeck says, and the fact that this moral is only a new verbalization of the "fate" in the old classic drama is what gives much of his work, particularly *Of Mice and Men*, the rounded inevitability of Greek tragedy. Thus, Edmund Wilson to the contrary, *Of Mice and Men* is not "a parable which criticizes humanity from a nonpolitical point of view" (or not principally), and the title doesn't mean that the utopian social plans of mice and men gang aft agley. It means what it says literally, that this is a book about mice and men: the mice that Lennie loves to pet (including Curley's wife) and the men who live with them in an ecological balance, until it is destroyed by violence (as it was in Burns's poem).

Just as ecology is Steinbeck's baby, teleology, which he defines as "the assumption of predetermined design, purpose or ends in Nature by which an explanation of phenomena is postulated" is the bath water he wants to throw out. Page after page in *Sea of Cortez* is devoted to a rambling philosophizing about teleologies, built up mostly from a heavy personal mysticism and some undigested field and quantum physics, and tied in by such phony devices as, after ten pages of Thoughts, "and all this against the hot beach on an Easter Sunday, with the passing day and the passing time." Teleologies, which assume purpose and causal relationship, are the factors that becloud the scientist, make the understanding of naked ecological behavior more difficult, and annoy Steinbeck so much that he rejects them all: religion, social progress, and George's faith that this time Lennie will do different.

Steinbeck's attitudes toward religion and radicalism have changed a great deal through the course of his work. His early Catholic priests in *The Pastures of Heaven* and *To a God Unknown*, fine and sympathetic men, have been succeeded by the comic characters who sanctify a pig in "St. Katy the Virgin," the foolish and dangerous figures in "The Forgotten Village" who fight germs with a crucifix, and now the teleologists of *Sea of Cortez*. His early heroic radicals of *In Dubious Battle* took on a Christian-martyr "complex" in a later short story called "The Raid," and have now, in *Sea of Cortez*, become collectivists who want to eliminate "the swift, the clever, and the intelligent," and rebels who forget that "while the collective state is free from capitalist domination, it is also free from rebels." It is curious that the high point both these strains reached was their fusion in the character of Jim Casy in *The Grapes of Wrath*, Steinbeck's most sympathetic radical as well as a quite literal modernized Christ (his initials the mystic J. C., his "call" derived from meditation in the wilderness, his last words a curious modern parody of Christ's: "You don' know what you're a-doin' "). Preacher Casy is repudiated by much in the new book.

Sea of Cortez also casts new light on a number of Steinbeck's other stock themes. Human sacrifice, which has always fascinated him and which is the focus of his early mystic novel, *To a God Unknown*, is described here as something which gives primitive peoples their sense of wholeness, and which Steinbeck suspects every whole man requires. Asceticism as a function of a call or mission, a central feature of Henry Morgan in *The Cup of Gold*, George in *Of Mice and Men*, and Tom Joad in *The Grapes of Wrath*, is now repudiated. No longer recognizing any valid call, Steinbeck jests at the ascetic and wallows in the scientist John Xanthus, who found time to leave a whole tribe of Indian bastards, as the proper symbol for the biologist, that "healthy, lecherous tenor of the scientific world." Fertility, the ecological ideal, is now Steinbeck's, and, as he did before in *To a God Unknown*, he raises it to the level of a mystical principle. The superhuman person, another favorite of Steinbeck's (Ma Joad in *The Grapes of Wrath*, Joseph in *To a God Unknown*, Slim in *Of Mice and Men*, and at least one person in almost every book, are explicitly described in superhuman terms), has now been replaced by the scientist, who gets the same sense of all-knowing, mystic oneness with the universe intellectually, like buying it wrapped in cellophane.

One of the arbitrary nuisances in this book is the conscious merging of the collaborators' personalities so that it is almost impossible to tell who wrote what, an important question if one is using the book as a key to Steinbeck's other writing. The only way to solve the puzzle is to assume that anything Steinbeck didn't write he is willing to take responsibility for—or he would not have permitted the editorial "we"—and to pin everything on him. That, unfortunately, makes him responsible for a great deal of pretentious mysticism, a small-boy or Hemingway glory in vulgarity ("We have wondered about the bawdiness this book must have if it is to be true"), and some of the corniest gags on record. On the credit side, the book has many valid and exciting ideas, a full measure of warm and delightful anecdotes (the Swedish tramp sitting in a ditch, ragged and dirty and drunk, saying to himself softly and in wonder, "I am rich and happy and perhaps a little beautiful"), and in spots a lighter, more genuine humor than Steinbeck has ever achieved before.

A good conclusion to an analysis of Steinbeck's whirlwind court-ship of science would be the old gag about marrying in haste and repenting at leisure. As Steinbeck admits in effect, the scientist is only an extension of the writer, and ends up just as disruptive of the ecological balance. "We could not observe a completely objec-tive Sea of Cortez anyway," he says, "for in that lonely and unin-habited Gulf our boat and ourselves would change it the moment we entered." Johnny Bear, unfortunately, can be a symbol for the scientist too, and most particularly for the scientific journalist.

Henry Thoreau

1. Henry Thoreau in Our Time

[1946]

IN JULY, 1945, we celebrated the centennial of Henry David Thoreau's retirement to Walden Pond. Almost twice as many old ladies as usual made the pilgrimage to Concord, to see the shrine containing his furniture, and to Walden, where they had the privilege of adding a rock to the cairn where his hut once stood and of opening a box lunch in the picnic ground that stands as his monument. The American Museum of Natural History staged a Walden Pond exhibit. The *Saturday Evening Post* ran an illustrated article. And to add the final mortuary touch, a professor of English published a slim volume called *Walden Revisited*. All in all, it was a typical American literary centennial. Henry Thoreau would probably not have enjoyed it.

A more significant Thoreau centenary would have been July, 1946, the hundredth anniversary of his going to jail. Every reader of *Walden* knows the story. Thoreau had not paid a poll tax for several years, as a sign that he had renounced his allegiance to a government that protected slavery and made war on Mexico, and one day when he walked into Concord to get a mended shoe from the cobbler he was seized and put into jail. That night the tax was paid for him, and the next morning he was freed, obtained his mended shoe, and went back to the woods to pick some berries for dinner. While he was in jail, placidly meditating on the nature of state coercion, Emerson is supposed to have come by and asked: "Henry, what are you doing in *there*?" to which Thoreau is supposed to have replied: "Waldo, what are *you* doing *out there*?"

It takes not much investigation into the story to discover that the actual details of Thoreau's first great political gesture were largely ridiculous. For one thing, the act itself was both safe and imitative, Bronson Alcott having given Thoreau the idea three years before by refusing to pay his taxes and going to jail, where he was treated quite well. For another, Thoreau in jail seems to have been not at all the philosophic muser he makes himself out to be, but, as the jailer later reported, "mad as the devil." For a third, Emerson certainly engaged in no such pat dialogue with him, for the jailer allowed no visitors, and Emerson's actual reaction to the event was to tell Alcott he thought it was "mean and skulking, and in bad taste." Finally, the person who "interfered" and paid his tax was Thoreau's old Aunt Maria, disguised with a shawl over her head so that Henry would not be angry with her for spoiling his gesture.

Why, then, celebrate the centenary of this absurd event? For only one reason. As a political warrior, Thoreau was a comic little figure with a receding chin, and not enough high style to carry off a gesture. As a political writer, he was the most ringing and magnificent polemicist America has ever produced. Three years later he made an essay called "Civil Disobedience" out of his prison experience, fusing the soft coal of his night in jail into solid diamond. "Civil Disobedience" has all the power and dignity that Thoreau's political act so signally lacked. "Under a government which imprisons any unjustly, the true place for a just man is also a prison," he writes in a line Debs later echoed, ". . . the only home in a slave state in which a free man can abide with honor." "I saw that the State was half-witted, that it was timid as a lone woman with her silver spoons, and that it did not know its friends from its foes, and I lost all my remaining respect for it, and pitied it." He summarizes his position, coolly, reasonably, even humorously, but with utter finality:

> I have never declined paying the highway tax, because I am as desirous of being a good neighbor as I am of being a bad subject; and as for supporting schools, I am doing my part to educate my fellow-countrymen now. It is for no particular item in the tax-bill that I refuse to pay it. I simply wish to refuse allegiance to the State, to withdraw and stand aloof from it effectually. I do not care to trace the course of my dollar, if I could, till it buys a

man or a musket to shoot with,—the dollar is innocent,—but I am concerned to trace the effects of my allegiance. In fact, I quietly declare war with the State, after my fashion, though I will still make what use and get what advantage of her I can, as is usual in such cases.

"Civil Disobedience" has been tremendously influential. It powerfully marked the mind of Tolstoy, and changed the direction of his movement. It was the solitary source book on which Gandhi based his campaign of Civil Resistance in India, and Thoreau's ideas multiplied by millions of Indians came fairly close to shattering the power of the British Empire. It has been the bible of countless thousands in totalitarian concentration camps and democratic jails, of partisans and fighters in resistance movements, of men wherever they have found no weapon but principle with which to oppose tyranny. In the relative futility of Thoreau's political act and the real importance of his political essay based on it, we have an allegory for our time on the artist as politician: the artist as strong and serviceable in the earnest practice of his art as he is weak and faintly comic in direct political action. In a day when the pressure on the artist to forsake his art for his duties as a citizen is almost irresistible, when every painter is making posters on nutrition, when every composer is founding a society devoted to doing something about the atom bomb, when every writer is spending more time on committees than on the typewriter, we can use Henry Thoreau's example.

Our first task in creating a Thoreau we can use is distinguishing the real man, or the part of him we want, from the various cardboard Thoreaus commentators have created to fit their wishes or fears. To Emerson, who should have known him better than anyone and certainly didn't, he was a bloodless character distinguished for his ascetic renunciations, a cross between Zeno the Stoic and a cigar-store Indian. Emerson wrote:

> He was bred to no profession; he never married; he lived alone; he never went to church; he never voted; he refused to pay a tax to the State; he ate no flesh; he drank no wine; he never knew the use of tobacco; and, though a naturalist, he used neither trap nor gun.

To his poet-friend and biographer Ellery Channing, Thoreau was the Poet-Naturalist, a sweet singer of woodland beauty, and to his young Abolitionist friend and biographer Frank Sanborn, he was a Concord warrior, a later embattled farmer. To Lowell, an embattled Cambridge gentleman, he was a Transcendentalist crackpot and phony who insisted on going back to flint and steel when he had a matchbox in his pocket, a fellow to the loonies who thought bran or swearing or the substitution of hooks and eyes for buttons would save the world. To Stevenson, full of Victorian vigor and beans, Thoreau was a simple skulker.

In our century Thoreau has fared little better. To Paul Elmer More he was one of Rousseau's wild men, but moving toward the higher self-restraint of neo-Humanism's "inner check." John Macy, one of our early Socialist critics, found him a powerful literary radical, but a little too selfish and aloof to be a good Socialist. To Lewis Mumford he was the Father of our National and State Parks, and to Léon Bazalgette, a French biographer, he was a savage, one of Chateaubriand's noble redmen in the virgin forest. Parrington makes him a researcher in economics, and *Walden* a handbook of economy to refute Adam Smith. To Constance Rourke he is the slick Yankee peddler out of vaudeville, who turns the tables on smart alecks, and to Gilbert Seldes he is an Antinomian.

Ludwig Lewisohn, an amateur sexologist and the Peeping Tom of our criticism, assures us that Thoreau was a clammy prig, the result of being hopelessly inhibited to the point of psychical impotence, or else hopelessly undersexed. The mechanical Marxists of the thirties are about as useful. V. F. Calverton conceded that he was "the best individual product of the petty bourgeois ideology" of his period, but hopelessly distorted by "Anarcho-individualism" and a probable sexual abnormality. Granville Hicks dismisses him with an epigram: "Nothing in American literature is more admirable than Henry Thoreau's devotion to his principles, but the principles are, unfortunately, less significant than the devotion." Van Wyck Brooks gives us Thoreau as a quirky, rather charming New England eccentric, his only vigorous feature an entirely fictitious hostility to the Irish, projected from Brooks's own discreet xenophobia. To Edward Dahlberg, a philosophic anarchist and disciple of D. H. Lawrence, Thoreau is a philosophic anarchist and earlier Lawrence. And Henry Seidel Canby, who manages to be one of the best biographers in America and almost the worst critic, sums up his excellent, definitive biography with the revelation that Thoreau was a neurotic, sublimating his passions in a loving study of nature.

From these cockeyed and contradictory extractions of Thoreau's "essence" we can reach two conclusions. One is that he is probably a subtler and more ambiguous character than anyone seems to have noticed. The other is that he must somehow still retain a powerful magic, or there would not be such a need to capture or destroy him, to canonize the shade or weight it down in the earth under a cairn of rocks. It seems obvious that we shall have to create a Thoreau for ourselves.

The first thing we should insist on is that Thoreau was a writer, not a man who lived in the woods or didn't pay taxes or went to jail. Other men did all these before him with more distinction. At his best Thoreau wrote the only really first-rate prose ever written by an American, with the possible exception of Abraham Lincoln. The "Plea for Captain John Brown," his most sustained lyric work, rings like *Areopagitica*, and like *Areopagitica* is the product of passion combined with complete technical mastery. Here are two sentences:

> The momentary charge at Balaklava, in obedience to a blunder-ing command, proving what a perfect machine the soldier is, has, properly enough, been celebrated by a poet laureate; but the steady, and for the most part successful, charge of this man, for some years, against the legions of Slavery, in obedience to an in-finitely higher command, is as much more memorable than that as an intelligent and conscientious man is superior to a machine. Do you think that that will go unsung?

Thoreau was not only a writer, but a writer in the great stream of the American tradition, the mythic and nonrealist writers, Hawthorne and Melville, Twain and James, and, in our own day, as Malcolm Cowley has been most insistent in pointing out, Hem-ingway and Faulkner. In pointing out Hemingway's kinship, not to our relatively barren realists and naturalists, but to our "haunted and nocturnal writers, the men who dealt in images that were symbols of an inner world," Cowley demonstrates that the idyllic fishing landscape of such a story as "Big Two-Hearted River" is not a real landscape setting for a real fishing trip, but an enchanted landscape full of rituals and taboos, a metaphor or projection of an inner state. It would not be hard to demonstrate the same thing for the landscape in *Walden*. One defender of such a view would be Henry Thoreau, who writes in his *Journals*, along with innumerable tributes to the power of mythology, that the richest function of nature is to symbolize human life, to become fable and myth for man's inward experience. F. O. Matthiessen, probably the best critic we have devoting himself to American literature, has claimed that Thoreau's power lies precisely in his re-creation of basic myth, in his role as the protagonist in a great cyclic ritual drama.

Central to any interpretation of Thoreau is Walden, both the experience of living by the pond and the book that reported it. As he explains it in the book, it was an experiment in human ecology (and if Thoreau was a scientist in any field, it was ecology, though he preceded the term), an attempt to work out a satisfactory relationship between man and his environment. He writes:

> I went to the woods because I wished to live deliberately, to front only the essential facts of life, and see if I could not learn what it had to teach, and not, when I came to die, discover that I had not lived. I did not wish to live what was not life, living is so dear; nor did I wish to practice resignation, unless it was quite necessary. I wanted to live deep and suck out all the marrow of life, to live so sturdily and Spartan-like as to put to rout all that was not life, to cut a broad swath and shave close, to drive life into a corner, and reduce it to its lowest terms, and, if it proved to be mean, why then to get the whole and genuine meanness of it, and publish its meanness to the world; or if it were sublime, to know it by experience, and be able to give a true account of it in my next excursion.

And of his leaving:

> I left the woods for as good a reason as I went there. Perhaps it seemed to me that I had several more lives to live, and could not spare any more time for that one.

At Walden, Thoreau reports the experience of awakening one morning with the sense that some question had been put to him, which he had been endeavoring in vain to answer in his sleep. In his terms, that question would be the problem with which he begins "Life Without Principle": "Let us consider the way in which we spend our lives." His obsessive image, running through everything he ever wrote, is the myth of Apollo, glorious god of the sun, forced to labor on earth tending the flocks of King Admetus. In one sense, of course, the picture of Henry Thoreau forced to tend any-one's flocks is ironic, and Stevenson is right when he notes sarcastically: "Admetus never got less work out of any servant since the world began." In another sense the myth has a basic rightness, and is, like the Pied Piper of Hamelin, an archetypal allegory of the artist in a society that gives him no worthy function and no commensurate reward.

The sun is Thoreau's key symbol, and all of *Walden* is a development in the ambiguities of sun imagery. The book begins with the theme: "But alert and healthy natures remember that the sun rose clear," and ends: "There is more day to dawn. The sun is but a morning star." Thoreau's movement from an egocentric to a sociocentric view is the movement from "I have, as it were, my own sun, and moon, and stars, and a little world all to myself" to "The same sun which ripens my beans illumines at once a system of earths like ours." The sun is an old Platonist like Emerson that must set before Thoreau's true sun can rise, it is menaced by every variety of mist, haze, smoke, and darkness, it is Thoreau's brother, it is both his own cold affection and the threat of sensuality that would corrupt goodness as it taints meat, it is himself in a pun on s-o-n, s-u-n. When Abolitionism becomes a nagging demand Thoreau can no longer resist, a Negro woman is a dusky orb rising on Concord, and, when John Brown finally strikes his blow, for Thoreau the sun shines on him, and he works "in the clearest light that shines on the land." The final announcement of Thoreau's triumphant rebirth at Walden is the sun breaking through mists. It is not to our purpose here to explore the deep and complex ambiguities of Thoreau's sun symbol, or in fact to do more than note a few of many contexts, but no one can study the sun references in *Walden* without realizing that

Thoreau is a deeper and more complicated writer than we have been told, and that the book is essentially dynamic rather than static, a movement *from* something *to* something, rather than the simple reporting of an experience.

Walden is, in fact, a vast rebirth ritual, the purest and most complete in our literature. We know rebirth rituals to operate characteristically by means of fire, ice, or decay, mountains and pits, but we are staggered by the amount and variety of these in the book. We see Thoreau build his shanty of boards he has first purified in the sun, record approvingly an Indian purification ritual of burning all the tribe's old belongings and provisions, and later go off into a description of the way he is cleansed and renewed by his own fireplace. We see him note the magic purity of the ice on Walden Pond, the fact that frozen water never turns stale, and the rebirth involved when the ice breaks up, all sins are forgiven, and "Walden was dead and is alive again." We see him exploring every phase and type of decay: rotting ice, decaying trees, moldy pitch pine and rotten wood, excrement, maggots, a vulture feeding on a dead horse, carrion, tainted meat, and putrid water. The whole of Walden runs to symbols of graves and coffins, with consequent rising from them, to wombs and emergence from them, and ends on the fable of a live insect resurrected from an egg long buried in wood. Each day at Walden Thoreau was reborn by his bath in the pond, a religious exercise he says he took for purification and renewal, and the whole two years and two months he compresses into the cycle of a year, to frame the book on the archetypal rebirth pattern of the death and renewal of vegetation, ending it with the magical emergence of spring.

On the thread of decay and rebirth Thoreau strings all his pre-occupations. Meat is a symbol of evil, sensuality; its tainting symbolizes goodness and affection corrupted: the shameful defilement of chastity smells like carrion (in which he agreed with Shakespeare); the eating of meat causes slavery and unjust war. (Thoreau, who was a vegetarian, sometimes felt so wild he was tempted to seize and devour a woodchuck raw, or yearned like a savage for the raw marrow of kudus—those were the periods when he wanted to seize the world by the neck and hold it under water like a dog until it drowned.) But even slavery and injustice are a decaying and death, and Thoreau concludes *Slavery in Massachusetts* with: "We do not complain that they *live*, but that they do not *get buried*. Let the living bury them; even they are good for manure." Always, in Thoreau's imagery, what this rotting meat will fertilize is fruit, ripe fruit. It is his chief good. He wanted "the flower and fruit of man," the "ripeness." The perfect and glorious state he foresees will bear men as fruit, suffering them to drop off as they ripen; John Brown's heroism is a good seed that will bear good fruit, a future crop of heroes. Ultimately Brown, in one of the most terrifying puns ever written, was "ripe" for the gallows. On the metaphor of the organic process of birth, growth, decay, and rebirth out of decay, Thoreau organizes his whole life and experience.

I have maintained that Walden is a dynamic process, a job of symbolic action, a moving *from* something *to* something. From what to what? On an abstract level, from individual isolation to collective identification, from, in Macaulay's terms, a Platonic philosophy of pure truth to a Baconian philosophy of use. It is interesting to note that the term Bacon used for the utilitarian ends of knowledge, for the relief of man's estate, is "fruit." The Thoreau who went to Walden was a pure Platonist, a man who could review a Utopian book and announce that it was too practical, that its chief fault was aiming "to secure the greatest degree of gross comfort and pleasure merely." The man who left Walden was the man who thought it was less important for John Brown to right a Greek accent slanting the wrong way than to right a falling slave. Early in the book Thoreau gives us his famous Platonic myth of having long ago lost a hound, a bay horse, and a turtle dove. Before he is through his symbolic quest is for a human being, and near the end of the book he reports of a hunter: "He had lost a dog but found a man." All through *Walden* Thoreau weighs Platonic and Baconian values: men keep chickens for the glorious sound of a crowing cock "to say nothing of the eggs and drumsticks"; a well reminds a man of the insignificance of his dry pursuits on a surface largely water, and also keeps the butter cool. By the end of the book he has brought

Transcendentalism down to earth, has taken Emerson's castles in the air, to use his own figure, and built foundations under them.

Thoreau's political value, for us, is largely in terms of this transition from philosophic aloofness. We see in him the honest artist struggling for terms on which he can adjust to society *in his capacity as artist*. As might be expected from such a process, Thoreau's social statements are full of contradictions, and quotations can be amputated from the context of his work to bolster any position from absolute anarchism to ultimate Toryism, if indeed they are very far apart. At his worst, he is simply a nut reformer, one of the horde in his period, attempting to "improve" an Irish neighbor by lecturing him on abstinence from tea, coffee, and meat as the solution to all his problems, and the passage in *Walden* describing the experience is the most condescending and offensive in a sometimes infuriating book. At his best, Thoreau is the clearest voice for social ethics that ever spoke out in America.

One of the inevitable consequences of Emersonian idealism was the ease with which it could be used to sugar-coat social injustice, as a later generation was to discover when it saw robber barons piling up fortunes while intoning Emersonian slogans of Self-Reliance and Compensation. If the Lowell factory owner was more enslaved than one of his child laborers, there was little point in seeking to improve the lot of the child laborer, and frequently Emerson seemed to be preaching a principle that would forbid both the rich and the poor to sleep under bridges. Thoreau begins *Walden* in these terms, remarking that it is frivolous to attend "to the gross but somewhat foreign form of servitude called Negro Slavery when there are so many keen and subtle masters that enslave"; that the rich are a "seemingly wealthy, but most terribly impoverished class of all" since they are fettered by their gold and silver; that the day laborer is more independent than his employer, since his day ends with sundown, while his employer has no respite from one year to another; even that if you give a ragged man money he will perhaps buy more rags with it, since he is frequently gross, with a taste for rags.

Against this ingenious and certainly unintentioned social palliation, *Walden* works through to sharp social criticism: of the

New England textile factory system, whose object is "not that mankind may be well and honestly clad, but, unquestionably, that the corporations may be enriched"; of the degradation of the laboring class of his time, "living in sties," shrunken in mind and body; of the worse condition of the Southern slaves; of the lack of dignity and privacy in the lives of factory girls, "never alone, hardly in their dreams"; of the human consequences of commerce and technology; of the greed and corruption of the money-mad New England of his day, seeing the whole world in the bright reflecting surface of a dollar.

As his bitterness and awareness increased, Thoreau's direct action became transmuted. He had always, like his friends and family, helped the Underground Railway run escaped slaves to Canada. He devotes a sentence to one such experience in *Walden*, and amplifies it in his *Journal*, turning a quiet and terrible irony on the man's attempt to buy his freedom from his master, who was his father, and exercised paternal love by holding out for more than the slave could pay. These actions, however, in a man who disliked Abolitionism, seem to have been simple reflexes of common decency, against his principles, which would free the slave first by striking off his spiritual chains. From this view, Thoreau works tortuously through to his final identification of John Brown, the quintessence of direct social action, with all beauty, music, poetry, philosophy, and Christianity. Finally Brown becomes Christ, an indignant militant who cleansed the temple, preached radical doctrines, and was crucified by the slave owners. In what amounts almost to worship of Brown, Thoreau both deifies the action he had tried to avoid and transcends it in passion. Brown died for him, thus he need free no more slaves.

At the same time, Thoreau fought his way through the Emersonian doctrine that a man might wash his hands of wrong, providing he did not himself commit it. He writes in "Civil Disobedience":

> It is not a man's duty, as a matter of course, to devote himself to the eradication of any, even the most enormous wrong; he may still properly have other concerns to engage him; but it is his duty, at least, to wash his hands of it, and, if he gives it no thought longer, not to give it practically his support. If I devote myself to

other pursuits and contemplations, I must first see, at least, that
I do not pursue them sitting upon another man's shoulders. I
must get off him first, that he may pursue his contemplations too.

Here he has recognized the fallacy of the Greek philosopher, free
because he is supported by the labor of slaves, and the logic of
this realization was to drive him, through the superiority and
smugness of "God does not sympathize with the popular movements," and "I came into this world, not chiefly to make this a
good place to live in, but to live in it, be it good or bad," to the
militant fury of "My thoughts are murder to the State, and
involuntarily go plotting against her."

Thoreau's progress also involved transcending his economics.
The first chapter of *Walden*, entitled "Economy," is an elaborate
attempt to justify his life and views in the money terms of New
England commerce. He speaks of going to the woods as "going
into business" on "slender capital," of his "enterprise"; gives the
reader his "accounts," even to the halfpenny, of what he spends
and what he takes in; talks of "buying dear," of "paying compound
interest," etc. Thoreau accepts the ledger principle, though he
sneaks into the Credit category such unusual profits on his in-
vestment as "leisure and independence and health." His money
metaphor begins to break down when he writes of the Massachusetts citizens who read of the unjust war against Mexico as sleepily
as they read the prices current, and he cries out: "What is the
price current of an honest man and patriot today?" By the time
of the John Brown affair he has evolved two absolutely independent
economies, a money economy and a moral economy. He writes:

> "But he won't gain anything by it." Well, no, I don't suppose he
> could get four-and-sixpence a day for being hung, take the year
> round; but then he stands a chance to save a considerable part of
> his soul,—and *such* a soul!—when *you* do not. No doubt you can
> get more in your market for a quart of milk than for a quart of
> blood, but that is not the market that heroes carry their blood to.

What, then, can we make of this complicated social pattern to
our purposes? Following Emerson's doctrine and example, Thoreau
was frequently freely inconsistent. (He was able to write in
Walden, "I would rather sit on a pumpkin and have it all to

myself, than to be crowded on a velvet cushion," and a few pages later, "None is so poor that he need sit on a pumpkin.") One of his chief contradictions was on the matter of reforming the world through his example. He could disclaim hoping to influence any-one with "I do not mean to prescribe rules to strong and valiant natures" and then take it back immediately with "I foresee that all men will at length establish their lives on that basis." Certainly to us his hatred of technological progress, of the division of labor, even of farming with draft animals and fertilizer, is backward-looking and reactionary. Certainly he distrusted co-operative action and all organization. But the example of Jefferson reminds us that a man may be economically backward-looking and still be our noblest spokesman, just as Hamilton reminds us that a man may bring us reaction and injustice tied up in the bright issue of economic progress.

To the doctrine of naked expediency so tempting to our time, the worship of power and success for which the James Burnhams among us speak so plausibly, Thoreau opposes only one weapon —*principle*. Not policy or expediency must be the test, but justice and principle. "Read not the Times, read the Eternities." *Walden* has been a bible for the British labor movement since the days of William Morris. We might wonder what the British Labour Party, now that it is in power, or the rest of us, in and out of power, who claim to speak for principle, would make of Thoreau's doctrine: "If I have unjustly wrested a plank from a drowning man, I must restore it to him though I drown myself."

All of this takes us far afield from what must be Thoreau's chief importance to us, his writing. The resources of his craft warrant our study. One of his most eloquent devices, typified by the crack about the Times and Eternities, is a root use of words—resulting from his lifelong interest in language and etymology—fresh, shock-ing, and very close to the pun. We can see the etymological passion developing in the *Journal* notes that a "wild" man is actually a "willed" man, that our "fields" are "felled" woods. His early writings keep reminding us that a "saunterer" is going to a "Sainte Terre," a Holy Land; that three roads can make a village "trivial"; that when our center is outside us we are "eccentric"; that a "landlord" is literally a "lord of the land"; that he has been "breaking" silence for years and has hardly made a "rent" in it. By the time he wrote *Walden* this habit had developed into one of his most characteristic ironic devices: the insistence that telling his townsmen about his life is not "impertinent" but "pertinent," that professors of philosophy are not philosophers, but people who "profess" it, that the "bent" of his genius is a very "crooked" one. In the "Plea for Captain John Brown" the device achieves a whiplash power. He says that Brown's "humanities" were the freeing of slaves, not the study of grammar; that a Board of Commissions is lumber of which he had only lately heard; of the Governor of Massachusetts: "He was no Governor of mine. He did not govern me." Sometimes these puns double and triple to permit him to pack of number of complex meanings into a single word, like the "dear" in "Living is so dear." The discord of goose-honk and owl-cry he hears by the pond becomes a "concord" that is at once musical harmony, his native town, and concord as "peace."

Closely related to these serious puns in Thoreau is a serious epigrammatic humor, wry quotable lines which pack a good deal of meaning and tend to make their point by shifting linguistic levels. "Some circumstantial evidence is very strong, as when you find a trout in the milk." To a man who threatened to plumb his depths: "I trust you will not strike your head against the bottom." "The partridge loves peas, but not those that go with her into the pot." On his habit of exaggeration: "You must speak loud to those who are hard of hearing." He reported that the question he feared was not "How much wood did you burn?" but "What did you do while you were warm?" Dying, he said to someone who wanted to talk about the next world: "One world at a time"; and to another, who asked whether he had made his peace with God: "We have never quarrelled." When Emerson remarked that they taught all branches of learning at Harvard: "All of the branches and none of the roots." Refusing to pay a dollar for his Harvard diploma: "Let every sheep keep but his own skin." Asked to write for *The Ladies' Companion*: "I could not write anything companionable." Many of these are variants of the same joke, and in a few cases, the humor is sour and forced, like the definition of a pearl as "the hardened tear of a diseased clam, murdered in its old age," or a soldier as "a fool made conspicuous by a painted coat." But these are penalties any man who works for humor must occasionally pay, and Thoreau believed this "indispensable pledge of sanity" to be so important that without some leaven of it "the abstruse thinker may justly be suspected of mysticism, fanaticism or insanity." "Especially the transcendental philosophy needs the leaven of humor," he wrote, in what must go down as an understatement.

Thoreau was perhaps more precise about his own style and more preoccupied generally with literary craft than any American writer except Henry James. He rewrote endlessly, not only, like James, for greater precision, but unlike James, for greater simplicity. "Simplify, Simplify, Simplify," he gave as the three cardinal principles of both life and art. Emerson had said of Montaigne: "Cut these words and they would bleed" and Thoreau's is perhaps the only American style in his century of which this is true. Criticizing De Quincey, he stated his own prose aesthetic, "the *art* of writing," demanding sentences that are concentrated and nutty, that suggest far more than they say, that are kinked and knotted into something hard and significant, to be swallowed like a diamond without digesting. "Sentences which are expensive, towards which so many volumes, so much life, went; which lie like boulders on the page, up and down or across; which contain the seed of other sentences, not mere repetition, but creation; which a man might sell his grounds and castles to build." In another place he notes that writing must be done with gusto, must be vascular. A sense of Thoreau's preoccupation with craft comes with noting that when he lists "My faults" in the *Journal,* all seven of them turn out to be of his prose style. Writing for Thoreau was so obsessive, so vital a physical process, that at various times he describes it in the imagery of eating, procreation, excretion, mystic trance, and even his old favorite, the tree bearing ripe fruit. An anthology of Thoreau's passages on the art of writing would be as worth compiling as Henry James's *Prefaces,* and certainly as useful to both the writer and the reader.

Thoreau's somewhat granite pride and aloofness are at their most appealing, and very like James Joyce's, when he is defending his manuscripts against editorial bowdlerizing, when he stands as the embattled writer against the phalanx of cowardice and stupidity. He fought Emerson and Margaret Fuller on a line in one of his poems they printed in *The Dial*, and won. When the editor of *Putnam's Monthly* cut passages from an article, Thoreau wrote to a friend: "The editor requires the liberty to omit the heresies without consulting me, a privilege California is not rich enough to bid for" and he withdrew the series. His letter to Lowell, the editor of *The Atlantic*, when Lowell cut a "pantheistic" sentence out of cowardice, is a masterpiece of bitter fury, withering Lowell like a premature bud in a blast.

Henry Thoreau's and John Brown's personalities were as different as any two personalities can be; one the gentle, rather shy scholar who took children huckleberrying; the other the harsh military Puritan who could murder the children of slavers in cold blood on the Pottawatomie, making the fearful statement, "Nits grow to be lice." Almost the only things they had in common—that made Thoreau perceive that Brown was his man, his ideas in action, almost his Redeemer—were principle and literary style. Just as writers in our own day were drawn to Sacco and Vanzetti perhaps as much for the majesty of Vanzetti's untutored prose as for the obvious justice of their case, Thoreau somehow found the most convincing thing about Brown to be his speech to the court. At the end of his "Plea" he quotes Brown's "sweet and noble strain":

> I pity the poor in bondage that have none to help them; that is why I am here; not to gratify any personal animosity, revenge, or vindictive spirit. It is my sympathy with the oppressed and the wronged, that are as good as you, and as precious as the sight of God.

adding only: "You don't know your testament when you see it."

"This unlettered man's speaking and writing are standard English" he writes in another paper on Brown. "It suggests that the one great rule of composition—and if I were a professor of rhetoric I should insist on this—is, to *speak the truth*." It was certainly Thoreau's great rule of composition. "He was a speaker and actor of the truth," Emerson said in his obituary of Thoreau. We have never had too many of those. He was also, perhaps as a consequence, a very great writer. We have never had too many of those, either.

2. Henry Thoreau Once More

[1962]

IN THESE PAGES too the *I*, or first person, will be retained. In 1946, in my twenty-seventh year, I published an essay called "Henry Thoreau in Our Time." With ironic suitability, it appeared in the *Atlantic Monthly*, a magazine to which Thoreau would not submit anything after its editor censored a "pantheistic" sentence. My essay, which ran to other heresies than pantheism, was an attempt to define a Thoreau who still spoke to our condition in 1946. I saw myself, with considerable presumption, as speaking for a young literary generation which had come through the strident politics of the 1930s, then the war, and now lived under a mushroom shadow.

I concluded that the essential Thoreau for our purposes was the *writer* who had made the diamond of "Civil Disobedience" out of the soft coal of his somewhat ludicrous night in jail. Thoreau's message, in brief, was that the writer's place is not on the picket line or even on the Admirable Cause Committee, but at his desk, writing the truth as he sees it. My essay went into other matters— it discussed the ritual cycles that underlie *Walden*, and it turned a mild Freudian eye on some images—but its real point was to find or create a Thoreau relevant to myself and to anyone who might share my predicament.

In the years since, I have been faithful to that image—I am a member of no incorporated body but the American Numismatic Society and the human race—but recently I have begun to think that my Thoreau must be hopelessly outdated, that in a world of space travel and Freedom Riders there must be newer images of

Thoreau. In quest of them I have read half a dozen recent books on the man, chosen at random, since I am no Thoreau scholar. I must report that I find no images of Thoreau more attractive than my own, and that some are considerably less attractive.

Henry Beetle Hough's *Thoreau of Walden: The Man and His Eventful Life* (1956), a popular biography, is the most inconsequential book of those I read, and its image most patently a travesty. Hough is the editor of a country weekly, the *Vineyard Gazette*, and the author of a number of benign books about small-town life. His Thoreau might be the folksy editor of the *Walden Gazette*, not the author of *Slavery in Massachusetts*, who picked up newspapers and "heard the gurgling of the sewer through every column."

This Thoreau has been mightily tamed. His *Walden*, in Hough's eyes, is "a book as native as the huckleberry bushes," and if it has the bad taste to say that the farmer spends his lifetime digging his grave with a plow, Hough will repair things: "the farmer deserved credit for being a farmer." Discussing Thoreau's signing off from the Unitarian Church, Hough writes: "There were surely lively discussions of this affair at the Thoreau home, and it must have distressed the family to see Henry making himself conspicuous and to some people offensive through his studied nonconformity. Majority feeling in New England was always against 'scenes' and this was a 'scene' of a kind." Commenting on Samuel Hoar's paying the poll tax Alcott refused to pay, Hough writes, having it both ways: "Governments would suffer more for their sins if it were not for men like Squire Hoar, and so would idealists like Bronson Alcott."

The phrase that perhaps most clearly shows Hough's absolute inadequacy to his subject is a reference to "the Thoreau sort of people." Hough really is a terrible cornball. He writes of Thoreau's letter to Lidian Emerson: "The phrases of the heart were such as any woman might prize coming from any man who loved her much." Hough describes Thoreau's prose as "sentences bold and rhythmic like the tall, swaying limbs of great trees." His own prose dissolves everything it touches, and it can digest even cellulose.

Leo Stoller's *After Walden: Thoreau's Changing Views on Economic Man* (1957) is a 1956 doctoral dissertation at Columbia, and is thus the view of a younger generation than my own. Its thesis, which is presented eloquently and well, is that Thoreau lost his faith in natural goodness climbing Mt. Katahdin in 1846, and as a consequence turned "away from utopian social thought and toward a new synthesis." This involved in principle "the acceptance of industrial capitalism," to be reformed and ameliorated rather than abolished, and in practice a yielding "to expediency" by surveying wood lots and thus contributing to their destruction.

In Stoller's view, Thoreau found a "union of principle and expediency" in the idea of forest management, which combines profits with forest preservation, and for Stoller this union typifies Thoreau's later social thought. Thus Thoreau "began to accept the industrial mode of production, to separate his concept of simplicity from handicrafts and subsistence farming, and to sketch a framework by which simplicity might be combined with industrialism." The "politics complementary to his economics," Stoller believes, was the young Republican Party, which should have been Thoreau's party.

This is an interesting and challenging thesis, but several things must be said. First, that Stoller sometimes reads Thoreau very badly—I did not trust him after page 50, when he identified "the journal of no very wide circulation" in *Walden* as *The Dial*, when it is of course Thoreau's *Journal*. Second, Stoller has no appreciation of the nature and importance of symbolic action, and writes flatly of "the failure of the Walden experiment." Third, his thesis is a considerable oversimplification of a much more complex social attitude, and there is plenty of evidence to the contrary, some of which Stoller presents.

Commenting on a demand for town forest-wardens in the 1860 *Journal*, Stoller observes that it is inconsistent with "Civil Disobedience." As he notes elsewhere, there is a strand of "Civil Disobedience" with which it is not at all inconsistent, that strand saying: "I have never declined paying the highway tax, because I am as desirous of being a good neighbor as I am of being a bad subject." Stoller properly notes that in his last years Thoreau turned against the institution of private property itself. But Stoller's quotations make this seem earnest and theoretical, not, as it was, gleefully subversive. Thoreau wrote to Harrison Blake welcoming the panic of 1857, with its failures of businesses and banks: "The statement that ninety-six in a hundred doing such business surely break down is perhaps the sweetest fact that statistics have revealed, —exhilarating as the fragrance of sallows in spring." As for the Republican Party, Stoller should take another look at "A Plea for Captain John Brown."

The Shores of America: Thoreau's Inward Exploration (1958), by Sherman Paul, is an intellectual or spiritual biography; "a biography of a vocation," Paul says. As such, it studiously and lovingly gives us the least important and least engaging Thoreau, the introspective self-important pest, the naturalist pursuing his soul with a butterfly net. Paul restores the Thoreau his contemporaries saw: heavily Transcendental and Emersonian. In this view, living at Walden was "the richest fulfillment of his life," and *Walden*, written "in his years of decay," "was written to summon it [that ecstasy] again." Everything becomes spiritual allegory: "the pond was the real self and the shore the empirical self"; "the pond was the soul"; "his vital heat [was] his faith" and so on. As a failure of nerve on Katahdin is helpful to Stoller's view, so a severe breakdown in 1850 is useful to Paul. Through the Pond experience all was harmonious; afterward "the remainder of his life had its own quiet desperation," with the "years of crisis" beginning in 1850. Yet as early as 1843, as Paul shows, Thoreau wrote that he was "a diseased bundle of nerves," and Paul himself calls the experience at the Pond "effective therapy."

Paul supplements his old-fashioned image of Thoreau with several more modish ones. Following Edward Dahlberg, he compares Thoreau repeatedly to Randolph Bourne; and following F. O. Matthiessen, he compares him to Hemingway, although chiefly in terms of "reportorial skill." Two other images are fresher. Thoreau was "what we would call today an inner-directed man," and he demonstrated what David Riesman calls "the nerve of failure." At the same time, he was an *Angst*-ridden existentialist, revealing in his *Journal* "the gathering despair of his life." (More properly, an *Angst*-ridden essentialist, since Paul quotes his statement in an early *Journal*: "What a man does, compared with what

he is, is but a small part.") Paul's book is, in short, a masterly means
to an unimproved end.

Consciousness in Concord (1958) is an edition of Thoreau's
hitherto "Lost Journal" of 1840–1841, edited with an extensive
commentary by Perry Miller. Miller is one of the few authors of
books on Thoreau who neither worships him nor identifies with
him, and Miller's tart maliciousness is a relief after all the cloying
sweetness. His editing of the *Journal* is exhaustive and resourceful:
noting revisions, tracing passages into print, identifying, explaining, raising the right questions and providing many of the right
answers. Miller's general line is that "the *Journal* is so thoroughly
a literary exercise that I am wary of biographical interpretations,"
but that does not keep him from finding in it an "embarrassing
revelation of Thoreau's primal urge to find a 'mother-substitute'
in impersonal nature," or anything else, when he chooses. As a key
to the life, Miller sees Thoreau as secretly wishing and courting
failure. Although all the Transcendentalists devoted themselves to
"perfecting devices for being let down by their friends," "with
Thoreau a luxuriating in friendship and in its inadequacies becomes
simply monstrous." Miller mocks Thoreau as "this home-centered
youth," writing "strangulated pages" out of "a syndrome of sensibility."

Nor is Thoreau his only butt. With Miller "we measure the
sublimity of Emerson's insensitivity"; we are introduced to William
Ellery Channing as "the poet who exalted the Transcendental
imperative into a long life of irresponsible whim"; Miller cuts a
letter from Isaiah Williams with the explanation: "A little bit of
his screaming will suffice." Miller's style is as lively as his opinions.
He squeezes the juice out of metaphors, he peppers parentheses
with exclamation points, his diction is classroom-breezy. At one
point I found Miller's book moving, when he introduces a long
footnote about Thoreau's love for music with the statement: "This
is one of those passages in Thoreau that break your heart." I
hadn't known that Miller had a heart, and I rejoice.

Walter Harding is our most tireless Thoreauvian, and his *A
Thoreau Handbook* (1958) offers itself as "a guide through the
welter of Thoreau scholarship." As such it is excellent, handling

an enormous amount of material with discernment and fairness in 200-odd pages. In regularly pointing out work that still needs doing, Harding sets useful targets for future Thoreau scholarship, although his principal demand—"we do not yet have a really satisfactory biography"—is easier to announce than to gratify.

In his own criticism of Thoreau in the book, Harding tends to warm tints, although there are occasional Millerite judgments: A *Week on the Concord and Merrimack Rivers* contains "passages vapid enough to have been written by Bronson Alcott"; the essay on "Love" contains, "as Krutch suggests, 'a real howler' "; the essay on "Chastity and Sensuality" is, if possible, "even more vapid." Harding ventures a few general interpretations: that Thoreau was no Stoic, that he is "America's greatest nature writer." But most of the book's value, in accord with its intention, is as a guide to other people's work, and as a mine of information. I did not know, for example, that the nudists have adopted Thoreau as a founding father, or that Gene Tunney read Thoreau as he trained for Jack Dempsey, and announced: "the spirit of Thoreau lends its luminous wisdom to man and nature wherever they meet," or that Lin Yutang regarded Thoreau as "the most Chinese of all American authors." I feel the better for the knowledge.

The latest of these books, Mark Van Doren's *Henry David Thoreau: A Critical Study* (1961) is also the earliest of them. It is a photographic reprint of Van Doren's undergraduate honors thesis at the University of Illinois, first published in 1916. As a piece of work by an undergraduate it is brilliant, even staggering, in my opinion the best criticism that Van Doren ever wrote.

Done under the supervision of Stuart P. Sherman, a pupil of Irving Babbitt's, and much influenced by Paul Elmer More, whom it describes as "Thoreau's most discriminating critic," the book takes the stand that was later to be identified as the New Humanism. Thoreau, along with Emerson, is accused of plunging "into shoreless seas of intellectual and moral egotism," of being ridden by "the intellectual demon." Van Doren sees Thoreau as emotionally defective, constitutionally lacking "a living heart," consisting of "little else than intellect." (Van Doren mockingly quotes John Burroughs—"If Thoreau had made friends with a dog to share his bed and board in his retreat by Walden Pond, one would have had more faith in his sincerity"—but does not realize how close his charges are to Burroughs'.) In one of the most whopping misstatements ever made about Thoreau, Van Doren writes: "Certainly the troubles of mankind caused him no disturbance."

In respect to Thoreau's emotional defects, Van Doren is misled by Emerson's obtuse tribute: "He had no temptations to fight against—no appetites, no passions." At the same time, Van Doren sees through Emerson's Stoic Thoreau, replaces it with an "out-and-out Epicurean" Thoreau, and then explodes that in turn with a Diogenes-the-Cynic Thoreau. (At least Van Doren makes it obvious to us that our Concord pea is somewhat too protean to stay under any of the walnut shells of Greek philosophy.)

Despite all of this nervous categorizing, the young Van Doren finds some aspects of Thoreau enormously attractive to him. He pleads for discounting: "Thoreau's permanent, best qualities—his sly and edged excellence, his leavening power—come into fuller recognition as his less essential qualities are subtracted and retreat." He asks that Thoreau be not read literally, but taken "with the sufficient allowance of salt." "If read as scripture, as some of his friends read him," Van Doren explains, "or as madman, as Lowell read him, he will yield nothing."

Early in his book, Van Doren announces that "the personality of Thoreau has never been presented in full, mainly because it has been treated in no case by any one who was not interested in proving a point." But Van Doren is as tendentious as his predecessors, as we all are and must be. He wants the "good hater and refuser," the nay-sayer, and he wants him as an image for himself and his generation. "Thoreau will be found a very satisfactory spokesman," Van Doren proclaims, "for one who feels driven into a position somewhat analogous to his position in 1840." Van Doren calls up "his support when it is necessary that one be unreasonable." Thoreau, he concludes, is "valuable as a protestant, valuable as an antidotal flavor."

Perhaps the new images of Thoreau by the young will come only when some of the recent and forthcoming *Walden* scholarship—including Shanley's study of the drafts (1957), Sherwin and Reynolds' *Word Index* (1960), and Harding's *Variorum* (1962)—

has been digested. The only example of such an image in the books I read—Stoller's compromiser—may be what the new generation wants, but it seems to me much less nourishing than Van Doren's refuser in 1916.

Paul's stab at an existentialist *Angst*-ridden Thoreau may be only the first of many such moves. Perhaps Henry Miller's "cool" Thoreau in his preface to *Life Without Principle: Three Essays by Henry David Thoreau* (1946)—the Thoreau "who would not run around the corner to see the world blow up"—will yet have a progeny of Beat and offbeat Thoreaus. "Civil Disobedience" has been a handbook for the Freedom Riders, as for Gandhi before them, and Integrationist Thoreaus are probably on their way. (I can even see a possible Black Muslim Thoreau, taking as its text the sneering contrast in *Walden* between the fake white runaway slaves and the real black runaway slaves.)

"There are probably words addressed to our condition exactly," Thoreau wrote in *Walden*. "I want something speaking in some measure to the condition of muskrats and skunk-cabbage as well as of men," he wrote in his *Journal* in 1850. The problem is, of course, knowing what our condition is. If we can discover it, and whether it is that of men or skunk-cabbages, we can find a Thoreau to speak to it. Perhaps the years since 1945 have been years of such demoralization and befuddlement that our condition escapes us. If we ever rediscover what we are, we can expect Henry Thoreau to have been there too a century before.

Until then we can ask a few simple things of books on Thoreau, or judge them by a few simple tests. One is that they allow him on occasion to have behaved badly. The obvious example is the lecture to John Field the bog hoer in *Walden*. Thoreau took shelter from the rain in Field's house and "tried to help him with my experience," advising him to give up tea, coffee, butter, milk, and meat; to build himself a "palace" like Thoreau's; and so forth. When Field properly ignored him, Thoreau concluded: "But alas! the culture of an Irishman is an enterprise to be undertaken with a sort of moral bog hoe." He ends the chapter: "Poor John Field!— I trust he does not read this, unless he will improve by it."

This is a Thoreau oblivious to his principles and contemptuous of another man's privacy in his ways; Thoreau being a bore and a prig. Had one of "the self-styled reformers, the greatest bores of all," come at Thoreau in his hut with a similarly patronizing up-lift, Thoreau would have booted him out the door. Characteristi-cally, Hough approves of the mission to John Field, Stoller objects to it for the wrong reasons (because Thoreau did not give him *practical* advice), and Harding ignores it but observes that in gen-eral Thoreau befriended Irish immigrants.

The second test for a book on Thoreau is that it recognize that he was primarily a writer, not a naturalist, reformer, or whatever. Here the recent authors seem finally to have gotten the point. For all the brilliance of his analysis, Van Doren could not see that primacy in 1916. He writes typically: "No other naturalist has been so malicious; no other transcendentalist has been so fastidious." But Stoller pays tribute to Thoreau's "greatness both as man and writer," and Paul announces: "If anything he was a writer."

One of the pleasures of reading books on Thoreau is that they quote lines one didn't know or had forgotten. Here are a few that delighted me: of Alcott, "the rats and mice make their nests in him"; in 1841, "I exult in stark inanity, leering on nature and the soul"; of November, "Now a man will eat his heart, if ever"; mys-teriously, in the "lost" *Journal*, "Every maggot lives down town"; of clergymen, that they cannot butter their own bread yet "make dipped toast for all eternity"; of a man who wanted to get rich to have leisure for poetry, "He should have gone up to the garret at once." Yet, like any writer, Thoreau is sometimes awful. He be-comes Thornton W. Burgess when he discovers a new species of fish and protests in his *Journal* that the importance of the discov-ery is not in the scientific gain, "but that I have a little fishy friend in the pond."

The last test I would recommend for works on Thoreau is that they stop telling us that he was a Transcendentalist and tell us instead how he transcended Transcendentalism. "In his writing and in his living," Van Doren notes, "his genius for the specific, his preoccupation with details, his love of facts, and his passion for real experience mark him off as distinctly as is possible from his transcendental brethren." Van Doren later adds Thoreau's handi-ness with tools and his humor. This all needed saying in 1916, and it still needs saying. Every time I have gone back to him Thoreau has seemed less Emersonian, and perhaps someday he will not seem Emersonian at all.

Matthiessen's *American Renaissance* (1941), which is *still* our best account of Thoreau (as it is our best account of Melville and so many others), said accurately: "His vitality as a revolutionary is still unexhausted." A young scholar, Wendell Glick, wrote in an article in 1952: "Thoreau's chief purpose in 'Civil Disobedience' was to wean men away from their adherence to an insidious relativism and to persuade them to return again to the superior standard of absolute truth." Perhaps those statements combine to make the best image of Thoreau we can take into the future: a revolutionary of absolute truth.

NOTE [1963]: One or two statements in the 1946 essay now seem to me to be misreadings, although I made no effort to correct them in the 1962 follow-up. I no longer believe, for example, that the self-justification in monetary terms in the first chapter of *Walden* (mentioned on page 34) was meant to be taken seriously. I now read it as irony, a bookkeeping deliberately exploded when more important values are introduced into the ledger. As for my remark about Thoreau and Lincoln (page 27), I wish that I had the knowledge of American literature that it presupposes. I cannot at present recall what lay behind so grandiose a generalization, and suspect that I had just read an anthology of American prose.

Notes on the Organic
Unity of
John Peale Bishop

[1949]

"Every poet over twenty-five must live with a critic.
He must not go to bed with him."

JOHN PEALE BISHOP, the poet responsible for that wicked
aphorism, went to bed with a critic every night of his life. The
simultaneous posthumous publication of Bishop's *Collected Poems*
and *Collected Essays* gives us a remarkable opportunity to study
the relationship between Bishop the poet and Bishop the critic.
The volumes themselves are triumphs of painstaking and devoted
editing by two of Bishop's friends, Allen Tate, who collected the
poems and wrote a preface and memoir, and Edmund Wilson,
who edited the essays with an introduction. On a few points we
might question them: Tate's decision not to attempt a complete
edition, with variant readings and all the juvenilia; Wilson's print-
ing of Bishop's piece on *Finnegans Wake* with "obvious errors corrected" in the text rather than in footnotes; the absence of any
kind of index, even one of the poems by title; the absence in either
volume of the good bibliography that the *Princeton University
Library Chronicle* printed in February, 1946, or any bibliography.
Yet all these seem outweighed by the simple excellence of both
books and by our debt of gratitude to the editors.

49

Despite the wealth of related material in the volumes, it is possible here only to suggest an approach (based on a theory of organic and functional unity among the different forms of a man's writing which I have tried to sketch out in my chapter on Eliot in *The Armed Vision*) through hurried notes on a handful of themes in the criticism that seem significant in the poetry.

The irony of the South as Rome. In his essay "The South and Tradition," Bishop suggests an approach to the South through the analogy of Rome. He writes:

> So much would seem to be the fact of the Cavalier South. The myth is something else again; possibly it is more important. For when all is said and done, a myth is far more exciting to the mind than most discoveries of mere things. So long as Rome was a myth, a matter for the imagination, stirred only by a few battered columns and a dismantled Forum, Europe was able to produce an architecture from its forms, through three centuries incomparable for fecundity. But as soon as Pompeii and Herculaneum were unearthed, the facts of the Roman world uncovered, classical architecture died and in its place succeeded only the lifeless excellence of archeology.

Bishop's use of "myth" here will be discussed later. The important thing to note about this odd quotation is that when Bishop says "Rome," unlike almost any other writer, he does not mean the living city, the Catholic center, or the ancient civilization either flourishing or decayed. He means quite simply a place entirely dead and buried, which art can utilize only until it is dug up, when reality ends art's necessary illusion. This, with slight modification, is the view of the South he suggests for the Southern poet; that is, for himself. One of the best-known and most impressive of Bishop's poems, "The Return," dramatizing the destruction of a civilization apparently Roman through some sort of fated flood, would thus be a symbolic poem about the South (this conjecture is strengthened by another poem in *Now With His Love,* "Apparition," in which a Virginia forest is seen as "undersea.") The ironic core of "The Return," the fact that the civilization at its height triumphed by means of the sea (the "old sea-fights") and is now swept away by the same sea or sea-god in rebellion ("Temples of Neptune invaded by the sea") is Bishop's metaphoric point about the South. The qualities that were its strength eventually destroyed it, the forces once successfully propitiated turned suddenly and devoured it.

This is, obviously, a sharply realistic, ironic picture, not at all the cozy "myth" Bishop pretends it to be. Where the fantasy of the South actually takes him in (as the racist nonsense "a mulatress; hence sensuous beyond either of its parents" does in the essays) we get such unsatisfactory poems about the South as the aimless relativism of "The Truth About the Dew," and the history vitiated by sentimentality of "Southern Pines." Only where he could see the South, not through a "myth," but through a viable metaphor, which seems consistently to have been Rome, do we get poems as fully achieved as "The Return" or the almost equally impressive "An Interlude," with its deeply poignant conclusion:

> In the meantime, the barbarians are back in the passes.
> Nothing is left but to stay devastation by tribute.

Poetry as discipline and technique. "In criticism of the arts," Bishop writes in his essay "The Infanta's Ribbon," "the technical approach is often the most profitable." His display of it in the essay, in an analysis of the musicality in Verlaine's "Clair de Lune," both amazes us with the precision of his eye and ear, and impresses us with the formidability of a poetics based on that sensibility. A later essay, "The Discipline of Poetry," rejects the tradition of Whitman, Lawrence, and Sandburg as deficient in precisely this sense of craft, and quotes Baudelaire: "Any poet who does not know exactly what rhymes each word allows is incapable of expressing any idea whatever." Only from this discipline, Bishop says, does the poem get "intensity," which seems to be his key word. "What matters is intensity," he writes, "and with intensity the poem may survive anything—even archaic language." In a review in the *Collected Essays*, Bishop defines the poetic faculty informally as "that unpredictable vision which brings separated things together in a way that continues to move us and disturb us." He makes it clear, however, that "unpredictable" means just what it says, not either "irrational" or "uncontrolled," and in an essay on "Chainpoems and Surrealism" he is properly contemptuous of our modern forms of spirit-writing. "The unconscious," he notes, "so far as we have been allowed to perceive it in poetry, is not in itself very interesting."

Bishop's poetry, as we might expect, reflects this consciously classical approach as well as Bishop's superior ear, and shows a precision of technical effect rare in our time (Blake's "Minute Particulars" was a remarkably apt title for one of Bishop's volumes of verse). His imagery is of the most precise: in "And When the Net Was Unwound Venus Was Found Ravelled with Mars," a wartime afternoon liaison with an Italian harlot is prepared by such scenic personifications as a "together" bed and an "adulterous" dusk; in "October Tragedy," a French bourgeois seeking mushrooms, who stumbles on the body of a working girl murdered in a sex crime, had been out gathering "esculent rumps" (this last would be what Kenneth Burke calls a "Bellerophontic letter," the whole action foreshadowed in miniature). Bishop's mastery of rhythm is equally great. Here is the last stanza of "Admonition":

> Find the loveliest shroud you own,
> Stilt a ceremonious
> Height on gilded heels. Then summon
> To a rarity grown common
> Starved arachnid, the dead-louse
> And whatever feeds on bone.

The mockery of the loose trochaic rhythm, culminating in the shocking spondee of "dead-louse" in the penultimate line, and the final heavy line in irregular iambics, produces a stanza almost perfectly orchestrated. Bishop's resourcefulness in rhyme needs no more example than the lines in "Fiametta":

> Her shadow restores the grass' green—
> Where the sun had gilded it;
> The air has given her copper hair
> The sanguine that was requisite.

where the delicate half-rhyme of "gilded it" and "requisite," combined with the chiming internal rhyme of "air" and "hair," produces a tonal supplement to Fiametta's elusive grace. Bishop's musical effects are of the most varied, from tiny diminishing and augmenting assonances and alliterations to such full chordal effects as the sequence of "breast," "waist," "beast," and "fresh" in the second stanza of "Metamorphosis of M" and the sharp jarring consonance of "parrot's irritable rage" in "Account of a Crime." Finally, Bishop's use of larger formal structures, mostly improvised, in the later poems is masterful, and the Alcaics, hendecasyllabics, *rime riche*, and the rest in the early poems show the amount of formal experimentation that went into them.

Myth and ritual. Bishop's criticism shows the curious paradox of a rich understanding of ritual and a thin and superficial conception of myth. In the essay "The Missing All," he notes that Hemingway, wounded and buried in a trench for four days during the war, "had been dead and brought to life again," and that he later found in the Spanish bullfight "his own apprehension reduced to a ritual"; that is, in our terms, found a collective public rite in which he could merge his individual symbolic rite of reliving the experience. We are inevitably disappointed, then, when we see Bishop using "myth," in the essay "The Myth and Modern Literature" and elsewhere, not as the verbalization, slowly concretized, of this collective ritual experience, but as a kind of "romantic conceit," as in "the myth of the Old South"; in other words, a lie. It is this basic relationship of myth to ritual that Bishop misses in his otherwise excellent piece on *The Golden Bough*. Unable to comprehend Frazer's central point about religion, which is precisely that the truth of the myth lies in the reality of the ritual experience, he gets into a sterile debate over whether or not the book "attacks" Christianity. If, instead of kidding Jessie Weston's "rather nasty and doubtless pedantic interpretation of the real symbolism of the Lance and the Cup," Bishop had learned this relationship from her, had followed the transmutation of orgiastic rite into pretty legend, we would have been spared the one indubitably silly piece in the *Collected Essays*, the piece on "Sex Appeal in the Movies." Many of Bishop's critical problems stem precisely from his failure to relate myth to ritual: he is dissatisfied with the concept of American folk arts as "pretty bedquilts and quaint portraits painted by itinerant talent," but has no clearer idea of what is missing than that it is something "European"; he finds that Eudora Welty's *Robber Bridegroom* does not make us feel "that terror of the forest which is always present in the tale of Grimm," but cannot understand why; he talks of poetry as "incantation," but seems in practice to mean no more than prestidigitation.

In his poetry, inevitably, Bishop is strong where he stays close to the reality of the ritual experience, weak where he goes off into his disembodied myth. The poem that seems to be popularly taken as his best, "Speaking of Poetry," states a theory of poetry in terms of the necessity of a "ceremony" or ritual that "must be found":

> Traditional, with all its symbols
> ancient as the metaphors in dreams;
> strange, with never before heard music; continuous
> until the torches deaden at the bedroom door.

It is this ceremony that will wed the "Desdemona" of form to the "huge Moor" of content (or the members of any comparable poetic dichotomy), and the poem demonstrates its theory by being itself such a ritual, and encompassing the marriage with moving beauty. The other poems framed around the ritual experience tend to be successful, if not to the same degree: "Wish in the Daytime" records a rebirth rite; "And When the Net Was Unwound," making a fertility ceremony of a casual copulation, roots the myth of Mars and Venus in the reality of experience; "The Coming of Persephone" and "Narcissus," with imagery related to that of the Mars-Venus poem (the three make an odd triad) also base their myths in the sex experience. Bishop's poems on classic themes, with sexual and ritual elements heavily emphasized, tend to be among his best. When he experiments with Christian mythology, however, he has no comparable sense of an underlying ritual experience, and such poems as "Easter Morning" and "The Emperor Also Was a God," both about the Crucifixion, fall into the sort of gossipy flatness that Robert Frost rewriting the Book of Job has made peculiarly his own.

Influence and imitation. For a heavily eclectic poet, Bishop wrote curiously little in his prose on the relationship of a poet to his predecessors and contemporaries. In the essay "Homage to Hemingway," he discusses Hemingway's relationship to such "ancestors" and "masters" as Twain and Flaubert, Sherwood Anderson, Ezra Pound, and Gertrude Stein, but the only generalization that emerges is "telling him what he must not do, for a young writer perhaps the most valuable aid he can receive." In an early review of Edgar Lee Masters, Bishop remarks that Masters' failure is due "to his determination to make poetry out of books which he has scarcely read." "It is not that fine poetry may not be created out of books and lonely meditation," he adds, but he gives no formula for this alchemy, other than that the poet who goes into the library for material must stay there "long enough."

Bishop's poetry reveals an enormous indebtedness. Merely to name a few of the more obvious influences, there are: Browning monologues ("Portrait of Mrs. C"); Cummings derivatives ("Riviera"); many Pound-influenced poems ("The Return" is the best of them); MacLeish imitations ("Occupation of a City"); a pseudo-Lindsay ("Mister Preval's Ball"); and any number of Yeats reminiscences (only "Hecuba's Rage" entirely comes off, but half a dozen others, among them "Young Men Dead," "A Defense," "Poor Tom's Song," "Divine Nativity," and "Whom the Gods Love" can stand comparison with a good deal of Yeats's work.) Sometimes the influence is a definite borrowing, probably unconscious, as where Eliot's two stanzas in "Whispers of Immortality" beginning "Donne, I suppose, was such another" and ending "Allayed the fever of the bone" boil down in Bishop's "John Donne's Statue" to:

> Proud Donne was one did not believe
> In heirs presumptive to a bone

and Webster's magnificent "Cover her face. Mine eyes dazzle. She died young" becomes the somewhat less magnificent "Give me your hand. She was lovely. Mine eyes blind" in Bishop's "Boudoir." In at least one case, the influence is consciously recognized and rejected in a parody, the marvelous burlesque of middle-period Pound in Bishop's "Frankie and Johnnie."

The impossibility of translating poetry. In a review entitled "On Translating Poets," Bishop confesses "I have spent some time, over a period of twenty years, trying to turn, now Latin lines, now lines written in some speech derived from the Latin, into an English that could be read without displeasure and without distrust." His conclusion is that it is impossible, that either you get a very different English poem or a useful "trot," but that either, for a number of reasons, is nevertheless worth doing. Bishop's own translations, printed as a section of the *Collected Poems*, seem to belie this: almost without exception they are impressive poems in their own right, and the few I have been able to check are unexpectedly faithful to the original. Bishop might be said to translate from six languages—Greek, Latin, Provençal, Spanish, French, and Arthur Rimbaud. His Rimbaud sonnet, "Venus Anadyomene," seems to me, along with some of Ben Belitt's work, the most impressive Rimbaud translation of our day. The other high point of the translations is a rendering of "Ieu M'Escondisc, Dompna, Que Mal Non Mier," from the Provençal of Bertran de Born, which succeeds, as an English poem, as fully as Pound's Provençal translations (I have no way of knowing whether it is as free). In his review, Bishop justifies translation as an exercise, as a way for the poet to "keep his pencil sharp" and "keep the hand in." His own work suggests that in addition translation sharpens the poet's skill in his original work and adds to his technical resources, and may also, apparently to Bishop's surprise, produce new poems of beauty and distinction.

Tragedy and the tragic sense of life. Bishop believes that "the tragic sense of life" is possible, at least to Spaniards, particularly to Hemingway's bullfighters (it would be interesting to see what Unamuno would make of *that*). Tragedy in the traditional sense, however, is now impossible. Bishop writes in "Moll Flanders' Way":

> It is precisely the greatness of the novel that it has been able to do this: that, in circumstances so small that they have lost the potentiality of tragedy, it has been able to find tragic possibilities, not in what was done, but in the failure of accomplishment. . . .

Our substitute for tragedy is what Bishop calls "dramatic irony," and the chief dramatic irony, for Bishop, seems to be the physical reality of death. The modern world is like Trimalchio's Sybil, he says in one place: it wants to die, but death is not the tidy abstraction it thinks. Bishop writes, in "The Poems and Prose of E. E. Cummings":

> The armies and the governments of this world had ignored the lonely man; but death had not ignored him. It was only to the

individual that death paid any attention. It was this contrast between the death of a man—I have seen them dug up out of the earth of France at Montfaucon—this death known in the flesh that lives and rots, and the impersonal casualty lists put out by the governments that gave everyone who went through the War a permanent distrust and horror of abstract forms of information.

The sharpest irony for Bishop is the relationship of life at its most vigorous, sex, to death; that is: love and war, Venus and Mars, or the Chaucer lines from which Bishop got the title of his second volume of verse:

> What is this world? What asketh man to have?
> Now with his love, now in his colde grave
> Allone, with-outen any companye.

A central image of Bishop's poetry is the corpse's corruption, the rotting of what was once young and lovely, or powerful and vigorous; whether the girl of "Admonition" with the dead-louse, the old king of "Night" "hideously exhumed and set upon his warhorse," the "young men rotted" of "In the Dordogne," or the girl with "the face rotten" and the drawers "maculate with blood" among the mushrooms in "October Tragedy." We thus have a sequence, in Bishop's thought, from tragedy, to the tragic sense of life, to dramatic irony, to death and sex, to the corruption of the flesh. The only possible tragedy for us would have to run that gamut, and end as the consciousness of worm and rot, seeing the skull beneath the skin. It is this limitation, I think, that deprives Bishop's poetry of a final dimension. A typical example is his poem "Twelfth Night," which, being about the journey of the Magi, suggests comparison with the Eliot poem of that title. The comparative failure of this poem, as against Eliot's, might have been discussed above in connection with Bishop's inadequate sense of sacrificial ritual underlying the Christian mythology, but the essential difference seems to me to be that Eliot succeeds in making the experience tragic where Bishop does not. Eliot's poem ends:

> We returned to our places, these Kingdoms,
> But no longer at ease here, in the old dispensation,
> With an alien people clutching their gods.
> I should be glad of another death.

Bishop's ends:

> But gray evasions shamed their skeptic eyes
> And the starved hands were suddenly boned with cold
> As plucking their gorgeous skirts they shook to go.

Eliot's Magi are dying that life may be born (that the crops may sprout out of their corpses, in fact), and the experience is tragic; Bishop's will die disappointed at seeing, not a god, "but a small child petulant with cries," and the experience is only ironic and pathetic.

Poetry and criticism. Bishop's metaphor for criticism, in his essays, is the mutilation of a living thing. "Decorticate a stem," he writes in "The Infanta's Ribbon," "split it into its fibres—it can no longer bear a flower. We cannot with the knife reveal its life; we can but sever it." And yet, he adds, the dissection may tell us something, and seems worth doing. His own criticism, or surgical equipment for dissection, progressed from a review of Pound's first Cantos in 1922, which confesses, "I shall have to learn at least three more languages and read seven years before I shall pretend to recognize all the references," to the piece on *Finnegans Wake*, published in 1940 and revised near the end of his life, which analyzes a key episode, that of the "prankquean," with an industry, learning, and imagination that make it, along with William Troy's work, the best criticism of that difficult book we have. Yet Bishop was always torn between an attraction toward criticism and a fear of its cutting edge, and some of his aphorisms in the *Collected Essays* are as short and brutal as "Critics are dissectors and scavengers." Nevertheless, not only is his criticism a body of valid creative art, but many of his poems are as much criticism as poetry. "An English Lady" is a critical evaluation, cruelly satiric, of a Baedeker approach to art; "The Hours," the long memorial poem to F. Scott Fitzgerald, is an interpretation of Fitzgerald's life and work by way of a tribute; "The Spare Quilt" is, like "Speaking of Poetry," a metaphoric poetics; "Meaning of a Lion" is an allegory on criticism and the artist; and two short previously unpublished poems, "To a Critic" and "This Critic," are in fact remote enough from primary art to be what Marx and Engels subtitled *The Holy Family*, a criticism of critical criticism.

Poetry and painting. Bishop's essays constantly relate poetry to the plastic arts. A lecture entitled "Poetry and Painting," read at Princeton in 1940, sets out to demolish the distinction Lessing so laboriously erected in *Laocoön,* and to grant painting a dimension of time, and poetry a dimension of space (it does not quite succeed, in my opinion). In it Bishop quotes Allen Tate's charge that "in some of my poems I lean very far toward the painters," and admits it with no qualms. Analogies with painting are constant in his criticism, particularly with Picasso's work in *papier collé,* which he uses for work as disparate as Cummings' poems and Masefield's narratives. Picasso's collage is obsessive with him, in fact, and at least three times in the *Collected Essays* Bishop refers to what seems to be its key image for him, the fact that in it Picasso utilized "scraps of wallpaper from demolished houses." In his prose, Bishop uses something of a collage technique (his poetry, compared to Pound's and Eliot's, notably does not) and some of his visual descriptions, like a fine one of Harry Lehr looking like "a Gibson man carved out of a potato," are pure paste-ups.

As Tate suggests, many of Bishop's poems lean toward the pictorial. The best of these, "Perspectives are Precipices," converts the Bluebeard tale into an ominous Dali-like vista disappearing into the horizon (a comparison that would be offensive, if Bishop's criticism did not show enormous respect for that talented charlatan). Several other poems are simply descriptions of pictures: "A Recollection" of a picture of a Venetian courtesan he either saw in his childhood or invented for an earlier fiction piece, "How Brakespeare Fell in Love With a Lady Who Had Been Dead Some Time"; "A Frieze" of a real or imaginery frieze; "Paolo Uccello's Battle Horses . . ." of a Uccello picture he also discusses in "Poetry and Painting." Still others are done in the styles of painters: "Ode" in Picasso's, "Riviera" in style of satiric dry-point etching like Peggy Bacon's, etc.

Art and society. Bishop is concerned with the social relations of art only in the most neutral or reportorial sense. "What conditions are necessary," he asks in "The Myth and Modern Literature," "that a body of literature come into being in a country, in a region, which hitherto has had little or none that was of more than local interest?" He is concerned with art and social classes in this same neutral sense, and his essay "Manet and the Middle Class" explores Manet's relationship to the social currents of his time in quite dispassionate detail. Bishop praises and quotes Marx, as an economic observer, half a dozen times in the essays, distinguishing between this "great and often profound thinker" and his absurd "disciples." What Bishop scorns, and seems to have scorned consistently from his early work to his latest, through the thirties as through the twenties, is political and social *commitment* in the artist, that aspect of Marx and Marxism, for example, that is *not* neutral social science. The *Collected Essays* include a furious letter to *The New Republic* in 1933, "The Social Muse Once More," appealing to poets to flee politics, "the besetting sin of poets and one which has done them and their craft more harm than all forms of drunkenness and debauchery put together." All such artistic commitment, Bishop insists, results in didacticism or false art, which he distinguished from true art in "Moll Flanders' Way":

> Like all the great novelists who were to follow him, Defoe both partakes of the middle-class view of conduct and surpasses it. And he opposes it in the only way that is open to the artist to oppose any set of abstract principles: not, as our proletarian novelists would do, by offering in their stead another, and supposedly better, set of abstract principles, but by confronting them with the passions of life and the consequences of action.

In another place, discussing Vardis Fisher, Bishop redefines this dichotomy: "We ask of the novel that it give us, not the illusion of real life, but the reality of the imagination." In still another place, quite seriously, he announces Baudelaire as the poet of "the common man."

Bishop's poetry somewhat shatters this neat illusion of the artist as a truncated man, a neutral observer on a plane above mortal strife. When he opposes the values of life and sex to those of war and death in "And When the Net Was Unwound" and similar poems, Bishop is clearly using poetry to propagandize against war, and producing not didacticism but art. When, on the other hand, he ruins the poem "Night and Day" with the final lines

> And the end what?
> More speed, more hunger.

the poem is bad, not because it is didactic, or because Bishop is committed against speed and hunger, but because the lines are flat, inadequately fused into poetry, and irrelevant. Bishop's poems against didacticism inevitably fall into counterdidacticism, like "Harder It Is to Sing":

> Harder it is to sing than shout
> And rotten, rotten is the age.
> But what are all these poets about,
> Their throats constricted by their rage?

"Art and Action," an elaborate complaint against the demands that the poet take a political position, gets its strongest effect, not from the satiric phrasing, but by running sixteen lines on two rhymes, and playing the tradition of its elaborate formalism against its content. Where Bishop is most successful, in fact, is in his poems like "This Dim and Ptolemaic Man" that furnish a counter-perspective to the social (in this case, the universal, with the last stanza suddenly projecting the farmer in his rattly Ford against the movement of the spheres, as Eliot before Bishop did with Sweeney).

The figure of the artist. Bishop's two heroic figures in the essays are Yeats, who said, "I could recover if I shrieked my heart's agony," yet remained dumb "from human dignity"; and Joyce, who dedicated his life to "an exploration into the unknown." The figure of the artist, proud as Yeats and priestly as Joyce, is a thread that runs all through the prose, but the artist of the poetry is a much more ambiguous figure. He is not only the "mighty" lion in "Meaning of a Lion," finally eaten by jackals; he is the comic lover in "To His Late Mistress" who begins as Fortinbras and is corroded into Hamlet; he is the dying old grandfather who kept peacocks "When other reasons for pride were gone"; he is the Roman Senator in "No More the Senator" putting off his insignia of office and going into a monastery cell because "multiplying manuscripts" will save those whom Christ cannot; he is the youngest hunter in

"Your Chase Had a Beast in View" who sings with erotic delight as the leopards are slaughtered; he is even Poor Tom, who sings:

> Alas, to make music I must withdraw
> Into a fool's experience.
> Only when hair's pranked mad with straw
> Do my words make sense.

As these notes suggest, Bishop is a rather more complex figure than we have tended to assume. If he is not a deep thinker, his criticism shows as sound a mind and taste as any we have had in our time. If he is not a major poet (and despite Eliot, we still have no idea how to tell major from minor, nor in fact whether the terms mean anything), he is one of a half-dozen lyric poets in America in our century (Stevens, Marianne Moore, Cummings, Aiken, Ransom come to mind) who without a "great" or large-scale work, have produced a body of poems that seems assured of survival. Bishop's criticism and poetry are substantially of a piece, the complementary work of a man imaginative, passionate, sensitive, dedicated to art, and deeply humanistic. Each reinforces the other, and both together, in these fine editions, show us the depth of our loss at John Peale Bishop's untimely death.

A Manifesto From
"The Deflowering of
New England"

Oᵁᴿ ʟɪᴛᴇʀᴀʀʏ ɢʀᴇᴀᴛs are doubly important to us: as writers working in America (or outside it) their example can guide us as we face the same problems; at the same time that their existence a century before us has very much altered the problems, and made it either easier for us to do certain things, or unnecessary. "Neither the New Testament nor Poor Richard speaks to our condition," Thoreau wrote in his *Journal,* but the *Journal,* or those parts of it Thoreau called "sentences uttered with your back to the wall," still *does* speak to our condition. What we ask of these oracles, in so many words, is how the writer functions in America. Economically, must he live off a wife or two, like Emerson, or on inherited property, like Adams and James? If not, must he take a hack job, an underripe political plum (in our day, journalistic plum), whether arduous like Melville's or relatively easy like Hawthorne's? Can he actually simplify his life, as Thoreau did, enough to live by a minimum of labor, at a time when the only possible version of Thoreau's slogan is "Complify! Complify! Complify!"? Must our writers still expatriate themselves, like James, or live straddling two continents, like Adams, or renew themselves peri-

63

odically by travel abroad, like Emerson, Hawthorne, and Melville, or can they remain contentedly parochial in their own land, like Thoreau again? Must the writer, in fact, leave Concord for Boston?

Assuming that the writer will live, somehow, somewhere, how and what is he to write? Can he find his form early and stick to it, as Hawthorne did with fiction, or must he move restlessly back and forth between poetry and prose, with Emerson and Thoreau, or go whoring after the theater, like James, or interrupt a respectable nonfiction career, like Adams, to write shamefaced novels, of which he prefers "any dozen pages" to all his proper work? Shall he stay close to his experience, to ask the old chestnut, and what does "close to experience" mean, anyway—is *Walden* actually closer to experience than *The Ambassadors*, or *The Blithedale Romance* than *Moby-Dick*? What are the writer's relations to be to his fellows? Can they rest on a basis of solid mutual respect, like those between Hawthorne and Melville, or be friendly with an edge of patronizing on both sides, like those between Emerson and Thoreau, or amicable but wary, like those between James and Adams? Why could James appreciate Hawthorne so magnificently, and find Thoreau "imperfect, unfinished, inartistic"; how could Emerson get the idea that neither Hawthorne nor Thoreau had ever quite panned out as a writer; what led Hawthorne to find Thoreau "the most tedious, tiresome, and intolerable" fellow alive, yet to brood so obsessively over his death? All these writers seem to have given each other plots and ideas, to have found jobs for one another and gotten one another's work published and puffed, but on the deeper level of community of mind, had they as much influence on each other as they had on men they never saw?

What can these writers tell us of the relation of the artist, *as artist*, to politics? Even the word "politics" means one thing in the case of Hawthorne, a machine Democrat in Salem getting political jobs; another in the case of Adams, descendant of Presidents and high-level maneuverer; still another in the case of Emerson, lecturing the citizens of Concord on the iniquities of the Fugitive Slave Law. What has happened in the half century between Thoreau's renouncing his allegiance to the state rhetorically in "Civil Disobedience" and James renouncing his citizenship quite literally with a recommendation from the Prime Minister of Great Britain "that he could both talk and write English"? If New England has decayed (and who, living and working in it, would dare to say that it hasn't?), has it any relation to this substitution of the real act for the symbolic one? Finally, there is the embarrassing and confusing question of the private and domestic lives of these writers, that is, not to put too fine a point on it, sex. On a scale of healthy and normal domestic life, Thoreau, priggish, terrified of women, dependent on his mother, and frigidly ascetic, would be at the bottom, followed closely by the spinsterish James; and Hawthorne and Adams, both of them fortunate in storybook marriages (until the death of Marian Adams), would be somewhere at the top. And yet, dare we say that the latter lives were fuller, or rounder, or even happier? Wouldn't a scale of tough-mindedness, of living in ecological balance with the world and dying with a minimum of whining be just as apt to run the other way? If Emerson's first marriage was passionate, short-lived, and tragic, and his second cold, long-lived, fecund, and contented, which one helped his work? What *is* the condition of "health" for the artist, is there any, and how would we know it if we saw it?

All these foolish examination-essay questions (discuss in five hundred words or less, use one side of the paper only) travesty the sort of thing we really want to know. The real questions are unaskable: what *good* is Emerson to us now, has Melville any use, will Thoreau help us if we call on him, can Adams feed us in the wilderness? How did they live, what did they *really* do, what were they *essentially*, how can we get to *be* them? What *is* the meaning of the American experience, of the American literary experience, of being a writer in this maddening country?

We waste our time going through well-bred critical biographies and literary studies with questions of this sort. Perhaps the critical biography, at least of American writers, is just an impossible form. The old American Men of Letters series, published by Houghton Mifflin about the turn of the century, foolish and outmoded as much of it is, had many things of value. The authors were themselves men of literary stature, like Oliver Wendell Holmes on Emerson, or they had known the subject in person, like Frank Sanborn on Thoreau, or they had something to say that had not been said before, like Thomas Wentworth Higginson on Margaret

Fuller. Yet none of them, certainly, is what we want and need, and even the best of them can no longer, in Thoreau's phrase, speak to our condition. A few isolated critical biographies of American literary men have been successful, the most imposing of them James's study of Hawthorne in the English Men of Letters series (for special reasons of sympathy and identification), and in recent years Newton Arvin's *Hawthorne* and neo-Marxist *Whitman* have been models of how much, within limits, the form can achieve. The blight on most of the recent efforts in the field has been the influence of Van Wyck Brooks's *Ordeal of Mark Twain* and *Pilgrimage of Henry James,* with their truncations, distortions, and simplistic "social" emphasis, encouraging such major falsifications by followers as Lewis Mumford's *Herman Melville.* It is amazing to see the Brooks doctrine still powerful enough for Van Doren to write of Hawthorne, in apparent seriousness: "He was crippled from the first, as so many Americans have been, by a suspicion of his own imagination."

Two works, however, seem to hold out hope that writing about American literary figures can yet come alive. The first of them is D. H. Lawrence's *Studies in Classic American Literature,* which cut to the heart of the American literary experience, and found it the mythic imagination. Lawrence's book has inspired few attempts along similar lines, however, except for Olson's *Call Me Ishmael* and Edward Dahlberg's egregious *Do These Bones Live?* Hawthorne's scenario for *Septimius Felton* frankly acknowledges the archetypal motif of "Medea's cauldron" in his plot (his retelling of Greek myths for children had at least served to bring them to his attention), but none of his commentators has had a comparable interest in his mythic patterns. The other work that should have had far more of a germinating influence than it has is F. O. Matthiessen's magnificent *American Renaissance,* which not only combines brilliant literary scholarship with keen aesthetic sensibility, but combines a Marx-influenced social criticism with a recognition of the value of Lawrence's approach and a fresh ritual emphasis of his own (Matthiessen was the first to point out, so far as I know, that *Walden* is a giant rebirth rite). *American Renaissance* remains the finest, if not the only serious, book we have on the great American writers.

There have been any number of recent biographies and critical studies, of varying degrees of merit. But none of them is entirely the book we want and need; and some of them bear no relation to it. Like Whitman before *Leaves of Grass*, we are all simmering, simmering; who will be the new Emerson, or even the exhumer of the old Emerson, to bring us to a boil?

NOTE [1963]: This excerpt is from a rather artificial debate. Richard W. B. Lewis, my friend and at that time my neighbor, was a fine literary critic who could not bring himself to publish any literary criticism. By way of getting him started, I split a batch of books for review with him. Our separate reviews appeared as "Two Views of the American Writer" in the Winter, 1950, issue of *The Hudson Review*. The next time I looked at the literary quarterlies, Lewis had articles in nine of them, so that apparently the scheme worked.

In *his* review, called "The Shock of Repetition," Lewis defines our philosophic difference. "Mr. Hyman is all for seeds, psyches, and material causes," he writes, "and I should confess that I am all for perfections, forms, and final causes." He goes on to remind me, in regard to my call for books giving us "living writers with guts inside them," that when Dante grew too interested in the scenes of hell, Virgil told him that "the desire to listen to these things is a vulgar (*bassa*) wish."

My own response to my demands was to write the next piece, "Melville the Scrivener," three years later. (I now regret that "scrivener." It means a professional public writer, which is the sense I wanted, but Melville used it to mean no more than "copyist," which is fatal to my intention.)

Melville
the Scrivener

[1953]

THE WORLD OF EVENTS, which was never too kind to Herman Melville in his lifetime, has been extremely thoughtful of him in the past year or two, by way of celebrating the centennial of *Moby-Dick*. The whaler *Anglo Norse* harpooned a great white whale in the Pacific. The leader of a group of Ku Klux Klan floggers in North Carolina turned out to be a lightning rod salesman. Attorney General McGrath, booted out of his job by President Truman, said as his last words in office, "God bless the President of the United States." On the flood of scholarly and critical works, omnibus volumes, radio programs, library displays, and centenary addresses, the Herman Melville Society (secretary Mr. Tyrus Hillway, Colorado State College of Education, Greeley, Colorado) floated happily, and a centennial edition of *Moby-Dick*[1] was published with 315 pages of notes and apparatus, more than half as long as the novel itself, justifying the editor's boast, "No other American novel has ever received such liberal annotation." In it Melville enthusiasts who had clapped for Tinker Bell as children could learn with some consternation that Sir James M. Barrie had modeled Captain Hook on Ahab. The author of a study of *Redburn* gave the present numbering of Melville's old home in Lansingburgh "for anyone who may wish to make a pilgrimage."

[1] *Moby-Dick: or, the Whale*, by Herman Melville. Edited by Luther S. Mansfield and Howard P. Vincent.

What are we to make of our Herman, "the phoenix of American letters" as Vincent puts it, "one of the foremost poetic imaginations in the world's literature" to Mr. Mason[2] in England, although he was "never more than a literary amateur"? What indeed are we to make of our Melville industry, with its radar post at Yale manned by Stanley T. Williams, its up-to-date electrocuting harpoons, its giant mechanized try-works, and its machinery for immediate canning or quick-freezing? We know so much about Melville, all of it patiently and marvelously won by our scholars: Sealts cataloguing Melville's reading, Vincent turning up the whaling documents he used, Anderson tracking him through the South Seas, Freeman straightening out the Budds, and all the others; we know it despite the ledgers and documents burned, the manuscripts destroyed or used as scratch paper by Melville himself, the letters cut up for signatures, the inscribed pages torn from books, and the correspondence thrown out by Harpers (which saved the contracts).

Our Melville scholars utilize each other's by-products in the most impressive of symbiotic relationships; the authors of all the current Melville studies acknowledge each other's moment-to-moment cooperation and bow individually to each of their predecessors—all except Mr. Thompson,[3] who crustily goes his own way, identifying all readings and interpretations not his own as misreadings and misinterpretations. The critics who have worked with Melville, whether mavericks like Edward Dahlberg and Charles Olson, who first gave us an insight into the importance of Shakespearean drama in fledging our phoenix, or respectable professors like the late F. O. Matthiessen and Newton Arvin, who gave us our first serious critical readings of Melville, have used this scholarship and have themselves contributed fact as well as insight to it.

What had first to be killed off was the biographical fallacy, brought to birth alongside the Melville revival by Raymond Weaver, that the early realistic novels are in large measure literal autobiography. Yet the most devoted exercise in exposing this fallacy, Gilman's study of *Redburn* as a work of fictional imagination,[4] is itself a mosaic of: "If young Pierre's presence at his father's

[2] *The Spirit Above the Dust,* by Ronald Mason.
[3] *Melville's Quarrel With God,* by Lawrance Thompson.
[4] *Melville's Early Life and Redburn, by* William H. Gilman.

sickbed had any foundation in life," "Herman may have experienced at this time the kind of fantasy he describes in *Redburn*," "If the experience Melville records in his story 'The Fiddler' is autobiographical," "if Melville, like Redburn," "Of Melville's further experiences in Liverpool, a few are identifiable with Redburn's and others may be safely assumed as true," "we must turn to allusions in his books for clues to his impressions."

We know so much about how Melville read the Bible, how he actually lived in the South Seas, what he took on a picnic in the Berkshires, but the man himself eludes us. We understand so little of what motivated this mysterious great writer that Gilman can explain, in all seriousness, that when Melville wrote Hawthorne in 1851, "What I feel most moved to write, that is banned—it will not pay," he meant "impassioned strictures on the evils of contemporary life"; Thompson can give us a Melville "sophomoric" and "of arrested development" writing Little Blue Books against God disguised as fictions; Mason can entirely miss the blunt sexual metaphor of "The Tartarus of Maids" and read it as "a bitter little descriptive essay on the indignity of mass labour"; Merrell Davis[5] can believe that the avengers of Aleema in *Mardi* are in the book as a carry-over from its earlier conception as a romance.

The publication of Jay Leyda's *Log*,[6] 900 pages of relatively unhewn biographical material, much of it new and striking or at least printed for the first time in full, gives us an unparalleled opportunity to study Melville for what he primarily was, a writer; to try to find out what being a writer in America was like or could be, how the artist lives, how he functions, and what he ultimately means. The people who write books and articles on Melville live almost without exception by teaching and write avocationally, and almost without exception they display an absolute incapacity to understand what writing professionally consists in and what it involves; they show an absolute unawareness that the area between writing for a living and writing for fun is at least as broad as the gap between the ranch and the dude ranch, or the brothel and the sorority house. "The literary career seems to me unreal," Arnold

[5] *Melville's Mardi: A Chartless Voyage*, by Merrell Davis.
[6] *The Melville Log*, by Jay Leyda.

wrote in *Essays in Criticism,* "both in its essence and in the rewards one seeks from it, and therefore fatally marred by a secret absurdity." In his copy of the book, after thirteen years in the Customs House, Melville wrote alongside the passage, "This is the finest verbal statement of a truth which everyone who thinks in these days must have felt." It is doubtful if many of our Melville authorities have felt or thought any such thing.

In the context of his society, Melville's outstanding characteristic would seem to be what Arvin in *Herman Melville* somewhat uncharitably calls "the tormented psychology of the decayed patrician." Impoverished and declassed, he could neither quite sustain the attitudes he had been trained in as a child nor substitute more satisfactory ones. He seems to have been a moderate Jacksonian Democrat all his life, drawn one way by loyalty to his brother Gansevoort, who was a fire-eating Tammany orator, and the other by the experience of his grandfather Thomas Melvill, a hero of the Boston Tea Party, who was callously fired from his job as Inspector of the Port of Boston by Jackson in 1829, an act that, according to a writer of the time, more "deeply shocked the moral sense of the community" than any other operation of the Jacksonian spoils system. Melville's writings show consistent awareness of the social issues of his day: Yoomy several times cries out against slavery in *Mardi;* Redburn's vision of the starving family in Launcelott's Hey is as terrifying a protest against society's iniquity as anything in *Capital; The Confidence-Man* is a bitter portrait of commercial America; the early books take up such "good" causes as the abuses of the missionaries, the horrors of flogging, the right of immigration, etc. "There is no telling who does not own a stone in the Great Wall of China," Redburn muses, and the imagery of marriage used for the fellowship between Queequeg and Ishmael, shocking as it is to our touchy age, seems to be the same mystic equalitarianism in another metaphor.

We have no way of knowing the intensity of Melville's concern with these matters. It comes as something of a surprise to note that the source for one of Melville's sharpest social criticisms —the story "Poor Man's Pudding and Rich Man's Crumbs," about the London poor fighting for leftovers from the Lord Mayor's banquet—is an amused and dispassionate record of the incident in his London journal, followed by the notation, "A good thing might be made of this." If Melville is not above working up social outrage for literary effect, we are entitled to distrust the degree to which any of the attitudes of his protagonists speak for him.

On the other great topic that agitated his time, religion, Melville is in approximately the same shifty middle position. We know that his irreverent language in conversation disturbed several of his friends. The note in Hawthorne's journal during 1856 is probably our best authority on Melville's views: "He can neither believe, nor be comfortable in his unbelief; and he is too honest and courageous not to try to do one or the other." Melville's own journal notes, on the voyage to Smyrna the next year: "Heartily wish Niebuhr & Strauss to the dogs.—The deuce take their penetration & acumen." None of this evidence of serious questioning accords with Thompson's contention in *Melville's Quarrel With God* that all the books are conscious, cleverly concealed tracts of heresy and blasphemy, but it probably accords no better with the view, omnipresent in our time, that "Billy Budd" is a final testament of Christian reconciliation. Melville's most elaborate discussion of the problem, *Clarel*, is a dramatic symposium where a number of conflicting viewpoints are posed and never reconciled, leaving us with Melville's own view as the sum and reduction of them all. Billy the Handsome Sailor is a Christian, if not a Christ, but this says little for his creator unless we are to assume that inventing Fedallah makes Melville a Parsee. At least we know from the record that he turned down that lightning rod.

Melville's reception by the special class of American society called reviewers was neither so bad nor so unanimous as we have been led to believe. Reviewing *Omoo*, Greeley recognized Melville as "a born genius," while George Washington Peck was attacking the book for "the perfect want of *heart* everywhere manifested in it"; *The United States Catholic Magazine and Monthly Review* added that its voluptuousness was not unreasonable, since its author was a Protestant. At least one anonymous reviewer, perhaps William Gilmore Simms, found *Mardi* "wild, warm, and richly fanciful." When Evart Duyckinck attacked

Moby-Dick idiotically in *The Literary World*, charging, among other things, that there was too much of Ahab, Hawthorne wrote him innocently that he thought the anonymous *Literary World* reviewer had missed the boat. Amid all the clamor of "bombast," "caricature," "clumsy as it is ineffectual," "sad stuff, dull and dreary, or ridiculous," "a monstrous bore," "maniacal," three or four reviewers praised *Moby-Dick* with qualifications, and at least one found it "a very superior" work, its final chapters "really beyond rivalry." If the *Boston Post* thought *Pierre* "perhaps the craziest fiction extant," and *The Albion* reported that "there is scarcely a page of dialogue that is not absurd to the last degree," we can at least see what they were talking about, and we can hardly quarrel with the *Anglo-American Magazine*'s description of the book as "a species of New York *Werther*," or with *Godey's Lady's Book*'s nastily accurate parody of its style. An article on Melville by Fitz-James O'Brien in *Putnam's Monthly*'s Young Authors series praised every work but *Pierre*; and a review of *The Confidence-Man* in *The Literary Gazette* attacked it by comparison with *Mardi*, "that archipelago of lovely descriptions," and *Moby-Dick*, "ghostly and grand as the great gray sweep of the rolling sea."

The real problem was sales. After the moderate popular success achieved by *Typee* and *Omoo*, Melville lost his audience with *Mardi* and never regained it, despite every effort. In America during the typical twenty-month period from August 1, 1876, to February 9, 1878, *Omoo* sold 33 copies, *Redburn* 35, *White-Jacket* 58, and *Moby-Dick* 66. From 1851 to 1887, *Moby-Dick* sold a total of 3,147 copies in this country. Melville wanted fame and adulation, but even more he wanted sales and needed money. After Harpers turned down *Typee* as obviously untrue and therefore "without real value," Melville's attitude toward publishers ranged from wary to contemptuous (Leon Howard,[7] a partisan of publishers against thoughtless and greedy authors, several times reproves him for this). Melville's letters to John Murray (reprinted as an appendix to *Melville's Mardi*), the English publisher of his first books, are a typical author's: cocky, patronizing, placat-

---

[7] *Herman Melville*, by Leon Howard.

ing, wheedling for money, suspicious that he is being cheated, and entirely unconcerned with the publisher's realities. He writes:

> In the first place, however, let me say that though your statements touching my previous books do not, certainly, look very favorably for the profit side of your account; yet, would it be altogether inadmissible to suppose that by subsequent sales the balance-sheet may yet be made to wear a different aspect?—Certainly,—without reference to the possible future increased saleableness of at least some of those books, on their own independent grounds, the success, (in a business point of view) of any subsequent work of mine, published by you, would tend to react upon those previous books. And, of course, to your advantage.—I do not think that this view of the matter is unreasonable.

Melville's growth to fame was a curiously organic process, but slow. For much of his lifetime he was the least-known serious writer in America. In 1856, less than five years after the publication of *Moby-Dick*, G. W. Curtis wrote him off with: "He has lost his prestige." So far as the record survives, he got only one mash note in his life, in 1857, from a Scottish girl named Eliza Gordon, who wrote:

> I have for this many a day been wishing to see you "to hear you speak to breathe the same air in which you dwell" Are you the picture of him you so powerfully represent as the Master peice of all Gods works Jack Chase?

A paragraph in the *New York Commercial Advertiser* in 1886 said Melville was "generally supposed to be dead." A column in the *Boston Post* replied that "such a state of things would be impossible here in Boston," where they had no trouble distinguishing the quick from the dead. When Melville died in 1891, the *Tribune* obituary said: "He won considerable fame as an author by the publication of a book in 1847 entitled *Typee*. . . . This was his best work, although he has since written a number of other stories, which were published more for private than public circulation." An obituary tribute in the *Times* was headed "The Late Henry Melville."

In England, Melville fared a little better. A review of *Typee* in *The Spectator* found it credible that an American sailor could have written the book, since the American lower classes were so much better educated than their English equivalents (Ah Gansevoorts!). Christopher North placed Melville with a review of *Redburn* in *Blackwood's*: "He will never have the power of a Cringle, or the sustained humor and vivacity of a Marryat, but he may do very well without aspiring to rival the masters of the art." If *The Athenaeum* found cause to dismiss *Moby-Dick* as "trash belonging to the worst school of Bedlam literature," *John Bull* reported that few books "contain as much true philosophy and as much genuine poetry" as this "extraordinary" book. If English reviewers tended to praise *The Confidence-Man* because it attacked "the money-getting spirit which appears to pervade every class of men in the States," or noted snidely that "few Americans write so powerfully as Mr. Melville, or in better English," the first serious appreciations of Melville's genius were by Englishmen, and a complete set of his works was in print in England as early as 1924, when only isolated volumes were available here.

The first active propagandist for Melville's work, and the man to whom all the volumes of Melville studies might fairly be dedicated, was William Clark Russell, a minor British sea novelist. In 1883 Russell tried to interest an American writer, A. A. Hayes, in doing a biography of Melville, "the greatest genius your country has produced." The next year he published an appreciation of Melville in an article entitled "Sea Stories" in *The Contemporary Review*, ranking him first among the "poets of the deep" and calling *Moby-Dick* his finest work, comparable to Blake and *The Ancient Mariner*. Russell wrote to assure Melville that "your reputation here is very great," corresponded with him, used every opportunity to praise his work as fit to rank with Elizabethan drama, dedicated *An Ocean Tragedy* to Melville, and in turn had *John Marr and Other Sailors* dedicated to him.

Shortly after Russell discovered Melville, two other Englishmen, James Billson and Robert Buchanan, took up the cause. Billson entered into correspondence as a fan, and Buchanan visited America and tried to locate Melville. He later wrote:

When I went to America, my very first inquiry was concerning Melville. . . . There was some slight evidence that he was "alive," and I heard from Mr. E. C. Stedman, who seemed much astonished at my interest in the subject, that Melville was dwelling "somewhere in New York," having resolved, on account of the public neglect of his works, never to write another line. Conceive this Titan silenced, and the bookstalls flooded with the illustrated magazines!

In 1885 Buchanan published in *The Academy* a poem in praise of Whitman, with a section devoted to Melville, "the one great imaginative writer fit to stand shoulder to shoulder with Whitman on that continent." A few years later a Nova Scotian professor named Archibald MacMechan entered into correspondence with Melville, and before Melville's death in 1891 Henry S. Salt had praised him in print, W. H. Hudson and Robert Louis Stevenson had become fans—the latter referring to him as "a howling cheese" in a letter—and a writer of boys' books named Charles St. Johnstone had walked up to Russell one evening and asked him casually whether he had ever read "the noblest sea book ever written, called *Moby-Dick*."

When this generation of English supporters died or retired from the battle, a new generation took it up, and D. H. Lawrence, E. L. Grant-Watson, and Viola Meynell were writing in highest praise of Melville's work before American writers knew it existed; Barrie paid it the sincerest form of flattery, while T. E. Lawrence write to a friend, "Melville is a great man," and found his war poems "magnificent." The tradition of English praise has continued down to the present, with Auden's perceptive study in *The Enchafèd Flood*. Only Mason's apparent ignorance of any English appreciation besides the Lawrences' and John Freeman's volume in the English Men of Letters series in 1926, enables him to publish *The Spirit Above the Dust* "in the hope of re-directing the interest of English readers and critics back to the swarming complexities and relevances of Melville's unusual art."

The growth of fame in America came much more slowly, and to this day probably fewer Americans would agree with Henry A. Murray that *Moby-Dick* is "of the same high order as the

Constitution of the United States and the scientific treatises of Willard Gibbs" than would agree with the summary of a contemporary reviewer in the *Boston Post* that Melville "has produced more and sadder trash than any other man of undoubted ability among us." In 1885, while Buchanan was complaining of his inability to meet the Titan, the New York correspondent of the Boston *Literary World* met "an old gentleman with white hair" in a bookshop, discovered him to be Herman Melville, and wrote his paper fondly, "Had he possessed as much literary skill as wild imagination his works might have secured for him a permanent place in American literature." In 1888, the year Russell dedicated his book to Melville as an avowal "of my hearty admiration of your genius," Charles F. Richardson wrote in the chapter "The Lesser Novelists" in his book *American Literature* that Melville "failed completely for lack of a firm thought and a steady hand." By 1900, when MacMechan had just published "The Best Sea Story Ever Written" about *Moby-Dick* in the *Queen's Quarterly*, Barrett Wendell's *Literary History of America* managed to say that Melville "began a career of literary promise, which never came to fruition."

The American revival began in 1919, the centenary of Melville's birth, with a two-part article by Frank Jewett Mather, Jr., in *The Review*, surveying all the works of "one of the greatest and most strangely neglected of American writers." The first full-length biography, Raymond Weaver's *Herman Melville, Mariner and Mystic*, appeared in 1921, a foolish and enormously influential book. By the next year Carl Van Vechten had written in *The Double-Dealer* that *Moby-Dick* "is surely Melville's greatest book, surely the greatest book that has yet been written in America, surely one of the great books of the world." All that remained to do was to rediscover the other works, a process in which we are still engaged, with two books on Melville in the twenties, one in the thirties, five in the forties, and at least half a dozen so far in the fifties. "You know perhaps that there are goodly harvests which ripen late," Melville wrote Bentley, "especially when the grain is remarkably strong."

Melville was perhaps no more and no less appreciated by his

fellow writers in America than is usually the case, "shock of recognition" theories to the contrary. Although Emerson, on the evidence of his journal and letters, was extremely interested in the legend of a great white sperm whale that attacked whaling ships, I know no evidence that he ever read any of Melville's writings, except possibly the anonymous "Hawthorne and His Mosses." Thoreau read *Typee* and mentioned an item of information from it in the first draft of *Walden*. Alcott also read *Typee* and mentioned in his journal that it was "a charming volume, as attractive even as *Robinson Crusoe*." Whitman reviewed it in *The Brooklyn Eagle* as "a book to hold in one's hand and pore dreamily over of a summer day," and reviewed *Omoo* in the same journal, recommending it as "thorough entertainment—not so light as to be tossed aside for its flippancy, nor so profound as to be tiresome." Longfellow noted in his journal, with a certain limitation of vocabulary, that *Typee* was "very curious and interesting," that he was reading *Omoo*, "a series of sketches of wild adventure," and that a day or two after *Moby-Dick* was published he "sat to read all the evening in Melville's new book, *Moby Dick or the Whale*. Very wild, strange and interesting." Margaret Fuller reviewed *Typee* in the *New York Daily Tribune* and advised, "Generally, the sewing societies of the country villages will find this the very book they wish to have read while assembled at their work."

George Ripley, who had attacked *Mardi* in the *Tribune* as Melville "leaving his sphere," reviewed *Moby-Dick* anonymously in *Harper's New Monthly Magazine* with greater perception than any of his fellows, writing:

> A new work by Herman Melville, entitled *Moby Dick; or, The Whale*, has just been issued by Harper and Brothers, which in point of richness and variety of incident, originality of conception, and splendor of description, surpasses any of the former productions of this highly successful author. . . . Beneath the whole story, the subtle, imaginative reader may perhaps find a pregnant allegory, intended to illustrate the mystery of human life. Certain it is that the rapid, pointed hints which are often thrown out, with the keenness and velocity of a harpoon, penetrate deep into the

heart of things, showing that the genius of the author for moral analysis is scarcely surpassed by his wizard power of description.

An editor at *Putnam's Monthly Magazine* wrote to Melville in 1854 that James Russell Lowell had read "The Encantadas" and "that the figure of the cross in the ass' neck, brought tears into his eyes, and he thought it the finest touch of genius he had seen in prose." There is no evidence that any of these authors ever wrote directly to Melville, or made any effort to meet him. A later generation of writers tried to get him to join the Authors Club in New York in the 1880s, but he pleaded that "his nerves could no longer stand large gatherings," rescinded his original acceptance, and only dropped in once or twice over the years. In 1890, a year before Melville's death, E. C. Stedman, perhaps persuaded by Buchanan, managed to get him to attend a literary dinner in his honor.

The only friendships Melville had with his fellow writers were with Oliver Wendell Holmes—who was his doctor in the Berkshires and, probably, the original of the doctor in "Me and My Chimney"—with Richard Henry Dana, Jr., and the celebrated friendship with Hawthorne. As early as 1846, Hawthorne had reviewed *Typee* in the *Salem Advertiser* noncommittally, noting that it would be extreme to call its "freedom of view" a "laxity of principle." When Melville's anonymous "Hawthorne and His Mosses" appeared in *The Literary World* in 1850, Sophia Hawthorne wrote to Duyckinck that the author was "the first person who has ever in *print* apprehended Mr Hawthorne. Who can he be, so fearless, so rich in heart, of such fine intuition?" At the same time, she and her husband spent part of their letters to Duyckinck praising the Melville books he had sent them. Hawthorne noted that *Mardi* "is so good that one scarcely pardons the writer for not having brooded long over it, so as to make it a great deal better." As the friendship between Hawthorne and Melville grew, and they saw more and more of each other at Pittsfield and Lenox, Sophia Hawthorne wrote in praise of Melville to her mother, affirming, with natural Peabody discretion, "I am

not quite sure that *I do not think him* a very great man." Melville
wrote Duyckinck in praise of Hawthorne's work, concluding, "Still
there is something lacking—a good deal lacking—to the plump
sphericity of the man. What is that?—He doesn't patronise the
butcher—he needs roast-beef, done rare.—Nevertheless, for one, I
regard Hawthorne (in his books) as evincing a quality of genius,
immensely loftier, & more profound, too, than any other American
has shown hitherto in the printed form."

Melville and Hawthorne spent their evenings together talking
"about time and eternity, things of this world and of the next,
and books, and publishers, and all possible and impossible matters." When Hawthorne in a letter appreciated and understood
Moby-Dick—which had been dedicated to him "In token of my
admiration for his genius"—to its author's satisfaction, Melville
wrote him, "But I felt pantheistic then—your heart beat in my
ribs & mine in yours, and both in God's"; asked, "Whence come
you, Hawthorne? By what right do you drink from my flagon of
life? And when I put it to my lips—lo, they are yours & not mine";
and concluded, "But truth is ever incoherent, and when the big
hearts strike together, the concussion is a little stunning." Melville wrote Sophia Hawthorne, in a statement that has been taken
too seriously by our scholars, that "the speciality of many of the
particular subordinate allegories, were first revealed to me, after
reading Mr Hawthorne's letter, which, without citing any particular examples, yet intimated the part-&-parcel allegoricalness
of the whole." Scholars interested in taking Melville's rhetoric
seriously might better have noted his special imagery for procreation, the paper mill, in the postscript to Hawthorne: "I should
have a paper-mill established at one end of the house, and so have
an endless riband of foolscap rolling in upon my desk; and upon
that endless riband I should write a thousand—a million—billion
thoughts, all under the form of a letter to you."

After this passionate drinking of the flagon of life together in
the Berkshires, there was little contact between the two until 1856,
when Melville visited Hawthorne at his consulate at Liverpool,
Hawthorne noting in his journal "we soon found ourselves on
pretty much our former terms of sociability and confidence."

There is no record that they ever quarreled except for Melville's
ambiguous "Monody" on Hawthorne's death:

> To have known him, to have loved him,
>   After loneness long;
> And then to be estranged in life,
>   And neither in the wrong;
> And now for death to set his seal—
>   Ease me, a little ease, my song!

The evidence suggests, however, that the big hearts only struck
together once, and then, stunned by the concussion, each darted
back into its own rib cage. In 1883, Melville told Julian Hawthorne
he was convinced Julian's father "had all his life concealed some
great secret," but failed to tell him, or us, what it was. Newton
Arvin has noted that their friendship began on an "astonishingly
sexual image," Melville's writing in "Hawthorne and His Mosses":

> Already I feel that this Hawthorne has dropped germinous seeds
> into my soul. He expands and deepens down, the more I con-
> template him; and further and further, shoots his strong New
> England roots in the hot soil of my Southern soul.

It ended, fittingly enough, on imagery of reticence and concealment.

If, as is generally believed, Hawthorne profoundly influenced
the final form of *Moby-Dick*, the only other contemporary writer
who seriously affected Melville's work may have been George
William Curtis. Reading for *Putnam's* in 1855, he advised J. W.
Dix, the new owner and editor, "I should decline any novel from
Melville that is not extremely good." When "Benito Cereno"
arrived, he reported: "Melville's story is very good. It is a great
pity he did not work it up as a connected tale instead of putting in
the dreary documents at the end," and the next day, "He does
everything too hurriedly now." Some months later Curtis wrote
Dix that before he printed "Benito Cereno" he should "alter all
the dreadful statistics at the end," and concluded, "Oh! dear, why
can't Americans write good stories. They tell good lies enough, &
plenty of 'em." The next year he wrote Dix praising "The Encan-

tadas" and "Bartleby." Howard believes that Curtis had the chance, and muffed it, to encourage Melville to build a novel like *Moby-Dick* out of "Benito Cereno." He suggests that it was submitted as notes for a novel, and that when Melville found he could sell it in its unaltered form he did so for the quick money, thus profoundly reshaping his career, which never again included a long prose work. If this oversimple but plausible conjecture has any truth, it would make Curtis at least as negatively influential as Hawthorne was positively influential. Curtis was the bad magician who bottled up the jinni that Hawthorne, the good magician, had briefly loosed.

Finances were at the heart of Melville's problems, and his whole life was a search for that viable economy for the writer that we have not found yet. A strong sense of insecurity was bred in him by what Gilman has charted as "four cycles of prosperity and adversity, or of promise and discouragement," in his first twenty-one years. *Typee* suggests the quality of Melville's memories of those years:

> There are none of those thousand sources of irritation that the ingenuity of civilised man has created to mar his own felicity. There were no forclosures of mortgages, no protested notes, no bills payable, no debts of honour, in Typee; no unreasonable tailors and shoemakers, perversely bent on being paid; no duns of any description; no assault and battery attorneys, to foment discord, backing their clients up to a quarrel and then knocking their heads together; no poor relations everlastingly occupying the spare bedchamber, and diminishing the elbow-room at the family table: no destitute widows with their children starving on the cold charities of the world; no beggars; no debtors' prisons; no proud and hard-hearted nabobs in Typee; or, to sum up all in one word—no Money! That root of all evil was not to be found in the valley.

A standard of living beyond his means was set for him by his mother, who, greatly to Gilman's displeasure, kept a servant in the worst period of adversity, although Gilman believes "she and her older daughters could have carried on the household without assistance." As early as 1847, when he was the successful and relatively prosperous author of *Typee* with *Omoo* due to appear, Melville started trying to get a job in the Treasury Department in Washington. Almost twenty years later, in 1866, Melville got his job as Inspector of Customs at New York at $4 a day. In the interval his writing had been unable to support him, writing and farming together were no more successful, and writing and lecturing had failed for the good reason that he was a dull and boring lecturer, although a Cincinnati paper found his voice "as soft and almost as sweet as the warbling of the winds in cocoa groves."

By 1875 he was a vanity author, publishing *Clarel* at his uncle Peter Gansevoort's expense (it set Uncle Peter back $1,200). Inspectors' pay at the Customs House was reduced to $3.60 a day, although the next year it was restored to $4. In 1877, Melville was almost dismissed, and his working hours were increased. He wrote to his aunt, Catherine Lansing:

> So it appears that I used in my letter to you the expression *"people of Leisure."* If I did, it was a faulty expression—as applied in that case. I doubtless meant people the disposition of whose time is not subject to another. But it amused me—your disclaiming the thing, as if there was any merit in *not* being a person of leisure. Whoever is not in the possession of leisure can hardly be said to possess independence. They talk of the *dignity of work.* Bosh. True Work is the *necessity* of poor humanity's earthly condition. The dignity is in leisure. Besides, 99 hundredths of all the *work* done in the world is either foolish and unnecessary, or harmful and wicked.

In 1886, the *New York Commercial Advertiser* noted that Herman Melville, generally supposed to be dead, "had, indeed, been buried in a government office" and "of late years he has done nothing in literature." In 1890 George Parsons Lathrop wrote to Horace Scudder, who had proposed that Lathrop do a Melville biography, "Melville, I believe, is alive still, clinging like a weary but tenacious barnacle to the N. Y. Custom House," although he had resigned five years before, and was now independent and even wealthy from good-sized legacies his wife and he had received. A columnist for a Boston paper wrote in 1889: "If I am not mistaken, Melville in his later years has been free from the drudgery of the custom house, but with him, as with many other literary men, pecuniary independence came too late to enable him to revive his powers of invention and description."

Few modern Melvillians, bolstered by academic tenure and two and a half cents a word from *The Walloomsac Review*, realize how seriously Melville tried to be a popular and successful writer. He was at least as practical about money as Wellingborough Redburn, who, down to his last penny after buying supplies for the voyage, pitched it into the water, noting that "if the penny had been a dollar, I would have kept it." Melville wrote to Hawthorne in 1851, just after finishing *Moby-Dick*:

> I am so pulled hither and thither by circumstances. The calm, the coolness, the silent grass-growing mood in which a man *ought* always to compose,—that, I fear, can seldom be mine. Dollars damn me; and the malicious Devil is forever grinning in upon me, holding the door ajar. My dear Sir, a presentment is on me, —I shall at last be worn out & perish, like an old nutmeg-grater, grated to pieces by the constant attrition of the wood, that is, the nutmeg. What I feel most moved to write, that is banned,—it will not pay. Yet, altogether, write the *other* way I cannot. So the product is a final hash, and all my books are botches.

Babbalanja in *Mardi* suggests the same split when he says that Lombardo was impelled to write by, "Primus and forever, a full heart. . . . Secundo, the necessity of bestirring himself to procure his yams," and adds that wanting the second motive, it is doubtful if the first would have sufficed.

Melville wrote Bentley in 1849, about *Mardi:* "But some of us scribblers, My Dear Sir, always have a certain something unmanageable in us, that bids us do this or that, and be done it must— hit or miss." Within a few months he was writing Lemuel Shaw to precisely the opposite effect about *Redburn* and *White-Jacket:*

> But no reputation that is gratifying to me, can possibly be achieved by either of these books. They are two *jobs*, which I have done for money—being forced to it, as other men are to sawing wood. And while I have felt obliged to refrain from writing the kind of book I would wish to; yet, in writing these two books, I have not repressed myself much—so far as *they* are concerned; but have spoken pretty much as I feel.—Being books, then, written in this way, my only desire for their "success" (as it

is called) springs from my pocket, & not from my heart. So far as
I am individually concerned, & independent of my pocket, it is
my earnest desire to write those sort of books which are said to
"fail."—pardon this egotism.

Melville's journal in London that fall noted that *Blackwood's*
was foolish to take *Redburn* seriously and "waste so many pages
upon a thing, which I, the author, know to be trash, & wrote it
to buy some tobacco with." The next month he wrote Duyckinck
thanking him for his review of *Redburn* and noting its general
favorable reception:

> I am glad for it—for it puts money into an empty purse. But I
> hope I shall never write such a book again—tho' when a poor
> devil writes with duns all around him, & looking over the back of
> his chair—& perching on his pen & diving in his inkstand—like
> the devils about St. Anthony—what can you expect of that poor
> devil?—What but a beggarly *Redburn*!

A year later he wrote Richard Henry Dana, who had praised
Redburn and *White-Jacket*:

> In fact, My Dear Dana, did I not write these books of mine
> almost entirely for "lucre"—by the job, as a woodsawyer saws
> wood—I almost think, I should hereafter—in the case of a sea
> book—get my M.S.S. neatly & legibly copied by a scrivener—
> send you that one copy—& deem such a procedure the best
> publication.

After *Moby-Dick* appeared, Sarah Morewood wrote to George
Duyckinck of their friend Melville, "I think he cares very little
as to what others may think of him or his books so long as they
sell well." Melville was willing enough to have a censored edition
of *Typee* published. He wrote Murray: "The book is certainly
calculated for popular reading, or for none at all.—If the first, why
then, all passages which are calculated to offend the tastes, or offer
violance to the feelings of any large class of readers are certainly
objectionable." *Redburn* was proposed to Bentley as very much
unlike *Mardi*, "no metaphysics, no conic-sections, nothing but
cakes & ale." At the end of his life, Melville noted in "Billy Budd,"
perhaps wryly, "There is nothing nameable but that some men
will undertake to do it for pay."

It is this apparent split in Melville—the desire for fame and money, and the desire to write exactly as he pleases, the spiritless complaisance and the stubborn integrity—that has puzzled commentators, who relax into a hopelessly split Melville. We see this symbolized best by the Leyda book's harpoon on the spine of one volume and Customs House badge on the other, its end papers contrasting a map of downtown New York with a map of the Pacific Ocean, a map of the environs of Pittsfield with a map of the whole world. Comprehending the unity of Melville requires a kind of critical vector analysis, calculating the point a professional writer reaches under the differing propulsions of "message" and "market," or, to change the metaphor, his point of greatest return in both economies. If *Mardi* is self-indulgent and *Redburn* hacking, or, to use a newer vocabulary, if the first is inner-directed and the second other-directed, *Moby-Dick* would seem to be the successful compromise. Here expression meets communication, poetic weds rhetoric, opposites fuse, and the result is a masterpiece.

If Melville found no satisfactory adjustment to the American economy, his relation to his domestic economy seems, on Leyda's evidence, better than has been supposed. We see his family and friends chiefly as they motivate and shape his writing, but on the superficial level his family impulses seem to have been strong, and he was an affectionate son and father and at least a dutiful husband. In the works themselves, in terms of symbolic action, things are somewhat more complicated. The biographers have made much of Melville's filling in his mother's name instead of his wife's as the mother of Stanwix on the boy's birth certificate, but this small Freudian slip can hardly compete with the intricacies of the mother-sister-wife ambiguity in *Pierre*. We have the testimony of his niece that Herman said his mother hated him, which may or may not be so, but of Pierre it would be more accurate to say his hates mother him. As Arvin has pointed out, the whale is a mother symbol as well as a father symbol and not only, I think, the mother in her role as castrator, the mythic *vagina dentata*. The thing to note is that the whale contains part of Ahab, his leg become whaleflesh (as Ahab has an ivory leg, whalebone become Ahabflesh); that is, they are consubstantial in the most literal sense, tied together by the umbilical cord of a harpoon line, and are thus in some sense patently mother and son.

As for Melville's wife Elizabeth, who wrote to her stepmother that part of each working day was spent making herself look "as bewitchingly as possible to meet Herman at dinner," she is a whole spectrum of fictional women, from Yillah to the shrewish wife of the narrator in "I and My Chimney." If she found *Mardi* full of "fogs," and tried to hush up the fact that her husband was writing poetry, she appreciated at least his physical presence, and during his absences found the house "utterly desolate." Henry A. Murray, in an address "In Nomine Diaboli" (which he has managed to present at five different colleges and publish twice to date),[8] revives all the old Lewis Mumford gossip about sex frustration and incompatible marriage "with wall shoved near." But generalizing from the work to the man, instead of vice versa, is always risky; and E. L. Grant Watson's ingenious conjecture, stated in Mason's book, that "Benito Cereno" is an allegory of marriage—presumably Melville's—is hardly the richest reading we have of that ambiguous story.

Melville certainly, like any writer, derived material from his family and friends, but that is a far cry from obsession. The rankling grievances of Major Melvill, cast out despite his Revolutionary War services, must have inspired *Israel Potter,* but using the story of Potter found in an old pamphlet as a vehicle for the emotion was an act of conscious craft. As the pamphlet story embodied his grandfather's grievance, we can see the treatment accorded his grandfather serving in turn as a vehicle for Melville's own sense of inadequate reward, but by this time we are as remote from Melville's biography as *Lear* is from Shakespeare's.

We get a similar interpenetration when we go after the family origins of "Billy Budd." On one level, Billy is certainly based on Melville's uncle Thomas Melvill, the major's son, who was court-martialed in 1832 for "yielding to paroxysms of passion" aboard the *Vincennes* and jumping "with his feet upon the breast of Thomas Spence an O. Seaman," and was found guilty but let off because of "the strong provocation given." On a deeper bio-

[8] Currently, in its Princeton version, in the *Princeton University Library Chronicle Moby-Dick* Centennial Issue, Vol. XIII, No. 2 (Winter, 1952).

graphical level he is Melville's young son Malcolm, who inexplicably shot himself at the age of eighteen; on still a deeper one he is Melville himself, the innocent victim of inflexible law. Lieutenant Guert Gansevoort, Melville's cousin, who helped to hang three alleged mutineers on the brig *Somers*—one of them went to his death, after his commander explained that "the honor of the flag and the safety of the crew required his hanging," saying "Yes, sir, and I honor you for it; God bless that flag!"—is certainly the original of Captain De Vere. Yet, equally, the first character is based on God the Son and the second on God the Father, neither of whom is known to have been either a Melville or a Gansevoort.

Gilman suggests that Melville's cousin Priscilla Melvill is the source of Isabel in *Pierre*, since her mother was French and she wrote impetuous and much-underlined letters revealing "a romantic and passionate nature," but, since we know nothing of Priscilla, that leaves us about where we were. Vincent's ingenious suggestion in *The Trying-Out of Moby-Dick* that Queequeg is based on Hawthorne gives us a wonderful metaphor for their friendship—the joint offering of burnt biscuit to a pagan idol—but not much additional insight. Finally, there is the matter of the origin of "Bartleby." We are told that it is "a portrait from life" and "based upon living characters," but nothing more than that. We know from Howard that Melville's philosopher friend George Adler spent his later life confined in an asylum with severe agoraphobia, and that may be the story's germ. Yet "Bartleby the Scrivener" is no more reducible to agoraphobia than *Hamlet* is reducible to abulia, and if Melville's overwhelming story of the terrible strength of weakness is a portrait from life, it is a portrait from our own lives. Gifts in Melville's household were always and characteristically books, and it is ironically typical of that bookish man that his family and friends should have come down to us as *literary* problems.

Narrowing the circle still further, we get the writer, finally, where he belongs, at work in his study. If his wife's testimony can be trusted—and the exaggerations of *Pierre* bear it out—Melville's schedule was rigorous. Living in New York in 1847, he spent his days: breakfast at eight, then a brief walk while his room was

cleaned, then to work until twelve-thirty, lunch, an hour's walk
with his wife, work again from two to four, dinner, reading what
he had written to his wife for an hour, a walk downtown until
eight, an evening with the family in the parlor until bed at ten.
When he moved to Pittsfield in 1850 and was at work on *Moby-
Dick*, the schedule altered: rise at eight, walk or split wood, feed
the horse and cow, breakfast, write from nine to two-thirty or
later, feed the horse and cow, dine, ride to the village, then the
evening in his room. This approximate schedule of five or six
hours of writing a day, barring interruptions and special events,
or a good day when he wrote until four or five o'clock, continued
until 1866, when Melville went to work in the Customs House
and became an evenings-and-Sunday writer.

In short stories like "The Happy Failure" and "The Fiddler,"
Howard says, Melville wrote away his ambition, and in "The
Lightning-Rod Man" he wrote away his fear. Howard thus sees
Melville's art as personal purgation. Mason calls the movement
from *Moby-Dick* to "Billy Budd" a progress from man's insanity
to heaven's sense, what we would call a movement from rejection
to acceptance. The opposed terms in Melville's own cathartic
dialectic were fact and fancy. He wrote Murray of the genesis of
Mardi:

> Well: proceeding in my narrative of *facts* I began to feel an in-
> curable distaste for the same; & a longing to plume my powers for
> a flight, & felt irked, cramped & fettered by plodding along with
> dull common places,—So suddenly standing [abandoning?] the
> thing alltogether, I went to work heart & soul at a romance which
> is now in fair progress, since I had worked at it under an earnest
> ardor.

In the course of writing *Moby-Dick*, Melville had written bitterly
to Hawthorne:

> What's the use of elaborating what, in its very essence, is so short-
> lived as a modern book? Tho' I wrote the Gospels in this century,
> I should die in the gutter.

With his view of the essential absurdity of authorship and its
incompatibility with a system of rewards and punishments, Mel-

ville took adverse reviews as entirely gratuitous, and in 1849, in a letter to Duyckinck, foreswore the practice: "I shall never do it again. Hereafter I shall no more stab at a book (in print, I mean) than I would stab at a man." By the next year, he had forgotten his resolution and took an anonymous stab at Cooper in print, and when he did later give up reviewing, it was because he wasn't popular enough to be asked, or because, as he wrote Duyckinck in 1863, turning down a book for review, "I have not spirit enough."

With travel and nonfictional narrative equated with cramping *facts*, critical writing equated with personal assault, and his exercise of fancy in romantic fiction unappreciated and unrewarded, Melville was left with his final and never entirely satisfactory equation, that of fancy and poetry. During the Civil War, he wrote his brother Thomas that he had sold a great lot of his "own doggerel" to a trunkmaker at ten cents the pound, which seems to be a self-deprecating way of saying that he had burned a batch of poems, an event commemorated by his bitter lyric "Immolated." An anonymous reviewer in *The Nation,* perhaps Charles Eliot Norton, dismissed *Battle Pieces* with "Nature did not make him a poet,"[9] and when *Clarel* was published at Uncle Peter's expense, Melville's first thought was not to put his name to it. His second, characteristically, was to hope it would revive his fame.

Within the formal organization of his books, of course, a writer lives more fully and much more satisfactorily. Insofar as they are individual rituals, symbolic actions for reshaping himself and his environment in a fashion he is unable to encompass realistically, each is essentially a dramatic operation. Gilman calls attention to the dramatic structure of *Redburn* as anticipating the fuller dramatism of *Moby-Dick,* and Howard notes Melville's conscious attempt to make *Moby-Dick* a dramatic romance resembling Shakespearean tragedy: the reference to Ahab as "a mighty pageant creature, formed for noble tragedies," the allusion to "tragic

---

[9] Mason has only expanded this when he writes: "Melville is not at all an easy poet to appreciate with fairness, for he attempts a lyric form with the slenderest of lyric equipment. His ear was poor, his rhythmic sense uncertain, his taste by no means infallible."

graces" to be woven around "meanest mariners," the stage directions, soliloquies, and curtain climaxes. The editors of the Centennial *Moby-Dick* remark on the dramatic titles and structures of a number of the chapters. Thompson's triumphant discovery of several different voices or viewpoints in the books, which he uses as evidence that Melville is gulling his readers, is actually a discovery of the novels' dramatic structure. The three viewpoints in *Redburn* he calls Wellingborough (the former naive self), Redburn (the narrator), and Melville (the author) are actually three of the dramatic personae in the action; and the split he proclaims of Melville's psyche into Ahab and Ishmael (we should add the whale) is precisely what Rank shows us as the way Shakespeare created Antony, Brutus, and Cassius by splitting the son's ambiguous relationship with the father into three simpler strands. This is the sense in which all dramas are internal to the dramatist. We can readily see Melville's attitude toward Christianity, say, split into warring voices in *Mardi* or *Clarel,* or his view of America break up dialectically in *The Confidence-Man.* It is entirely fitting that "Billy Budd," the last work, should have converted so readily into a play and an opera.

Only Arvin, so far as I know, has taken the view that *Moby-Dick* is not dramatic, and beyond that, that Melville's "imagination was profoundly nondramatic." "The structure of the book has only a superficial analogy with that of tragedy or of drama in general," he writes, and prefers to find it epic, with its movement forward "not from climax to climax in the sharp dramatic sense, but from one wave-crest to another." Which is, really, only to isolate as essence one aspect of drama, its climaxes, while ignoring drama's more characteristic essence, its dialectic progress of the action through conflicts or agons, which allows us to say that epics as well as novels may have dramatic structure.

The trio of great short fictions, "Bartleby," "Benito," and "Billy Budd"—one might say Melville was concerned with B-ing—develop single aspects of *Moby-Dick*'s totality. Bartleby represents another phase of Ahab's quest for the absolute, although an Oriental, Nirvana one rather than Ahab's Western sacrificial immolation. Gilman describes Melville's "isolatoes"—Taji, Redburn, and Ishmael (why not Bartleby?)—as in a tradition of American

writing from *Walden* to "Prufrock"; Mason lists the "Melville
men" as Bulkington, Plinlimmon, and Bartleby, describing the
theme of "Bartleby" as "the victory of the passive and independent spirit over the engaged energies of social or moral compulsion"
and finding it an anticipation of Kafka; and Arvin toys with "schiz-
ophrenia" and "dementia praecox" for "Bartleby" before settling
for "the bitter metaphysical pathos of the human situation itself."
Our own primary grouping of "Bartleby" would probably be with
Ahab, an exploration of *"non serviam"* in passive rather than
daemonic rebellion.

Similarly, "Benito Cereno" explores the "secret of dominance,"
as Howard suggests, in other terms than Ahab's, inverting the
master-slave relationship, as "Bartleby" inverted the employer-
clerk relationship. Appearance is an illusion, an inversion of
reality (Gilman says this conflict is the theme of all Melville's
principal works) as Don Benito is revealed to be not the master
of his ship but the slave of his slave. What then of Ahab, in
effective command of the ship and his men, but mastered by the
whale, by Fedallah, by his own blind drives and black inexorable
passions, and far beyond emancipation? Finally, then, the last
story, "Billy Budd," takes up the problem once more, this time
through the Christian metaphor—as "Bartleby" had used the
Buddhist and "Benito" the Platonic—and raises it to the level of
tragedy. This innocent youth, made a proper tragic hero, if we
follow Aristotle, by the *hybris* of uncontrollable temper, or if we
follow the Bible, a sacrificial victim relatively without blemish,
must die to restore order on the ship, that is, for our salvation.
Like Ahab he must slay and be slain, but here the ritual is chan-
nelized, public, tribal, Catholic—not lonely, romantic, Protestant
—and its ultimate mood is acceptance. Ahab has come full circle.

Melville's "fables" are warnings against the absolute, Howard
says, quoting from a letter to Hawthorne: "But what plays the
mischief with the truth is that men will insist upon the universal
application of a temporary feeling or opinion." The icon of his
father is in this view the same lying prophet to Pierre that Fedallah is to Ahab, and Plinlimmon's horological time, the life of
l'homme moyen sensuel, like Ishmael, is the solution. To Melville, Howard adds, Ahab was suffering from what we would call

a "transference neurosis." Mason finds Bartleby's death "creative" whereas Pierre's was "wasted," and sees Bartleby as Plinlimmon's triumph. With these lonely defiers he equates Hunilla's "lonely submission," and, for Mason, Melville is as resolute an advocate of the absolute as Howard would have him its opponent. Vincent, in *The Trying-Out*, noted that all the characters in *Moby-Dick* are extensions or dramatic projections of Ishmael, but warned that the whale represented Evil to Ahab, not to Ishmael, and certainly not to Melville. The conception of ritual or symbolic action avoids these problems of identification by insisting that the book is a symbolic experience for the writer as well as for the reader, that he *undergoes* it and is altered by it, so that asking whether Melville agreed with Ahab is rather like asking whether Jonah agreed with the whale.

Too much of our criticism has discussed Melville's symbolism in terms of stasis rather than action, as though the symbols were fixed counters. The learned editors of the Centennial *Moby-Dick* find the chapter "Cutting In" a chapter "of pure exposition, without symbolic or special narrative purpose," which puts them in the position of the ichthyologist whose nets had holes an inch in diameter, and was able to assure the world that there were no fish in the water smaller than one inch. Vincent earlier, in *The Trying-Out*, noted the documents foreshadowing and embodying all a book's actions, what Burke calls "Bellerophontic letters" —the sermons in *White-Jacket* and *Moby-Dick*, Plinlimmon's pamphlet in *Pierre*—and thus could be expected to know that actions can be symbols too. Mason says Melville chose the symbolic rather than the allegorical method as Keats chose a life of Sensations rather than of Thoughts, and that the dramatic intensity of his symbolic imagination was able to fuse symbol into myth; Moby Dick thus becoming the "grand god" to Ishmael and presumably to us. For Richard Chase in *Herman Melville: A Critical Study*, however, everything is a dream-book allegory: the ship *Bachelor* "represents America sailing off evasively toward an archaic utopia," while the *Jereboam* "is America seeking with equal evasiveness a futurist utopia," and so forth.

Our commentators have been enormously interested in Melville's symbolism of white and black. Howard notes Melville's "black" truth opposed to the conventional darkness of error; Mansfield and Vincent trace Melville's "blackness of darkness"— used in "Hawthorne and His Mosses" as well as *Moby-Dick*—back to *Sartor Resartus*; Mason asserts curiously that Melville's white is, in White-Jacket's jacket, say, both evil and innocent. They tend to treat both symbols in isolation, rather than as the extremes of a spectrum whose middle section is gray. "Benito Cereno," for example, begins with everything gray: sea, sky, fowl, vapors, shadows. Melville's journal shows his reaction to the ambiguities of Jerusalem: "The color of the whole city is grey & looks at you like a cold grey eye in a cold old man."

In many of these questions, style must be our guide. At twenty, Melville was writing letters to his brother Allen in a dialect style that suggests Pound's letters at their most self-indulgent. Unlike Pound's, his development from there was toward steadily increasing discipline and control. Melville could be playfully funny in letters, like the suggestion to Duyckinck that pen and ink should be taken away from a Mr. Hart "upon the same principle that pistols are withdrawn from the wight bent on suicide," but the comedy in his works was always serious. Gilman, as Melville's friend Joann Miller did, finds parts of *Redburn* and other books very funny, but the words he uses—"comedy," "irony," "satire," "burlesque," "jollity," "whimsy"—suggest that he is talking about a number of different things and blurring their distinctions. Davis compares parts of *Mardi* to Rabelais, and certainly some of the chapters in *Moby-Dick* deserve this comparison more than the one Thompson makes with Sterne, noting with what appears to be real distaste some of *Moby-Dick's* dead-pan phallic punning. Where Melville's irony was sharp, as in his dedication of *Israel Potter* to the Bunker Hill Monument, the resemblance is to Swift, and it is the traditional devices of satire that create the layers of belief and disbelief that Thompson devotes so much effort to peeling apart.

Duyckinck first noticed, although unsympathetically, the audacious punning in *Moby-Dick* on whaling and blubbering, climaxed by the whaler *Rachel* weeping for her children; and the preface to *Typee* contains a bold pun (lost in our blunter time) on the disadvantages to the Polynesians of "their promiscuous intercourse with foreigners." This is all pretty far from humor, and actually represents a serious compression of meaning, as Egyptian sacred texts are packed with puns to increase their magical efficacy. We can see the technique clearly in the ambiguities later attached to Biblical names like Ishmael (the outcast redeemed in exile, the wild man made blessed and fruitful), a name Melville began by using in *Redburn* as a simple synonym for outcast. Mansfield and Vincent note that the name "Moby Dick" may come from the Biblical "Moab," in Hebrew "seed of the father," but fail to note what "Dick" is apt to mean in this context. It is an evidence of Thompson's basic lack of perception, and may suggest how absolute the willful refusal to read can be, that he gets the significant name "Steelkilt" as "Steelkit" throughout his book.

Melville wrote Hawthorne in a famous passage, perhaps echoed by Eliot later, that he "had no development at all" until he was twenty-five, and that it was from that time that he dated his life. *The American Review* of New York, reviewing *Mardi* on publication, noted shrewdly that it had been shaped as a more pretentious work than the two that preceded it by a particular "flattering unction" from English critics, the "astonishment expressed that a common sailor should exhibit so much reading and knowledge of literature." Like Blake's, Melville's mind naturally concretized abstractions. One of the ideas that gradually became symbolic in the works was conscious diabolism. Melville wrote on the margin of his copy of *Lear*, "The infernal nature has a valor often denied to innocence." Referring to *Moby-Dick*, he wrote Hawthorne of "the hell fire in which the whole book is broiled," and suggested that its secret motto was Ahab's "*Ego non baptiso te in nomine patris, sed in nomine diaboli.*" He wrote Sarah Morewood not to buy or read the book: "A Polar wind blows through it, & birds of prey hover over it." When an anonymous large sperm whale destroyed the whaler *Ann Alexander* almost on publication day, Melville wrote Duyckinck, "I wonder if my evil art has raised this monster." But that this evil art was a process, not a condition, in Melville's mind is obvious from the statement to Hawthorne that beautifully anticipates the concept of symbolic action in literature, "I have written a wicked book, and feel spotless as the lamb." When Henry Murray refers to the book as "a great product of the demi-urge," he is, along with a whole segment of psychoanalytic thought, simply ignoring the rebirth part of death-and-rebirth rites.

Melville's formal intellectual development could be called a progress from the naive Rousseauism of *Typee*, in which man is born free but is everywhere (except Typee) in chains, to the equally naive Schopenhauerism of his last year, when he underscored in his copy of *The World as Will and Idea* the line "the preponderating magnitude of the evil and misery of existence." More in his fashion, Sensation rather than Thoughts, was his re-experiencing of Shakespeare's insights, as Keats did in his last years. On his first serious reading of Shakespeare, in 1849, Melville wrote, absurdly, to Duyckinck "if another Messiah ever comes twill be in Shakespeare's person." By the next year he was back on his feet, and beside the statement in his edition of Chatterton "and though Shakspere must ever remain unapproachable," he wrote "Cant. No man 'must ever remain unapproachable.'" Whether Melville ever approached the Stratford Messiah or not, a similarity of pattern emerges from Mason's very suggestive chain of comparison: *Moby-Dick* with *Lear*, *Pierre* with *Hamlet*, *The Confidence-Man* with *Timon*, and "Billy Budd" with *The Tempest*.

One of the causes of Melville's recent shift, in a year, to this side idolatry in regard to Shakespeare may have been his rather comic American chauvinism, which reached some sort of peak in 1850. At a dinner party that August, when Holmes laid down some propositions on the general superiority of Englishmen, Melville attacked him so vigorously that Holmes was led to suggest that within twenty years the United States would grow men sixteen and seventeen feet high, "and intellectual in proportion." "Hawthorne and His Mosses," written the same year, proposes that since America has so many literary geniuses, "let her not lavish her embraces upon the household of an alien." It is remarkable that Melville's reaction of fascinated distaste to London was so much like what we can presume Eliot's to have been that he put down in his journal notes for what can only be *The Waste Land*:

> While on one of the Bridges, the thought struck me again that a fine thing might be written about a Blue Monday in November

London—a city of Dis (Dante's)—clouds of smoke—the damned &c—coal barges—coaly waters, cast iron Duke &c its marks are left upon you, &c &c &c

"If an inhabitant of another planet should visit the earth," John Jay Chapman is alleged to have said, "he would receive, on the whole, a truer notion of human life by attending an Italian opera than he would by reading Emerson's volumes. He would learn from the Italian opera that there were two sexes; and this, after all, is probably the fact with which the education of such a stranger ought to begin." Whether an inhabitant of another planet would learn from Melville's volumes that there were two sexes is a question of some interest. He might deduce that there were three, or none, or one, or many. He would learn from *Moby-Dick*, for example, of the Canaller "ripening his apricot thigh" on the sunny deck; from a letter to Duyckinck that Fanny Kemble Butler seemed so masculine on the stage that "I should be curious to learn the result of a surgical examination of her person in private," and from another that Melville loved "all men who *dive*." From the journal he would learn that Leigh Murray had "the finest leg I ever saw on a man"; that harem ladies in Constantinople "look like nuns in their plain dress, but with a roundness of bust not belonging to that character"; and that a picture of Lucretia Borgia in Rome showed a "Good looking dame—rather fleshy." If he read the American edition of *Moby-Dick*, as against the English, which deleted a number of suggestive references in "The Counterpane" and "Nightgown" chapters, he would learn that Queequeg's grasp was of a "bridegroom," that his hug was "matrimonial," and that they finally went to bed "in our hearts' honeymoon." In both editions he would learn of Stubb's supper of penis steak, of Stubb's wild phallic dream about kicking, and of the mincer's curious garment, arraying him as for an archbishoprick. If he came from a Freudian planet, the visitor would not fail to note such imagery in *Mardi* as Taji's description of Yillah as "my shore and my grove, my meadow, my mead, my soft shady vine, and my arbour," or her conception as a blossom fallen into the "opening valve of a shell," or Yoomy's poem about a maiden who may or may not be Yillah in the imagery of valley, soft meadow, and dell. Then when he read a biography he would be further confused to learn of Melville's marginal checking of Shakespeare's twentieth sonnet, which Arvin calls "the most frankly epicene of the sequence," and bewildered by beachcomber gossip that Melville had a child by the original of Fayaway. He might run to Italian opera for relief, or even to Emerson.

Finally, then, we are left with Herman Melville, a writer in America a century ago. We have photographs, and the fragments of a physical picture: Duyckinck reports a worked satin vest, Willie saw him "with his cigar and his Spanish eyes," Hawthorne as "a little heterodox in the matter of clean linen," a man named Field as "the most silent man of my acquaintance," and a young visitor noted on his first encounter, "His countenance is slightly flushed with whisky drinking." We know that Melville had weak eyes, that he developed severe rheumatic pains in his back in 1855, suffered the next year from "neuralgic complaints in his head and limbs" and "a morbid state of mind," and that his nervous system was disturbed by a bad spill in a carriage in 1862. He had what was apparently some sort of nervous collapse while reading proof on *Clarel* in 1876, and, on his wife's testimony, couldn't receive even his sisters. The next year Herman was "*morbidly* sensitive, poor fellow" in his wife's correspondence, and later, "poor fellow he has so much mental suffering to undergo (and oh how *all* unnecessary) I am rejoiced when anything comes into his life to give him even a moment's relief." About that time he wrote a postscript assuring his brother-in-law, how seriously we cannot tell, that he was *not* crazy. The next year he suffered from paralysis of the hands, then a kind of "rheumatic gout." By 1888, his memory had weakened, and he took a four-year-old granddaughter to Madison Square Garden, forgot her there, and had to go back and get her. Many of his symptoms suggest a psychosomatic complaint, but lay diagnosis of a stranger over a century's gap is not without its hazards.

All his life Melville flirted with anonymity. The piece that made him his first literary friendship and ultimately helped to shape *Moby-Dick*, "Hawthorne and His Mosses," was published anonymously. Melville proposed publishing *Pierre* anonymously, then *Clarel* (giving up only on "the *very strong* representations of his publishers"), and *John Marr* was so published. In "Hawthorne and His Mosses" Melville writes:

> Through the mouths of the dark characters of Hamlet, Timon, Lear and Iago, he craftily says, or sometimes insinuates the things which we feel to be so terrifically true, that it were all but madness for any good man, in his own proper character, to utter, or even hint of them. . . . Tormented into desperation, Lear, the frantic king, tears off the mask, and speaks the same madness of vital truth.

If all these basic questions about Melville, from his view of the absolute to his sexual leanings, are unanswerable, and if Melville is like Shapespeare ultimately unknowable, it is due to our inability to penetrate this mask, which is simply the mask or persona of art. Behind it the artist sits in darkness and anonymity, perhaps, as Joyce suggests, paring his nails. "Strike through the mask," Ahab exhorts us. How can we? Why in fact should we? In the last analysis it is the mask itself we want, and the face we see mirrored in it can only be our own.

Forays Into Hostile Territory

Psychoanalysis and the
Climate of Tragedy

[1956]

PSYCHOANALYSIS AND TRAGEDY are not easy matters to discuss from a mere reading knowledge, with no experience either behind the footlights or on the couch. Yet if we take tragedy not as a subdivision of drama but as a larger complex of attitudes and actions found in many literary forms, and psychoanalysis as a cultural rather than a medical phenomenon, specialists have written little enough to our purpose, and the overlap between the two areas has been so inadequately discussed that a critic of literature may perhaps be pardoned for stepping in brashly where theater people and analysts hesitate to tread.

Tragedy as we know it had its first and greatest flowering in fifth-century Athens, in the plays of Aeschylus, Sophocles, and Euripides, and its fullest theoretical formulation in the *Poetics* of Aristotle. The forms of Attic tragedy, as Aristotle half knew from tradition, derived from the sacrificial rites of Dionysus, in which the god in bull or goat form was annually slain, dismembered, and resurrected. The plots of Attic tragedy came principally from Homer, and the bloody stories of incest and murder fit the ritual forms so well because the Homeric tales themselves, as Rhys Carpenter has shown most fully in *Folk Tale, Fiction and Saga in the Homeric Epics*, derive from similar rites far from Mount Olympus. Out of the *agon* or dramatic conflict between the god in human form and his antagonists evolved the ethical concepts of *hamartia* or shortcoming, the tragic flaw; and *hybris* or pride, the imperfect insight into man's true stature in relation to destiny and the gods. These defects motivated the action, and for the spectators, in Aristotle's formulation, the tragic action aroused pity and terror and symbolically purged them through catharsis. The moral ingredients of tragedy are thus: the flawed protagonist swollen with pride; *peripeteia*, the sudden pitiable and terrifying change in his fortunes; and a cathartic climax that Herbert Weisinger in *Tragedy and the Paradox of the Fortunate Fall*, borrowing the phrase from Isaiah, has called the "small moment," that desperate awaiting of the fateful outcome when all seems in doubt.

Buried in the Old Testament there are tragic dramas, particularly the very Greek story of Saul and his "bloody house" in the books of Samuel, but the later priestly theology has imposed its institutional conception of the sacrificial animal without blemish on the earlier *hybris* stories, and revised such obvious tragedies as Jonah and Job, the former into a curious redemptive comedy that concludes on the parable of the gourd, the latter with an ending that begs all its questions and blandly returns all Job's earthly property twofold. On the basis of a theology where the only sins are disobeying God or worshiping rival gods, and the consequences of those are never in doubt, no agonistic form is possible, and the Judaic tradition has produced nothing like a tragic or dramatic literature.

Building on this tradition, Christianity too seems incompatible with a tragic literature, as Weisinger among others has shown. The great Christian drama of the Passion cannot be tragic because the perfection of Jesus eliminates *hybris* or any shortcoming, neither pity nor terror in Aristotle's sense is possible because of our inability to identify our own flawed human nature with the image of perfect goodness suffering absolute injustice, and the final victory is always certain. Drama with a human protagonist, insofar as it is Christian, cannot be tragic, since the issue has been settled once and for all by the victory of Jesus in His Incarnation, and His Atonement makes all subsequent private atonement unnecessary for the Christian,[1] who needs only some combination of Faith and Grace to

---

[1] I am leaving this statement in as a curiosity. I cannot imagine what came over me when I wrote it, since I know better and knew better then. Actually,

participate in the antecedent act. Dante properly recognized this in identifying his great poetic drama as a divine comedy. When tragic possibility is reintroduced in Christian history it is invariably repudiated as heresy: the Manichean belief that the issue has not yet been finally settled, denying Incarnation its victory; or the Pelagian repudiation of Original Sin, obviating divine Atonement.

Nor have the great Oriental faiths produced anything we could properly call tragedy. Since their common sacrificial figure, as William Empson reminds us in *Some Versions of Pastoral*, is not the Western Dying God, typified by Jesus on the Cross, but an antithetical image of The Sincere Man at One With Nature, typified by the Buddha under the Bo tree, no Passion is possible, and there can be neither struggle nor victory. Lacking our characteristic Western philosophy of change, the great Oriental faiths seem to lock man in a permanent dualism, which does not become resolved in time, but has always been transcended in a higher unity pre-existent in the blinding moment of eternity.

I would submit that the great tragic literature of the modern world has escaped divine comedy by being only nominally Christian, and in fact deeply heretic at key points. Shakespeare may be Christian in *Measure for Measure* and *The Tempest*, but *Lear* and *Macbeth*, *Othello* and *Hamlet* are Christian only in their insistence on the radical imperfectibility of man. They exist in a Manichean and Pelagian universe where the Incarnation has never happened and the Atonement consequently did not occur. In this universe proud man is locked in mortal struggle with the inner forces of evil, and must win through to some private redemption and true-seeing by means of his own suffering, with no otherworldly allies. The great tragic novels like *Karamazov* and *Moby-Dick* are similarly Manichean and Pelagian, with Jesus appearing in person in the first to hear from the Grand Inquisitor the failure of His Incarnation, and Ahab in the second, striking through the mask of the Christian Atonement and finding his own sacrificial atonement,

---

Christian orthodoxy insists that Christ's Atonement makes atonement by the Christian necessary, and in fact Christ's Atonement is the event that makes later atonement possible. Christ, in short, is the Christian's representative, not his substitute. My 1956 statement is not far from the Antinomian heresy, that justification by Grace exempts from the moral law. [1963]

that of a Pelagian man-god, in the consubstantial mystery of immolation with the great whale.

The rise of rationalism, whether in its characteristic eighteenth-century form as mechanical determinism or its characteristic nineteenth-century form as optimistic perfectibility, killed the tragic possibility that had coexisted with Christianity in pagan survival and Christian heresy. Francis Fergusson has defined the tragic rhythm of action in *The Idea of a Theater* as the movement from "Purpose" through "Passion" to "Perception" (acknowledging his debt to Kenneth Burke's *"poiema," "pathema," "mathema"*). Taking, as Aristotle did, Sophocles' *Oedipus Tyrannus* as the archetypal tragedy, Fergusson has discussed later dramatic literature as the hypertrophy of one or another phase of the tragic rhythm. In his terms, the rationalist world of mechanical determinism would permit no Purpose because we can have no free will or choice, no Passion because suffering becomes meaningless where we "understand" all and forgive all, and no Perception because no increase of self-knowledge could come from the discovery that everything has been externally caused. In the Victorian world of optimistic perfectibility (to return to our earlier terms) *hybris* can be dissipated by a bracing daily cold bath, *peripeteia* waits only on improvements in the social machinery, and what small moment of terror, doubt, or despair could survive the splendid teleological faith that the Heavenly City is at this moment having its building plots laid out on earth?

It is my belief that the writings of Sigmund Freud once again make a tragic view possible for the modern mind. Insofar as psychoanalysis is a branch of clinical psychology aimed at therapy, it is optimistic and meliorative (although Freud, in such statements as "Analysis Terminable and Interminable," was far more pessimistic about the difficulties and ultimate limits of cure in biological "rockbottom" than the majority of his followers). Insofar as it is a philosophic view of man and a body of speculative insights that can be turned on every area of culture (that is, what Freud called "applied" psychoanalysis), it is gloomy, stoic, and essentially tragic. Its basic recognition is the radical imperfectibility of man, a concept it derives not from the Christian Fall, but from the Darwinian

Descent. Freudian man is an imperfectible animal, and, as the biological punishment for having risen in the scale beyond the microorganism, a dying animal. The first protoplasm "had death within easy reach," Freud observes in *Beyond the Pleasure Principle*. For Freud, the aim of human existence is the reclamation of some cropland of ego from the "Zuyder Zee" of id, and the limited victory in this bitter struggle is achieved primarily through the traditional philosophic means of self-knowledge. Man's animal nature is to be controlled and channeled in the least harmful direction possible, not changed or abolished, and cure lies not in extirpating animality but in facing it and living with it.

Human life "is hard to endure," Freud says in *The Future of an Illusion*, but we must learn "to endure with resignation." "If you would endure life," he recommends in "Thoughts for the Times on War and Death," "be prepared for death." In such essays as "An Apology of *Raymond Sebond*" and "That to Philosophie, is to Learn How to Die," Montaigne confronted death as nobly and resolutely as Socrates in Plato's *Phaedo*, but without Socrates' eloquent faith in individual resurrection and the afterlife. Since many of us are not Socratics but skeptics, and our problem to adjust not to the dying animal that will be sloughed off to free some eternal spirit but to the dying animal that becomes putrid meat and nothing else, we might do well to eschew the easy consolations of religion and turn to whatever grimmer satisfactions exist in Freud's stubbornly materialist view. Here we can find not only an Original Sin—the Freudian myth of the expulsion from the Eden of the womb added to the Darwinian myth of the origin of death—in which the modern mind can believe, but some terrestrial hopes for redemption and the good life.

In terms of Greek tragedy, the Oedipus complex is another phrasing of *hybris* (of King Oedipus' own *hybris*, in fact), the child's swollen pride that he is a fitter mate for his mother than the tall stranger. Libido, the blind energy of sexual impulses, is equivalent to the ancient Greek "wild Ate," the daughter of Zeus and Strife, the wrath or madness that seizes the hero and moves him to senseless violence, destruction, or self-destruction. Sublimation is the small moment, the reintroduction of possibility, the birth of art and all human culture out of filth. Sublimation allows St. Francis to create a life of goodness out of an impulse to bestiality, or Bach to compose for an organ that is not the one with which psychoanalysis is preoccupied. Even the curative procedure of analysis itself, the transference, is a scapegoat mechanism, and Freud in his whole life and work is a sacrificial figure, almost a Dying God, even without the benefit of such probably apocryphal anecdotes as the one of Freud dashing out of his office shouting, "Why must I listen to such swinishness!"

If the human condition is ultimately animal, even swinish, man is nevertheless capable of moral action and sometimes of a life of sacrificial good, as Freud himself was. In terms of Ruth Benedict's somewhat oversimple dichotomy between shame cultures and guilt cultures, the Freudian neuroses are our own guilty or introjected equivalents for the public shame of wrongdoing in Attic tragedy, and they motivate an internal symbolic action like the redemptive ritual on the stage. For Freud, the choice is a newer dialectic statement of the old dualism, truly "beyond the pleasure principle": destroy others or turn the destruction inward. The ancient Zoroastrian divinities Ormuzd and Ahriman that Mani brought into Christianity are still locked in mortal combat in Freud's "exquisitely dualistic conception of the instinctive life," now called Eros the life instinct and Thanatos the death instinct. "The death instinct turns into the destructive instinct" when it is directed outward to the external world, Freud writes in "Why War?" and he concludes the grandest of his philosophic works, *Civilization and Its Discontents*, with the extremely moderate hope:

> Men have brought their powers of subduing the forces of nature to such a pitch that by using them they could now very easily exterminate one another to the last man. They know this—hence arises a great part of their current unrest, their dejection, their mood of apprehension. And now it may be expected that the other of the two "heavenly forces," eternal Eros, will put forth his strength so as to maintain himself alongside of his equally immortal adversary.

In essence, this prophetic statement, written as long ago as 1929, asks no more than the old horseplayer's reasonable prayer, "Lord, let me break even, I need the money."

If Freud produced a climate of opinion in which tragedy could again flourish, an important group of his followers in this country, the neo-Freudians or "revisionists," have done their best to dispel it as quickly as possible. In half a century of existence, psychoanalysis has raced through the whole religious cycle from revolutionary prophetic truth to smug Sunday sermon, and almost as soon as Freud's philosophy began to have an effect on our culture it was hushed up and denied in his name. The revisionists, principally the late Karen Horney, Erich Fromm, and the late Harry Stack Sullivan, along with a number of others of similar views, have put Freudian psychoanalysis into what Emerson called the "optative mood."

All began by publishing independently, but Horney and Fromm had had some contact in Berlin, where they had been influenced in varying degrees by Wilhelm Reich's "Freudo-Marxist" movement. Horney, who has written most extensively about the causes of her defection, has explained that she could not swallow either the views of feminine psychology Freud published in the *New Introductory Lectures* in 1933, or the death instinct, the former as a woman but the latter as a citizen. "Such an assumption," she writes of the death instinct in *New Ways in Psychoanalysis*, "paralyzes any effort to search in the specific cultural conditions for reasons which make for destructiveness. It must also paralyze efforts to change anything in these conditions. If man is inherently destructive and consequently unhappy, why strive for a better future?" In his more articulate strivings, befitting a social psychologist, Fromm found the gloomy fixities of biological instincts equally incompatible with hopes of improving the human condition by first making over society. Sullivan, from a very different background in clinical psychiatry, primarily with psychotics, came to similar conclusions. All three have influenced one another, first by their publications, later through direct discussion and a kind of uneasy collaboration. Their views and approaches, however, remain different enough so that one can choose to be a Horneyite, a Frommian, or a Sullivanite, and in some cases, like that of Clara Thompson, one can make several of these choices in succession.

The leading neo-Freudians, as well as their shifting followers, appear to be entirely sincere and dedicated psychoanalysts and psychiatrists, convinced by developments in the social sciences or by their own clinical experience that Freud was culture-bound, masculine-biased, cancer-morbid, or for some reason blind to what they can see. The result of their revisions has nevertheless, in my opinion, been not to improve or modernize psychoanalysis, but to abandon its key insights both as a science and as a philosophy. Their effect has been to re-repress whatever distasteful or tragic truths Freud dug out of his own unconscious or his patients', and to convert the familiar device of resistance into revisionist theory.

Freud always believed that "prudish America" would welcome his theories and water them down with equal enthusiasm, and his expectation has not been disappointed. The passion of Americans for constant reassurance that they live in the Garden of Eden (which Horney characteristically refers to as "the greater freedom from dogmatic beliefs which I found in this country") was in evidence as far back as 1912, when Jung wrote Freud from America that he was having great success in overcoming resistance to psychoanalysis by playing down sexuality, and Freud wrote back that he need not boast, since "the more he sacrificed of the hard-won truths of psychoanalysis, the less resistance he would encounter." Even predicting this American bowdlerization, however, Freud could hardly have imagined the extent to which it would be done in his name, in books worshipfully acknowledging his teaching or fulsomely dedicated to his memory. Paradoxically, with the aim of making psychoanalysis more scientific, the neo-Freudians have made it less so: where Freud was descriptive, they are hortatory; where he was the humble therapist, they are faith healers, inspirational preachers, be-glad-you're-neurotic Pollyannas.

The question of whether in fact Horney, Fromm, and Sullivan are Freudians or psychoanalysts at all seems to me of relatively minor importance, and is probably impossible to answer authoritatively anyway. In *The History of the Psychoanalytic Movement* in 1914, Freud reserved the right, as the founder of psychoanalysis, to say what it was and what it was not, but his various statements of the criteria involved shift disconcertingly. In the *History*, he calls the theory of "repression" in the unconscious the pillar on which the edifice rests, "really the most essential part of it," along with the empiric facts of "transference" and "resistance." "Every investigation which recognizes these two facts and makes them the starting-point of its work may call itself psychoanalysis," he writes, "even if it leads to other results than my own." Later in the book he describes the dream as "the shibboleth of psychoanalysis," and a few pages later declares that Jung's approach "no longer has the slightest claim to call itself psychoanalysis," apparently because it discards the sexual nature of the libido and the reality of the Oedipus complex. In other works, Freud makes the infantile sexual etiology of the neuroses the test of psychoanalysis, or remarks "a psychoanalytic, that is, genetic explanation."

If any investigation starting from the mechanisms of the unconscious may call itself psychoanalysis, the theories of Horney, Fromm, and Sullivan are probably psychoanalytic. They certainly recognize the existence of resistance and repression, and Horney even calls the concept of resistance "of paramount value for therapy." On the genesis of the neuroses from infantile sexualty, they are considerably less orthodox, since they recognize early sex frustrations as causative in some cases but insist that factors like "anxiety" or "the current life situation" are more relevant. They use the term "transference," but mean not a repetition of an infantile attachment, Freud's "cure through love," but, with Sullivan, a significant new sort of interpersonal relation, the first break in the patient's chain of "parataxic" distortions; or, with Horney, simply that human relationship of the patient's which is easiest to study, control, and explain to him. "As for the transference, it is altogether a curse," Freud wrote in a bleak letter to Pfister in 1910; it never occurred to him that he could solve the problem by a little Draconian redefinition.

If we take Freud's sexual concepts, so unattractive to Jung's American contacts in 1912, as basic, there is no likelihood of calling Horney, Fromm, and Sullivan Freudian psychoanalysts. I would take these basic concepts to be: *libido*, the volcanic sexual instinct; *id*, the caged beast of the unconscious ("a cauldron of seething excitement," Freud called it in a different metaphor); and the *Oedipus complex*, the destructive rivalry with one parent and attachment to the other. In varying degrees, the revisionists have denied all three or modified them out of recognition. For Horney, the libido concept is harmful nonsense suggesting discouraging limitations to therapy; the id is a "debatable doctrine" (what she keeps of Freud she calls "findings," what she rejects, "doctrines"); and the Oedipus complex does not exist in healthy adults, but is produced accidentally in neurotics, as Adler had suggested earlier, by parental sex-stimulation or parent-fostered anxiety. For Fromm, as for Jung, the sexual libido is simply an assumption "one does not share"; what Freud called id is largely eradicable drives produced by the culture; and the Oedipus complex is, Fromm agrees, the central phenomenon of psychology and the nucleus of all neuroses, but it is not a nasty sexual attraction to one parent and a murderous rivalry with the other, but merely a normal and healthy struggle against parental authority in the quest for freedom and independence. For Sullivan, sexual difficulties tend to be symptoms rather than causes, so that libido and id simply do not exist, and a variety of interesting interpersonal attachments take the place of the Oedipus complex.

The neo-Freudians insist on the importance of sociology and anthropology for knowledge of the ways in which the culture determines personality and character, or at least limits their possibilities. A good deal of their sociology, however, seems to be about as profound as Fromm's ingenious formulation "the most backward class, the lower middle class," and their anthropology is typified by Thompson's statement that Benedict has shown in the Kwakiutl or the Dobu "a whole society of psychically crippled and unproductive people," and that certain primitive cultures seem to be "predominantly destructive of man's best interests." If Fromm has read more modern anthropology than Freud, he has apparently been less affected by it, and cultural relativism has not laid a glove on him. In *The Sane Society*, Fromm equates all ethics with "Greco-Judaeo-Christian" ethics, a moral absolute, and remarks casually, "natural ethics, the Decalogue," with the engaging footnote: "Minus the first commandment, which bears on man's destiny and not on ethics."

The opportunity, vastly greater than Freud's, that the neo-Freudians have for acquiring some accurate information about the nature of man in society seems to have resulted only in cheerier illusions. Malinowski in *Sex and Repression in Savage Society* would appear to have confirmed the universality of the Oedipus

complex by finding among his matriarchal Trobrianders an equivalent, the male child's rivalry with the culture's father surrogate,
the mother's brother. The neo-Freudians have taken it instead to
show that, in Horney's words, "the generation of such a complex
depends on a whole set of factors operating in family life"; in other
words, that all such unwholesome manifestations are socially produced and could be eliminated by social change. If Freud generalized a universal human psyche from an early practice consisting
largely of neurotic Jewish middle-class women in turn-of-the-cen-
tury Vienna, a reading of *The Golden Bough*, and his own self-
analysis, all we can say is that the ingredients of that curious stew
simmered down to more wisdom than all the resources of American
industriousness have brought the neo-Freudians. Socrates sitting on
a stone in the market place still knows more about the world than
Alexander conquering it.

Ultimately, the differences of Horney, Fromm, and Sullivan with
Freud reduce themselves to a contrasting view of human nature, to
philosophic disagreement. The revisionists see man as fundamentally good, innocent, and unfallen; thus they inevitably have a different conception of human drives, relationships, and the aims of
therapy. In Horney's view of the child frustration, sibling rivalry,
the Oedipus complex, and similar factors are not ultimately determining; the important matters are "such parental attitudes as having real interest in a child, real respect for it, giving it real warmth,"
and "such qualities as reliability and sincerity." As for adults:

> It is so much easier for a woman to think that she is nasty to
> her husband because, unfortunately, she was born without a penis
> and envies him for having one than to think, for instance, that
> she has developed an attitude of righteousness and infallibility
> which makes it impossible to tolerate any questioning or disagree-
> ment. It is so much easier for a patient to think that nature has
> given her an unfair deal than to realize that she actually makes
> excessive demands on the environment and is furious whenever
> they are not complied with.

Horney cannot countenance the Freudian view because it would
allow "no liking or disliking of people, no sympathy, no generosity,
no feeling of justice, no devotion to a cause, which is not in the last
analysis essentially determined by libidinal or destructive drives."

The aim of therapy is not Freud's modest relief from neurotic difficulties, but "true happiness," to which most patients, she says, had never even dared aspire. "The enjoyment of happiness is a faculty to be acquired from within," she adds, and the end of analysis for the patient is "to give him the courage to be himself," or in another formulation, "by rendering a person free from inner bondages make him free for the development of his best potentialities." Horney never doubts that when the patient has the courage to be himself it will be a good self, or that he has best potentialities to develop, because she shares Rousseau's faith that "the spontaneous individual self" is born free and good but is everywhere in environmental chains. Beneath everything there is some sort of ultimate, absolute "genuineness" in the personality, and it is this that gives her her faith, against Freud's "disbelief in human goodness and human growth," that "man has the capacity as well as the desires to develop his potentialities and become a decent human being."

Fromm charges that Freud may have been inspired in his theorizing by "an unsolved problem in the relationship to his own mother," but nothing in Fromm's background has given him cause to doubt "the unconditioned love of the mother for her children *because they are her children*." The slogan of his "humanistic psychoanalysis" is "productive love," which enriches both parties and surpasseth understanding. Fromm's first book, *Escape From Freedom*, carries as its epigraph the unlovely Talmudic saying, "If I am not for myself, who will be for me?" His second book, inevitably entitled *Man for Himself*, explains how he got his key term ("Genuine love is rooted in productiveness and may properly be called, therefore, 'productive love' "). Since only a person genuinely capable of loving himself is capable of loving others, self-interest is a social good, as it was for Bernard Mandeville and Adam Smith. Fromm writes:

> The failure of modern culture lies not in its principle of individualism, not in the idea that moral virtue is the same as the pursuit of self-interest, but in the deterioration of the meaning of self-interest; not in the fact that people are *too much concerned with their self-interest*, but that they are *not concerned enough*

*with the interest of their real self; not in the fact that they are
too selfish, but that they do not love themselves.*

Even the superego in *The Sane Society* is loving and productive, "a
voice which tells us to do our duty, and a voice which tells us to
love and to forgive—others as well as ourselves."

The aim of therapy is naturally to free this true self for its true
productive loving self-interest. "Mental health is characterized by
the ability to love and to create," he writes, and "creation" as an
ideal is defined rather broadly: "an ever-increasing number of people paint, do gardening, build their own boats or houses, indulge in
any number of 'do it yourself' activities." As for the nature of man,
"we look upon human nature as essentially historically conditioned," and Freud's Manichean dualism becomes the Christian
certainty of victory for God's Party: "the forward-going life instinct
is stronger and increases in relative strength the more it grows."
We know that our redeemers live, even if they are only people in
the French Communities of Work with "a resilient spirit of good
will," "people who have said 'yes' to life"; not yet the truly "awak-
ened ones" like "Ikhnaton, Moses, Kung Futse, Lao-tse, Buddha,
Jesaja, Socrates, Jesus."

Sullivan's underlying philosophy seems essentially similar, although its expression is a good deal more rugged and considerably
less inspirational. In *Conceptions of Modern Psychiatry*, Sullivan
defines love as a "state of affectional rapport," which has "great
adaptive possibilities" and produces "a great increase in the con-
sensual validation of symbols." In *The Interpersonal Theory of
Psychiatry*, he redefines it in even clammier terms:

> Intimacy is that type of situation involving two people which
> permits validations of all components of personal worth. Valida-
> tion of personal worth requires a type of relationship which I call
> collaboration, by which I mean clearly formulated adjustments of
> one's behavior to the expressed needs of the other person in the
> pursuit of increasingly identical—that is, more and more nearly
> mutual satisfactions, and the maintenance of increasingly similar
> security operations.

For Sullivan, perhaps because so much of his clinical experience
was with psychotics rather than neurotics, the aim of therapy is less

ambitious: better interpersonal relations, better communication, and a positive direction toward goals of collaboration and of mutual satisfaction and security. He is less impressed by the miraculous "unique individual self" that will flower than Horney and Fromm, and his vision of the nature of man is not so much Rousseau's uncorrupted innocent as a neutral network of interpersonal relations, as capable of good, bad, or indifferent functioning as a telephone switchboard. How far it is from a tragic vision we can see in such comments as: "When difficulties in the sex life are presented by a patient as his reason for needing psychiatric help . . . the patient's difficulty in living is best manifested by his very choice of this as his peculiar problem."

Other neo-Freudians show similar optimism. Franz Alexander, the head of the Chicago Psychoanalytic Institute, sponsors a shorter and more directed therapy, in line with his idea that the therapist is not dealing with the stubborn sexual libido, but with three basic human tendencies he has named: to receive or take, to retain, and to give or eliminate. Clara Thompson believes with Fromm in "creative productive love," as a consequence of which she sees the aim of therapy as "calm self-possession," the patient "free to develop his powers." Like Horney, Fromm, and Sullivan, she simply cannot believe in the existence of evil. Surely a child "in a perfectly benign environment" would not show "serious destructiveness," and any child warped by bad parents can be readily redeemed "if a teacher, a Boy Scout leader or some other hero of childhood presents a consistently different attitude." Bruno Bettelheim, the principal of the Orthogenic School at the University of Chicago, calls on psychoanalysis to emphasize "positive human emotions and motivations," and to interpret behavior in terms of "inner freedom and human autonomy" and "man's inherent dignity." Beyond these, there are Fay B. Karpf's "Dynamic Relationship Therapy," and what Patrick Mullahy, a Sullivanite trained in philosophy, describes as "the sense of adequacy, competence, and power which comes from self-respect and respect for others—a rational feeling of power." An inch or two further, and we are lying down in green pastures beside Norman Vincent Peale.

The question is not what degree of therapeutic success these doctrines give, since the evidence suggests that any internally consistent system of interpretation accepted by the patient, from shamanism to the miraculous grottos of Zurich, can cure,[2] but rather what happens to literature in a culture that has shaped them and is in turn somewhat shaped by them. If tragedy requires Freud's stoic winning through to the perception of harsh truth, and all the influence of our psychology goes directly against it, then perhaps we should be content with comedy or even farce. Unfortunately, the neo-Freudian doctrines could as readily be shown, I think, to be uncongenial to art of any sort. Comedy and farce, like dreams, are the disguised fulfillment of repressed wishes. As the dream is organized in reaction to the commanding injunctions of the superego, so the comic arts get their structuring from a similar ethical conflict, the opposition of accepted what-ought-to-be to what-is. In the cultural determinism of the interpersonalists, where whatever happens is no individual's fault, comedy is as impossible as tragedy.

Lionel Trilling, who has been uniquely distinguished among modern literary critics by his defense of Freudian orthodoxy against vulgarization and revision,[3] has remarked that one of the greatest contributions of psychoanalysis to literature is its image of the mind as a kind of poetry-making machine, so that it constitutes almost a science of tropes. Insofar as literary or artistic form and dream form are the products of similar devices, and operations analogous to condensation, displacement, and the rest shape the poem, Freud has given us one of the great critical tools for literary analysis. Where the revisionists deny genetic and dynamic factors and insist on "the current life situation," here, as on so many occasions, they repudiate insight and hobble art. Burke has written in *The Philos-*

---

[2] In *New Statesman* for January 7, 1956, Dr. H. J. Eysenck of the University of London printed some disconcerting figures on psychoanalytic cure, based on a review of the published material. Of neurotic patients treated by means of any kind of psychotherapy, approximately two out of three recover. Of neurotics who receive no therapy whatsoever, approximately two out of three recover. In other words, two out of three is apparently the percentage of spontaneous recovery. Since then, none of the letters in *New Statesman* taking issue with Dr. Eysenck's conclusions has challenged these figures.

[3] Since this was written, Trilling has published his 1955 Freud Anniversary Lecture, *Freud and the Crisis of Our Culture*, with its bold and and brilliant vision of Freud's biological limitation as a sanctuary against the omnipotent tyranny of culture.

ophy of Literary Form that the poem consists of three aspects: dream, prayer, and chart. The neo-Freudian poem has for its dream, The validation of all components of personal worth; for its prayer, Help me to stop making excessive demands on the environment; for its chart, To thine own self-interest be true.

Perhaps a good measure of the fault lies in our country itself. In a paper, "Freud in America: Some Observations," read at the 1954 meeting of the American Psychological Association, Joseph Adelson discussed the resistance to Freud in terms of the deeply entrenched American idea of "the indefinite perfectibility of man" that Toqueville noted as early as 1835. Adelson writes:

> American feeling is animated by a zest for freedom; it cries out against constraint. While men may vary in what they achieve, their destinies are open and infinite. We may fall into error or failure, yet we do so, not because of an inner taint, but through circumstance; and circumstance, the American feels, can be rectified. Original sin, even in its most secular versions, has not attracted our thought. In changing the external, in modifying situations, men, we feel, can make and re-make themselves. It is in the idea of man's perfectibility and in the vision of a tractable world that Americans find their way to life's meaning. Throughout its history American feeling has struggled against the concept of limitation and has been held by the attitudes of hope and optimism.

Adelson summarizes Freud's contrary vision of human life, and adds:

> The American mood is substantially different. We experiment enthusiastically, trying this and that, all of our efforts informed by a vigorous faith in the endless plasticity of the human organism. It is my impression that we tend to disregard the dark and archaic components of the personality; at the very least we deprive them, rhetorically, of their vigor. Think of how Freud expressed the intensity of the instincts or of the superego— "oceanic," "surging," "raging." American psychology uses much blander adjectives. We tend to emphasize the ego's resources, its ability, somehow, to drive its way to health. In fact, the systems of Rogers, Horney, and Sullivan have in common the explicit assumption that the organism autonomously moves forward to growth. We incline to see the therapeutic task, then, as involving

the strengthening of ego capacities. A friend of mine puts it this way: "We don't try to kill the weeds; we feed the clover and hope that *it* will kill the weeds."

If Freud, *in conjunction with* other intellectual and social forces, succeeded in denting this Emersonian optimism in the period between the two world wars, many of his most articulate followers have since labored to hammer it back into shape. No one can say that any given work of art is affected by any given body of ideas, but we must assume in general that ideas have consequences. It is instructive to note how many important contemporary writers have followed their earlier tragic work with later mellowings. Hemingway is a classic example. Where *The Sun Also Rises* and *A Farewell to Arms*, if not masterpieces, are authentically tragic, moving from Purpose through Passion to Perception; such later novels as *For Whom the Bell Tolls* and *Across the River and Into the Trees* are merely bathetic; and if Robert Jordan or Colonel Cantwell commits *hybris*, the author seems no longer aware of it. Where "The Undefeated" was a truly cathartic work of art, its recent rewriting as *The Old Man and the Sea* is almost a Frommian parody ("If I am not for myself, who will be for me?"). Faulkner has moved similarly from a fiction of ritual tragedy in *The Sound and the Fury* and *Light in August* to optimistic comedy or fairy tale, as have Steinbeck, Caldwell, and so many others. Such dissimilar poets as Frost and Eliot traveled the same route from earlier bleak stoicism to such later chatty affirmations as *A Masque of Mercy* and *The Confidential Clerk*. If on the whole our poets have been less affected than the novelists by the retreat from tragic insight, it is perhaps only that not many of them were ever there to begin with.

We would all enthusiastically welcome the psychoanalytic good society, where every psyche was well and whole, and no one had impulses that could not or should not be gratified. To the extent that a good part of our literature depends on our being deeply and irremediably sick, renouncing it would be a small price to pay for general psychic health, just as Hegel was prepared to slough off art as an inferior form of communion when the stage of perfect communion was realized. Even within our limited experience at present, we can see how much our great literature depends on and is informed by the patterns of neurosis in our culture. To an unacculturated Cheyenne, King Lear would be simply an old man behaving very badly; to those gentle socialists the Mountain Arapesh, the whole disordered story of ungrateful children and rival claims to power and property would be meaningless. In real life, we are sure, Mr. and Mrs. Othello have no problem that a good marriage counselor couldn't clear up in ten minutes, and any of our clinics would give Iago some useful job around the grounds allowing him to work off his aggressions in some socially approved fashion.

Unfortunately, Mr. and Mrs. Othello do not exist in real life but in art, where their deadly misunderstanding is essential to our own well-being, and Iago is permanently out of the therapist's clutches. The psychoanalytic good society seems no nearer of achievement now than it did in Vienna in 1900, and to many of us it seems further off. Meanwhile all the Cheyenne are acculturated and apt to behave almost as badly as Lear, given similar provocation. If the Mountain Arapesh have not yet learned the joys of private property and early toilet training from our movies, they soon will, and one day they will all wear thin bow ties and know what bites sharper than the serpent's tooth. The trouble with the revisionist Freudians is not that they would give up art for the psychoanalytic good society, but that they pretend that it is already here, that we are well when we are in fact desperately ill, and they drive out art when it is almost the only honest doctor who will tell us the truth.

If Freud showed us that human life was nasty, brutish, and short, and had always been, he was only holding the mirror up to our own faces, saying what the great philosophers and the great tragic writers have always said. If we are serious, our reaction to this bitter truth is neither to evade it with one or another anodyne, nor to kill ourselves, but to set out humbly through the great tragic rhythm of pride and fall, so curiously alike in psychoanalysis and literature. At the end of this hard road we can see faintly beckoning that self-knowledge without which, we are assured on good authority, we live as meanly as the ants.

Jesting at
Scars

[1956]

Such questions as what song the sirens sang, or what name Achilles assumed when he hid himself among women, Sir Thomas Browne assures us, though puzzling, are not beyond all conjecture. Now that Dr. Bruno Bettelheim, principal of the Orthogenic School at the University of Chicago, has published in *Symbolic Wounds* his theory that puberty rites and a great deal else are expressions of male envy of the female, we can make a new stab at conjecture. The song the sirens sang to each virile hero must have been "Come to Me, My Melancholy Baby," and the name Achilles assumed was of course "Thetis," the name of the mother with whom he was identifying.

This is bold stuff, despite Dr. Bettelheim's very moderate manner, and his book is of some significance as one of the latest attempts to revise Freudian theory drastically, in Freud's name. At a time when psychiatrists are becoming increasingly overbearing in areas of discussion they only dimly apprehend, such as literature, and seem to develop a splendid assurance in inverse proportion to the mousiness of what they bring forth, it is a pleasure to see at least one Freudian psychologist and psychiatrist making major challenges to theory, and large-scale forays into anthropology and culture, all with a tentativeness and humility akin to Freud's own. Even in the act of disagreeing with him, one

121

must welcome the fashion in which Dr. Bettelheim puts his views: speculatively, offering alternatives, and hedging them with such disclaimers as "This is obviously a very complex question," "This interpretation of course may be correct only in individual cases," "I am still unable to explain," and so forth.

Symbolic Wounds is shaped around seven "hypotheses" about the meaning of puberty rites among nonliterate peoples. These are, in the author's words:

1. Initiation rites, including circumcision, should be viewed within the context of fertility rites, which play a primary role in primitive society.
2. Initiation rites of both boys and girls may serve to promote and symbolize full acceptance of the socially prescribed sexual role.
3. One of the purposes of male initiation rites may be to assert that men, too, can bear children.
4. Through the operation of subincision men may try to acquire sexual apparatus and functions equal to women's.
5. Circumcision may represent an effort to demonstrate sexual maturity or may be a mutilation instituted by women, or both.
6. The secrecy surrounding male initiation rites may serve to disguise the fact that the desired goal is not reached.
7. Female circumcision may be partly the result of men's ambivalence about female sex functions and partly a reaction to male circumcision.

The traditional Freudian explanation of initiation rites involving circumcision, subincision, scarification, the knocking-out or filing of teeth, or any ritual physical mutilation interprets them as symbolic castration of the young by their elders, an expression of Oedipal hostility. In place of this, Dr. Bettelheim argues a basic male motivation which he calls "vagina envy," equivalent to the Freudian "penis envy" in females. It is this "vagina envy," subsuming childbirth and nursing functions, which he believes inspires symbolic wounds and male puberty rites, and he strongly suggests that Freud was unable to recognize "vagina envy" because of the androcentric nature of his psychology. Dr. Bettelheim's interest in initiation rites originated in his clinical experience with disordered children at the Orthogenic School, when four of the pubescent children, two girls and two boys, invented a secret society with a monthly ritual in which the boys were to draw blood from their index fingers or some "secret place of their bodies" and mix it with the girls' menstrual blood. "At this point," Dr. Bettelheim says unhappily, "it became necessary to interfere," but he decided that the children's fantasy resembled primitive initiation rites he had read about, and apparently he went on to read widely in modern ethnography and ethnology. It is his claim that his theory of "vagina envy" and his other hypotheses fit such clinical experience as the four children, and the anthropological evidence he has read, better than traditional Freudian theory does.

Insofar as this is an ambitious revision of psychoanalysis, it displays several promising features. The first is Bettelheim's realistic weariness of what he calls the "deceptively pat biological model," the idea that such laws as Haeckel's "ontogeny recapitulates phylogeny" (the principle that the development of the individual repeats the evolution of the group) can be more than metaphors for psychology, if indeed they are more than that for modern biology. The second is Bettelheim's real cultural relativism, his insistence that "any event may be experienced, and its meaning understood, in vastly different ways in different societies," and that the same culture trait will produce varied results not only in different social configurations but on different personalities within the culture. The third, and most remarkable in a school principal who first encountered initiatory rites in the antisocial behavior of his disordered adolescent pupils, is a recognition of the high importance of rituals, the collective emotional experiences of nonliterate cultures, as neither institutionalized neurosis nor fantasy gratification (although they contain ingredients of both, surely), but as significant actions in the real world, filling vital social, psychological, and aesthetic needs that are less adequately filled in our own literate culture.

Psychoanalysis can stand serious modification in freeing it from the biological sciences and adjusting it to developments in other cultural sciences. Unfortunately, Dr. Bettelheim does not stop there. His major disagreement with Freudian psychology is in areas of philosophic depth and profundity where it is least in need of revision and has suffered from it most. If Freud's aim was laboriously to reclaim a little ego from the swamps of id, Bettelheim's policy is: ignore id, let us have only "ego psychology." Psychoanalysis, he says, is wrong to view "social institutions as mainly resulting from or expressive of man's destructive or irrational instinctual tendencies"; perhaps this was inevitable in those old fellows, fighting "entrenched denial and repression," but now with ego psychology we emphasize "positive human emotions and motivations."

For many of us, the answer to this was given by Freud himself in *The History of the Psychoanalytic Movement*, in response to the first of the "ego" psychologies, Alfred Adler's splintering in 1910. Freud writes, in Brill's translation:

> Psychoanalysis has a greater interest in showing that all ego strivings are mixed with libidinal components. Adler's theory emphasizes the counterpart to it; namely, that all libidinal feeling contains an admixture of egotism. This would have been a palpable gain if Adler had not made use of this assertion to deny, every time, the libidinal feelings in favor of the impelling ego components. His theory thus does exactly what all patients do, and what our conscious thinking always does; it rationalizes, as Jones would say, in order to conceal the unconscious motives.

Freud's conclusion is flatly that Adler's psychology "signifies an abandonment of analysis and a secession from it," and it would appear to this writer that Bettelheim's psychology signifies just about the same thing.

In his quest for "positive human emotions and motivations," Bettelheim consistently reinterprets the evidence in the cheeriest possible fashion. Thus sadistic impulses, such as the fantasies of some of his boy patients about tearing out female genitalia, represent only envy (sadism is not mentioned in *Symbolic Wounds*). Initiation rites are not imposed on the young by the old, but gratify constructive desires in the young (masochism is not mentioned either); if they are imposed they are imposed for the youngsters' own good. "What psychoanalysis has viewed so far as originating mainly in the id, the unconscious, and as the expression of unintegrated, destructive tendencies, may be much more the result or expression of ego tendencies that try, through ritual, to integrate chaotic instinctual desires and anxieties," Bettelheim writes. Instead of basely submitting to the father, the initiate bravely identifies with the mother; circumcision "clearly occurs because of the people's desire for it, not because of pressure from above"; "society may thus have been founded not on the association of homicidal brothers (postulated by Freud) but on a joint effort of men to master a common problem." Finally, Bettelheim asks rhetorically: "Under which frame of reference can human behavior best be understood, that of inner freedom and human autonomy, or that of coercion by blind instinctual forces or by the insensible powers of custom and tradition?" His answer, of course, is the former, since the latter does "injury to man's inherent dignity."

Unfortunately, such authorities on "man's inherent dignity" as the great tragic writers from Aeschylus to Joyce and the great stoic philosophers from Socrates to Freud himself seem consistently to have disagreed. What this is, as terms like "integrate," "joint effort," "inner freedom and human autonomy," and so forth make clear, is the same inspirational revision of Freud that Fromm, Horney, and the neo-Freudians have been purveying over the years. Water down libido, deny id, replace the Oedipus complex with something like Bettelheim's Christine complex, and heal and be healed by *caritas*. Bettelheim, whose earlier title *Love Is Not Enough* suggests that he should know better, trots out as usual "the child treated with love and tolerance," or finds "severe oral deprivation" traumatic for the newborn child "particularly when accompanied by cold and indifferent handling." "Important enterprises of human beings," he concludes, "and certainly those that have continued for centuries to give satisfaction, must serve positive rather than negative ends." Accentuate the positive is the slogan; love everybody or you will be left out of all the nice games. What Freud, to whose memory the book is dedicated, would have made of all this treacle can readily be imagined.

On examination, this "ego psychology" looks suspiciously like old-fashioned rationalism. A pyromaniac boy who set fires at the Orthogenic School out of urethral obsession was "rehabilitated" (ah, that word from the Bowery Missions) by "being permitted to set small, safe fires under supervision and to extinguish them by throwing jets of water from a hand fire pump." When he turned the stream of water through the window of his motherly counselor's room, that speeded up the rehabilitation. Bettelheim speaks of "the rather unusual custom of eating part of the female genitalia," or remarks cheerily, "Female pubic hair is a matter of great interest to modern children." His basic metaphor for primitive initiation is teaching or learning (where it is not integrating or adjusting). Other metaphors are less overt: he believes that nonliterate peoples consciously add new rites to their ceremonies in an attempt to gain new effects (the primitive as stage manager), and impose taboos with similarly conscious ends in mind (the primitive as legislator). Myths are invented "after the rites of the cult with the intention of explaining them," and we may compare myth "with the experiences of a young and unsophisticated child."

Bettelheim devotes a great deal of attention to Jewish religion in his book, and here his Freudianism is rather more orthodox, since he recognizes that such Jewish customs as infant circumcision obviously do not fit his voluntaristic theories. *Symbolic Wounds* suggests somewhat more familiarity with Roellenbleck on traces of Magna Mater cult in the Old Testament and Zimmerman's theory of Jewish circumcision as permanent erection (to name two of his more abstruse citations) than it does with the Bible itself. Bettelheim speaks of "the original nature of Jahwe as a fire god, who appeared to Moses in the burning thornbush," and he is orthodox Freudian in seeing fire as a phallic expression, and Judaism as thus by extension a "phallic religion." All this seems unnecessarily labored. There appear to be traces of many primitive worships in the Old Testament, among them the sacrificial blood of the lamb and bread of life, later to flower in the New, but the characteristic god of the earliest J text is neither the priestly compilers' fire god of the altars who savors the smell of burned kidney fat (Exodus 29:13), nor the sky god of the E text who lives on mountain tops like Zeus and sends down storms and victories. It is a very primitive phallic deity, Buck Mulligan's "collector of prepuces," who makes male nakedness sacred (Genesis 9:23) and can show only his back parts to Moses (Exodus 33:23); who is appealed to by means of a genital oath (this has become a commonplace reading of Genesis 24:2 and

47:29) and in return confers fertility (Genesis 49:25); whose symbol of power is the rod that turns into a serpent (Exodus 4:3) and whose altar is a phallic herm on which oil is poured (Genesis 28:18) or a cairn of stones on which the sacred meal is eaten (Genesis 31:46). Judaism is an ancient religion containing such a variety of survivals that neither Bettelheim nor Freud can reduce it to any primitive monotheism, and its customs and taboos are magical, not practical, as Bettelheim recognizes when he insists that modern medical circumcision is the ancient sacrifice to the phallic deity "camouflaged as a hygienic or prophylactic manipulation." "I ignore medical rationalizations," he says grandly at one point.

The problem is, ultimately, the matter of motivation. Bettelheim quotes an Australian aboriginal's explanation for the *Kunapipi* ceremonies (a lengthy initiation rite involving circumcision and subincision) and adds "I cannot accept the obvious rationalization." When a Nandi in Africa explains tribal clitoridectomy with "We are Nandi. We don't want such a hanging down thing in our women," Bettelheim comments, "I believe that the custom originates in more positive desires." Rationalization is, of course, the name one vocabulary of motivations reserves for another. When an Australian informant justifies subincision of the young men with "It makes the old men strong," he is saying that it contributes to the psychic well-being of the tribe, which is precisely what Bettelheim is saying in another phrasing. Any monist interpretive system insists, "This is why they think they do it, but I will tell you why they *really* do it." In actual fact there are no motivations in the situation (except the neutral one that it is believed to be a good thing to do); they are put in by the interpreter, and you come out with whatever explanation your vocabulary smuggled in. Aristotle's fourth or Efficient Cause, God's inscrutable purpose, is here simply being argued against his third or Final Cause, man's motive, with various secular equivalents for the deity.

Bettelheim's conclusion, that initiation rites are "efforts at acquiring the functions of the other sex," begs this question: are they efforts in the minds of the initiates, the initiators, the tribe, the field worker, Bettelheim, Freud, History, or God? We would be better off, I think, accepting the fact that causation is relative to the vocabulary used and ultimately unknowable. Bettelheim recognizes that rites can "now satisfy needs different from those they served in the past"; he accepts Benedict's statement that rites continue stable while their associated symbolic meanings (myths) vary; and he admits "interpreting rituals on the basis of their possible symbolic meaning is hazardous." He has, however, a characteristically psychoanalytic distrust of Malinowskian social function, arguing that what Malinowski sees as means may in fact be the tribe's end and vice versa, and that functional explanations do not explain the individual's own wish. Of course they do not, which is why we need psychoanalytic explanations too, and both, along with other motivational systems, for a rich and meaningful interpretation. Our job is to learn how to translate from one vocabulary into another, to build bridges between systems, and insofar as Bettelheim limits his pluralism within one system and denies the validity of others, we must build his bridges for him.

Despite all these failings, *Symbolic Wounds* is a useful book. It points up the real need to revise Freud, not in the neo-Freudian direction of bowdlerizing or re-repressing his profound insights, but in putting them undiminished into a context of our later knowledge. Thus, as Kenneth Burke suggests in the section "The Temporizing of Essence" in *A Grammar of Motives*, we must translate what Freud called his "vision" of the Primal Horde from its characteristic nineteenth-century form as a theory of prehistoric "origin" back into its true form as a statement about the nature or "essence" of the Oedipal situation, generally recognizing all such statements of temporal priority as actually statement about logical priority. We must additionally replace the inherited "memory traces" (with which Freud anticipated Jung's racial unconscious) by cultural transmission, and adapt in general to new discoveries in sociology, anthropology, and mythology, which would include throwing out not only Freud's Moses the Egyptian (as Bettelheim does) but Moses the historical figure (as Bettelheim does not). *Symbolic Wounds* in addition points up the need for a serious reconsideration of the role and relationship of the sexes, transcending both Freud's androcentric view and the gynocentrism of Bettelheim's authorities: Mead, Bateson, Ashley Montagu. (They seem to be a new Cybele cult, convinced that all the boys want to be girls.) Here we would start from the post-Malinowskian recognition of a universal Oedipus complex shaped differently in different cultures, and seek to balance in our own society the importance of the female-dominated childhood and the male-dominated adult world. Finally, *Symbolic Wounds* suggests the enormous importance of ritual. "Rudimentary forms of religious beliefs and rituals were probably the first inventions of the human mind," Bettelheim says, aware of ritual origins; "envy must be hidden and expressed only through ritual," he adds, alive to function. In the last paragraph of his book Bettelheim calls for "more civilized, less magic and more satisfying institutions" as our equivalents for primitive rites. These are, for some of us, the imaginative organizations of art, ritual structures more significant than factors of ritual origin and function, and they bring us whatever of psychic well-being our poor bedeviled tribe has.

From Bali to
Geselland

[1956]

HERE, THEN, we have those mysterious children popping in and out of the house, and how are we to discover what makes them tick? We might do well to listen to "the new field of personality and culture," or "personality *in* culture," which is apparently the coming integrative science of man, in which anthropology, psychiatry, psychology, child development, and other disciplines will find their place. At least that is the opinion of Margaret Mead and Martha Wolfenstein, who have produced a substantial anthology[1] on childhood as seen by various experts in the collaborating fields. American parents are "comrades rather than a *couple* in the French sense," says Françoise Dolto, and "The gangster has become the substitute father of American boys." How does she know? True, she has never been to America, but she is a French child analyst and has had a number of American patients. American piano lessons tend to be sterile drudgery, suggests Colin McFee. How does he know? He helped a group of Balinese boys form a *gamelan* orchestra, and they learned music in a more creative fashion. Learning is "the primary basis for social stratification, at least in principle," in Jewish culture, says Mark Zborowski, and this emphasis "has diminished little in in-

---

[1] *Childhood in Contemporary Cultures,* edited by Margaret Mead and Martha Wolfenstein.

tensity on different levels of acculturation" in America. How does he know? He grew up in an Eastern European *shtetl*, and he and colleagues have interviewed many Eastern European Jews in the United States. "The German child is prepared in the home to become an independent individual, who, through the practice of willing obedience to parental rules, has learned to obey all rules of his own accord and who, through painful experience, has trained his will to master the problems of life," says Rhoda Métraux. How does she know? She has been reading German child-guidance books.

As these examples may suggest, the study of personality in culture seems to produce insights of varying authority and value. One problem is the relationship of any significant trait to the larger configuration. In 1949, Geoffrey Gorer and John Rickman published *The People of Great Russia,* placing great emphasis on swaddling of the child as a determinant of the later adult character, and Ruth Benedict's "Child Rearing in Certain European Countries" appeared posthumously in *The American Journal of Orthopsychiatry,* warning that swaddling might have a variety of effects, depending on the cultural configuration. These were apparently the poles of opinion in the Columbia Research in Contemporary Cultures project Benedict had inaugurated. In 1954, Mead, who had inherited the project when Benedict died in 1948, published "The Swaddling Hypothesis: Its Reception" in *The American Anthropologist.* Here, in the name of clearing up "some of the confusions which have arisen during the last four years regarding the study of cultural character," Mead led a strategic retreat to what was essentially the Benedict position.

Much of *Childhood in Contemporary Cultures* reflects this new sophistication, with the emphasis on configuration rather than the isolable trait. Mead writes in her introduction:

> But, while striking differences in behavior may give rapid clues to important differences in the whole pattern, it is important to realize that it is not any single item of child-rearing practice or of culturally patterned child behavior—not the presence or absence of feeding bottles or slates, skates or hoops or balls, prayers or homilies or bribes—which is significant in isolation. It is the way in which all these thousands of items, most of which are

shared with other cultures, some of which are shared with all other cultures, are patterned or fitted together to make a whole.

Some of the contributors, however, are still unreconstructed. One of Wolfenstein's contributions, "Some Variants in Moral Training of Children," a cross-cultural study involving interviews with parents of Chinese, Czech, Eastern European Jewish, and Syrian origin, was first published in 1950. It cites Benedict's article, then goes happily ahead showing how characteristic modes of nursing, swaddling, and toilet-training determine personality and character.

The emphasis on these readily discernible "striking differences" in national character arose during the war, when anthropology was mobilized to study the cultures of occupied and enemy countries that could not be studied in the field, and here we encounter the much-debated "study of culture at a distance." I would say that Margaret Mead is one of the finest field workers alive, and that one of the reasons she is so good is that she is a natural snoop. "Peeking over a house wall, one may see . . ." she writes in her marvelous essay, "Children and Ritual in Bali." (In *Growth and Culture*,[2] an earlier book on Balinese children done in collaboration, Mead admitted that the Balinese village she worked in was chosen in part because its household walls were "loosely constructed fences through which it was easy to see what was taking place.") It is precisely this quality of texture, of the richness of intimately observed behavior—in short, of snooping—that is lacking in her article written with Elena Calas, "Child-Training Ideals in a Postrevolutionary Context: Soviet Russia." Where Wolfenstein is studying culture at a distance (a thematic analysis of "The Image of the Child in Contemporary Films") she is terrible; where she gets closer to it (French children observed in the park) she makes some convincing observations; where she is saturated in it (clinical experience with "Two Types of Jewish Mothers" and their children) she is wonderful. When Wolfenstein describes Mrs. S, one of her two types of Jewish mother, warning her son that a woman across the street was actually aggravated *to death* by her son, she is talking about something; when she

---

[2] *Growth and Culture*, by Margaret Mead and Frances Cooke Macgregor. Based upon Photographs by Gregory Bateson analyzed in Gesell Categories.

generalizes from half a dozen Italian films that "An older ideal of womanly purity and virtue, which seems to have lost its hold on other western cultures, remains in the ascendant in Italy," she is talking about nothing, and the significant difference in the language shows it.

From the perspective of personality in culture, another recent book on childhood, *Child Behavior*,[3] a publication of the Gesell Institute of Child Development, speaks for a culture that is neither Western civilization nor the United States, but a place we might call Geselland. The language of Geselland uses exclamation points as the Hottentot tongue uses clicks, so that Gesells say, "The mother-child relationship! The first, and one of the most important and exciting that the human being ever experiences!" In Geselland every couple has one child who occupies their exclusive attention (although they borrow another one, apparently, for the sibling rivalry rites). They live in cities where the schools have psychologists and guidance teachers, the mothers are "modern mothers in their wish to follow modern methods," the fathers take the children to the dentist "to overcome resistance," and both parents are preternaturally eager to learn anything that will contribute to the welfare of their child, although reading about problems like "insecurity" makes them worry. Wolfenstein needs an article to summarize the behavior of French children in the park, but Ilg and Ames have been down to the Geselland playground so many times that they can recreate it in a paragraph:

> However, even by the time some children are two and a half, you can help them to develop techniques for getting along with friends. You can tell Joey, "Talk to Jimmy, don't hit him," if Joey is a hitter. Or, "What can Danny have instead?" if you are addressing a grabber. Or, "Let Mary have a turn now," or, "You can have it after Betty is finished."

This is perhaps unfair, since *Child Behavior* is a popularization, pieced together from a syndicated newspaper column of the same name that Ilg and Ames produce. One would never guess from it that Dr. Ames was the author of "Precursor Signs of Plantigrade Progression" in *The Journal of Genetic Psychology*,

[3] *Child Behavior*, by Frances L. Ilg, M.D., and Louise Bates Ames, Ph.D.

or Dr. Ilg a collaborator in equally learned publications. But popularization is a kind of projective test too, and it often shows more nakedly than technical writings the tendencies of a movement. Just as the Balinese child is seen as a small adult, the Syrian child as a vessel to be filled, or the German child as a plant to be cultivated, so the child in Geselland is seen as a fertile seed or egg that "grows" and "unfolds" according to some built-in plan. "Growth, growth," says Dr. Gesell's foreword to the book. "Behavior grows!" the authors begin, with a click. The emphasis is on order, measure, "norms and standards of development," "watching the growing infant as he unfolds" or twitching nervously when growth "possibly doesn't unfold or move."

The metaphors that cannot be countenanced see the child as something limitlessly plastic, "a lump of clay," or as something primarily determined by the culture or "mother's treatment of the baby." This seed-egg figure may be a popular image deliberately substituted for the Gesell group's more scientific and dialectic image of the spiral of development, but it may equally reflect an unconscious ideal in the authors. There is at least one certainly unconscious metaphor for the child buried deep in *Child Behavior*, underlying the suggestions of a newspaper in a corner of the bathroom floor for difficult excretory cases, a police whistle to summon the dilatory child, and a muzzling adult hand for the biter.

In this culture, the nature of the child is known, not only because it is all built in from the start, but because it classifies readily into easily identifiable physical and temperamental types: Sheldon's constitutional typing of endomorph, mesomorph, and ectomorph; a division into "focal" and "peripheral" personalities; Kanner's "autistic" personality and its sociable opposite; and even an ultimate typing, "Children can almost be placed in two different groups, those who love peanut butter and those who don't." From the vantage point of these fixities, syndicated shamans can do a number of things for parents: consoling ("You can be prevented from feeling too much surprise or discouragement"); coaching ("And don't be above using guile"); indoctrinating ("Try to recognize and respect your child's basic, inborn individuality"); laying down the law ("We do not recommend spanking for this behavior"); and cooling off ("This information may help you to keep down your expectations").

In all this emphasis on growth and culture, it is not surprising that the voice chiefly identified in our time with fixity and biological limitation, Sigmund Freud's, is seldom heard. Erik H. Erikson is the only contributor to *Childhood in Contemporary Cultures* who overtly resists the prevailing cultural emphasis. His article on "Sex Differences in the Play Configurations of American Adolescents" notes "how many questions remain unanswered if a one-sided cultural explanation is accepted as the sole basis for the sex differences expressed in these configurations." Wolfenstein has Freudian moments, as when she gives the traditional phallic reading of "Jack and the Beanstalk," or suggests brilliantly that American "fun morality" may be "a new kind of defense against impulses," or ends her concluding chapter on a tribute to Freud's humanistic vision. Else Frenkel-Brunswik turns briefly to "depth psychology" for a "dynamic" dimension to her environmental study of family backgrounds. Robert Sunley finds in studying nineteenth-century American child-rearing literature, somewhat to his surprise, that American Calvinist ideas about the child were more realistic in recognizing his sexual and aggressive drives than later optimistic thought. (The paper on "Freud, Infant Damnation, and Total Depravity" remains to be written, and would clear the air wonderfully.)

Child Behavior is, as could be expected, sharply anti-Freudian. When little girls attempt to urinate standing up, "This is a perfectly normal experiment and not in our opinion a sign that they have 'penis envy' or have been overexposed to little boys." The emphasis is always away from the psyche: "Reasonable experimentation with laxatives and experimenting with a relaxing diet should certainly be tried before you conclude that your child's constipation is an 'emotional' problem." There is even a slash of Occam's Razor at Freud: "However, in keeping with the principle of never seek a complicated explanation when a simple one will do, don't seek 'deep' reasons and complicated therapy unless you're sure that something simple will not suffice"—which we might translate as "Never seek a reason when a rationalization will do." With endomorphic personalities, quoting Sheldon,

"Nothing is ever choked or held back. There is no emotional inhibition"; when the authors encounter an uncontrollable little boy with no discernible superego, they conclude sourly "this boy's personality was the thing at fault"; when they encounter the little boy who prefers to dress up as a girl and play with dolls, he is "the feminine" type. Characteristically, masturbation is always treated as a "tensional outlet," and the remedy for it, as for all childhood sexuality, is "providing ideas for something better to do." For adolescent sexuality, the remedy is "providing a child with a view of himself and his life plan and life role which is not consistent with getting early sex expression and fulfillment." Against adult sexuality, that well-known tensional outlet, something worse to do, and disrupter of life roles, the authors tactfully offer no recommendations.

Despite all the emphasis on culture, social and economic realities seem to play little part in it. All the people of Geselland are middle class, and they apparently have their days free for child-watching. In *Childhood in Contemporary Cultures*, Mead notes the value to the child of the extensive adult leisure in her Balinese village, but never relates it to wealth-getting activities or economic margin. Her conclusion to the book contains one of its few mentions of class differences as a factor in child care in our own culture. The most interesting case is that of Frenkel-Brunswik, who compares an authoritarian and a democratic family while specifically excluding "social and economic determinants" from consideration, choosing families of roughly similar stations. Nevertheless, she is so strongly concerned with social implications, noting "fascistic attitudes" in her authoritarian family (which is of German origin) and how they might come "to the fore" after "social upheavals of a major sort," that it finally becomes obvious that she is writing a political parable, a cautionary tale about Good Germans, Bad Germans, and the rise of Hitler.

Through all the glossy new gadgetry of method in these books a kind of old-fashioned rationalism peeks out. *Childhood in Contemporary Cultures* deals extensively with such symbolic expressions as art and rituals, but it is never in their own terms, always as didacticism or projective test. Mead sees works of literature as clear designs whose intentions "miscarry" if the audience gets anything not "carefully and creatively planned," and the hopeful directions of her conclusion—constructively loaded juvenile books, constructively loaded dramatic performances, and pious group conferences—are neither so novel nor so innocent as she might think. Wolfenstein shows in some comments on Dickens and Dostoevsky that she has only the dimmest sense of how novels differ from tracts, and her one impressive literary insight, the significant "national character" difference in the endings of *Oliver Twist* and *Huckleberry Finn*, turns out to be W. H. Auden's. Ilg and Ames remark, "They seldom ask, 'How shall I tell him about war?'— though war, to our way of thinking, is much harder to explain than sex." This would be rather a nice joke if it were a joke, but it is apparently a serious statement, suggesting that the authors will recognize Eros, the life instinct, at least as a tensional outlet, but never Thanatos, the death instinct. A letter they quote approvingly shows how beautiful death can be when "The cemetery has no tombstones permitted and truly looks like a beautiful park." They simply do not credit the possibility of hostile or destructive elements in the personality. In their culture, the adopted child is always "a chosen child—desired, selected and doubly cherished for this reason," never, say, a vessel the adopting parents fill with the guilts and reproaches they feel about sterility.

All these ladies have a curious owlish quality, humorless and gullible. Wolfenstein gives a weighty analysis of a French child's drawing of an arrow, which the child explained was a picture of a hunter shooting a bird, the hunter not in the picture because he had released the arrow, the bird not pictured because it had been missed. (This, doctor, is a joke.) Frenkel-Brunswik finds her democratic home admirable in part because the mother, a social worker who has been analyzed, divorced but "on good terms" with her husband, talks about her daughter as follows:

> "I do hope that she will do something that will make her happy and at the same time be constructive. I hope the girl will have experience early enough that she can integrate it and lead an outgoing, constructive life; that she won't have to spend so long working out her aggression that she finds herself no longer young —not that I wish to spare my daughter the suffering and experience necessary for development, but I hope she may get it early

and fast. I feel that I can help by giving a lot of trust and confidence in the girl. I do feel that at times in the past I may have expected too high a performance for the sake of my own gratification, and that may have troubled Peggy. The child has been given more responsibility than the average, but as a rule it hasn't seemed to be a strain."

It never occurs to Frenkel-Brunswik that the easy jargon of understanding can be as readily used to obfuscate relations as to reveal them, and if her account of the authoritarian family is like taking the cover off a sewer, this is like riffling through the yellowing pages of *PM*.

These attitudes are characteristically accompanied by a general contempt for the arts of language. *Child Behavior* is written entirely in Gesell, the click of exclamation points and the soft wet thud of nursery school slogans. German and French are translated in *Childhood in Contemporary Cultures* as one gets cocktail onions out of the bottle, with savage jabs, and the contributors quickly shift from English to Newspeak. Even David Riesman's enormously impressive chapter from *The Lonely Crowd*, showing the dangerous nonsense in a children's book called *Tootle*, ends at the apocalyptic moment when "the self-confirming process of the peer group pushes preference exchange to the point of parody." The use of the first-person plural in these books seems significant. Ilg and Ames have a chummy "we" that includes authors and reader-parents, as in "We can try to smooth over the child's 'worse' stages." Wolfenstein attacks the false and misleading "we" of the nursery school, as in "We don't hit," which pretends that teacher and child are age-mates. Her own first-person plural goes to the other extreme. In "We have come to consider the child's nature as totally harmless and beneficent," or "In America we tend quickly to forget on the conscious level what we have put behind us or outgrown," it excludes herself and simply means "you benighted readers."

It is hard to separate problems of methodology raised by these approaches from the personal limitations of authors and editors. Ilg and Ames are solidly configurational, insisting, "But here as always the total child in the total situation should be the primary consideration." Much of *Childhood in Contemporary Cultures* is similarly enlightened. But cultural configurations can over-simplify and distort too (as Boas showed in his comments on Benedict's *Patterns of Culture*, noting that one would never realize from it that her aggressive and destructive Kwakiutl were warm and kindly parents). Studying the total child in the total situation, whether the nursery school and clinic of Ilg and Ames, or Mead's "live children" in "play groups" and "real children in analytic situations," runs us into the variant of Heisenberg's Uncertainty Principle that bedevils the social sciences, the fact that the very act of observation dislocates things to the point where accurate observation is impossible. When Mead and Macgregor tried to validate the Gesell categories for a nonliterate culture in *Growth and Culture*, they properly found that the categories had to be altered at key points. When Mead announced that what Gesell calls "ulnar grasp" (holding with the fingers furthest from the thumb) relates to general Balinese "lack of goal orienta-tion," she was engaged in using the categories as though they were already valid for Bali, and was trying to put what she had decided from field study as though it had been learned or could be learned from motor behavior.

Another problem is of course the reliability of the informant. Anthropologists have increasingly been coming to realize that many of their pictures of primitive cultures are no more than what the old men (who tend, for a variety of good reasons, to be the principal informants) wish were so or believe was so in the happier past. Some of *Childhood in Contemporary Cultures* is obviously idealized reality of this sort, particularly the Zborowski article, which tends to picture Eastern European *shtetl* life as a golden age of piety and learning. His statement, for example, that the Jewish ideal of male beauty was and is pale, deep-set-eyed, and scholarly seems to me (perhaps because I am a florid endomorph) extraordinarily unlikely. In Geselland, inevitably, only one wise old informant is ever used, and the authors clear up disputed matters with the simple "Dr. Gesell has commented on this subject."

Where these works are most useful, in my opinion, is in their strongly implied criticisms of our own culture. One of the articles in *Childhood in Contemporary Cultures*, Benedict's classic 1938 paper, "Continuities and Discontinuities in Cultural Conditioning," demonstrates the crippling discontinuities in our own culture (in which the child learns roles of irresponsibility, submission, and asexuality which it must then painfully unlearn to function as an adult) by showing how various American Indian and Pacific cultures avoid these discontinuities or minimize them through such devices as age grades and ritual ceremonies. Erikson's remarkable "Sex Differences in the Play Configurations of American Adolescents" shows how much can be made of projective behavior when the analyst feels the sting of the culture on his own hide, whether by being enough moved by a withdrawn girl to permit himself "the clinical luxury of one nonstandardized question," or by being painfully aware of wider significance when a disturbed Negro boy dramatizes ultimate "lowness" by building his structure of blocks *under* the table.

Ilg and Ames love their culture, and even welcome television for "its real educational value," but they too sometimes suggest that the culture has not entirely encapsulated all virtue. They note that some primitive peoples feature "the self-demand and self-regulation schedules which many pediatricians now recommend," and some of their anecdotes, such as one in which a newborn baby "sent" daily gifts from the hospital to his sib and was welcomed on arrival home, suggest the advantages of cultures in which gift-giving and reciprocity are ceremonial and institutionalized. In *Growth and Culture*, Mead notes that anthropological findings are welcomed in America if they underline plasticity and resisted if they document limits. She makes it clear that the book's intention is not primarily to tell us about Bali but to "give us much greater understanding of what is happening to our children," and concludes, "We can develop our culture" in certain preferable Balinese directions.

As critics of America, these ladies have certain obvious difficulties. Mead and Wolfenstein have produced an ethnocentric and culture-bound book, not by intention, surely, but because the cultures they could get suitable child material on, except for Bali, are all too similar, more like subcultures of Western civilization than independent organic wholes (here some of Mead's own work on the Manus or Arapesh would have helped enormously). Ilg and Ames have not set foot outside Geselland for many years. The personality and culture field seems to be inevitably gynocentered, and Mead remarks sharply, "Although there are distinguished male workers in the field . . . it is probably not an accident that all of them have worked closely with woman teachers or collaborators." She appears to recommend "collaborative two-sex teams" (why not three-sex or four-sex?) in line with the general faith of our time that teamwork and integration will solve whatever problems individuals cannot. *Growth and Culture*, we might note, involved the collaboration of a dozen people, plus a theoretical hash of Gesell, Erikson, Lawrence Frank, Cybernetics, and a group conference of other experts. With all these voices joining in, debate gets promptly onto a high level of philosophic abstraction: growth or training, determinism or plasticity, biology or culture, nature or nurture. Through all this hubbub, the child crawls ignored between the adult legs, relieving tension by picking his nose, growing up as best he can.

The Dead Sea
Scrolls

1. Clergymen and Mischief-Makers

[1956]

ANY DISCUSSION of the ancient scrolls, found in caves at Wady Qumran near the Dead Sea beginning in 1947, has to be dated, like a news story, since the situation changes almost daily. This review was written in February, 1956, after the unrolling and identification of the last and most stubborn of the seven original scrolls as not the Book of Lamech it had been thought, but a fuller Aramaic text of four chapters of Genesis; and before the disclosure of the "secret" of the Jordan government's copper scroll, unrolled at Manchester, announced for the summer of 1956. With not-yet-identified fragments of at least sixty different manuscripts found in Cave IV alone, the revelations seem hardly begun. The two books that occasioned this review, now in their fourth or fifth printings and selling sturdily, are already outmoded, as this review will undoubtedly be by new developments before it appears in print.

The scrolls, which are unquestionably authentic, are of enormous importance in half a dozen scholarly fields, in none of which this reviewer is competent to talk about them, but their principal interest for the folklorist seems to lie in one area, the relationship of myth to history. It is the contention of some students of the scrolls that they belonged to an ancient Jewish religious community, probably the Essenes, and that they demonstrate that at some time like 100 B.C. this community believed in a Teacher of Righteousness or

suffering Messiah who was persecuted and done to death by a
Wicked Priest or Man of the Lie, perhaps betrayed to the gentiles
and crucified, but who returned again in glory or would return. The
community celebrated a sacred baptism and a communion meal
involving sacred bread and wine blessed by a priest, and had many
teachings and ethical doctrines resembling those of the New Testament, including elements of the Lord's Prayer. Various scholars
defend various details in this summary, with no one accepting it
all. If any substantial part of it turns out to be true, it would be the
strongest documentary evidence yet to support the view that Jesus
was a mythical rather than a historical figure. For this reviewer,
who is relatively unconcerned with the historical origins of Christianity, but inclined to generalize with Lord Raglan that sacred
books and myths are never the record of history but always narratives based on rituals, it would be a demonstration of the ritualists'
contention in a particularly telling case, where we apparently know
so much historical reality, from His trade to His remarks on various
public and private occasions.

One would hardly guess any of this significance from Millar
Burrows' *The Dead Sea Scrolls*, which is a learned and comprehensive summary of every aspect of the scrolls and every theory about
them, written at a temperature just above freezing. In the whole
welter of controversy, the only certainty on which Burrows is prepared to insist is that all the scrolls were written before A.D. 68, when
he believes they were left in the cave at Wady Qumran, and that
some of them probably go back to the second or third century B.C.
Whether the enemy they refer to as the "Kittim" are the Seleucids,
B.C., the Romans, A.D., or neither, cannot be established by any
evidence "definitely conclusive"; a body of ideas in the scrolls may
or may not be Gnostic, despite many resemblances; and the community itself "was more closely related to the Essenes than to any
other group known to us," but may not have been the Essenes at
all. Much of the scholarly material that Burrows describes as a
background to the scrolls is fascinating new information to a layman, particularly his account of a solid paleographical sequence of
Hebrew square script from the fifth century B.C. to the eleventh
century A.D., and a sequence of archaic Hebrew script examples not
much less solid from the ninth century B.C. to the ninth century A.D.

Burrows' book is magnificently equipped with maps, illustrations, an enormous bibliography, and an appendix of complete translations of two of the scrolls, the Habakkuk Commentary and the Manual of Discipline, and a related manuscript, the Damascus Document, along with partial translations of two other scrolls. It has, however, neither footnote citations nor an index, and an item once lost in it is gone forever. This fits in curiously with Burrows' general reluctance to be pinned down at any point. He insists that there is no danger that the scrolls will "require a revision of any basic article of Christian faith," noting that he has studied them for seven years and "I do not find my understanding of the New Testament substantially affected." Burrows is a professor of Biblical Theology at Yale, he has worked on the scrolls almost from the beginning and edited the scholarly publication of several of them, he is one of the world's few authorities on *both* Testaments, and the fairest ultimate judgment of his value is probably Professor William F. Albright's in a review of the book for the New York *Herald Tribune*:

> He is well known among scholars for his prudence in dealing with relatively familiar areas of investigation and for his extreme caution in probing the unknown. He has never been a pioneer, but he is generally a safe guide in mapping well explored regions.

Edmund Wilson's *The Scrolls from the Dead Sea* is something very different. It is a popular account and digest of the story, in about a quarter of Burrows' wordage, for a different lay audience, the readers of *The New Yorker* (where it first appeared), who are presumably more interested in the adventure of the discoveries and the controversies they aroused than in having the texts. This is not to say that Wilson's book is more superficial than Burrows'; in fact, Wilson seems far more aware of the issues and significances involved than Burrows, and he weighs the various theories as though he were interested in determining some facts, not in canceling everything out at zero. Wilson appears to share the views of Professor A. Dupont-Sommer of the Sorbonne, but he is careful to note the disagreement of scholars with some of Dupont-Sommer's translations and interpretations, as well as some scholarly concurrence with his findings. Wilson's reporting is as ingenious as his summaries of theory are scrupulous, and he brings the story to life with a variety of journalistic color: quotations from the diary of Professor Sukenik, under fire in Jerusalem, calmly buying up scrolls; a re-creation of a hyperthyroid Czech scholar named Flusser; an identification of Dupont-Sommer with Renan; and a final image of Metropolitan Samuel of the Syrian Jacobite Church, unenlightened by all the events he had precipitated but one quarter of a million dollars richer.

It is thus particularly disturbing to see Wilson, despite so much journalistic shrewdness and insight, entirely miss the big point of the story, where missing it seemed inevitable for Burrows' pussy-footing divinity school conservatism. Wilson recognizes that Jewish and Christian spokesmen have been deeply disturbed by the scrolls, but he believes that they fear for, respectively, the authority of the Masoretic text and the uniqueness of Jesus, rather than the much more serious threats to their respective impositions on history, monolithic Judaism and the historical Jesus. Wilson pictures a historical Jesus (with a historical cousin John nicknamed "Baptist") who "may well have found prepared for him, by the teaching of the Dead Sea sect, a special Messianic role, the pattern of a martyr's career." He cannot figure out why the Essenes disappeared from history, concluding flatly, "We do not know what became of the Essenes," although as long ago as 1864, in his book *The Essenes,* Christian D. Ginsburg recognized clearly that "The Essenes as a body must have embraced Christianity," that they *became* the primitive Christians, in fact.

At one pole in the controversy over the Qumran scrolls are those scholars, Christian and Jewish, who resist some of their implications so strongly that they refuse to date the scrolls in antiquity. A typical example is G. R. Driver, professor of Semitic Philology at Oxford, who dates the scrolls at A.D. 400 or later, denying the accuracy of the archaeological evidence, and casting doubts on the paleographical evidence by observing that one of the principal texts used for comparison, the Nash Papyrus, was "touched up" by the late Professor F. C. Burkitt so it would photograph better. Another is Professor Solomon Zeitlin of the Dropsie College, who dates the scrolls even later, in the Middle Ages, attacking the whole concept of Hebrew paleography as an exact science.

At the other extreme are the radical interpreters: Professor Dupont-Sommer, who has insisted that the Qumran covenanters were Essenes, that their enemies the Kittim were the Romans in the first century A.D., and who introduced the Passion, Resurrection, and Epiphany in his translations; and Dr. John Allegro, a thirty-two-year-old assistant lecturer in Comparative Semitic Philology at the University of Manchester, who helped unroll the copper scroll and was one of the international team authorized to study the later fragments in Arab Jerusalem, and who added to the story the Teacher's Delivery to the Gentiles, Crucifixion, and Burial. Dupont-Sommer's arguments have been published in two books available in English as *The Dead Sea Scrolls* (1952) and *The Jewish Sect of Qumran and the Essenes* (1954); but Allegro's contentions have so far only been available in garbled accounts in the American press of two talks he delivered over the B.B.C. network, January 23 and 30, 1956. I quote from accounts of them in the *New York Times*. Allegro spoke of a "recently discovered manuscript" making it probable that the Wicked Priest gave the Teacher of Righteousness "into the hands of his Gentile mercenaries to be crucified," after which the disciples "reverently buried the body of their Teacher in a tomb nearby" and settled down "to await his glorious return as Messiah of God." This recently discovered manuscript is apparently entitled "The Order for All the Congregations of Israel in the Last Days," but beyond that nothing is known about it in this country, and it may or may not be the copper scroll whose contents are to be kept secret until summer.

Until some additional description of this mysterious document is available here, Allegro's arguments cannot be evaluated, but some conclusions are possible about Dupont-Sommer's reliability. On page 5 of his second book, Dupont-Sommer opposes "too rigid a resort to the criterion of the pottery," when it seems apt to contradict his dating; on page 7, "archaeology now provides valuable corroboration," when new dates for the pottery support his theories. He accuses his critics of lacking "the necessary strictness of scientific method," but his own free translations and emendations of the text (which differ widely from Burrows' translations at key points) do not inspire confidence. Dupont-Sommer may have, as one of his critics, Dr. W. H. Brownlee, concedes, "an uncanny knack for being ultimately right (or nearly so), even when his views are initially based on the wrong texts!" but it hardly sounds like "the necessary strictness of scientific method."

Somewhere in the middle, between the terrified orthodox and the bold heterodox, are Jewish scholars like Ralph Marcus, in a series of articles on the scrolls, welcoming the Dead Sea Essenes as the legitimate left wing of a whole spectrum of Judaism in antiquity; and Christians like Ginsburg, in his book on the Essenes, undisturbed by his convictions that the Sermon on the Mount is a description of Essene life, that Jesus was probably an Essene, and that "primitive Christianity was nothing but an offshoot from Essenism."

Ginsburg has the excuse of writing in 1864 for his euhemerist faith that myth is the record of history, but later commentators should know better. Burrows recognizes that one of the scrolls, "The War of the Sons of Light with the Sons of Darkness," is as apt to be eschatological as historical, "a purely apocalyptic vision or a liturgical religious drama," and that it "seems more like a ballet than a battle." The same possibility, however, never occurs to him for the events in the other scrolls, and much of his book is taken up with speculation about the precise historical identification of the Teacher of Righteousness, the Wicked Priest, and other characters. Wilson is equally anxious to read myth as history, and even Dupont-Sommer and Allegro, although their Teacher of Righteousness, as the Messiah, is properly vague, identify the Wicked Priest as Aristobulus II and John Hyrcanus II (Dupont-Sommer) and Alexander Jannaeus (Allegro).

The mythic school of Gospel interpretation does not seem to exist any more, having been derided out of our sophisticated climate of opinion along with Haldeman-Julius' Little Blue Books, but it may yet have the last laugh, and the old rationalist titles —The Pre-Christian Jesus, Did Jesus Live 100 B.C.?—come back ironically as awareness of the scrolls grows. There is an especial melancholy in the fact that John M. Robertson, the greatest and most solid of the mythic school, did not live to see the discoveries at Wady Qumran. When one ambiguous early Church book, the *Didache* or "Teaching of the Twelve Apostles," was discovered in his time and published in 1883, Robertson insisted that it was a pre-Christian work with what he called "Christist interpolations," and built a good part of his case against the historicity of Jesus on it. We now know that the *Didache* was just what Robertson surmised, we can identify it as an Essene manual similar to the scrolls, and before the scholars are finished we may have scores like it.

As the implications of the Dead Sea Scrolls began to emerge, we were favored with a mounting chorus of warnings from the clergy. Dr. J. Carter Swain told the First Presbyterian Church of Jamaica, Queens, in December, 1955, that the scrolls "will not radically alter our picture of Christian origins, because the essential features of Jesus' ministry are too well known and established for that." Dr. John Sutherland Bonnell welcomed the discoveries in a sermon at his Fifth Avenue Presbyterian Church in January, assuring Christians that they need not fear, since "the place of Jesus Christ in history is unchallengeable." After Allegro's broadcasts, an unnamed English Catholic spokesman was quoted as saying "any stick now seems big enough to use against Christianity," and another, or perhaps the same one, called the broadcasts "atheist in spirit." The *New York Times* carried comments by Catholic, Protestant, and Jewish clergymen under the heading "Dead Sea Scrolls Held Overvalued." The priest, the Very Rev. John J. Dougherty of the Immaculate Conception Seminary of Darlington, New Jersey, attacked the views of Wilson and Dupont-Sommer in *America* as "mischief" but "nothing new"; the rabbi, Dr. Samuel Sandmel of Hebrew Union College, warned against Wilson, remarking "seldom have so many readers been lead astray by one man"; and the minister, the same Dr. Bonnell, confined himself to urging Allegro to slow down.

In an atmosphere as charged as this, the student of folklore, if he claims to be serious, has special responsibilities. They are, quite simply, to find out the truth as best he can, unintimidated by the massed firepower of the clergy or any other group of special pleaders, and to teach and publish it as he sees fit. Burrows and Wilson have set off a few squibs, but the real fireworks may be yet to come.

2. The Dead Sea Scrolls, or What You Will

[1957]

THE RECENT BOOKS on the Dead Sea Scrolls and the Jewish monastic community at Qumran that produced them almost unanimously disavow a scholarly audience. Allegro calls his Pelican paperback[1] "a small popular volume" attempting "to give to the general public some conception of the extent and importance of recent discoveries in this area." Fritsch[2] is somewhat more equivocal, stating, "It is my purpose to relate these thrilling discoveries and present their significance for Biblical studies in a way that will catch the imagination of the general reader, and at the same time be practical for the student who may wish to pursue the subject more thoroughly." Gaster[3] writes flatly: "This book is addressed to laymen." Graystone[4] says he is reprinting his articles from a theological quarterly "in the hope that they may be of interest to a wider public." Whitman's stapled pamphlet[5] defines its intention as "the hope that it can, in some small measure, alleviate" the "tremendous need that Americans in all walks of life were beginning to feel for a full but concise treatment of the subject, in layman's language." Only Rowley[6] makes no concession to a popular audience, but then his book turns out to have been published in 1952, and reissued unchanged after widespread interest in the subject had been created. All in all, no laymen need feel abashed in the presence of these volumes, even if he reads no Semitic language and does not know a palimpsest from a carbon 14 dating.

The principal by-product of the scrolls to date seems to be controversy. "Some of the discussions have savoured of propaganda and a needlessly sharp note has been frequently introduced," Rowley says in his moderate way. "This has prejudiced the discussion and has made more difficult the attainment of agreed solutions."

[1] The Dead Sea Scrolls, by J. M. Allegro.
[2] The Qumrān Community: Its History and Scrolls, by Charles T. Fritsch.
[3] The Dead Sea Scriptures, in English translation with introduction and notes by Theodor H. Gaster.
[4] The Dead Sea Scrolls and the Originality of Christ, by Geoffrey Graystone, S.M.
[5] The Dead Sea Scrolls and What They Mean to Protestant, Catholic, Jew, by Arthur Whitman.
[6] The Zadokite Fragments and the Dead Sea Scrolls, by H. H. Rowley.

The debate with one bold scholar, he adds, "has not always been carried on with the serenity of a purely scientific discussion." Putting it more graphically, Gaster says the controversy has been as hot and dark as the caves themselves. Yet the principal impression the reader gets from the six books under discussion is not so much of controversy as of a Sunday outing on the madhouse lawn, with everyone mumbling his own fancies and no one listening to anyone else. So much, apparently, can the scrolls be made to demonstrate precisely what the demonstrator already had in mind that it is hard to believe that these writers are talking about the same documents.

John Marco Allegro is thirty-four years old, a Comparative Semitic philologist at the University of Manchester, and one of the international team of scholars piecing together scroll fragments at the Jerusalem Museum in Jordan. Allegro may be a prodigy of philology, but he does not seem characterized by the scholarly temperament or habits of caution. After some sensational interpretations of the material in talks on the B.B.C. in January, 1956, had produced dissents from his fellow scholars at the Museum and a public reproof from his colleague and former teacher Rowley, Allegro backed down, and *The Dead Sea Scrolls* omits some of his bolder reconstructions. In *The New Statesman and Nation*, October 27, 1956, Edmund Wilson reviewed Allegro's book enthusiastically, identifying him as one of the "scholars with no clerical commitments" of whom Wilson says: "They are free, as the ordained scholars—sometimes Protestant and Jewish as well as Catholic—do not always seem to be, to piece a story together, to speculate on what must have happened."

As Wilson says, Allegro apparently has no religious bias, aside from traces of a conservative Christianity that calls the doctrine of justification by grace "the warmth of a familiar hearth," and identifies the New Testament miracles of feedings and healings as eschatological ("signs of the ultimate victory") rather than humanitarian. However, his book shows at least one marked bias, pro-Arab and anti-Israel, which may be natural or may be the artificial protective coloration of a scholar working under the Jordan government. Allegro writes of brave little Jordan:

> Every penny has to be put to urgent use, and development schemes cry out for attention if the meagre resources of the

country are to be stretched to support an abnormally swollen population. With an enemy at her gates, she must for ever keep a standing army at the alert, which, even with outside help, drains her reserves intolerably.

Noting that for many years before the discoveries the Bedouin had been collecting guano in the scroll caves and selling it in Bethlehem, Allegro suggests wittily (and ungrammatically) that it is not at all improbable "that the Jewish orange groves near Bethlehem were fertilized with priceless ancient manuscripts written by their forefathers."

The real problem is that, like pro-Arab Englishmen generally, Allegro is a retarded adolescent romantic. His account of the discovery and purchase of the scrolls is written in the language of the cheap thriller:

> Events now had taken a sinister turn. If Jabra's fears were justified, it meant that this dealer and his confederates were willing to go to any length to avoid interference in their territory. It was clear that from now on the game would be played to very high stakes, perhaps to higher values than mere money.

Allegro's ultimate interest in the scrolls seems to lie in constructing a melodramatic story: the evidence regarding the Qumran community "points to the early influence of a very strong personality"; he deduces (from no evidence) that the sect's Teacher of Righteousness probably set up as a rival High Priest to Alexander Jannaeus, the Wicked Priest in his interpretation, and as his book's high point Allegro creates a garish cinema confrontation scene between them:

> In any case, the scene as these two priests faced one another must have been dramatic enough. The one, haughty and proud, scarred by the wounds of many battles, and the ravaging of a lifetime of greed and lechery, the other, white-robed and saintly, gazing scornfully on his enemy, secure in his simple trust in God and the hope of resurrection to eternal life.

As for ties between the Qumran sect and Jesus, the withdrawal into the desert for forty days "is the key to the whole life and teaching of Jesus," and Jesus threw down his challenge to the Devil and his forces "perhaps only a mile or two from Qumran itself."

Charles T. Fritsch is a Presbyterian clergyman, an associate professor of Old Testament at Princeton Theological Seminary, whose visiting lectureship at the American Schools of Oriental Research in Jerusalem seems to have occasioned *The Qumrān Community: Its History and Scrolls*. Fritsch writes in the pulpit style of ringing clichés so democratically shared by all the religions in America— "Little did the unsuspecting Bedouin realize," "to date with uncanny accuracy"—and displays the clergy's special fondness for the *non sequitur*—"The large natural caves have been used by Bedouin shepherds through the centuries, so that the archaeological evidence in them is very meager."

Fritsch shows a curious literalness in reading the scrolls. Alone of these six writers, he takes "The War of the Sons of Light and the Sons of Darkness" to refer to a literal rather than an apocalyptic war, at least to the extent of assuming from it that the community "had numerous banners and a complicated military organization." Following out its apocalyptic fantasies, he sees the tiny Qumran community of a few hundred studious ascetics lined up in serried ranks of thousands, hundreds, fifties, and tens. Fritsch is as pro-Jewish as Allegro is pro-Arab: quoting A. Dupont-Sommer's "fitting tribute to these fallen heroes of Israel"; welcoming the undercover purchase of the Metropolitan Samuel's four scrolls for Israel so that "once again all the manuscripts discovered in Cave I will be together in the land and among the people that gave them birth two thousand years ago"; taking the Hebrew documents from the time of the Second Revolt found in the cave at Murabba'at as evidence "of the high cultural level of common people" among Jewry at the time; even noting the ironic implications of the guano traffic without any of Allegro's nasty bite: "it is quite possible that the orange groves around Bethlehem were fertilized with fragments of papyrus or skin from the caves."

All of this adds up to the scrolls as an affirmation of the common "Judaeo-Christian" heritage so important to liberal Protestantism. Fritsch welcomes all connections, and ends with theology as a seamless garment. The early Church Father, Origen, who tells of the findings of manuscripts in a jar near Jericho during the reign of Caracalla, may have taken scrolls from these very caves. Like the later Christians, Fritsch holds, the Qumran community had a genuine baptism, not a rite of lustration, in that they believed "The Holy Spirit, and not water, cleanses a man of his iniquities," and they had a sacramental meal "at which the Messiah was present." Furthermore, their Messiah was not the traditional Jewish Davidic king in glory but the Suffering Servant of Deutero-Isaiah. "The way was now theologically prepared for the coming of God's Son," Fritsch writes, "in whom the Messianic hopes of Israel were to be fulfilled and the mission of the Servant realized. These profound Messianic teachings of the Essenes must have been known by Jesus."

Theodor H. Gaster, professor of Comparative Religion at the Dropsie College and visiting professor of History of Religions at Columbia, is an outstanding Hebraist and Semitic philologist. *The Dead Sea Scriptures* offers itself as "a complete and reliable translation of the celebrated Dead Sea Scrolls," and its bellyband shrieks: "For the FIRST time the ACTUAL TEXT of the DEAD SEA SCROLLS." Gaster has worked scrupulously in every case "from the facsimile plates, not from the editors' transcriptions," and he announces his intention of following this volume with another explaining and justifying its translations. The present book, he assures us, "does not gear these renderings to any particular theory, but allows the documents to raise their own voice and give their own testimony amid the din and hubbub of current controversy about them."

On the basis of his notes and explanations, some of Gaster's versions seem remarkably free. He reverses the meaning of one passage in the Zadokite Document (the manuscript that preceded the cave finds, discovered in a Cairo *genizah* and published by Solomon Schechter in 1910 as "Fragments of a Zadokite Work"). As Gaster says in his notes, the text of a rule for the Sabbath reads:

> If a human being falls into a place of water or into a place of . . . let no man bring him up by a ladder or a rope or by any other implement.

Gaster renders it as:

> If a human being falls into a place of water or into a dark place, one is to bring him up by means of a ladder or a rope or some other instrument.

His justification is that the text's reading "would be against the universal Jewish rule that Sabbath laws may be broken in cases of life and death." Elsewhere Gaster inserts whole lines with such explanations as: "This restoration is based on the assumption that there is once again a play on the expression 'lift up'," or, "in order to bring out the nexus of thought I have had to result to a certain amount of expansion and paraphrase." At other times he ends a hymn with a Shakespearean couplet, or alternates what he calls "Biblical English" with such slang as "will 'put their bite' on thee," or omits from a text "a series of esoteric glosses."

Oddly accompanying this liberal theory of translation, and apparently justifying it, is a conservatism in interpretation more extreme than that of any other scholar on the scrolls whom I have read. Gaster devotes a whole section of his introduction to a warning against attempts to "historicize" the scrolls, "that is, to detect in them precise and specific historical allusions," or even "to speculate about historical allusions." It is this tendency, he believes, that has "compromised (or at least embarrassed)" the "true understanding" of the scrolls to date. As for the parallels so many scholars have found between the scrolls and Christianity, the covenanters "were in no sense Christians and held none of the fundamental theological doctrines of the Christian faith." There is in the scrolls "no trace of any of the cardinal theological concepts—the incarnate Godhead, Original Sin, redemption through the Cross, and the like—which make Christianity a distinctive faith."[7] At the same time, the religious ideas of the scrolls "served largely as the seedbed of the New Testament."

What motivates Gaster seems to be a familiar combination of Jewish pride and exclusiveness. *The Dead Sea Scriptures* is dedicated "To the Memory of the Men of Qumran," and the preface explains:

> More than to all the foregoing, however, the writer adheres to the view that the Dead Sea Scrolls should be regarded as something

[7] Some scholars have found: if not Incarnation, at least God's begetting the Messiah (of which more later); definite Atonement and Redemption through Faith; Fritsch has Baptism and a kind of Communion; Dupont-Sommer has detected the outline of the Gospel story, including Passion, Resurrection and Epiphany; Allegro has added Delivery to the Gentiles, Crucifixion, Burial, and Return in Judgment.

more than the subject matter of a scholarly controversy. For those who will read them sympathetically, they possess value in their own right as conveying the religious message of men who gave up the world and were able to find God in a wilderness, simply because they preferred nakedness to motley and because they realized that, in the larger analysis, crucifixion can itself be resurrection.

In Gaster's hands, the scrolls demonstrate high Jewish religious experience independent of Christianity, but comparable to its ethical and aesthetic heights. It is this that leads him to call them Scriptures and translate them as eloquently as possible, to reverse the doctrine about pulling people out of wells on the Sabbath, to deny Christian identifications while affirming later Christian dependency.

For Gaster, high religious experience appears to be primarily mystic, and there is a running comparison in his book between the religion of the scrolls and the experiences of mysticism. The Qumran covenanters "achieved, in short, what mystics term the 'unitive state' "; they believed "in a constant cyclic repetition of primordial and archetypal elements"; they resemble the medieval Waldensian Brotherhood; the literary conventions of their hymns "should no more dull our ears to the underlying passion and authenticity of feeling than do the mannered conceits of a Donne or a Herbert or a Vaughan"; they use "the standard and characteristic idiom of mystical experience"; their recurrent despair at God's "seeming remoteness" is comparable to that of St. John of the Cross in *The Dark Night of the Soul*, and their sense of renewal and rebirth to that of George Fox's *Journal*. In sum:

> The desert to which they repaired was not simply the desert of Judah; it was also the mystic's Desert of Quietude—what John Tauler called "The Wilderness of Godhead, into which He leads all who are to receive this inspiration of God, now or in eternity." In that wilderness, they would not merely receive a renewal of the Covenant; they would also have the vision of the Burning Bush. Removed from men, they would acquire an unobstructed view of the divine. Thirsting in an inhospitable wild, they would drink the unfailing waters of God's grace. Shorn of earthly possessions, theirs would be the poverty of the mystics—that poverty which

Evelyn Underhill has described as "complete detachment from all finite things." Burned by the scorching sun, they would see the *semplice lume* of Dante, the "infused brightness" of Saint Teresa, and by that light they would not be dazzled.

In 1950, when he published his invaluable *Thespis: Ritual, Myth and Drama in the Ancient Near East* (with its revealing epigraph from Psalm 39, "Surely every man walketh in a vain shew"), Gaster apparently agreed with Gilbert Murray and Jane Harrison on the primacy of ritual over either belief or the believer's subjective state. In *The Dead Sea Scriptures*, there is one page relating the War Scroll to the ancient Near East seasonal combat, but Gaster now seems to see religion as essentially a matter of inner experience, and to present the scrolls as evidence that Jewish inner experiences are second to none.

Geoffrey Graystone, at thirty-five only a year older than Allegro, is an English Marist Father who has taught Scripture and Theology in Marist seminaries in England and Ireland. *The Dead Sea Scrolls and the Originality of Christ,* dated from Rome and published in America with the imprimatur of Bishop Jerome D. Hanna of Scranton, is a reprinting of a series of articles that appeared in the *Irish Theological Quarterly.* Three articles are on the scrolls themselves and a fourth takes issue with Edmund Wilson's book. (Graystone has published another series of articles in the *Tablet,* not yet in book form, one of which takes issue with Allegro.) Graystone is as passionately unwilling as Gaster, from very different premises, to acknowledge any relationship between Christianity and Judaism, and the effort of his book is to play down the significance of the scrolls as far as possible. He writes characteristically: "Much of what has been writen was a little premature," or, "a number of theories and opinions, one or two a little advanced, have been ventilated on this question." Graystone argues that "Christianity did not in any sense owe its origins to the Qumran sect," and, with a stroke so shrewd it should make the Jesuits look to their laurels, demonstrates that not only are the scrolls remote from Roman Catholic Christianity, but that they display nothing of the essence of Christianity "as it is understood by leading liberal scholars" (that is, by Protestants).

For Graystone, the issue is a simple dogmatic one: Christianity did not evolve from earlier ideas like a worldly doctrine, but was revealed instantaneously and uniquely by the Passion of Jesus. The Qumran covenanters speak of their "New Alliance" ("New Covenant" in most translations, "New Testament" in King James English), but it is "nothing more than a renewal, however complete, of this old alliance of Sinai," whereas "The Christian 'New Alliance' was effectively established for all men through the blood of Christ, shed in sacrifice on Calvary, and thereby the Old Alliance, concluded between one people and their God at Mount Sinai and sealed by the blood of animal victims, was abrogated." Graystone's distinction between any idea in the scrolls and its Christian analogue is always that the former "is not based on the teaching and example of the Son of God," and his conclusion is that the scrolls do not challenge the originality of Christ, as Wilson and others had claimed, but rather "bring into greater relief the uniqueness of Christ." Graystone's view is best summed up in a sentence he quotes approvingly from an article by R. E. Brown in the *Catholic Biblical Quarterly:* "It should be evident that the basic difference between the two theologies is Christ."

Except for Brown and Canon J. Coppens of Louvain, Graystone does not find Catholic orthodoxy orthodox enough for his taste. He gives a history of the Qumran sect as "the Dominican Fathers actually working on the Cave material in Jerusalem would put it," but he does not agree with the "Catholic scholars of note" (even Coppens to some extent) who "are so struck with the similarities of vocabulary instanced above that they admit that the New Testament writers, particularly John and Paul, borrowed formulae and expressions from the scrolls." Graystone admits no such thing, and dissolves all similarities of vocabulary in the uniqueness of Christ.[8]

---

[8] On one scholarly point Graystone seems incredibly confused. The conventional view of an apocryphal work called "The Testaments of the Twelve Patriarchs" has been that it is a Jewish document with heavy Christian interpolation. Graystone, with a few other recent Catholic scholars, argues that its origins are Christian. Parts of one of the testaments, the Testament of Levi, were found in the Qumran caves in Aramaic, and some fragments were in the Cairo *genizah* with the Zadokite Document. Graystone and his fellows argue that Levi "is a distinct and pre-Christian work" incorporated in the Testaments. (This decision seems to be made empirically to explain its finding, and not on internal evidence, if I can judge by R. H. Charles's scholarly edition in *Apocrypha and Pseudepigrapha of the Old Testament.*) On p. 104 of his

Graystone's tone toward Judaism is always patronizing. He says of the hymn appended to the Manual of Discipline (where in his opinion "the religious sentiment of Qumran attains its high water mark") : "No one will deny the loftiness and sincerity of these sentiments, which sum up much of what was best in Jewish piety and prepare the way for the Christian revelation." Qumran theology is always limited by un-Christian qualities: "the rigid exclusiveness of the sect, their narrow view of predestination, their sharp and inexorable distinction between Sons of Light and Sons of Darkness." The best Graystone can say for the scroll sect is that considered alongside the Pharisees bitterly attacked by Jesus in the Gospels, "the comparison is very much in favor of the sectaries." The only enthusiastic use Graystone seems prepared to make of the scrolls is to bolster Catholic dogma. He welcomes their evidence of Jewish celibacy, since it shows that the Jews in the last century B.C. were less benighted than some have alleged, and argues, "let no one now object against the virginity of Mary or her virginal marriage with St. Joseph that voluntary celibacy for a higher motive was a thing unheard of and morally impossible among the Jews of that time."

Harold H. Rowley is professor of Hebrew Language and Literature in the University of Manchester, Allegro's senior colleague and former teacher. His book *The Zadokite Fragments and the Dead Sea Scrolls* consists of three lectures delivered at Canon Coppens' University of Louvain in March, 1952, attempting to summarize the state of our knowledge about the scrolls. Much of each page is filled with footnotes and citations, and the bibliography of works consulted covers thirty-five pages and consists of almost a thousand books and articles in a dozen languages. Rowley has seriously attempted to read and digest all the scholarship and opinion on the scrolls, and somewhere in the middle of his book he ventures his own tentative view in a sentence: "The wicked Priest could be identified with Menelaus with much appropriateness, and Onias would appear to be the Teacher of Righteousness."

book, Graystone says: "The influence of *Jubilees* and the *Testaments* on the Qumran documents and especially the Damascus Document is also incontestable." If Graystone believes that the Testaments are a Christian work, written A.D., how does he think they influenced the Qumran documents, by general agreement (including his) written B.C.?

Rowley seems to be inhibited by no religious or theoretical bias, but to have the temperamental caution of the scholar to an inordinate degree. His preface explains:

> For a long time I refrained from forming any judgment on the age of the Scrolls or on the period which they reflect, and one of my good friends, Mr. J. Leveen, has frequently reproached me for sitting so long on the fence. It seemed to me wiser to suspend judgment until access could be had to all the facts, than to rush to conclusions on very inadequate evidence. Although the full evidence is not yet available, and it may be a long time before all the Scrolls are unrolled and published, there would seem now to be enough access to the facts to warrant a reasonably based view, though I would emphasize that it can only be tentative until all the texts are available.

This tone contrasts sharply with Rowley's statement against Allegro after the abashed broadcaster had backed down, as reported in *Time*, April 2, 1956:

> I deplore as unscholarly the presentation to the world of what scholars everywhere have supposed—as I supposed—to be specific statements in an unpublished text to which Mr. Allegro alone had access, when they are only his deductions from evidence which is capable of other interpretations. . . . Mr. Allegro was one of the most promising students I have ever had, and he is capable of doing fine work. I think it is a pity that he was entrusted with the editing of texts far from supervision. . . . Important documents, for which scholars in all countries are eagerly waiting, should not be used to give immature scholars a spurious authority.

Rowley's voice only rises, one gathers, when the deepest taboos of the tribe are violated.

I know nothing of the biography or qualifications of Arthur Whitman, except what emerges from a study of his pamphlet. It comes under unimpressive auspices, as a drugstore quickie smeared on the front cover with "NEW REVELATIONS FROM THE CRADLE OF CHRISTIANITY" and "THE STORY OF THE GREATEST RELIGIOUS DISCOVERY OF MODERN TIMES," and on the back with a giant question mark and a series of teasing questions, ending, "did they claim a superior knowledge of creation . . . ? did they in fact have a superior knowledge . . . ?" The writing is as dramatic as Allegro's, with a physical description of the Arab boy who found the first scrolls that could only have been invented, and a great deal of melodrama about the buried treasure of gold, silver, and incense described by the copper scroll found in one of the caves, concluding "one of the greatest prizes known to mankind—the fabulous lost treasure of the ancients." There is a certain amount of clumsy writing, and some deliberately low-brow analogies, including one justifying the disagreements of scholars over the scrolls by "the vast differences of opinion that exist within the field of medical practice" over such matters as miracle drugs. Whitman makes a number of curious statements, including, "Zadok became the first King Solomon"; he does not seem to know what "the Law" means among Jews; and he is unfamiliar with Qumran archaeology.

Yet, on the whole, *The Dead Sea Scrolls and What They Mean to Protestant, Catholic, Jew* is enormously better than its merchandising would suggest. Most of its information is solid, its interpretations are sensible, its tone is moderate, and it is probably a less slanted picture of the consensus of opinion about the scrolls than any of the other books except Rowley's. The "questions and answers about the scrolls" that constitute the last chapter are neither the dogmas of catechism nor the half-truths of sensationalism, but a summary of what has gone before in the form of intelligent questions and sensible answers. Whitman's bias in discussing Palestine's history seems to be markedly pro-Israel, so that it is only "oil-rich Arab leaders who objected to Jewish colonization," and as for the Israelis: "Against enormous odds, they outmaneuvered and outfought the Arabs, forcing them after long and bitter fighting to accept the boundaries the U.N. had established." His religious bias, even more surprisingly, appears to be extreme liberal Protestant. In its paraphrases of scholarly and clerical opinion, the pamphlet gives most emphasis to the views of A. Powell Davies, pastor of the Unitarian All Souls Church in Washington, as stated in his book *The Meaning of the Dead Sea Scrolls*. Whitman concludes:

> Most scholars will agree with the views of writers such as Rev. Davies, and their agreement is, in fact, implicit in most of their writings, even though they may not state it each time they prepare a scholarly article to be read by their colleagues.

In short, the spectrum is fairly wide. For Allegro, the scrolls are scripts for historical melodrama. For Fritsch, they document the continuity of the "Judaeo-Christian" heritage. To Gaster, they show the mystic beauties of Jewish religious experience, and to Graystone its inadequacies compared to Roman Catholic Christianity. For Rowley, they occasion scrupulosities of scholarship, and they enable Whitman to write a Unitarian tract sugar-coated with sensationalism about buried treasure. Other books seem just as varied in their approaches. For Edmund Wilson's hero, Professor A. Dupont-Sommer of the Sorbonne, the scrolls are occasions for elaborate theorizing about pre-Christian Christianity in Essenism, and the imaginative reconstruction of history. A characteristically bold Dupont-Sommer reading finds in the sentence in the Zadokite Document, "God, through his Anointed, hath made known his Holy Spirit," "something like a Trinitarian theology." For A. Powell Davies, if I can judge by the paraphrase of *The Meaning of the Dead Sea Scrolls* in Whitman's pamphlet (for I have not yet had an opportunity to read the book), the scrolls are a reaffirmation of the traditional Unitarian or humanist "Jesus the Teacher," the good man deified rather than the god incarnated. For Henry Neumann in *The Dead Sea Scrolls*, a pamphlet published by the New York Society for Ethical Culture, the scrolls naturally show the glories of ethical culture.

Nor have I yet had an opportunity to read *The Dead Sea Scrolls and Modern Scholarship* by Solomon Zeitlin, professor of Rabbinical Literature at the Dropsie College and Gaster's colleague. From accounts in these books of the series of articles he has published in his *Jewish Quarterly Review* and elsewhere, Zeitlin seems to be engaged in one of the most remarkable King Canute performances in recent scholarship. Zeitlin has dated the script of the scrolls at various times from the seventh to the eleventh centuries A.D., or quite a few centuries after everyone else, and he has claimed that its paleographic resemblance to the text of the Zadokite Document Schechter found in the Cairo *genizah* "is so striking as to indicate that they are of the same locality and the same period, i.e. the Middle Ages." Zeitlin suggests that the scrolls were never actually in the caves or in the jars, since no reputable European or Jewish scholar ever saw them there. He has dismissed the hymns that Gaster finds so impressive as flat and poor, with little poetic quality, a poor copy of the Psalms. In a letter to the *New York Times*, March 30, 1956, Zeitlin denied that "scrolls written by semi-literate persons could have any influence on Judaism." His articles have such titles as " 'A Commentary on the Book of Habakkuk': Important Discovery or Hoax?," "Scholarship and the Hoax of the Recent Discoveries," "The Alleged Antiquity of the Scrolls," "When Were the Hebrew Scrolls 'Discovered'—in 1947 or 1907?," "The Antiquity of the Hebrew Scrolls and the Piltdown Hoax: A Parallel," "The Fiction of the Recent Discoveries near the Dead Sea," "A Note on the Fiction of the 'Bar Kokba' Letter," "The Propaganda of the Hebrew Scrolls and the Falsification of History," etc. As words like "alleged," "hoax," "fiction," and "falsification" make clear, Zeitlin apparently sees the scrolls as a plot by much of the scholarly world against him and against the sanctity of Hebrew studies.

In his pamphlet *The Hebrew Scrolls*, G. R. Driver, professor of Semitic Philology at Oxford, has much more moderately resisted the dating of the scrolls in antiquity. Professor J. L. Teicher of Cambridge, editor of the *Journal of Jewish Studies*, has identified the scrolls as products of the Christian heretic Ebionites in the first century A.D., explaining the Teacher of Righteousness as Jesus and his adversary the Wicked Priest as Paul. Finally, for G. Lankester Harding, director of the Jordan Government Department of Antiquities and the man responsible for most of the excavation at Qumran, they are the occasion for not only a great deal of sober digging but for the liveliest speculation yet. In an article in the *Illustrated London News*, September 3, 1955, Harding suggests that Jesus may very well have visited the Qumran monastery. If before the year is out further excavation turns up a visitors' book with the signature "Joshua ben Joseph, Nazareth," Harding will presumably not be surprised.

When the scrolls so neatly, like the Apostle Paul, can be all things to all men, it is not surprising that scholarly disagreement exists on the most basic matters. For Dupont-Sommer and Burrows, an outstanding characteristic of the scrolls is their revelation of Jewish Gnostic dualism, making the Fourth Gospel suddenly not the least Jewish of the Gospels, but the most. Gaster's only comment on the dramatic dualism in his texts, in passages on "the two spirits of man" and "The War of the Sons of Light and the Sons of Darkness," is "see A. Dupont-Sommer," and his only comment on their equally dramatic Gnosticism is "This is scarcely to be confused with the later more elaborate doctrine of the Gnostics." For Gaster, reference to "exile in the desert of Damascus" in the Zadokite Document is "figurative geography" for "voluntary withdrawal from the normative forms of Jewish life," for Graystone "Damascus" is "almost certainly a symbolic name for Qumran," for Fritsch it is a real migration to the real city of Damascus. The Zadokite Document and a cave fragment say that the members of the community must be thoroughly versed in the "Book of Hagu." Allegro thinks the Book of Hagu is a scroll we have not yet turned up, "although it is possible that we have it without knowing." Fritsch believes it is the Manual of Discipline itself. Zeitlin doubts that there ever was a Book of Hagu, attributing it to the imagination of the author of the Zadokite Document. Gaster simply translates the problem out of existence, rendering the Book of Hagu "the Book of Study" and giving his reasons. Gaster does the same with the Teacher of Righteousness, identified by most scholars as the founder, leader, and sometimes Messiah of the sect, and the subject of an enormous amount of historical speculation. "Teacher of Righteousness," Gaster says, is a mistranslation for the "correct expositor" or "right-teacher" title given to whatever priest had the office of expounding Torah throughout the sect's history. (This does not prevent Gaster from himself using "Teacher of Righteousness" later in his book.)

Sometimes differences of opinion depend on variant readings of the manuscripts. Allegro translates from a fragmentary Manual of Discipline: "When [God] begets the Messiah," explaining "this word could conceivably have been used here with the weakened sense of 'produce' or the like, or it could, as the editors suggest, be a scribal error for 'leads,'" but that he has been convinced in favor of "beget" by the sect's Messianic use of the familiar Christian proof text from 2 Samuel 7:14, "I will be his father, and he shall be my son." Gaster translates the passage "if the anointed king of Israel happens to be present," and comments:

> We may safely leave out of serious consideration the alleged occurrence in this text of a phrase reading, "If [God] begets the Messiah." This bizarre statement rests on nothing more substantial than an arbitrary reading of a faded word and an even more capricious restoration of a lacuna. Such a statement, it need scarcely be observed, would be utterly preposterous to a community of Jews committed to belief in the Torah and in the traditional doctrines of their faith. This whole document, in fact, has been egregiously misunderstood.

Where there are no variant readings, the translations nevertheless show remarkable differences, apparently reflecting differences of theology and religious vocabulary. Burrows translates from the Manual:

> for they shall all be in true community and good humility and loyal love and righteous thought, each for his fellow in the holy council, and they shall be sons of the eternal assembly.

Gaster translates the same passage:

> All of them will thus be members of a community founded at once upon true values and upon a becoming sense of humility, upon charity and mutual fairness—members of a society truly hallowed, partners in an everlasting communion.

Where Graystone's translation has the hymn at the end of the Manual say that stumbling man will be aided by "God's graces," Gaster translates "God's mercies" and "God's righteousness"; and where Graystone's text asks, "What is the son of man?," for Gaster the text asks, "What is mere mortal man?"

In an earlier review of the Burrows and Wilson books, I tried to define the significance the scrolls had for the student of mythology and comparative religion, principally their strong evidence for pre-Christian patterns of Christianity and their increasing the likelihood that Jesus was a mythic rather than a historical figure. (One more chastening example, obviously, of What You Will.) Assessing the meaning of the scrolls now seems a great deal harder, and there may be as many meanings as readers. One of the interesting features of the scrolls is the open polytheism of their Old Testament manuscripts. The text of Deuteronomy 32:43 found in the caves reads: "Rejoice, O ye heavens, with him, and all ye gods worship him." The Septuagint reads: "Rejoice, O ye heavens, with him, and let all the angels of God worship him," while the Hebrew Masoretic text (and all our Christian and Jewish Bibles based on it) says simply: "Rejoice, O ye nations." It is Wilson's contention in *The Scrolls from the Dead Sea* that one of the factors underlying the resistance of Jewish scholars to accepting the scrolls and their implications has been "a fear of impairing the authority of the Masoretic text." Allegro does conclude that the authority of the Masoretic text has been somewhat impaired, with more authority established for the Septuagint where it differs, and "a remarkable vindication" of the Samaritan Pentateuch. Fritsch's conclusion from the same evidence, however, is the opposite; he finds the scrolls "supporting the fidelity of the Masoretic tradition."

The threat to Jewish peace of mind that seems to me much greater than challenges to the Masoretic text is the scrolls' evidence that monolithic Judaism is a modern invention retrospectively imposed on history. The Qumran Jews apparently considered themselves orthodox, and were considered orthodox, despite some remarkable innovations. They did not sacrifice in the Temple in Jerusalem (here the Manual of Discipline disagrees with the Zadokite Document, which says that under certain conditions, and perhaps at another time, they did). They had a solar rather than a lunar calendar, so that holidays and even Sabbaths did not coincide with orthodoxy's. (The late Ralph Marcus suggested in "Pharisees, Essenes and Gnostics" in the *Journal of Biblical Literature*, 1954, that they did not carry out their unorthodox calendar in practice, "otherwise these covenanters would have been stigmatized as heretics," but Marcus may simply have been assuming the monolith.) Many of their views we would certainly stigmatize as heretic, including their celibacy, ritual baptism, and wildly uncanonical scriptures. Their keeping of the Sabbath, even if it came on a Wednesday, seems to have been extraordinarily rigid: despite Gaster's emendation, it is not at all unlikely that anyone unlucky enough to fall into a well on that day was allowed to drown, and they certainly dispensed with that invaluable jesuitical institution, the *shabbos goy*—the Zadokite Document says flatly: "No one is to commission a Gentile to transact business for him on the Sabbath day." Like the earlier orthodox Jews of Elephantine in Egypt in the early sixth century B.C., whose papyri reveal that their god had a female consort named Anat Yahveh, and who had apparently never heard of the Law, the Patriarchs, or the Sabbath, the Jews of Qumran would find it harder to make the grade today.

While the Dead Sea Scrolls were being hawked around Jerusalem, a new edition of Sir Frederic Kenyon's *Our Bible and the Ancient Manuscripts* was in press with the statement, "there is no probability that we shall ever find manuscripts of the Hebrew text going back to a period before the formation of the text which we know as Massoretic." The example suggests that it is well to be tentative about these matters, when the next discoveries may overturn everything we know. In our time there has been a wild fascination with the discoveries of Near East archaeology, or any archaeology, and one popular summary after another has become a best-seller. One widespread theory is that all those book buyers are in quest of religious certainty, or even documentation (for Christian doubters, perhaps the authenticating texts of such reassuring apocrypha as Pilate's Letters or Peter's Gospel; for Jewish doubters, perhaps fragments of the original Ten Commandments or Noah's Ark). Here the example of the scrolls seems to suggest that less certainty comes from more documents and artifacts, that new evidence only serenely confirms everyone in the line he was already pursuing.

There is a great deal of solid information to be acquired from these six books: Allegro prints translations of the variant Bible readings in tabular form; Allegro and Fritsch, in photographs and descriptions, give us the physical reality of the site, the caves, the jars, and the script itself; Gaster gives us readable translations of the texts, and a superb analytic index of their ideas and of Bible quotations and parallels; Rowley chews and digests the millions of words written on the subject for us; even Graystone and Whitman add to our knowledge. Around this well-lighted clearing there are the shifting figures of theory dancing in the shadows, and the animal growlings of passion and prejudice. Out there you venture at your peril.

A Critical Look
at Psychology

[1959]

A CONSIDERABLE PRESUMPTION is involved when a man criticizes a field not his own, particularly when that field is as multiverse as psychology. The presumption increases when the criticism is based on a reading acquaintance with only the tiniest fraction of the literature in one small area, and a few friends in the field who must be thoroughly unrepresentative, in that they exhibit none of its defects or failings. All I can say in extenuation is that it is the engagingly old-fashioned habit of literary criticism to insist that it still takes all knowledge to be its province, and that the impulse is friendly, based on an enormous respect for the field of psychology and a sharing of its aspirations. Sometimes an amateur can see things that the professional misses, or at the very least his insolence can annoy the professional into considering matters usually outside his specialized sphere. Still, perhaps "look" in my title is overambitious. Call it "glance" or "squint."

Psychology arose historically as a branch of philosophy (where it is still ensconced in some booksellers' catalogues, if no longer in academic departments). The earliest development of its insights, however, came from writers. Sigmund Freud repeatedly credited the poets with anticipating his discoveries (by delving into their own psyches, he said), and how could he have acknowledged the debt more prettily than by naming the complex he considered nuclear after the protagonist in two plays by Sophocles? Thomas Hardy knew psychoanalysis, Freud once told C. P. Oberndorf, meaning it in the sense in which we rediscover the mechanisms of depth psychology each time we open Shakespeare.

In noting these anticipations and intuitions, however, we must not minimize the difference between writers and psychologists. Athenian tragedies are, in fact, oddly unpsychological (someone remarked that there is more psychology in a page of Proust than in the whole extant corpus of Greek drama), in that in them character always arises out of action, never the reverse. King Oedipus, we must remember, has no explicit Oedipus complex in Sophocles' play of that name: he killed his father and married his mother in all innocence, although he *is* oddly short-tempered with gentlemen of his father's generation, and he seems to have shown no reluctance about marrying a widow well along in years. Oedipus' daughter Antigone has something that looks much more like a traditional complex, although even here it is not very explicit. Sophocles' predecessor Aeschylus is fuller and clearer about motivation in such characters as Clytemnestra in the *Agamemnon*, but only by the time we get to Euripides do we begin to rival case history: the marvelous comic *agon* between anal-character father and anal-character son in the *Alcestis*; the classic disintegration of the repressed homosexual personality of King Pentheus in the *Bacchae*.

Even in the adventure stories of that busy syndicate we call Homer, as E. R. Dodds has pointed out, there are touches that stagger us by their psychological truth: the boy Astyanax's terror of his father's great erect helmet crest in *Iliad* 6; Penelope's dream of the eagle and geese in *Odyssey* 19, with its eloquent wish fulfillment and elaborate condensation and displacement. Nor did the ancient Greeks have a monopoly on psychological insight. The other major progenitor of Western culture, the Hebrew Bible, is fully as knowledgeable, and it should be a chastening experience for the modern psychologist to reread (or read) the history of Saul and his "bloody house" in the books of Samuel, and see the complexities of emotional relationship in the odd triangle of mad hostile Saul, smitten Jonathan, and ambivalent David.

All this is perhaps a long running start for some strictures against current American psychology, except insofar as the literary critic, with his tiny capital invested in Homer and the Bible, Greek drama and Shakespeare, Proust and Thomas Hardy, can fairly ask what the new management thinks it is doing to the old firm. Perhaps, to paraphrase a cynical saying, every country gets the psychologists it deserves, but I am not sure that justice is that poetic. In any case, I should like to suggest five limitations in current American psychology as I have encountered them.[1]

The first is an inadequate history and culture, ranging from simple provincial ignorance to a self-righteous hostility, strongly Calvinist in nature. Many psychologists seem to be ignorant even of the history of their own field, or to despise their founding fathers as obsolete unscientific old fuddy-duddies. "We *know* so much more than they did," T. S. Eliot says, phrasing a similar attitude in regard to the poets of the past, and he answers it, "Precisely, and they are that which we know." I have heard a young psychologist dismiss as ludicrous the most enthralling case history I have read, Morton Prince's *The Dissociation of a Personality*, because Prince had the misfortune to write it in 1905 rather than 1958, to know less depth psychology in 1905 than my young acquaintance does in 1958, and not to be equally aware that the successive personalities Miss Beauchamp developed might be artifacts of Prince's own creation. Yet the imaginative power and breadth of Prince's picture of the human personality make the case still a revelation to read, and Prince was improvising his theory as he went along, like Charcot, Janet, or Freud. When Drs. Corbett H. Thigpen and Hervey M. Cleckley published the record of a similar case as *The Three Faces of Eve* in 1957, with far less excuse than Prince for being unaware that the successive personalities might be artifacts of the therapists', their book, written as sensationally and badly as Prince's book was written with dignity and style, was introduced rapturously by a past presi-

[1] The examples are drawn almost entirely from the human-adjustment psychology we outsiders get to read about—psychoanalysis, psychiatry, clinical psychology—but no evidence suggests that these things are less true of the manipulators of earthworms and golden hamsters.

dent of the American Psychological Association, and apparently was taken seriously in the field.

If many American psychologists know little about the history of their own discipline, they seem to know less about the history and values of anything else. When they are concerned with literature or the arts at all, it is as simple projective tests for revealing the warp of the individual or the culture, and they are far more likely to take their examples exclusively from films, soap operas, and comic strips than from Cervantes, Pushkin, or Montaigne. This seems much less true of the European-born among American psychologists, perhaps because their education was broader, perhaps because they have been encouraged to see themselves as heirs of the culture, rather than as new settlers building on its ruins. How far we have come from the ideal of a man like William James, at home in half a dozen disciplines, or Freud, reading eight languages and their literatures, studying archaeology and anthropology, collecting antiquities and Yiddish jokes.

The second weakness I see in American psychology is a philosophical shallowness and superficial optimism. I have already stated my views along these lines in "Psychoanalysis and the Climate of Tragedy" and elsewhere, and I do not here propose to repeat those chillingly blithe quotations about human nature and destiny from such neo-Freudians as Karen Horney, Erich Fromm, and Clara Thompson. I have since, however, encountered a book that seems to me a representative specimen of inspirational psychology, *Why You Do What You Do: A Guide to Self-Understanding*, edited by two laymen, Robert N. Linscott and Jess Stein. Here one can learn from "a leading American psychiatrist" that adolescent hostility and aggression can be cured by "a well-organized social program," or see "one of New York's leading psychiatrists" solve the problems of impotence and frigidity with such vulgar wisdom as "Encouragement by a wife, even a well-placed bit of flattery after a successful contact, may pay enormous dividends." I hope there is no need to quote further. A similar philosophic shallowness and optimism, it seems to me, distinguishes those psychologists at the other end of the tonal spectrum from these cheery oracles, the cynical whores of motivation research who are so contemptuous of mankind that they believe we are easier to be played on than a pipe (a phrasing, incidentally, from the pen of the creator of one of the earliest motivation analysts in literature, Dr. Iago).

Third, I should like to note the tendency of American psychology toward oversimplification, its apparent preference for the reductive and the mechanistic rather than the complex tangled bank of life. This, among the experimental psychologists, produces a passion for quantification and for results expressible in statistical tables. These rigors are always defended as the only way in which psychology can become a true empirical science, yet in reality they are the only way psychology can eliminate so many factors not susceptible of quantification as to become as shapely and remote from life as classical economics. Where the experimental psychologists want quantification, many clinical psychologists appear to want a similarly reductive empirical success: tests that will have a high diagnostic efficiency even if the actual relationship of manifestations to meanings remains as mysterious as augury; short-cut treatments that will calm or cure as magically as exorcism. And so many psychoanalysts and psychiatrists seem principally to want a showy new term or theory they can call their own, an "Orestes" complex or a "gambling" neurosis. The latter term, by the way, I get from a book, Edmund Bergler's *The Psychology of Gambling*, which has one of the funniest unconscious puns I know, the author's boast that a patient he treated for impotence "is today one of the pillars of the bar association." Perhaps all of these—tables and statistics, tests and short-cuts, terms and theories—similarly can be pillars of the impotent.

My fourth criticism is the related matter of narrowness and overspecialization. I would regard psychology's characteristic myopic preoccupation with a segment of an approach to one aspect of a problem as primarily responsible (cultural inadequacy is certainly a factor too) for the awful prose in which most current psychology seems to be written. Early in the twenties, I learn from Frederick J. Hoffman's *Freudianism and the Literary Mind,* a girl named Mercy Rogers read through 102 books on psychoanalysis and allied subjects and then killed herself. In the fifties, she could not have gotten through the curdled and clotted prose of half that number anywhere in the field of psychology before turning on the gas.

We have for so long been told of the gains (and they are impressive gains) obtained through specialization, teamwork, and interdisciplinary co-operation, that it is about time we began to notice the losses. As long ago as 1950, in *Childhood and Society,* Erik H. Erikson warned that interdisciplinary teamwork was "a kind of halt-and-blind cooperation, in which a social scientist with little psychological vision carries in a piggy-back fashion a psychologist who has not learned to move with ease in the larger events of this world, so that together they may grope their way through contemporary history." In the Summer, 1958, issue of the *Northwest Review,* a political scientist, Lucian C. Marquis, delivered a full-scale attack on interdisciplinary teamwork. "It is time," he suggests, "that we call for a cease-fire, in order to assess the price of our victory and to count the casualties," which include, in his view, the loss of initiative, independence, creativity, and invention; "thwarted individuality and the leveling of tastes and interests." Specialization seems inevitably forced on the modern social scientist, and some co-operation of specialists must follow as a consequence, but none of the by-products is inevitable, least of all the new "team man," with his extraordinary efficiency in a narrow groove, his unconcerned and routine respect for all fellow specialists, and his nervous resentment of anything intuitive, imaginative, sweeping and uncategorizable, or anything that might menace the easy money for projects in which everyone is a neatly fitting cog.

My final stricture, and the only one perhaps less valid now than in the past, is the amazing tolerance of psychology for superstition and occultism. I am aware that my own hero, Freud, was an incorrigible sucker for telepathy (as he was for the curious theory that the Earl of Oxford was William Shakespeare), but at least he had the good sense to make it extracanonical. Freud wrote to Ernest Jones: "When anyone adduces my fall into sin, just answer him calmly that conversion to telepathy is my private affair like my Jewishness, my passion for smoking and many other things, and that the theme of telepathy is in essence alien to psychoanalysis." Carl Jung, on the other hand, has made an impressive range of occultisms part of his dogmatic system, of which the possibility of flying saucers is only the latest and funniest.

I am not, however, primarily referring to such famous aberrations as these, but to the tolerance and even respect accorded by American psychology to a wide variety of charlatans and necromancers. I would instance Wilhelm Reich and the "orgone" box as an example of the former, and J. B. Rhine and "parapsychology" as an example of the latter. Before he died Reich was put out of business, not by any organization of psychologists, but by the Food and Drug Administration. Rhine continues to prosper in an academic institution, while his experiments are respectfully repeated in a number of places, as if one were to reproduce the experiments of the Fox sisters in table-rapping. When a poltergeist recently manifested itself on Long Island, in a household containing two adolescent children, the representatives of psychological science who investigated it were not the child psychologists we might expect, but a team of parapsychologists from Duke, and their learned report concluded that "psychokinesis" (the manipulation of matter by mental powers) seemed the likeliest explanation. It is a disturbing experience to look up "Psychologists" in the New York classified telephone directory and see the listings for "metaphysician," "psychometaphysical healing," "auto-suggestion," "mental healing," "Yoga," and "astrological interpretation of human nature."

I should not like, in this foolhardy endeavor, to create either of two false impressions: that I undervalue the enormous wealth of knowledge and benefit psychology has produced in its brief history; or that I believe the field of literature to be free of comparable failings. Even where the two disciplines come together, literature has often been more sinning than sinned against. For the work of every I. A. Richards, creating something like experimental conditions in which to study the reading of poems, or Lionel Trilling, bringing the full range of Freud's tragic vision to bear on literature, or Kenneth Burke, synthesizing a complex and rewarding eclectic psychology for the uses of literary criticism, there are surely a hundred critics for whom psychology is a narrowly reductive positivism, a chance to become a pundit of parlor psychoanalysis and play Peeping Tom with impunity, or a weapon with which to mutilate the corpses of the illustrious dead. After all, it was a literary critic, not a wild-eyed psychologist, who indicted the California orange as "an extraverted thing."

Nevertheless, the imaginative insights of the literary arts can broaden and enrich the field of psychology. Psychologists must approach them, however, with humility and even a touch of awe, not with the arrogance and self-assurance that seem to go with an M.D. in the field. I have in mind Edmund Bergler, pontificating in *The Writer and Psychoanalysis* about the mysteries of "the creative process" after analytic experience with a handful of neurotic hacks, or A. Bronson Feldman, in his contribution to *Explorations in Psychoanalysis*, exploring Dante, Goethe, and Shakespeare primarily as repressed homosexuals with castration complexes, paranoia, and masochistic cyclothymia.

Let us be clear, for example, about just what that masochistic cyclothymic William Butler Yeats is saying when he writes in "A Prayer for My Daughter":

> It's certain that fine women eat
> A crazy salad with their meat

or in "Two Songs From a Play":

> Whatever flames upon the night
> Man's own resinous heart has fed.

or in "The Circus Animals' Desertion":

> Now that my ladder's gone,
> I must lie down where all the ladders start,
> In the foul rag-and-bone shop of the heart.

He is not, for one thing, parading his neurotic symptoms for us, although they were plentiful enough, certainly. He is not making a series of denotative statements or pseudostatements about reality, ranging from the truism (that ladies eat tossed salads), through the mistaken (that the heart is a pine knot rather than the large muscle we know it to be), to the meaningless (that unspecified lost ladders can be retrieved in an unattractive junk shop somehow associated with the circulatory system, or, perhaps, the emotions). Nor is he projecting his hopes and fears as they are triggered by phantasms, nor pouring out his free associations, nor even producing a kind of entertaining nonsense patterned by meter and rhyme. What he is doing is telling us the profoundest truths he knows about the human condition, in a metaphoric language not paraphrasable in any other words, and he is giving us these truths in as controlled and impersonal a fashion (although the manner of discourse differs) as any experimental scientist reporting his conclusions.

Characteristically, Yeats's insights are neither optimistic nor cheering. They suggest that man is a wounded animal condemned to die, his impulses nasty and destructive, his hopes largely confined to enduring his condition and controlling his nature. These are the traditional conclusions of the gloomier philosophers and poets, and we call them the tragic vision if we choose to emphasize the brightness of the flame as the resinous heart burns, or stoicism if we focus on the charred tissue itself. There is less difference than twenty-two centuries might suggest between Freud's remarks in *The Future of an Illusion* on "the painful riddle of death, for which no remedy at all has yet been found, nor probably ever will be," and Callimachus' epigram on Charidas of Cyrene in the Greek Anthology:

> "What is it like below, Charidas?"
> "Very dark."
> "And what about the resurrection?"
> "All lies."
> "And Pluto?"
> "A fable."
> "Then I am done for."

What are traditionally called the humanities can furnish psychology, or, more properly, psychologists, with this bitter yet ultimately most rewarding vision of human nature and destiny. Actually, the relationship is wholly symbiotic, since literature in turn needs and must increasingly lean on this sort of deeper and truer psychology (along with a comparably enriched sociology and anthropology, and perhaps eventually a great unified science of man, clearing *all* the jungles). Beyond the parochial concerns of the literary critic, the whole world needs a better, more profound, and more influential psychology. It was easy enough to get into our present predicaments in innocent ignorance, like the younger son in fairy tales, but only that combination of knowledge and virtue that we call wisdom seems likely to get us even partway out.

NOTE [1963]: This broadside was delivered by invitation at a convention of the American Psychological Association. I expected to be chewed to pieces, but the response was tepid and consisted mainly of confessions by psychologists to some of my charges, at least on behalf of their colleagues. When the essay appeared in *The American Scholar*, it drew some letters defending the discipline and attacking me. A few of these were published in the magazine. Of those that were not, the most interesting is a letter from a psychologist saying that he had decided to test my general reliability by checking one surprising statement that I had made, that Morton Prince had been mayor of Boston. He had looked the matter up and was able to inform me that Prince had never been mayor of Boston. He left implicit his conclusion about the reliability of the rest of my remarks. My source for the statement was Ernest Jones's *Sigmund Freud: His Life and Work*. It turned out that Jones had confused Prince with Prince's father, who *was* mayor of Boston. The reference has been removed from the text.

I think now that I was somewhat unfair to the psychologists in charging that they condone charlatans and necromancers in their field. I find that they *do* make all sorts of legal efforts to have their profession defined and safeguarded against the telephone book quacks, but that so far their efforts have had little success.

The Dialectic
of Christianity

[1960]

I HAVE BEEN STUDYING the history of Christianity, in connection
with a course I give in the Bible, and one of the books I have
found most useful as a theoretical approach is Paul Radin's *Primitive Religion*. Christianity is far from a primitive religion, although
it is built on primitive foundations, but so much of Radin's theory
seems relevant that he may be dealing with universal constants in
the religious experience. (The other possibility, that his ideas have
been unconsciously shaped by the dominant Christian pattern of
our culture and that my application of them is thus entirely tautological, is one I prefer to reject.)

The three ideas of Radin's that I find particularly applicable have
in common the recognition of dialectic process, considering the results with which we are confronted to be the synthesis of oppositions. The first sees religious doctrine, dogma, or orthodoxy as a
precarious compromise between the opposed needs and temperaments of the two religious types into which Radin divides societies:
the extroverted lay mind (in our terms, this group would include
many clergymen) craving material satisfactions and security; and
the introverted religious formulator craving less tangible things,
among them power. The second idea sees the motivations of the
religious formulator himself, priest or prophet or shaman, as a tension between his genuine neurosis, expressed in disorientation and
suffering, and the practical manipulations and sly self-aggrandize-

178

ment of "priestcraft." The third sees notions of deity, ranging from the simplest name to the most complex theology, as a synthesis of ambivalent impulses of love and hate, originally directed elsewhere. Radin is not the inventor of these dialectic concepts—the first is in a general way familiar to all our thinking about religious history; the second is implicit in Bogoras, Jochelson, and others on the Siberian shaman; and the third comes from Freud, and has been elaborated as an approach to religion by such Freudians as Theodor Reik—but in combination, as a general dialectic of process in the study of religion, they represent a substantial theoretical contribution on Radin's part.

It has been customary to see the history of Christian dogma or belief as a series of great debates: St. Athanasius against Arius on the Trinity, St. Augustine against Pelagius on Original Sin and the need for Grace, St. Thomas Aquinas against St. Bonaventure on the Immaculate Conception of the Virgin Mary, Luther against the Pope or his spokesmen on Faith and Works, Arminius against Calvin or such Calvinists as Gomar on Free Will. In this simplistic view, one argument won out, the loser was stigmatized a heretic like Arius or Pelagius, or became a minority line of thinking in the Church like Bonaventure and Arminius, or founded a schismatic Church of his own like Luther or Calvin.

In a less simplified view, orthodoxy does not win out over heresy, but emerges as a tension between two heresies. A clear-cut example is the Council of Chalcedon, convened in 451, which formulated the orthodox doctrine of the Incarnation, the Christian paradox that Christ was both fully God and fully man. The Church Fathers of Alexandria, principally Clement and Origen, emphasized His divinity to the point where their Incarnation resembled Theophany and the Monophysite denial of Christ's humanity. The Church Fathers of Antioch, among them St. John Chrysostom and Theodore of Mopsuestia, emphasized His humanity to the point where their Incarnation resembled Inspiration and the Adoptionist denial of Christ's divinity. In the words of the *Oxford Dictionary of the Christian Church*,[1] "It was these two opposite tendencies which the

---

[1] Edited by F. L. Cross. Most of my references can be found in this volume. I have noted its High Church Anglican bias in a review, but its factual information is detailed, reliable, and invaluable.

Chalcedonian formula sought to hold in proper balance." Yet the real opposition the Formula resolved was not between the extremist theologians of Alexandria and Antioch. It was between Alexandrian theology and the body of Christians, including many of the five hundred bishops present, unconcerned with the abstractions of Incarnation but rallying in defense of the suffering human Jesus of the Synoptic Gospels; and between Antiochene theology and the same body of Christians, rallying in defense of the divine Jesus of St. John's Gospel and St. Paul's Epistles. The Council of Chalcedon, in other words, was not a compromise between opposed religious formulators, but a double compromise between formulators and the body of laymen with a vested interest in Scripture (and its securities in this world as well as the next). As the example shows, the Chalcedonian Formula reflects an earlier compromise of precisely the same sort by the Synod of Carthage in 397, when it fixed the canon of the New Testament.

Let us look at another contribution of Clement of Alexandria and Origen, the doctrine of Apocatastasis, that all share in salvation, attacked by St. Augustine and stigmatized a heresy by the Council of Constantinople in 543. We see it developing in the Old Testament as a denial of the exclusive salvation of the Chosen People: it extends the Covenant to the Moabite Ruth and to the heathen of Nineveh to whom Jonah is sent; it is formulated by "Deutero-Isaiah" in Isaiah 49:6, "I will also give thee for a light to the Gentiles," and Hosea 2:23, "And I will say to them which were not my people, Thou art my people." The universality of the glad tidings of redemption is the central message of the New Testament: it is the point of the descent of the Holy Ghost on the Apostles at Pentecost, giving them the gift of various tongues (thus neatly reversing the Tower of Babel story) in Acts 2:4; and it is the essential Pauline message, typically in Galatians 3:28, "There is neither Jew nor Greek, there is neither bond nor free, there is neither male nor female: for ye are all one in Christ Jesus." Yet from the sixth century on universalism is Christian heresy, affirmed only by a few Anabaptist and Arminian sects and the small Universalist Church, while predestined damnation for many becomes the central tenet of Calvinist Protestantism, which proceeds to divide the modern world into sheep and goats.

Clearly when the interest is evangelical, as in the optimistic stages of Judaism when Jonah and Deutero-Isaiah were written, or the early days of Christianity when it was attempting to break out of the limiting confines of Judaism and spread through the whole Roman world, the emphasis is on universality. When the interest is consolidation, and a going church needs the power to punish by withholding salvation, the emphasis suddenly returns to a Chosen People or a predestined Elect. The exclusivist religious formulator, whether the compiler of the Pentateuch or John Calvin, rediscovers the doctrine of limited salvation, the laymen defend their material and spiritual stake in it, and the religious thinker out of step with the times is anathematized if he is lucky and burned to a crisp if he is not.

We get a dialectic including both Church and State in the great Arian controversy. The heresiarch Arius, early in the fourth century, taught a position somewhere between the Trinitarian and the Unitarian, in which the Son was subordinate to the Father but created by him "of like substance," *homoiousios*. Against him, Athanasius argued the doctrine of the Trinity later formulated in the Nicene Creed, that Father and Son were equal and "of one substance," *homoousios*. The Emperor Constantine, not much concerned with theology but very much concerned that Christianity, which he had made the official religion of the Roman Empire, unify it instead of disuniting it, convoked the Council of Nicaea in 325. It decided in favor of Athanasius, and Arius and the bishops who supported him were banished. A few years later, the Emperor, somewhat persuaded of Arianism by his sister Constantia, asserted his new role of Pontifex Maximus by himself banishing Athanasius, by that time Bishop of Alexandria, and restoring Arius to favor. Soon after Constantine died in 337, his son and successor Constantius openly embraced Arianism, and Athanasius fled to Rome. Constantius had been a joint emperor with his brothers Constantinus and Constans until their deaths, and he did not like power-sharing for either God the Father or himself. During the next two decades, the influence of Arianism grew. Its high point was the adoption by a double council of Eastern and Western bishops at Sirmium in 359 of a compromise formula that Father and Son were *homoios*, similar; St. Jerome, who was seventeen at the time, commented, "The whole world groaned and marvelled to find itself Arian." Two years later Constantius died, the conservative semi-Arian bishops lost their nerve, and the pendulum swung back. Despite everything a later Arian emperor of the East, Valens, could do, orthodoxy was re-established at the Council of Constantinople in 381, although Arianism continued among the Teutonic tribes in Europe for a long time after.

Here we have the party of the laymen, led by Constantine and his successors, and the party of the religious formulators, whether the ascetic and saintly deacon Arius or the equally ascetic and saintly deacon Athanasius, locked in complicated combat. The final decision, by which the Nicene Creed was reaffirmed orthodoxy, and Athanasius became bishop and saint and Arius the chief of heresiarchs, was determined neither by their arguments nor by the cabalistic magic of the iota of difference between *homoousios* and *homoiousios*, but on the basis of considerations of Imperial polity, Imperial whim, and the accidents of Imperial survival.

Or we might consider the history of Antinomianism, the doctrine that Grace or Faith frees from the Law. Its roots are again in the Old Testament, in the protests of the Prophets against the priestly ritual of sacrifices in Deuteronomy and Leviticus. The protest is most eloquently stated in Micah 6:8, insisting that the Lord asks not burnt offerings, "but to do justly, and to love mercy, and to walk humbly with thy God." It flowers in St. Paul, in the idea of a New Covenant that frees from the Old Covenant, the Pentateuch or Torah, particularly in the Epistle to the Romans 3:28, "Therefore we conclude that a man is justified by faith without the deeds of the law," and 6:14, "For ye are not under the law, but under grace." Developed by the heretic Marcion in the second century, this becomes the doctrine that Love (Christian love, Paul's *Agape* of 1 Corinthians 13) frees from the Law, and with an irony that has sometimes accompanied Christian love in history, it led to violent anti-Semitism. Marcion rejected the entire Old Testament and anything in the New that seemed to him under Jewish influence or to be inspired by the despotic Jewish God of Torah as against the new Christian God of Love, so that Marcion's Scripture contained only ten Pauline Epistles and a de-Judaized Gospel of St. Luke. Marcion was excommunicated. What in Paul's milder form was a necessary relaxation of Jewish rigidities to facilitate extensive proselytizing of the gentiles, in Marcion's more extreme form was the subversion of Church authority and a denial of its claim to traditional ancestry. Marcion's followers continued to be a problem for several centuries.

Antinomianism took other forms among the Gnostics and Manicheans in the early Christian centuries, and was strongly revived in the Reformation by Luther's return to Romans 3:28 and the doctrine of justification by faith alone, without works. As the Protestant churches developed their own bureaucracies, Antinomianism became the property of such smaller protesting groups as the Anabaptists. In our own day, neo-Marcionism as represented by such a writer as the Jewish-born Simone Weil has an intellectual currency in fashionable literary circles, but pure Antinomianism is widespread in England and America, if one can judge by the popularity of Graham Greene's novels or James Gould Cozzens' *By Love Possessed* (in which Love frees from the Law in the most literal sense).

The Donatist heresy is equally instructive. Donatus and his followers in Numidia in the fourth century refused to recognize a new bishop on the grounds that he had been consecrated by an apostate, and that sacraments conferred by the unworthy are invalid. Other factors, among them personal rivalries, African nationalism, and economic unrest, were involved, and the Donatists eventually split off from the Church and took to marauding. The doctrine that the efficacy of sacraments depends on the worthiness of the minister survived them, however, as it survived St. Augustine's argument that the true minister of sacraments is Christ, the priest only his vessel. Julian the Pelagian, in controversy with St. Augustine in the fifth century, argued that St. Augustine was himself an unworthy minister, whose concept of Original Sin was based on his Manichean youth. In the Middle Ages, the monk Henry of Lausanne revived the argument that the sacraments have no objective efficacy, but depend on the worthy character of the priest. His preaching had no effect beyond getting him periodically jugged for heresy, but when another monk, Martin Luther, preached the same Donatist doctrine four centuries later, it tore the Church apart. Here corruption among the clergy (still Radin's easygoing laymen) would be thesis, protest by rigorist reformers (Radin's formulators) antithesis, and the sudden miraculous transformation whereby cor-

ruption puts on incorruption, synthesis, to become in turn the new
Protestant thesis and begin to corrupt. (It is amusing to note that
those rigorist Protestants, like Barth and Niebuhr, who preach
against the worldliness and secularity of their Church in our time,
do so not in the name of Donatus, their true progenitor, but of his
antagonist St. Augustine.)

With the Reformation, the alliance between Church and State,
Christ and Caesar (what cynical historians, following Gibbon, call
"the Chi and the Kappa"), took radically new forms, as well as
continuing some of the same old Catholic forms. At their simplest,
these forms are the alliance for extortion that Radin shows in *Primitive Religion* (quoting Gayton) between chief and shaman among
the Yokut. At the other extreme, they are the great events of history. Luther, advocating the merciless extermination of the Lutheran peasants in the Peasants' Revolt, lost a considerable part of
his mass following, but from then on the German princes were
devoted Lutherans, and the safety of Protestantism against Catholic armed repression was assured. Calvin, if no more bellicose than
Luther in temperament, managed by one symbolic action to make
the point even more vividly than Luther did in his stand on the
peasants. When Michael Servetus denied the Trinity and the divinity of Christ, arguing a very modern-looking Unitarianism, one
of Calvin's people denounced him to the Catholic Inquisition, he
fled to Geneva for safety, and there Calvin had him burned.

The princes were thus assured that no dangerous revolution was
in the saddle, while the real Calvinist revolution, social and economic, went on invisibly, the oxidation of rust rather than burning.
Whereas Luther still condemned the lending of money at interest,
the old Catholic sin of Usury, Calvin approved it, and the *Institutes*
developed a new ethic for the rising class of burghers who consti-
tuted Calvin's chief support. "While a natural consequence of
belief in election might be expected to be to weaken or destroy
moral effort," the *Oxford Dictionary of the Christian Church* remarks ingenuously, "history in fact does not bear out this deduc-
tion, even in the case of those holding an extreme form of the
doctrine." From the work of Weber, Sombart, and Tawney, we
have learned the relation between the Protestant ethic and the new
society. Tawney explains in *Religion and the Rise of Capitalism*:

In their emphasis on the moral duty of untiring activity, on work as an end in itself, on the evils of luxury and extravagance, on foresight and thrift, on moderation and self-discipline and rational calculation, they had created an ideal of Christian conduct, which canonized as an ethical principle the efficiency which economic theorists were preaching as a specific for social disorders.

Here the shaman figure, John Calvin, speaks for the practical laymen in a rarely efficient synthesis.

Radin defines as "the fundamental trait of all shamans and medicine men everywhere," emphasizing it with italics: *They must be disoriented and they must suffer.* "Solitude and suffering open the human mind," a Caribou-Eskimo shaman told Rasmussen. In the simpler societies, Radin generalizes, "neurotic-epileptoid individuals predominate among the medicine men." He defines the traits of the shaman:

> his ability to fall into a trance state involuntarily and to put himself into one voluntarily; his capacity to transform himself into an animal; his power to travel through space and time and to journey to the spirit-world; and, finally, the fact that he is possessed by some spirit either unrelated to him or an ancestor. To this we may add his dual character: unconscious at one moment, and not only conscious at the next moment but the most practical of men.

If we discard the shape-shifting into an animal (and even here there are analogues) we get a remarkable description of the priest-prophet figure in Christian history. In the Old Testament, the prophets are called *nebi'im,* which seems to mean something like "ravers," and are obvious shaman types; Jeremiah 29:26 makes the flat equation, "For every man that is mad, and maketh himself a prophet." In the New Testament, the shaman figure runs from John the Baptist (robed in camel's hair, crying in the wilderness) early in the Gospel story, to St. John the Divine (with his ecstatic visions of journeying to the spirit-world, full of animal transformations) in the last book.

The most fully developed shaman figure in the New Testament is of course St. Paul, glorying in his infirmities, with his epileptoid conversion like that of the Ashanti priests whose initiation is described by Rattray, "They hear the voice of some god or fall down in a fit or, it may be, go into a trance." Radin might be writing of Paul when he says of the shaman, "His projections, his hallucinations, his journey through space and time, thus became a dramatic ritual and served as the prototype for all future concepts of the religious *road of perfection.*" Yet at the next moment, Radin reminds us, the shaman is not only conscious but the most practical of men. Here are the conflicting tasks of the religious formulator in the more highly organized primitive societies, as Radin defines them:

> As a thinker, for instance, he is impelled to transform coercion into willing consent; yet, as one who has most to gain by accentuating the difficulties of the approach to the spirits and the gaining of their help, he must insist on attention to minutiae which play right into the hands of the very magical practices he wishes to displace. As a theologian he must give the deities real definiteness and separate them, as far as he can, from the turmoil of life; as a medicine-man or priest whose power depends on the ordinary man he must, on the contrary, emphasize their closeness to this average man by indicating their relationship to his food supply and his life values. Finally, to satisfy his own artistic-intellectual temperament he must elaborate the attitudes of humility, reverence, other-worldliness, and willing subjection to divine control. Yet these are apt to lead him to a subjectivism which, precisely among those primitive societies where the medicine-man or priest is politically dominant, is regarded as definitely anti-social.

It is almost a synopsis of the Pauline Epistles.

In early Christian history, the shaman pattern is obviously continued in the waves of hysterical martyrs, who die crying, "I am the wheat of Christ! I am going to be ground with the teeth of wild beasts!" and their successors the mad anchorites and stylites. We find it less obviously in the ascetic early Fathers of the Church: St. John Chrysostom who ruined his health by his austerities as a hermit, or Origen who castrated himself on the strength of Matthew 19:12 ("there be eunuchs, who have made themselves eunuchs for the kingdom of heaven's sake"). A few saints have been fortunate in the possession of attested powers of bilocation, the ability to be in two places at the same time, among them St. Alphonsus Liguori, St. Anthony of Padua, and St. Philip Neri. Others, beginning with St. Francis of Assisi in the thirteenth century, have been granted stigmata, the five wounds of Christ on the Cross, which do not become septic and which resist ordinary treatment, but are liable to periodic bleedings, mostly on Fridays and during Lent and Passion Week. There have been 330 known stigmatics since St. Francis, about sixty of whom have been beatified or sanctified. In addition to stigmata, saints sometimes display powers of levitation, bilocation, and telepathy, symptoms of hysterical lameness or blindness, and the ability to abstain from food and sleep. St. Gemma Galgani, an Italian stigmatic who lived into the twentieth century, enjoyed frequent ecstasies and marks of scourging in addition to her stigmata. Therese Neumann, a stigmatic apparently still alive in Bavaria,[2] is said to have taken no solid food since 1922, and since 1927 no nourishment whatsoever but daily Communion. She has visions during which she is able to read consciences and discern the authenticity of relics, and her home has become a place of pilgrimage.

The Church has varied in its attitude toward the insane. In the early Church, they were admitted to Communion but barred from ordination. In the medieval Church a surprising number of them attained to the priesthood, and some founded orders and were eventually canonized. Under Henry VIII in England, Foxe's *Acts and Monuments of the Christian Martyrs* reports, an insane man named Collins saw a priest holding up the host over his head, and held up a little dog over his own head in mimicry of the action. For it he was tried, condemned, and burned; and the dog with him. (This suggests two different treatments of the insane, that they were burned for blasphemy and that they sat in judgment.) At least two of the stigmatics, St. Francis and St. Catherine of Siena, were oustandingly rational and practical in other phases, adept organizers and shrewd power manipulators.

Radin identifies the curing techniques of primitive shamans as projections of their own "neurotic-epileptoid mental constitution." Christian healing has not been without its shamanistic features. In the first seven Christian centuries, recovery from illness was regu-

[2] She died in 1962. [1963]

larly expected from the sacrament of Extreme Unction, and in the Roman Catholic Church Unction is still given "for the health of soul and body." The possession of a gift for healing was regarded in the early Church as a recommendation for holy orders, and the curative miracles of saints, their relics, and their shrines have continued in Roman Catholicism to the present. The Reformation rejected all Christian healing as Romish superstition, but the tradition continued in tiny splinter sects like the Plumstead Peculiar People of London, who reject medical aid and heal each other with oil and prayer, on the basis of James 5:14 ("Is any sick among you? let him call for the elders of the church; and let them pray over him, anointing him with oil in the name of the Lord"). The great recent flowering of Christian faith healing has been the Christian Science Church, founded by Mary Baker Eddy after her own miraculous recovery, in the classic pattern of the shaman, from a variety of ailments.

The primitive priest-thinkers' descriptions of religious phenomena, Radin explains, are "often specifically conditioned by economic-social considerations, such as, for instance, the validation and justification of their authority, the maintenance of their rights and their privileges, and the justification of their desire for prestige." Sometimes in Christian history these religious conceptions, however disoriented and suffering, seem to have been designed primarily to advance the conceiver's privileges and prestige. This has been the traditional Protestant view of Catholic miracles, that they are, to quote Foxe, "feigned and forged of idle monks and religious bellies, for the exaltation of their churches, and the profit of their pouches." Like healing, however, this sort of visionary careerism has had a Protestant apotheosis in recent history. In the eighteenth century in Switzerland, two brothers named Christian and Hieronymus Kohler founded the sect of the Bruegglers, claiming that they and a girl named Elizabeth Kissling were Father, Son, and Holy Ghost, and that certain remarkable sexual freedoms followed from this fact. At the end of the century, in England, Joanna Southcott announced that she was the Woman of Revelation 12 ("clothed with the sun, and the moon under her feet, and upon her head a crown of twelve stars") and that she was to give birth to the

Prince of Peace in 1814. She sealed thousands of believers into the company of the elect for fees ranging from twelve shillings to a guinea. Always a loyal member of the Church of England, she left a box of prophecies to be opened after her death only by the Archbishop of Canterbury, and well into the twentieth century her followers were pestering successive Archbishops to open the box, "to save England from ruin," employing for persuasive purposes a press agent and sandwich men in the streets. A few decades after Joanna's death, H. J. Prince, who had been a curate in the Church of England, and his rector, Samuel Starky, seceded to found the Church of the Agapemone. They announced at various times that they were the Holy Ghost, the Prophet Elijah, and the Two Witnesses of Revelation 11 ("These have power to shut heaven"), acquired a body of followers, and went in for varieties of scandalous wrongdoing until (Marcion having been wrong) the law caught up with them. The thinly veiled claims of Father Divine to be God in our own time and country are too well known to need comment.

On the subject of primitive ambivalence toward deity, Radin presents some extraordinarily suggestive material. Among the Baila of Northern Rhodesia, according to Smith and Dale, the high god Leza is called by a variety of names. In Radin's view, the oldest are those concerned with the bad side of his ambivalent character: He-Who-Besets-Anyone, He-Who-Persecutes-Anyone-with-Unremitting-Attentions, He-Who-Stirs-Up-to-Do-Good-or-Bad-by-Repeated-Solicitation, He-Who-Trades-on-a-Person's-Good-Name, He-Who-Asks-Things-Which-He-Has-No-Title-to-Ask-For. Radin sees the second group, the praise-names, as created by the priest-thinkers to offset the popular ambivalent names: The Creator, The Moulder, The Constructor, The Everlasting-and-Omnipresent, He-from-Whom-All-Things-Come, The Guardian, The Giver, Deliverer-of-Those-in-Trouble. "But the answer of the lay realist was devastating and mordant," Radin says of the third group: Dissolver-of-Ant-Heaps-but-the-*Maumbuswa*-Ant-Heaps-Are-Too-Much-for-Him, He-Can-Fill-Up-All-the-Great-Pits-of-Various-Kinds-but-the-Little-Footprint-of-the-*Oribi*-He-Cannot-Fill, and The-Giver-Who-Gives-Also-What-Cannot-Be-Eaten. Among the Ewe of West

Africa, Radin says (crediting Spieth), the high god Dente "had no less than twenty-five epithets associated with him," such as:

> I am the king of the cave; I am he who drags the cliff; When you serve Dente, you are serving a real king; Dente is the great *tro* of Kratsi; Dente is the owner of the town; Kwasi died in vain, for it is I, Dente, who killed him and took possession of his things; Bestower of gifts; Dente is bad because the people of Kratsi are bad; I am he who sees the occult; I seize the sinner in his sin; I confuse the people; if you see anything beautiful, give it to your guardian-deity; I break without reason; I break certain things and I destroy others; If your grandfather gives you nothing, do you believe that your guardian-deity will give you something?; I, who adorn myself with trifles, visit the people at night; I am the great liar of the world; I am the *tro* of the tribes; I am he before whom the great kings kneel; I am the great hunter who gives nourishment to those who wish me to be with them; If you will not give it to me, I will take it from you; I am the great pot; I send the rain; Do not forget him who helps you; If no other *tro* can help you, I, Dente, can do so.

Radin concludes, "The whole history of religion, primitive and civilized, is epitomized in these names."

It would be a useful project to go through Scripture culling names, descriptions, and attributes of deity exactly comparable, but it is not feasible in these pages. It is possible, however, to note a few of the wilder heresies that have appeared in Christian history, most of them in the first fanatic centuries, showing similar ambivalence. Some are patently priest-thinkers' excesses, some lay realists' counterstatements, some an ambiguous tension of the two. The Adamites advocated undoing Adam's Fall and returning to Eden by going naked. The Cainites held the God of the Old Testament responsible for all the evil in the world, worshiped those who withstood him—Cain, Esau, Korah, etc.—and had an apocryphal Gospel of Judas Iscariot. The Collyridians, in Thrace in the fourth century, worshiped the Virgin Mary and sacrificed cakes (Greek *kollyris*) to her. The Ophites worshiped the Eden Serpent as the Liberator and Illuminator of Mankind, and held the Fall to be a progress from ignorance to knowledge and an advantage to mankind. Their branch, the Naasenes, called the Serpent by his Hebrew name, *nachash*, instead of the Greek *ophis*. The Migetians, in Spain in the eighth century, held that God had revealed himself successively in David as Father, Jesus as Son, and St. Paul as Holy Ghost. The Stercoranists (from the Greek *stercor*, excrement), in the twelfth century, held that God embodied in the Blessed Sacrament is digested and evacuated by the recipient, thus carrying the orthodox doctrine of Transubstantiation to its logical end.

It seems unlikely that many Christians in our day believe that Elizabeth Kissling was the Holy Ghost, or Judas the Savior, or H. J. Prince the Prophet Elijah, but it also seems unlikely that they believe most of the traditional theology of their churches. The evidence suggests that if most practicing Christians in the United States believe in the divinity of God the Father, they are Arian or Adoptionist regarding the divinity of Jesus and the reality of the Holy Ghost. Whereas the churches are Augustinian and Calvinist, the laity are Pelagian, Arminian, and Origenist, assuming natural innocence, free will, and that Hindus and agnostics are about as apt to be saved as they are. If they believe in an afterlife they give no sign of it in this life. The last word in the American synthesis seems to be that of Radin's lay realist: the shamans have filled the Good Book and the Creeds with their fancy ideas, but a Christian is a man whose wife takes the children to church on Sunday.

Who Reads Dictionaries?

The Oxford Classical
Dictionary

[1949]

THE OXFORD CLASSICAL DICTIONARY, edited by M. Cary and others, is a labor of scholarship in 971 double-column quarto pages. Although it lacks such essentials as an index, any classified listing of its contents, or any account of the qualifications of its contributors and is full of inexplicable gaps, on many questions of fact and scholarship it is serviceable and will reward the casual reader with such fascinating information as that the Romans had loaded dice, the ancients washed clothes with urine rather than soap, the suitors of Penelope played marbles for the bride, and 147 different wounds are mentioned in the *Iliad*. Anyone reading through its articles on literature, myth, and ritual for a full and authoritative statement on those subjects, however, is apt to feel that a cruel joke has been played upon him. The articles on literature are, with few exceptions, woefully superficial and incomplete: C. M. Bowra on Homer ignores almost every significant view and controversy on the subject, and ends with a historical blind old Homer, who may, he notes, be two men of the same name; the articles on Antony, Autolycus, Brutus, Caesar, Cleopatra, Coriolanus, and Troilus do not even mention Shakespeare, although the one on Timon inexplicably does; A. W. Pickard-Cambridge's article on tragedy ignores or dismisses every serious treatment of the subject but Aristotle's, which it attacks.

Most of the articles on mythology are done by H. J. Rose, who also does many of the articles on rites and customs, and who would seem to be almost the worst choice imaginable. Rose is the king of the euhemerists, convinced of the possible historicity of everyone from Agamemnon ("probably an historical person") to Theseus ("there is no proof that any real person lies behind the legend, but that is not impossible"), and such discrepancies as Agamemnon's worship as Zeus at Sparta, and the probable etymology of Theseus' name, do not at all disturb him. Rose gets much of his material from Farnell's two books on Greek cults and Roscher's *Lexikon*; his chief concern with myth is whether the hero was a god or a man, a question as meaningless as the one about angels and pins; he notes that the Greek deities were consistently theriomorphic and remarks that there is no evidence for Greek totemism, as though *that* were not major evidence for Greek totemism; he says that the Erinyes "are often confused" with the Eumenides, presumably by Aeschylus; he suggests that the Harpies may be based on the filthy Indian fruit-eating bat; he argues that Hephaestus is lame because in early fighting communities lame men would naturally become smiths (as, we might add, Odin is one-eyed because in early fighting communities old men would tend to have lost an eye); he dates many Greek rites as late because they are not mentioned in Homer, and finally admits on page 492 that Homer suppressed primitive material "due to his dislike of the grotesque." Almost the only useful thing Rose does with myths, besides tell them in all their muddled detail, is note some motifs in Stith Thompson's index, and it is characteristic that the one time he draws on a nonclassical myth for comparison, comparing Prometheus with the American Indian trickster Coyote, he has learned about Coyote through German scholarship.

The other writers on myth and ritual in the dictionary, chiefly F. R. Walton, M. P. Nilsson, and G. M. A. Hanfmann, are little better: almost equally euhemerist, superficial, and oblivious to or biased against all the theories of our century. The book displays very little over-all consistency. Rose notes that Cadmus was both a culture-hero and a serpent-figure, then J. E. Fontenrose notes the same thing of Cecrops, then Rose states the same curious correlation in connection with Erichthonius; in no case is any explanation attempted, or any reference made to the other two. Sometimes we get flat contradictions of fact between authorities: Hanfmann says Nessus gave Deianira the garment that later killed Hercules; Rose says Nessus gave Deianira some of his poisoned blood, which she smeared on a garment; both cite Sophocles' *Trachiniae* as their authority. Sometimes the contradictions come in the same article: Walton says that the goddess Atargatis punished with illness eaters of fish, and suggests that the taboo "may have originated in the unwholesomeness of the local species" (a theory of primitive taboo as hygienic measure that no one has taken seriously for a generation); he then remarks *in the next sentence* that the priests of Atargatis ate fish daily in a ritual meal. In short, the *Oxford Classical Dictionary*, if it is as unreliable and useless in general as it is on these topics, might better be pulped now and the paper used for comic books.

The Standard Dictionary
of Folklore

1. Dissent on a Dictionary

[1950]

I SAY "DISSENT"—not yet, three months after publication, having seen a single review, assenting or otherwise—because such a book[1] can hardly fail to impress. The sum of twelve years of research, it appears to be a monument of industry, scholarship, and love, a production by American folklorists finally to rival the giant compendiums of their European fellows. This initial volume, covering the first nine letters of the alphabet in 531 double-column quarto pages, includes more than three thousand entries and forty long encyclopedia articles, written by twenty-eight prominent specialists. It is, or seems to be, a mine of reliable information as a reference book, and a grab bag of delights for anyone reading or just skimming it: here are a Russian household spirit who lives in the toilet bowl, a Hindu deity worshiped by barren women and wrestlers, a cellarful of cadavers accidentally tanned in a Dublin church crypt, a Chinese dragon king devoted to fire engines, a Crow ceremony involving "a throwing away of wives," and a Borneo cult that worships Chinese green porcelain jars. For serious researchers, there are many brilliant and perceptive entries, and a number of distinguished articles, outstanding among them Charles Francis Potter on such subjects as Funeral Customs and Infanti-

[1] *Funk and Wagnalls Standard Dictionary of Folklore, Mythology, and Legend.* Vol. I: A–I. Edited by Maria Leach.

cide, R. D. Jameson on Cannibalism and the folklore elements concealed in patent-medicine advertising, Thanksgiving gluttony, and the form of hospitable wife-lending called "entertaining buyers," Theresa C. Brakeley's symbolic account of Drums, and Jerome Fried's dramatistic account of Games. Most particularly, there is the work of Gertrude Prokosch Kurath, both in individual entries on dances and ceremonies throughout the world and in her remarkable long article on Dance, which constitutes the first complete and tabulated account of the subject, and represents a major triumph of the method she calls "ethnochoreography." Mrs. Kurath's combination of exhaustive learning, passionate concern for meaning and function, economy of style, and wit alone warrants the cost of the book, and substantially exempts her from the strictures to follow.

Despite this admirable effort, and all these good and useful things, the book is seriously and essentially flawed, almost to the point of becoming a joke, by a number of things that seem, risky as such generalizations always are, to be thoroughly characteristic of American scholarship in the field. Its faults, in short, are our faults, and need examination. The fact that most of the entries are regrettably unsigned makes it difficult to exempt individuals other than Mrs. Kurath (who seems to have signed everything she did), but I suspect in any case that the disease is epidemic, and that we shall all soon perish. Here are a few notes on what seems to me the critical sickness of folk study in America, as its symptoms are evidenced in the *Standard Dictionary*.

Provincialism and bias. Although a good number of these contributors were trained in anthropological relativism, the special position of the Anglo-Saxon heritage and the Christian religion seem hardly questioned. A list of hybrid languages, for example, will include "pidgin English, lingua franca, kuan hua, beche le mer, Yiddish, Canuck, Swahili, and Romany," never English. The writer on Indian and Persian Folklore obviously expects illiterate peoples to be "inarticulate," since she twice denies, in two adjacent paragraphs, that the Indians are. Abraham and other Old Testament figures are rightly treated as mythological, while equally mythological New Testament figures and saints are not. Alexander H. Krappe remarks quaintly, "monotheism, too, may have its myths: the Old Testament is full of them." Mohammed's daughter Fatima is denied virginity because she bore children; will Christ's mother Mary be treated similarly in the next volume? Will the promised entry on Jesus (there is nothing under "Christ") begin, like others in the book, "A wonder-working god believed by Christians to have become incarnate as man. . .".?

Obliviousness to literature. For all the dictionary's concern with folklore, it never takes up the problem of folk literature except to discuss specific texts; yet surely it is with folk material as art—song, story, drama, picture—rather than as custom and belief, that we are essentially concerned. Artists fare no better. The entry for Aeneas mentions an undefined "*Aeneid,*" but no Virgil. An entry for Flying Dutchman that cites Austin's *Peter Rugg* and Coleridge's *Ancient Mariner* stands out in the book as almost the only formal literary reference. Of technical and stylistic discussion, that essential part of folk study concerned with "structure," there is hardly a trace.

Ignorance. Our scholars simply do not know enough, and what they do know they shockingly fail to understand, as Americans are said to know more things and to know less about them than anyone else. The simplest way to show the absurdly deficient scholarship of the dictionary is to check an entry against a comparable one from the English *Oxford Classical Dictionary,* itself no monument of perfection. Here is the *Standard* on Baubo:

> BAUBO. In the Orphic tradition of Greek religion, one of the daughters of Celeus of Eleusis (elsewhere she is called Iambe), who by a jest and by obscene gestures made the grieving Demeter smile. The jesting and the gestures formed part of the Eleusinian rites, and probably the story was invented to explain these after the fact. Baubo is also considered by some the nurse of Demeter, or the nurse of Iacchus who in one of the common versions of the story himself made the gestures at Demeter's sorrow.

Here is the *Oxford Classical* entry:

> BAUBO (*Babo*), a female daemon of primitive and obscene character, doubtless originally a personification of the *cunnus*. She appears in the Orphic version of the Rape of Kore (Kern, *Orph. Frs.* 49ff) and on inscriptions from Paros and Asia Minor, and is

mentioned by Asclepiades of Tragilus (Harpocration s. v. Dusaules) as mother of the Anatolian Mise. She has been thought to have a part in the Eleusinian Mysteries (Ch. Picard in *Rev. Hist. Rel.* xcv (1927), but see L. Deubner, *Attische Feste* (1932), 83, n. 3. She survives in modern folklore (R. M. Dawkins in *JHS* xxvi (1906). Other references in Picard, l.c. and W. K. C. Guthrie, *Orpheus and Gk. Rel.* (1935), W. K. C. G., 136.

These authorities of the *Standard* are not only ignorant and superficial, they are so often gullible and wrong. The author of the entry on Boogie-Woogie states earnestly that it was invented by Jimmy Yancey at Chicago rent parties in the early 1920s; Krappe argues that the presence of King Noble, the Lion, in medieval beast epic and fable "militates most strongly against the theory of a European origin," which suggests an ignorance of the European lion, still in Greece in classical times—an ignorance incredible in anyone who had read Herodotus or Aristotle; the entry on Friar Tuck is so oblivious to his existence outside the Robin Hood cycle as to be embarrassing; MacEdward Leach's knowledge of the ancient sources of Pennsylvania Dutch hex would be greatly improved by a reading of, say, E. M. Butler's *Ritual Magic*; and the author of the entry on Intaphernes' Wife doesn't even suspect matrilineal relations behind the rationalization for her choice of her brother's life rather than husband's or son's.

Evasion. This ignorance and superficiality is characteristically tricked out in all the proper question-begging and weasel words: "it is believed" (by whom?), "and strangely enough," "for some reason," "physical anthropologists have drawn interesting conclusions" (*what* conclusions?), "it was inevitable that," "something sinister about crossroads," "it is a fair presumption," "the whole subject, however, is still very imperfectly known," "these questions seem so intangible," etc. Where this is not evasive it is simplistic: the writer or writers on herbs cannot understand why basil should "paradoxically" be both sacred and dedicated to the Evil One, or why some peoples think a poisonous herb is a cure for poison.

Bad writing. It is hard to trust a group of scholars who cannot write an English sentence. A plural subject and singular predicate in the entry on Aeromancy make it impossible to understand how the process operates, Chinese Ancestral Tablets are described mysteriously as "finding their source much earlier than their origin," and so forth. The choice of words is generally so inexact —"inflict" for "afflict," Oedipus guilty of "murder" rather than "parricide"—that when Jameson, the only real stylist in the book, uses correctly a word like "nubile," it comes as a shock. With their foreign-born authorities, like Jonas Balys, the editors' failure to correct such half-English as "falsificators," "every house and smallest cabin," "at the end of his laborious life," "he confessed frankly what were his own creations," constitutes cruel irresponsibility. Finally, the undefined jargon is so heavy that occasional entries read like nothing so much as Benchley parodies:

> All dead people become bongas except uninitiated children who become bhuts, and women who die in childbirth and are not cremated. These become curins.

Euhemerism. The besetting foolishness of the book, as of so much American folk scholarship, is the idea that mythic figures were or may have been historical, such as Arthur, Buddha, Christ, Cormac Mac Airt, Evadne, Guinevere, Herakles, Hiawatha, and so on interminably. Far more pernicious, however, is the attitude of some of the more sophisticated authorities, who dismiss this simple euhemerism as "not quite satisfactory" or not "a fully explanatory method," and take a position that might be called neo-euhemerist. Thus Richard A. Waterman and William R. Bascom argue against accepting legends as accurate history, smuggling in the idea that they are *in*accurate history; the entry on Hyperboreans says they were "probably a reminiscence of some tribe or tribes along the amber routes"; the entry on Aeolus dismisses him as legendary but looks around for his real island; similarly, there is no attempt to make Cuchulain historical, but the remains of his *dún* or fortress can still be seen today in County Louth; most purely, Dr. Johannes Faustus is a mythic figure based on the small-time German sorcerer George Faust (rather than a mythic figure derived from ritual who acquired, like Atli in the *Volsunga Saga* and many others, someone's approximate name).

"*American folklore.*" "We can now safely assume that there is such a thing as 'American folklore' and not 'only European (or African, or Far Eastern) folklore on the American continent,'"

B. A. Botkin says proudly in his article on the subject, while noting the excellent division of the field—into English, Negro, and other immigrant survivals, and native Indian lore—made by the American Folklore Society in 1888, which makes nonsense of his statement. It is this pious desire to have a native folklore like the other kids that involves the dictionary in its most dreadful junk, all taken seriously: Joe Magerac and Bowleg Bill, manufactured by dialect writers after the pattern of Paul Bunyan, himself manufactured by lumber trade papers; even more mechanical atrocities, like Dingbelle, Fifinella, and the Gremlins, Col. Bogie the imaginary golf opponent, and assorted side-hill dodgers and whifflepoofs; any song sung popularly, like "Auld Lang Syne" (we can expect "Sweet Adeline" in the next volume); and such representatives of "the folk" as Hilaire Belloc, who wrote alphabet rhymes, the basement entertainers who composed a parody of "The Boll Weevil" about the housing shortage, Walt Disney, and Joe Hill. The scholarly entries on these frauds and popular amusements are an effront and an abomination in a work of reference. A Balys article exhaustively exposes the nineteenth-century scholars and collectors who fouled their nest by faking Estonian lore; why was not the same job done on the omnipresent American fakers? (There is not even a suspicion in the book, for example, that John Jacob Niles invented such "folksongs" as "Black Is the Color," "Venezuela," and "I Wonder as I Wander.") Where the American material is not a fraud, the authors have no feel for it: the entry on "The Gray Goose" sees no connection between it and such ancient totemic songs as "The Cutty Wren" and "The Darby Ram" (itself dismissed as a "tall tale"); the poker superstitution known as "Dead Man's Hand" becomes "*The* Dead Man's Hand" and the fine joke of "G-string" gets wrecked in "gee string"; there is no sense at all that the title of the Negro dance "Balling the Jack" is not the respectable railroad slang it seems.

Narrow specialization. Most of the contributors seem happiest when assigning some nonsensical date, based on the date of given texts, to a form: ballads developed in the Middle Ages, the best English carols were composed in the fifteenth century, the oldest French folk songs may go back to the twelfth century; or finding some equally inane place of origin: Cinderella is probably orig-

inally Oriental, "human castration seems to have begun in Meso-
potamia," ballads originated in southern France. When not involved in these absurd pigeonholings, they debate whether the
Biblical Behemoth was a hippopotamus or an elephant, or the
wonderful question of whether deification precedes or follows
legend. No two contributors even seem to agree on what folklore
is; the dictionary gets around this rather admirably by letting
twenty-four of them submit separate definitions (what a state
that shows in a field!), but confusion is worse confounded when
they all use the same words to mean different things. In any case,
their true definitions consist of their entries, and here the kind of
insight we get is the contributor who notes that the idea that
blood transmits racial characteristics has been exposed as "pure
myth."

Amateurism. All these tidy little bins suggest a developed and
even overspecialized field, but in fact most of our folk scholars are
amateurs or specialists in something else: anthropologists, literary
men, linguists, musicologists, artists, etc., and the few professional
folklorists tend to be full-time teachers. These varied backgrounds
would create an ideal situation were there genuine co-operative
effort, but in most cases what is pooled is largely waste by-products.
Anyone writing a farce about a group of collaborators on a folklore dictionary would sketch out the inevitable cast of characters: the elderly comic clergyman who collects autograph albums,
the social scientist who contributes entirely irrelevant notes on
African marriage systems, the urbane and witty international
traveler hunting out bawdy material with deadpan relish, the dull
scholar with his decimal-point classifications, the voluble French-
Canadian nationalist interested in proving that the true home of
French culture is Canada, the Air Force veteran who wants to tell
funny stories about the Gremlins *he* saw. Here they are, every one.
There will be little serious work done until the study of folk material in this country writes its declaration of independence from
all such eccentrics, as well as from the omnipresent anthropologists
who write most of this book, constitute most of the American
Folklore Society, and, at best, patronize the field and regard it as
one of the less reliable techniques anthropology has at its disposal.

The shape of the problem. In *The Kenyon Review* for Summer, 1948, I attempted to define a comprehensive folk study that would embrace the three related questions of origin, structure, and function, and this triple concern still seems to me the criterion for judging any approach. On origin, the dictionary tells us: "the story-telling mind would naturally incorporate the example," or "the idea of dog-headed beings may have originated from real robbers, using the pelts of dogs for masking," or "vivid imaginations fed by dreams and shadows account for most such legends." Structure is hardly discussed. On function: the idea of cave paintings as fertility magic, although the animals at Lascaux, for example, are characteristically pregnant, is "conjectural," cumulative songs "are sung purely for fun," the purpose of myth is "to explain phenomena otherwise unexplainable," the purpose of rite is to make religion palatable to the uneducated. In all this, it is *process*, some sense of the operations of the "folk work," that is lacking. Apollo Sminthius must be "either the protector or destroyer of mice," not just a mouse god; the Manx Hunting of the Wren represents "hostility to wrens" (as a ceremonial dismemberment of Osiris might represent "hostility to Osiris"); the association of the Hindu god Ganesa with the rat "suggests a humble origin," or the slum side of the heavenly tracks; ribbons wound around a staff "became the serpents of the caduceus." Casting about for help, Krappe rejects "the ill-supported and wholly unsound fancies of Freud and his pseudo-science," and chooses instead that queen of the sciences, "psychical research"! Stith Thompson boasts that his "historic-geographic method" ignores origin, structure, and function to give "the history of an item of folklore." MacEdward Leach tosses out the English anthropological school on one page and writes the Blood article from Frazer, Hartland, and Crawley on another. All the marvelous work of English scholarship goes ignored or denigrated: Marian Cox gets five grudging lines, Hartland is thrown the sop of "able," Frazer is credited with a "remarkable" collection of data and "somewhat dubious" conclusion, Jane Harrison, Raglan, and the others go unmentioned. The patient, in short, sends the doctor packing. Let the patient beware.

2. *Notes Toward a Second Edition*

[1951]

THE *Standard Dictionary* is a long-awaited, badly needed, useful, and very defective book. Since I have already discussed some of the general implications of its failures as weaknesses of our folk scholarship, it seems best to confine myself here to specific criticisms and suggestions, each with an example or two, which might be thought of as Notes Toward a Second Edition. All the examples are drawn from Volume I, since the body of this review was written before the appearance of the second volume, but they could as readily be drawn from either. All subsequent criticism should be read against a general background of praise and gratitude for the labors involved, appreciation of the utility of a major portion of the work, and real admiration for some of the contributions, particularly Gertrude Kurath's magnificent work done on Dance and Ritual and the kind of serious scholarship typified by Katherine Luomala's article on Indonesian Mythology and Theodor Gaster's articles on Semitic Folklore and Semitic Mythology.

Many of the entries need filling out. Mrs. Leach acknowledges gaps in her preface, explaining that "completeness was an end never contemplated," and calling the book "a representative sampling." In that case, perhaps *Standard Dictionary* is a misnomer, and the work should have been entitled something like *Tid-Bits of Folklore, Mythology, and Legend*. But even by Mrs. Leach's criteria the book is unrepresentative and incomplete. What can we do with a discussion of Caldrons of Regeneration that mentions only Celtic ones, a discussion of Charms that gives only South American material, an entry on Contests that confines itself to North American Indian contests? Surely a list of legendary Caesarian children that doesn't mention Caesar can have little point. Or a list of those born with teeth that includes only one, the Roman tribune Lucius Sicinius. Or an entry on the Roman Fates that doesn't give their names. In the last case, however, the inadequacy of the entry is explained. It was, like many others in the book, taken bodily from an unspecialized reference work, without further research. The *Standard Dictionary* reads:

FATES. The three Roman goddesses who determined the fate of every human: a development of the idea of the *fatum* or spoken word of Jupiter which could not be altered. The Fata Scribendi wrote the destiny of the child at birth: this may be a goddess or goddesses. Since the Fates performed their duties at birth, they were identified with the Parcae. See MOIRAE: NORNS.

My copy of the eleventh *Britannica* reads:

FATE, in Roman mythology, the spoken word (*fatum*) of Jupiter, the unalterable will of heaven. The plural (*Fata*, the Fates) was used for the "destinies" of individuals or cities, and then for the three goddesses that controlled them. Thus Fata Scribunda were the goddesses who wrote down a man's destiny at his birth. In this connection, however, Fata may be singular, the masculine and feminine *Fatus, Fata*, being the usual forms in popular and ceremonial language. The Fates were also called Parcae, the attributes of both being the same as those of the Greek Moerae.

It might be noted that not only is the *Britannica* article inadequate as a source, but that it has been further oversimplified and inaccurately copied.

The dictionary must be revised to give sources, evidence, and citations. When, for example, the entry on "Blow the Man Down" says "in the Bahamas it is still sung by Negro fishermen for 'launching' their boats, by which they mean hauling them up on shore in the fall," the reader has no idea whether this statement is based on any more material than the single use of the tune, to new words, recorded at Nassau in 1935 for the Archive of American Folk Song and issued by the Library of Congress (in which, incidentally, the text makes it clear that "launching" means "launching"). The statement regarding the cantillation of "Oriental Jews" (whatever *they* are), that "the unfixed melodies of their style are believed to have some part in the development of cante flamenco," is entirely meaningless unless we know *who* believes this on what evidence, *what* part they are believed to have had, and *how*. The entry on Brutus is the first one in the book to perform the elementary job of a work of reference and say "The legend is told in" with a list of sources; the entry on Cain is the first one to cite analogues adequately; the article on Chinese Folklore is the first one with an annotated bibliography.

Many of the entries need re-assembling, rewriting, and cross-referencing. All the square dance terms, for example, are scattered as separate entries—All Eight Balance and All Eight Swing under A on page 36, Grand Right and Left under G on page 463, etc.—which means that until the appearance of the index (and perhaps afterward) these terms have to be known before they can be learned. Many of the entries are written with a maddening informality and no sense of the requirements of a dictionary: that on Buzzard, for example, begins, "If you wear a buzzard feather behind your ear you will never have rheumatism," not "A diurnal bird of prey found . . ." The book's cross-referencing leaves a great deal to be desired. The entries on Augurs and Augury and Haruspices appear to have been boiled down from the *Britannica*, but in the process of boiling all relationship between them has disappeared; the entry on Building Ceremonies doesn't mention "London Bridge is Falling Down" in connection with mural inhumation, but the article on Games does; the entry on Hashish never suggests that it is known in this country as marijuana. Anyone interested in the theory, accepted by many Bible scholars on excellent evidence, that Mordecai and Esther in the Old Testament are Marduk and Ishtar in disguised forms, goes through the entries on characters in the Book of Esther without finding a mention of the theory, and finds the briefest possible "it is conjectured" under Ishtar with no conjecturer named.

A good deal of the *Standard Dictionary* needs outright correction. The entry on Francis James Child remarks that "New variants of some of the 305 ballads in his collection have occasionally been discovered, but no new ballads." This is superficially true—Child was a compiler, and almost all the ballads were discovered well before his time—but to the extent that it suggests that Child's list is the complete canon, it is nonsense: I count twenty-one ballads in the *Oxford Book of Ballads* without Child numbers, some of them patently worthy of inclusion. The entry on Forbidden Fruit states that Adam was created mortal and stood to gain immortality by eating forbidden fruit, rather than, as every Sunday School folklorist knows, the reverse. Whatever authority picked up the information on Demeter from British sources apparently didn't know that the "ear of corn" in the Eleusinian mysteries was an ear of wheat, not what corn means in this country, Indian maize. Sometimes the book cheats: the statement that "Emperor and Abbot" "has been found in every ethnic group of which the collection of folktales has been adequately surveyed" is of the sort that can never be disproven, since any body of folk tale lacking it has obviously never been "adequately surveyed." Or a statement is entirely absurd, like the explanation for an insane person's being called "cuckoo": "perhaps in reference to the traditional cuckoo clock which always is out of order and tweets at the wrong time, etc."

Credits and attributions should be treated in a less carefree fashion. Freud's Moses theory is identified only as "one interesting conjecture." The entry on Cailleac, the personification of the last sheaf of grain, is a digest of Frazer's material in Part V of *The Golden Bough*, and neglects to say so or to mention Frazer's name. The entries on "Cap o' Rushes" and "Catskin" ignore Marian Cox, who first compiled and studied these tales. Henry Carrington Bolton, who did the authoritative study of *The Counting-Out Rhymes of Children* in 1888, from which Charles Francis Potter lifts much of his article on Counting-Out Rimes, is identified only as an anonymous "collector of children's rimes in the 80's," while Potter's article on Eeny, Meeny, Miny, Mo has only a reference to an "H. C. Bolton of the Smithsonian Institution" who "once wrote" an ignorant statement on the topic—the whole apparently a peculiarly shoddy attempt to conceal the fact that a definitive book on the subject exists and has been plundered. The character of Big John the Conqueror is credited to Stetson Kennedy's book *Palmetto Country*, published in 1942, although Zora Neale Hurston published the same material in *Mules and Men* in 1935, and all the evidence suggests that one of Mr. Kennedy's principal folk sources is Miss Hurston.

The dictionary should be edited and rewritten for consistency. On page 50, "Amulets are primarily preventive and are to be distinguished from talismans which transmit qualities," but by the next page, in the same article, the distinction has been entirely forgotten, and "Amulets of animal parts or substances depend frequently for their efficacy on the sympathetic transference of the characteristics or qualities of the animal from which they are acquired," while on page 81 the same author speaks of ashes "used as a talisman against thunder and lightning." The author of the entry on "Cupid and Psyche" contradicts himself within one column, remarking at its head that the story is "relatively uncomplicated with other great folktale themes," and at its foot, "Familiar motifs abound in this tale" and listing some of the great folktale themes that complicate it. Not even the euphemisms are made consistent: on page 304 Nessus attempted to "rape" Deianira, on page 492 he attempted to "violate" her, and on page 370 he attempted to "abduct" her.

New material must be added, and old material defined and explained. Listing the topics not discussed in the book is an impossible job: the index of any book in the field, opened to any letter and checked against the dictionary shows the gaps—Aeschylus, agon, alpha and omega; Balum monster, black magic, bridge of souls; Cerridwen, Cherubim, circles of stone; etc. The omissions of authorities who have achieved two dates are equally scandalous: there is a biographical note on the American, Frank Clyde Brown (1870–1943), but none on S. Baring-Gould, Pierre Bayle, Ruth Benedict, or Henry Carrington Bolton; there is a biographical note on the American, Mellinger Edward Henry (1873–1946), but none on J. O. Halliwell, Jane Harrison, J. G. Herder, or Eleanor Hull. A good deal of material goes begging for an explanation: the author of the entry on Davy Jones doesn't seem to care why the sea should be personified with so odd a name; nor the authority on "Dead Horse Chantey" why sailing ships should have had a dead horse rite; nor the authority on "Edward" *why* the implication of the mother should be "sudden and unexpected"; nor the authority on Hephaestus why so many mythological smiths should be lame. Words are used maddeningly without definition: the reader of the entry on Bones is supposed to know what olisboi are; the entry on Cám Khan refers mysteriously to "women who have borne Con lōn"; "deiseal" is used repeatedly for sunwise circumambulation and not defined until page 202; the entries on Chang-hko and Chinūn Way Shun suggest that "nats" are Kachin spirits, but the reader will not be certain until the second volume.

Lest the additions here suggested make the book impossibly bulky, it seems only fair to note examples of the kind of thing that might well come out. The larger part of the American material, from Almanacs to Industrial Lore, is trashy and fraudulent, and should be tossed into the wastebasket. There should be no space for medical notes like "Negroes of the southern United States use alum to stop bleeding"; the many purely sociological entries on Afro-American mating systems; asides like "for I got it by oral tradition through 12 generations from Elizabethan England"; a listing of the advantages of membership in the American Folklore Society; the comic Negro dialect on page 99 and elsewhere. Stories and examples appear to be chosen for inclusion at random and could be ruthlessly pared: there seems no better reason for two Coyote tales and two Anansi tales as separate entries after adequate entries on Coyote and Anansi than that someone wanted to tell stories. Repetitions could be readily and profitably eliminated: on page 55 the entries on Andromeda and Andromeda Theme repeat the same material; the same story told on page 127 as Bear Taken for a Cat is retold pointlessly on page 153 as "Bogle in the Mill"; the authority on Chinese folklore remarks of shape-shifting foxes:

> Inasmuch as foxes can become invisible and hear everything that is said and read everything that is written, the wise scholar will tell only flattering stories about foxes and keep silent about their wickedness.

Later discussing the same beings by name, he writes:

> The hu hsien, being invisible, know everything that is written about them and scholars are afraid to write the truth lest the hu hsien take revenge.

The *Standard Dictionary* is, as reference works go, extraordinarily slipshod. There are innumerable typographical errors: some of them significant, like the misspellings of MacCulloch and Tylor in adjacent lines of the entry on the Anthropological School which suggest that the topic fell into the wrong hands; some of them comic, like a misprinting of the magic name in the entry on Gírle Guairle that manages to ruin the point of the story. All the book's spellings should be made consistent, instead of depending on the whim of the contributor. Pronunciations should be given for every foreign name and term: at present, there are only a few in the book, and those given without even any consistency within one man's work, so that we are told that Bodb is pronounced bōv, but have to guess that Badb is pronounced bāv. Most essential, every contribution must be signed. Some authorities, like Gertrude Prokosch Kurath and Alfred Métraux, seem to have signed everything they wrote, even if it was no more than a sentence; others, like MacEdward Leach and R. D. Jameson, to have signed some of their work; still others, like Archer Taylor and Stith Thompson, to have signed little or nothing. With signatures, we could weigh the competence behind statements, discount for bias, check contradictions and inconsistencies, assign blame for fraud and theft where it belongs, assign praise where *it* belongs. Without signatures, I am afraid, we are left like those who traditionally have dealings with the devil, never quite sure whether it is gold pieces or goat droppings we are carrying home.

Words and
Sensibilities

AT TIMES of upward social mobility, the etiquette books appear, to teach the rising groups how to behave almost indistinguishably from the groups they join or supplant. In the modern world such books have appeared in spurts, from Castiglione's *Courtier* in the Renaissance to Emily Post, and I suspect that when the Babylonians replaced the Sumerians they promptly produced cuneiform tablets teaching table manners. Language habits are particularly sensitive indicators of class and education, as we saw in the recent British controversy over "U" and "Non-U" speech (the "U" standing for "University," and thus by extension "Upper-class"). The relationship of language to status is less absolute in this country, but as the advertisements offering to increase your earning power by increasing your vocabulary make clear, there it is. A generation or two ago it was the problem of Jiggs's Maggie, who needed simple correct grammer to go with her new wealth, or greenhorn cousin Shmelka, who needed English idioms and more certainty about *v*'s and *w*'s when he talked to customers in the store. Now the problem is more complicated. Maggie's daughter Marlene lives in Larchmont and addresses the PTA, and Schmelka's grandson Stuart works in advertising and is a Young Republican. What *they* need is some handy guide to the difference between *factious* and *factitious*, *fictious* and *fictitious*, or reliable information on the nuances of meaning between *harangue* and *tirade*. Dictionaries are of no use because they note alternatives in most cases without recommendation, they are not concerned with transitory subtleties of fashion, and they are a nuisance because each word must be looked up separately. To fill the special needs of Marlene and Stuart, handbooks of usage come into being.

A *Dictionary of Contemporary American Usage*, by Bergen and Cornelia Evans, does not attempt to evade these delicate matters of status. "Respectable English," the preface says, "means the kind of English that is used by the most respected people, the sort of English that will make readers or listeners regard you as an educated person." Certain "perfectly intelligible" usages "are not used by educated people and hence are regarded as 'incorrect' and serve as the mark of a class." The Evans book is offered as a guide to "what is currently accepted as good English" in the United States; "It is designed for people who speak standard English but are uncertain about some details." Thus an entry will conclude characteristically, "This construction is condemned by some grammarians, but in the United States it is accepted and used by well educated people"; or, of something disapproved, "Speech of this kind shows that one's friends aren't bookish people."

For Marlene and Stuart, many of the book's distinctions are useful and informative. *Loving* is chaste as an adjective (*a true and loving wife*), concupiscent as a noun (*I need loving*). *Costive* does not mean *costly* but *constipated*, *noisome* does not mean *noisy* but *obnoxious*. *Recrudescence* is the breaking-out-again only of something thoroughly unpleasant in England, of anything at all here. It may even be helpful to know that "The plural of the tailor's *goose* and of the improper gesture is *gooses*." Some of the examples look as though they were aimed at making the diner-out civil, if not necessarily a wit, so that remarks on the plural of *asparagus* conclude, "The food is always treated as a singular, as in *this asparagus is good* and *how long did you cook it?*" The most useful thing the Evans (Evanses? their book gives no clue) do is hammer away insistently at clichés: *bowels of the earth* "has been in constant service since 1593 and should be retired"; *brown as a berry* "has been repeated ceaselessly for more than five hundred years and is entitled to at least that long a rest"; *brown study* "should be avoided"; and so on endlessly. Phrases like *it stands to reason that* are dismissed as "no more than a clearing of the throat." Sometimes the authors offer constructive alternatives to clichés in the form of less bedraggled clichés. They remark of *as thick as thieves*:

> For those who want to avoid it but still feel the need for some such comparison, there are many established alternatives waiting: as thick as hail, as thick as hops, as thick as huckleberries, for those who wish to emphasize profusion; as thick as porridge, for those who have specific density in mind; and for chumminess, a fine old Scotch simile, as thick as three in a bed.

The decision sooner or later forced on all such books is when to ride the hobbyhorse of common usage and when to dismount. The authors will accept *like* for *as* in *Winston tastes good like a cigarette should* (as Mr. Evans suggested in his television program), but their appeal is not to its victory in oral currency, but to examples in Shakespeare, More, Sidney, Dryden, Smollett, Burns, Southey, Coleridge, Shelley, Keats, Darwin, Newman, Brontë, Thackeray, Morris, Kipling, Shaw, Wells, Masefield, Maugham, and the eleventh *Britannica*. The authors tend to follow usage in most cases, but periodically they take a stand against it. They disapprove of the debasement of a word like *agony* in *I was in agony in those new shoes*, proposing instead *My feet hurt*; but they record without comment the similar debasement of the word *passion*, from the Passion of Christ on the Cross to *She had a passion for fresh strawberries*. They regularly protest such meaningless business jargon as *enclosed please find, under separate cover*, and *enclosed herewith*, although usage is overwhelming. They have odd nostalgias for old forms, even remarking of the obsolete spellings *hickop* and *hicket* for *hiccup*, "It's a pity they've been lost." Noting the addition of *Babbitt* to the language, they propose that *Snopes* and *Sartoris* "deserve currency."

On the short sharp words of prejudice, the Evans make no pretense of following common usage, but deliberately set out to reform it. Of *Jew* they remark characteristically: "It is a word of incomparable dignity and immeasurable scorn and everything in between. It used to be a word of great comic range but that, at least, is fading. Its colloquial uses as an adjective or a verb are all offensive. The guidance to the 'correct' use of the noun does not lie in any dictionary but in the heart and mind of the user." There are no entries for words like *Kike* and *Sheeny*. Under *mulatto* the authors state their general principle: "All racial designations illustrate the difficulty underlying euphemism: contempt or disdain or dislike cannot be made acceptable to its victims by a mere change of words"; but under *Negro; nigger; nigra; darky* they insist: "Negro is the proper and, in formal writing, now the only permissible name." The entry on *African* suggests special pleading, concluding: "In English as used in South Africa no white man is a *native* (even though native) and no black man is a *South African* (even though he and his ancestors have lived in South Africa for many generations)."

Some of the information in *A Dictionary of Contemporary American Usage* would seem relatively useless, in terms of the book's stated intentions or by any criteria. *KLM*, it turns out, stands for the Dutch airline *Koninklijke Luchtvaart Maatschappij voor Nederland en Kolonien N. V.* The plural of *caryopsis* is *caryopsises* or *caryopsides*, not *caryopses*; the plural of *coccyx* is *coccyxes* or *coccyges*, not *coccyces*; the plural of *dialysis* is *dialyses*. The correct Arabic singular is *jinni* and the plural *jinn*. Other information is certainly misinformation. The authors confuse the *aegis* of Zeus, forged by Hephaestus, with that of his daughter Athena, with the Gorgon's head in its center, and they pontificate, "There is only one aegis and in its classical sense the word does not have a plural." They understand *feral*, in use at least since 1659 to mean a domesticated plant or animal that has run wild, as meaning simply *wild* or *animal* (although they quote Darwin's "The dovecote pigeon . . . has become feral in several places" as their example). Consequently they identify it as "solely a literary word" (although it is an accepted technical term, and in fact the only term, in several sciences), connect it with one of Mr. Evans' pet peeves, the legends of children reared by animals, and laugh it away. The authors think *skittles* and *ninepins* "are two names for the same game," although skittles can be an entirely different game played with a spinning disk or top. They claim that the ending of *Spaniard* is "the derogatory formation seen in *coward, sluggard, drunkard*, and so on," but make no attempt to explain *wizard, poniard, galliard*, and the rest.

The comparison that A *Dictionary of Contemporary American*

Usage provokes on every page is with Henry Watson Fowler's *A Dictionary of Modern English Usage*, published in 1926 and the standard reference work since. The Evans book may be read as a running argument with Fowler and his rigors, and at times the Evans resemble nothing so much as modern, permissive parents battling the authoritarian, curmudgeonly old grandfather. On *asset:* "Fowler regards it with stern disapproval and adjures his readers to shun it. Yet it is a common word in our language now and a useful one. It is an asset to the language. That it is a false singular is of no importance." Fowler lists *donate* among back-formations too irregular to be used, but it is "now a fully accepted word." The Americanism *caption*, for a legend under a picture, "has given some purists a conniption. . . . 'Rare in British use,' grumps Fowler, '& might well be rarer' "; but the Evans embrace it: "now standard usage." They write: "Fowler inveighs against the use of *conservative* as an adjective to mean *moderate* when qualifying a noun such as *figure* or *estimate* as 'perhaps the most ridiculous of slipshod extensions.' But the processes of language are indifferent to ridicule," and, in short, "Certainly in American usage *conservative* is now standard in the meaning of *moderate.*"

On *fiddle:* "Fowler incites us to rebel in the old word's defense. . . . But it is a lost cause." Of *Frankenstein* for the name of the monster: "None the less the term is now established ('almost, but surely not quite, sanctioned by custom,' cries Fowler in a plea which he must have felt to be futile)." Regarding *frock:* "Fowler called it 'a nurseryism of the same kind as *nighty* & *shimmy*' but it did no good." Of *phenomenal:* "Fowler foresaw this loose extension of the word's meaning and sternly condemned it as 'a sin against the English language.' But his condemnation, though reiterated by a host of lesser authorities, could not stay the word's efflorescence or degradation. Its primary meaning now is certainly 'extraordinary' or 'prodigious'." The entry on *elevator* must be quoted entire:

> Fowler's classification of *elevator* as a "superfluous word," his designation of it as "a cumbrous and needless Americanism," and his stern suggestion that it be at least restricted to "its hardly-avoidable commercial sense of grain-hoist," fall on modern ears with all the tinkling quaintness of a harpsichord. It is now standard in American usage, established beyond challenge, too common

to be cumbrous. *Lift*, which Fowler would have used in its stead, is, of course, so used in England, but even to traveled Americans it seems comic and to most Americans it would simply be incomprehensible.

Beneath these disagreements, as the tone suggests, admiration and even envy bubble. On *electrocute* the Evans note "Fowler's assurance that this 'barbarism' jars the nerves of Latinists 'much more cruelly than the operation denoted jars those of its victim' must be accepted as a linguist's grim humor." They quote admiringly his rhetorical question on *meticulous*, "What strange charm makes this wicked word irresistible?" Sometimes they join him in his hopeless causes: fighting for *belly* as "a good, sensible, established, time-honored word" against the imprecise nice nellies who say *stomach* or even (horrors!) *tummy*; complaining that *banal* was borrowed from France when the English "had a dozen good words at home to choose from"; protesting that people debase the language by using *literally* to mean *figuratively* as in I'*m literally melting*; or announcing that *onomatopeiac* is the preferred form of the adjective, with no reason given (Fowler's reason for preferring *onomatopeic* is that *onomatopoetic* "inevitably suggests, at least to those who do not know Greek, irrelevant associations with poet").

Sometimes the Evans take a strong Fowlerian tone: "How our hearts sink at a prefatory *frankly*, for we know some brutality is to follow, and a craven brutality, too." At other times they are weakly Fowlerian, identifying a phrase that "has now become a pompous cliché if used seriously and a feeble jest if used facetiously." Sometimes it is Fowler's sort of indignant metaphor:

> Prudery moves on prurience as a snail in its own slime and leaves the trail of this slime over all that it touches. The gallant cock and the patient ass are forever banished from our speech and we have only the nursery equivalents of *rooster* and *donkey*.

The Evans are most Fowlerian, perhaps, in their divagations. The entry on *hemlock*, explaining that the American hemlock is not Socrates' poisonous variety, has some of the bold digressiveness of Fowler's entry on *fir, pine*, beginning "Most of us have wished vaguely & vainly at times that they knew a fir from a pine." Under *dog's life, lead a* we get a wild surrealist essay on the conditions of canine existence, culminating in:

> Certainly today, with the veterinarian's bill often exceeding the pediatrician's, with canine psychiatrists, with dog sitters, with vitamin-enriched canned dog food, with quilted coats and fur-lined booties, with rubberfoam mattresses, boarding houses, schools of etiquette and even orphanages, a dog's life can no longer serve as the trope of wretchedness and all phrases that so imply must be discarded as clichés.

The entry on *fit for a king* concludes:

> But the glory of kings has departed. Except for three or four housebroken survivors, a monarch's life today is not a happy one. What is now fit for a king? Shabby rooms in a hotel on the Riviera, overdue bills, the hissing conspirator, the yawning waiter, the sneering reporter, the gossip columnist, and in the shadow the assassin. *Fit for a king* is now a ghoul's cliché. Let it be mercifully abandoned.

Apparently language usage books are now in the pioneering stage dictionaries were in in Samuel Johnson's day—vehicles for the cranky and opinionated individual voice, which will eventually be supplanted by the more uniform, authoritative, and duller collaboration of anonymous scholars. We can get a vivid picture of the personality behind *A Dictionary of Contemporary American Usage*. For convenience let us call it "Bergen Evans," a figure we already know to some extent from his books and television programs. (This is unfair to sister Cornelia, an author and public figure in her own right, but it is probably inevitable in any collaboration with a television personality, and we can enter the reservation that any given feature of "Bergen Evans" may be hers.) The jacket says that Evans grew up in Ohio and England, studied at Miami and Harvard and was a Rhodes scholar at Oxford, is now an English professor at Northwestern, has written two books debunking popular fallacies and is "the informative and witty moderator" of television programs. We could have guessed Harvard from the book's mockery of the *Boston accent* in a long entry, ending with the suggestion that if God no longer speaks in Hebrew, "He at least has a Boston accent"; or the book's indignant denial of the existence of anything that might be called a "Harvard" accent, the entry under that heading beginning "*Harvard accent* is a cliché of resentment that mingles malice and ignorance in about equal proportions." We can see traces of the debunking books in the confusion about *feral* mentioned earlier, and an entry on *lone wolf* repeats Evans' obsessive concern that no one continue to think wolves hunt in packs. The pattern is superficially Johnsonian, in its odd combination of provincial and metropolitan culture, and Johnson too had a doctorate. Evans clearly has the great lexicographer in mind: Johnson anecdotes and quotations run through his book; and in at least one place, echoing some strictures of Fowler's against *psychological moment*, he goes far beyond Fowler's tone to the authentic rhythms of the Grand Cham himself: "The phrase was woolly in its inception, confused in its translation, affected in its adoption, and misunderstood in its application. It is pompous, meaningless, and tedious."

Evans' true prototype, however, is neither of these British gentlemen but America's own Henry L. Mencken, and there is some evidence that it is Mencken's whopping jackboots Evans is attempting to fill. There are considerable differences (it is hard to picture Mencken as a Rhodes scholar or a Harvard Ph.D., or as fiercely democratic in Evans' fashion) but there are even more considerable resemblances, and the special field Evans has claimed for himself, combining negative debunking of nonsense with positive labors on behalf of the American language, was Mencken's own. Evans has many of Mencken's irritating provincialities: he mocks the jargon of heraldry in *bar sinister* ("It's much simpler to say 'He was a bastard' "); he scorns the use of Latin quotations ("It serves only to mark one as either a hopeless pedant or an affected ass"); and he snipes at modern literature ("Spenser, in the manner later employed by T. S. Eliot, went out of his way to be obscure"). Evans has all of Mencken's ambivalent fascination with popular culture. He praises *L'il Abner*, *Pogo*, and *Mad*; tells Goldwyn jokes; draws his examples from "The Stag at Eve" and Ogden Nash; goes out of his way to promote *Come Back Little Sheba* as "a moving treatment of a slattern"; and has a long, fascinated entry on Stephen

Potter's *gamesmanship*, which he traces back to Chaucer. Unfortunately, Evans is just as likely to be wrong as right in these references: in a long article on *nicknames* he refers learnedly to *"Hot Lips* Paige," although the name is Page, and his friends called him "Lips." "In the cynical terminology of bebop" Evans defines: "A *square*, to the zoot-suit cognoscenti, is one who is not *hep*," although zoot-suit is a stage earlier than bop, and of course the word is *hip*.

Evans has much of Mencken's smart aleck quality, although, since he makes the astonishing claim that *smart aleck* has amatory connotations, and has been "replaced by the humorous, less disparaging, slang term *smarty pants*," perhaps we should say, much of Mencken's smarty pants quality. Evans remarks of *bright and early*, "The airlines report more delays because of fog in their early morning flights than at any other time of the day." Of *crossword puzzles*, "the malady lingers on." Of *stag*:

> In colloquial American usage it designates a man unaccompanied by a woman at a social gathering or a special party for men unaccompanied by their wives. It also means a swine which has been castrated after the maturation of the sex organs. There is no known etymological connection between these last meanings.

Some of Evans' entries are terribly cute, running to vulgar suggestions about saltpeter, comic differentiations ("Many trusties have been recruited from the second sort of trustee"), and such examples as, for *science*, "Boy, he's got that down to a science!"

Evans tries to dismiss each cliché with its own little joke: *"a feather in one's cap* is now bedraggled and droopy and no feather in anyone's stylistic cap"; as an image, *the apple of one's eye* "seems repulsively bloodshot and grotesque"; *"fresh as a daisy* is a wilted metaphor"; on *grin and bear it*, "one must bear it, but the grin has long since faded"; *"to feather one's nest* is strictly for the birds"; and so on. He advises his readers to reply to "Alas, poor Yorick" with "What, has this thing appear'd again tonight?" and other funny quotations from *Hamlet*. The best example of Evans' odd ambivalence toward mass culture is his attitude toward *Time*. He finds it "deft with this ploy" of gamesmanship, and mocks its pretence of omniscience, but is awed by the "brilliant creations" of its portmanteau words, adducing *cinemactress* in evidence. Even Mencken, who praises the "terse and dramatic words" of comic strips in one of the *American Language* books, would not have prostrated himself before the brilliance of *cinemactress*.

The portrait of H. W. Fowler that emerges from A *Dictionary of Modern English Usage* is very different. We could have guessed that he was a schoolmaster and classical scholar, Tory, High Church Anglican (from the entry under *Catholic* that will not allow the term to be monopolized by Roman Catholics), Blimpish (recommending *doctress*: "Everyone knows the inconvenience of being uncertain whether a doctor is a man or a woman"), snobbish, and prejudiced. He is the oracle of the club, and he has the authentic voice: Here are examples:

> No; a barbarism is like a lie; it has got the start of us before we have found it out, & we cannot catch it; it is in possession, & our offers of other versions come too late.

> Poor old *foreword!* your vogue is past, your freshness faded; you are antiquated, vieux jeu, passé, démodé; your nose is out of joint.

> Fie! fie! a Greek tragedy and *protagonists?*

> Can any man say that sort of thing & retain a shred of self-respect?

> *Sensitize* is a word made for the needs of photography, & made badly.

> If an epoch were made every time we are told that a discovery or other event is epoch-making, our bewildered state of ceaseless transition from the thousands of eras wc were in yesterday to the different thousands we are in today would be pitiful indeed. But luckily the word is a blank cartridge, meant only to startle, & not to carry even so imponderable a bullet as conviction.

Fowler is learned and literate but insistently not *literary;* "literary critics' word" is almost his strongest abuse: "*Distinction,* as a literary critics' word, is, like *charm,* one of those on which they fall back when they wish to convey that a style is meritorious, but have not time to make up their minds upon the precise nature of its merit." Fowler must have kept the club members laughing their heads off, if we can judge by the entry under *pun.* He calls the automatic discrediting of puns "a sign at once of sheepish docility & desire to seem superior. Puns are good, bad, & indifferent, & only those who lack the wit to make them are unaware of the fact."

Fowler's characteristic posture is that of King Canute commanding the waves to cease ("So strong is the false belief that every bully must be a coward that acts requiring great courage are constantly described as cowardly if they are so carried out as not to give the victim a sporting chance"). He himself never fights unless he is hopelessly outnumbered, and it is never in the hope of victory, only to keep defeat from being total: "Is it too late to suggest that 'my betrothed' . . . should be given another chance?"; anyone who uses *nice* "in its more proper senses . . . does a real if small service to the language"; of *obnoxious* in the old sense of *open to attack*, "we may hope that scholarly writers will keep it alive." When Fowler surrenders, it is only after the last cat and rat have been eaten, and no one is left to man the ramparts: "Though *pandar* is the older & better form, it is useless to try to restore it"; "any attempt to keep *tetchy* alive seems due to a liking for curiosities." When Fowler accepted "sixteenmo" as proper for "sextodecimo," something died in Jacobite hearts all over the world.

Yet, there is a stubborn practicality in him that tempers the purism, a Sancho Panza coexisting with Don Quixote: "We will split infinitives sooner than be ambiguous or artificial"; even, "Seriously, our learned persons & possessors of special information should not, when they are writing for the general public, presume to improve the accepted vocabulary." Fowler's real heresy is what might be called Adamist, the idea that everything has its *true* name, the name God gave it, or as *Modern English Usage* phrases it, "among these names there is usually one that may be regarded as the thing's proper name, its *kurion onoma* or dominant name as the Greeks called it." He was, altogether, an original and a redoubtable figure, and it may be just as well that we shall not soon see his like again.

At which, inevitably, appears A *Dictionary of American-English Usage: Based on Fowler's Modern English Usage*. It is Fowler rewritten for those eager customers Marlene and Stuart by Margaret Nicholson, head of the Contract and Copyright Department of The Macmillan Company. Her preface admits that "to tamper with Fowler has taken both humility and courage—or perhaps fool-hardiness," and states the conditions of her venture fully:

> New words and idioms have come into the language since the publication of *Modern English Usage;* there are peculiarities of American speech and writing not recorded by Fowler; and many of us today, English and American, have neither the time nor the scholarship to follow through the fascinating but sometimes exasperating labyrinth of Greek and Latin parallels and Fowler's Socratic method of teaching by wrong examples. *American-English Usage* is an adaptation of MEU, not a replacement. AEU is a simplified MEU, with American variations, retaining as much of the original as space allowed. Many of the longer articles had to be shortened, many of the more academic ones and those less pertinent to usage today were omitted, to make room for new entries and illustrations. Fowler's own mannerisms and pedantries —and I am sure he would have been the last to deny them— have been left untouched. There was a temptation sometimes to soften the sting of "illiterate," "journalese," "lady novelists," "uneducated writers"; perhaps Fowler himself would have tempered some of them had he revised his book, but only Fowler could decide that. They have been left as he wrote them.

Miss Nicholson has perhaps not tampered with Fowler quite enough. She leaves many of his pronunciations untouched, even where, as in *parliament* ("Pron. par'*lament*"), many Americans join me, I think, in saying "par'lyament." To Fowler's strictures against pronouncing the *t* in *often*, which he says is "practiced by two oddly consorted classes—the academic speakers who affect a more precise enunciation than their neighbors'" and "the uneasy half-literates who like to prove that they can spell," she adds a parenthesis noting that the *Oxford English Dictionary* and Webster "more charitably" allow the pronunciation as an accepted regional variation. (It should be recorded that the Evans book offers no guidance to pronunciation, for no stated reason.)

Miss Nicholson has cut Fowler's explanation of *genteelisms* and his long list of examples, but has neglected to add any mention of the English U and Non-U controversy, which was precisely over the class associations of these paired words: lower-class people using the genteel *serviette* where their blunter betters say *napkin.* She has left in and even amplified Fowler's instructions (for Ernest Bevin's generation, perhaps) on how to address a lord, although it would be more useful for Marlene and Stuart to know how to address a congressman, and she has retained his complaint that the Japanese example has ruined the fine old simplicity of British titles. She has preserved the little gem of an essay on how to tell firs from pines, although she has changed Fowler's "most of us have wished . . . they knew" to the more colloquial "most of us have wished . . . we knew." Miss Nicholson has omitted Fowler's indignant entry on *frock*, but has not replaced it with some explanation for the confusing *negligee*; she has added a brief entry on *O.K.*, an Americanism which Fowler scorned to notice (she removed his *okapi* to do it), but nothing on *Hi*; she has added *ingenuous* but not *disingenuous*; she omits many words that since Fowler's time have come into general use, such as *denture*, or general misuse, such as *fulsome*.

Miss Nicholson adds an entry on *pinch hitter*, and takes a properly Fowlerian line to it, that it is often misused to mean an inferior rather than, as it does in baseball, a superior substitute. She keeps Fowler's two explanations of *burlesque* as a form of caricature, without taking any notice of the fact that, in the Evans' words, "In America *burlesque* has a special meaning, one probably much better known to the masses than its older meaning: a theatrical entertainment featuring coarse comedy and dancing." She preserves Fowler's assurance that those who wish to mark their adherence to the technical sense of the word *myth*, rather than the popular sense, do so by pronouncing it *mīth*—although if there ever were any such people they have certainly long since gone. Miss Nicholson retains Fowler's entry on *phallus*, which consists in its entirety of the statement that the plural is *phalli* (the words ought to be *phallos* and *phalloi*, there being no reason to take a Greek word in the Latin form), and she makes no mention of *penis*, which has become the general respectable word in America, popularized I suspect by nursery school teachers and people Fowler would call doctresses.

Miss Nicholson's principal alteration has been to give up on Fowler's lost causes, surrendering in each case to the waves of popular usage. Where he says that the singular *aborigine* "is felt to be anomalous & avoided or disliked," she says, "though gaining in popularity, even among scholars, is still avoided or disliked by

many." Like the Evans, she repudiates Fowler and accepts *asset*
("through usage has been accepted in both US and Brit."), *caption*
("firmly established in US"), *donate* ("chiefly US"), *electrocute* (no
mention), *elevator* ("standard US, *lift* Brit.), *Frankenstein* ("Most
US dictionaries now give as a second meaning of *Frankenstein* the
monster so created"), and many others. Where Fowler took no
stand, she can give in even more readily, with the typical comment,
"The misuse is so frequent as to be almost established," or "undoubtedly right, but the battle is in vain." Thus Webster gives the
pronunciation as *Gren'wich* Village, "but it is not commonly so
called there"; and although the OED says the pronunciation *trōkĕ*
for *troche* is "in vulgar and commercial use," "Nevertheless it
is now so pronounced, US & Brit." Miss Nicholson quotes Sir
Ernest Gowers accepting *I will go* for simple future tense with the
slogan "If we go by practice rather than by precept," and on that
basis even accepts *up* as an intensive (*eat up your food*), at which
we can imagine Fowler roaring like the Father Bear.

Despite her introductory statement, Miss Nicholson omits
Fowler's strictures against *banal, banality* ("These are LITERARY
CRITICS' WORDS, imported from France by a class of writers whose
jaded taste relishes novel or imposing jargon") and a number of
other diatribes and harangues, as she omits his eight pages of
French words with phonetic pronunciation, his examples of poetry
and much else that gives his book its color and variety. What she
has added is mostly of a specifically American character: a protest
against *irregardless*, which he had probably never heard; notes that
words like *exotic* and *facet* have become American "VOGUE WORDS"
(the second replacing Fowler's entry on *facetiae*, apparently not an
American vogue word); and so forth. On *vase*, Fowler says flatly,
"Pron. vahz (not vawz)"; Miss Nicholson says, in a burst of pa-
triotism, "For most Americans the natural pronunciation is vās.
This is not a 'US illiteracy'; it was the earlier pronunciation in England." Where Fowler says the plural of *dwarf* is *dwarves*, and the
Evans say "The plural is *dwarfs*, not *dwarves*," Miss Nicholson com-
promises, "Usually *dwarfs*, rarely *dwarves*."

Much of her effort, not surprisingly, has been with Fowler's race
prejudices. His remarkable entry on *nigger*, "Applied to others than
full or partial negroes, is felt as an insult by the person described,"

becomes in her hands "Sometimes used familiarly between two Negroes with affection. Used by a non-Negro it is offensive." Where Fowler's only entry on *darky* consists of instructions for forming the plural, she writes, "Spell *darky*, if used; pl. *darkies*. (Colloq., often offensive.)" Fowler's entry on *Hebrew, Israelite, Jew, Semite* contains the statement that the word *Jew* is sometimes avoided because it "has certain traditional implications (as usury, anti-Christianity) that are unsuited to the context"; her entry on *Hebrew, Israelite, Israeli, Jew, Semite* says nothing of the sort. Miss Nicholson oddly reprints without alteration Fowler's statement that "the normal uses" are *A Chinaman* and *Three Chinamen*, as against the Evans' much more accurate "In the United States the preferred form is *Chinese*, as in *one Chinese* and *two Chinese*."

Miss Nicholson is in personality and opinion apparently very unlike her predecessor. Where he saw the United States as a nation of semi-literate aboriginals, she is at least defensively American: "To reject these words simply because they are 'chiefly US' is evidence of a sorry lack of faith in our own culture." Where he is backward-looking and austere, she is forward-looking and chatty. Fowler might have admired her distinction "*Eatable* implies a measure of palatability, whereas even tripe is *edible*," but what would he have made of the world casually assumed by her entry on *sloe-eyed*, "The mystery and romance writers who describe their heroines thus seem to be thinking of the effects of sloe gin rather than the bluish-black plum"?

What one sees in the usage books, in short, are the crotchets of strongly marked personalities, but behind them and ultimately determining the issue are the shifting patterns of the culture. To speak respectably and be regarded as an educated person are perhaps not very impressive ideals, but beyond them lie more impressive visions of *being* genuinely respectable and educated. The entry in the Evans book on *genteel; gentle; Gentile* points out that all three words are from the Latin *gentilis*, of the same clan or tribe. Some of the fun of reading usage books is watching the ceaseless quest for gentility inevitably undercut by the tendency of every euphemistic word, however delicate in inception, to become as vulgar as the word it supplants. *Cuspidor* was taken from the Portuguese as a refined way to say *spittoon*, and *cemetery* ("sleeping place") was a nice euphemism for *graveyard* or *boneyard*. *Privy* (a place to be private) was succeeded by *toilet* (a place to dress), then *bathroom*, soon *washroom* and its Latin form *lavatory*, eventually *powder room*; yet the veneer never stays on for long. It is more delicate to say *pluck* than *guts*, although *pluck* too means intestines, and it is much more delicate to say "Poppycock!" than some coarser equivalent, although the Evans assure us that it is a colloquial Dutch word for a cake of pap-shaped semi-liquid dung. These matters may be ultimately not in the dictionary but in the heart and mind, as the Evans say, or buried deep in the culture's history. Those not of the dominant clan, Marlene or Stuart, pursuing *gentility* or *Gentility*, might better pursue the truly *gentle*, that archaic characteristic of gentlefolk, and respect the language, like any tool, to keep it sharp. Perhaps a lord has sensibilities too, like a Chinese, and is hurt when incorrectly addressed; perhaps even a word bleeds when you cut it.

The Oxford Dictionary
of the
Christian Church

[1958]

T HE IMPOSING *Oxford Dictionary of the Christian Church,*
the first of its sort, offers itself "not only to those who through
Holy Baptism have been admitted to membership in the Body of
Christ, but to all who take an intelligent interest in contemporary
culture." The preface continues:

It is addressed to the needs not merely of those whose primary
vocation lies in the Christian ministry or in the professional study
of theology or church history, nor even only to the general body
of professing Christians who seek information about their faith
and its growth, but to the educated public as a whole.

The present reviewer, by the dictionary's definition an "infidel"
("A person who has a positive disbelief in every form of the
Christian faith"), raised in the Jewish faith but infidel there too,
and without pretensions to the professional study of theology, has
no justification for this review beyond the hope that he is a
member of the educated public to whom the book is addressed.

The ODCC, as the dictionary asks that we abbreviate it, is the
work of the Rev. F. L. Cross, Lady Margaret Professor of Divinity in the University of Oxford and Canon of Christ Church,

his staff, and over a hundred scholars, a great many of them clergymen in the Church of England. Since "in order to secure the maximum uniformity it was agreed at the outset that all contributions should be subject to such editorial modification and reconstruction as seemed desirable, and that anonymity should be preserved," the book has a unified character and viewpoint lacking in such pluralist signed works as the *Oxford Classical Dictionary*. Its viewpoint throughout is High Church Anglican, finding its clearest identification with the Tractarian or Oxford revival of the nineteenth century, which sought to restore the Church of England to its Catholic, credal, and ritualistic traditions. The book's particular hero is Cardinal Newman, the leader of the Oxford Movement and before his conversion to Roman Catholicism its boldest Tractarian. The entry on Newman concludes: "His genius has come to be more and more recognized after his death, and his influence both on the restoration of RC-ism [Roman Catholicism] in England and the advance of Catholic ideas in the C of E [Church of England] can hardly be exaggerated." Secondary heroes are E. B. Pusey, the leader of the movement after Newman's defection and Cross's predecessor as Canon of Christ Church. (Pusey was so strong in the faith that he was suspended from the Oxford pulpit for two years for teaching Roman Catholic doctrine), and John Keble, the brilliant Tractarian and poet.

The aim of the ODCC seems to be no less than the undoing of the Reformation, at least for the Church of England. Thus an entry on *Middle Ages* remarks: "Once viewed as a sterile period, it has come to be regarded as one of the most creative and fruitful periods in the world's history." In general, the Protestant character of the Established Church is denied, and its traditions are repudiated. Here, of course, the great stumbling block is the Thirty-Nine Articles of the Church of England, agreed upon by convocation under Queen Elizabeth in 1562, which affirm many of Martin Luther's basic principles: that "Holy Scripture containeth all things necessary to salvation" (Article 6); "That we are justified by Faith only" (Article 11); that "The Church of Rome hath erred" (Article 19) as General Councils of the Church "may err, and sometimes have erred" (Article 21); that the use of "a tongue not understood of the people" is "a thing plainly repugnant to the Word of God" (Article 24); that the Roman doctrine of Transubstantiation in the Eucharist is not only "repugnant to the plain words of Scripture" but "hath given occasion to many superstitions" (Article 27); that the laity must be given the Eucharistic wine as well as the bread (Article 30); that "the sacrifices of Masses" are "blasphemous fables, and dangerous deceits" (Article 31); that marriage is lawful for the clergy (Article 32); and so forth.

Until 1865, "subscription" to all thirty-nine Articles was required of the clergy of the Church of England and members of the universities of Oxford and Cambridge. Since then there have been no tests of faith at the universities and the clergy has been required only to "assent" to the Articles in general. The ODCC explains: "Assent is generally understood to imply a less definite form of adherence than subscription, but there is apparently no official explanation as to exactly what it involves. Perhaps the term may be explained as an undertaking to refrain from teaching anything directly opposed to the standard of doctrine implied, without requiring positive agreement in detail in one's personal opinions." The dictionary entries seem to assent only in this loose sense to a number of the Articles, and when they are discussed the emphasis tends to be on the range of permitted disagreement. A typical comment is: "Much variety of interpretation has been put upon many of them without improperly straining the text, and probably this license was deliberately intended by their framers," giving as an example the "masterly ambiguity" of Article 17, on predestination.

Insofar as John Foxe's *Acts and Monuments,* commonly known as "The Book of Martyrs," has been the principal household work keeping alive the old Protestant fury in England, one of the consistent efforts of the High Church party has been to discredit Foxe, beginning with attacks by S. R. Maitland, the librarian at Lambeth Palace, more than a century ago. Although Foxe's general reliability has since been solidly re-established by J. F. Mozley (in a study published by the Church of England's Society for Promoting Christian Knowledge), the *Oxford Dictionary* says flatly of Foxe's book: "As a work of history, its value is impaired by its author's credulity and bitterness." Where Foxe and his party glory in the execution of Roman Catholic martyrs in England, the ODCC says of Fisher and More, "Their execution in 1535 was universally mourned." Even Richard Hooker, the "architect" of the Church of England, is not Catholic enough, and the biographical entry on him complains of the liberality of his doctrine on episcopal ordination and the Eucharist. The tone used for such modern critics as John Kensit, who opposed "what he believed to be romanizing tendencies in the C of E," is almost petulant: "increasingly violent and individualist," "causing considerable friction and disturbance wherever he went."

Historically, the great Protestant critics of the Roman Catholic Church have not been distinguished for their temperateness. Wycliffe called adherents of the Pope "the twelve daughters of the diabolical leech," Luther characterized the denial of Communion wine to the laity and other abuses as "the Babylonian Captivity." The spirit of the Oxford Dictionary is about as far from this as can be imagined. The traditional pre-Reformation martyrs of Protestantism are for the most part blandly repudiated: the Albigenses "were animated by an implacable hatred against the Church" and "because of their unsocial doctrines were a menace not only to the faith of the Church but to ordered society"; "grave excesses and fanaticism brought ill-odour" on the Anabaptists; and so on. "Since the Reformation," an entry on Antichrist remarks, "the identification of the Pope with Antichrist has been frequently made, esp. in the less educated circles of Protestantism." From this one would hardly guess that Archbishop Cranmer died affirming it, that such an identification was one of the 104 Articles that the Church of Ireland adopted in 1615, or that it is a tenet of the Lutheran Book of Concord of 1580, to which many Lutheran churches still subscribe.

Many of the dictionary's entries on aspects of Roman Catholicism maintain a nice impartiality, such as one on the nineteenth-century Cardinal Antonelli, Papal Secretary of State, that concludes: "A statesman rather than a prelate, he was loaded with praise by his friends, but regarded as unscrupulous by his enemies." The entry on Massacre of St. Bartholomew's Day is rigorously dispassionate. On such phenomena as the eighteen manifestations of the Virgin Mary to St. Bernadette near Lourdes, the dictionary confines itself modestly to noting how they are commemorated in the Roman Catholic Church. The cult of saints' relics, the ODCC explains, "is based on the natural instinct of men to treat with reverence what is left of the dead they loved." (Article 22, less impressed by natural instinct, says, "The Romish Doctrine concerning Purgatory, Pardons, Worshipping, and Adoration, as well of Images as of Reliques, and also invocation of Saints, is a fond thing vainly invented, and grounded upon no warranty of Scripture, but rather repugnant to the Word of God".) The *Oxford Dictionary* is critical in two main areas. It hits hard at the wicked and dissolute Popes in history (though no harder, certainly, than many Roman Catholic historians); thus it remarks bluntly of an inept Pope, St. Celestine V, "His pontificate was astonishing and disastrous." Hagiography gets equally short shrift, and the typical description of a saint's history is "An apparently worthless legend."

In the book's effort to define the Church of England as a Catholic Church, a great deal of space is expended on justifying the legitimacy of its holy orders. A long article on *Anglican Ordinations* defends their historical continuity in a line going back to Divine institution, asserting against Roman Catholic polemic that even if the Apostolic Succession was broken with Archbishop Parker under Queen Elizabeth, it was regained with Archbishop Laud at the Restoration. The article on Parker is nevertheless careful to remind readers of his consecration "by four bishops who had held sees in Edward VI's reign." The entry on *Anglicanism* does not seem embarrassed by the fact that "the C of E tolerated, esp. in the later years of the 19th cent. and the earlier years of the 20th, a considerable infiltration of Liberalism," but the entry on *Liberalism* suggests that the recovery has been more or less complete. The biography of A. H. Stanley, Dean of Westminster, notes that he "gave much offense to orthodox Churchmen by his invitation to all the scholars who had produced the RV [Revised Version of the Bible], among them a Unitarian, to receive Holy Communion in the Abbey." The entry on *Essays and Reviews* (1860), "A collection of essays by seven authors who believed in the necessity of free inquiry in religious matters," deals chiefly with its violent condemnation by the

Church of England. It neglects to mention that one of the condemned authors, Frederick Temple, later became Archbishop of Canterbury.

As the Oxford Movement in the Church of England paralleled Ultramontanism in the Roman Catholic Church, the dictionary points out, so was there a parallelism between Anglican Liberalism and Roman Catholic Modernism. Modernism was quickly crippled by the excommunication of J. J. I. von Doellinger in 1871 and by the enormous pressures put on Lord Acton, and it was finally extirpated by the condemnation of Modernist doctrines as heretic by St. Pius X in 1907, and by the excommunication shortly afterward of such Modernist priests as Alfred Loisy in France and George Tyrrell in England (in Tyrrell's case, for protesting against the Papal encyclical in two letters to the *Times*). Excommunication "has in fact been very rare in the C of E," the dictionary notes, perhaps proudly, thinking of Dean Stanley and Archbishop Temple.

Balancing the ODCC's emphasis on the Catholic tradition of the Church of England in matters of ritual and sacramentalism, there is an equally strong identification with Protestantism in the welcome accorded the revival of Calvinism by Barthian theology, with Karl Barth a hero to balance Newman. The article on St. Paul's Epistle to the Romans, the key New Testament book for Barth, notes that it was equally important to St. Augustine, Luther, Calvin, and Wesley. The enthusiastic entry on Reinhold Niebuhr says, "He has been much influenced by the Dialectical Theology of K. Barth," and adds that he goes even beyond Barth to reject "the theology of the Creeds in its traditional form" as giving "insufficient place to original sin." In the entry on *Arminianism* the dictionary speaks of the recent "theological revival of Calvinism under the influence of K. Barth," and the article on *Calvinism* concludes:

> Calvinism suffered severe setbacks through rationalism in the 18th and 19th cents., but recently it has once more come to the fore esp. through the work of K. Barth, whose influence has been considerable not only in the Protestant Churches on the Continent but also in the C of E. Its attraction for the modern re-

ligious mind is probably due to the stress it lays on the omnipotence of God and the nothingness of man as a reaction against the easy humanitarianism of 19th cent. liberal Protestantism. Along with the debt to John Calvin, the dictionary explains, Barth's Dialectical Theology "drew its inspiration from thinkers in revolt against the humanist ideal," principally Kierkegaard and Dostoevsky. Both are treated to very respectful biographical articles, the one on Kierkegaard concluding, "His total influence on contemporary thought is very considerable," and the one on Dostoevsky similarly noting that his ideas "have had a profound influence on the Continent."

The entry on *Atonement* says that in recent years "there has been a return to traditional views" under the influence of Barthian theology and its "determination to put the Cross rather than the Manger at the centre of the Christian Creed." The article on *God* expounds yet another aspect of the Barthian revolution: "The main trend in the present century has been against immanentism, with a reaffirmation of the Divine transcendence." The book's only criticism of Barth, so far as I could see, is the suggestion under *Incarnation* that "Neo-Protestant theology, under the influence esp. of K. Barth and his school, has sometimes been so emphatic in its denial of immanence as almost to imperil belief in a real Incarnation altogether." "In recent times," the ODCC explains, "renewed interest has been taken in the theology of the Church by Catholics and Protestants alike." This revival of theology is regarded as being almost single-handedly due to Barth: "His influence has been very deep on the Continent as well as in Great Britain and America, where it has done much to break the reign of the more negative elements of German criticism."

The higher criticism of the Bible, in other words, has been replaced by something more positive. "Since the World War of 1914–18," the dictionary explains (Barth's commentary on Romans appeared in 1919), "the approach of scholars to the NT has shifted. A 'post-critical' period has begun, in which the interest in literary and historical questions has declined. More attention is paid to the theology of the Bible and to the interrelation of different parts of the OT and the NT." Under Bible *Exegesis* the dictionary notes: "K. Barth is the chief representative of a return to a more dogmatic and conservative method." The tendency of the ODCC is to dismiss the higher criticism of the Bible as a mere nineteenth-century aberration, although Origen in the third century and Eusebius and St. Jerome in the fourth were higher critics in every sense of the term, as were many of the Reformers.

The writers of the ODCC in general take a fairly conservative line on Bible criticism. They accept or at least treat respectfully its more moderate conclusions, particularly where the agreement of scholars is overwhelming. In regard to the Old Testament: "large sections" of the Book of Jeremiah were not written by the prophet; "The popular belief that David was the author of the whole Psalter can no longer be sustained"; the Song of Solomon "is prob. an anthology of love poems of varying length, ascribed to Solomon and his beloved (the 'Shulamite') and their friends"; the Books of Ezra and Nehemiah are "generally supposed by modern scholars" to have been written much later than the time of Nehemiah, that is, to be pseudepigraphic. Similar judgments are made about the New Testament: the author of the Book of Revelation is neither the John of the Fourth Gospel nor the Apostle John; "it is widely held" that parts of Second Corinthians do not belong in it; "some modern scholars" have questioned the genuineness of the Epistle to the Ephesians, "but the problems have not received any agreed solution"; along with Origen and Luther modern scholars "almost unanimously consider" the Epistle to the Hebrews pseudepigraphic; the authenticity of the Pastoral Epistles "has been frequently denied by NT critics."

For the bolder conclusions of higher criticism, or the more radical critics, the dictionary shows little respect. C. C. Torrey questioned the historical existence of Ezra, "but this drastic critical hypothesis has received little support"; F. C. Baur denied the Pauline authorship of all except four Epistles, but his book "roused a storm of controversy"; W. C. Van Manen rejected the authenticity of *all* St. Paul's Epistles, but "his opinions attracted attention more as curiosities than for their intrinsic importance." The theory that Jesus was a mythic rather than a historic person is misunderstood by identifying it with Strauss's *Life of Jesus*, which certainly assumes a historical Jesus, and the theory's actual proponents are ignored or dismissed. C. F. Dupuis,

P. C. A. Jensen, Georg Brandes, and P. L. Couchoud are not mentioned; Arthur Drews is tossed aside as a "German anti-Christian apologist"; and the leader of the movement, J. M. Robertson, gets no biographical entry, but along with W. B. Smith is named as among "a small group of critics" who denied the historical existence of Christ and were promptly refuted by P. W. Schmiedel. The long article on *Jesus Christ* entirely ignores the myth theorists, and none of their many volumes is listed in the extensive bibliography of "Other works from many different standpoints."

Where the *Oxford Dictionary* does not repudiate higher criticism, it sidesteps it in a variety of fashions. Thus the Eden story contains "a fundamental truth about man in his relation to God, even if the truth is held to be there conveyed in legendary form"; the purpose of Genesis "is not so much to offer exact science and accurate history as to record the progressive character of the Divine revelation and to indicate the spiritual mission of the Israelite people"; the Gospel according to St. Mark "gives us a patchwork of tradition; but on analysis every part of it bears witness, in its own way, to a 'Jesus of History' behind it." Sometimes the treatment seems almost disingenuous. A tiny entry on the prophet Elisha says: "He had not the individuality or strength of character of his predecessor" Elijah, but significantly neglects to mention that he anticipated many of the miracles of his successor Jesus, among them healing, raising the dead, and multiplying the loaves. An entry on *Bethlehem* nowhere says that it translates as "house of bread," and is thus a peculiarly fitting birthplace for Him who said of the bread: "Take, eat; this is my body." There is the repeated claim that the Gospels were written by their reputed authors, since "It is unlikely that tradition would wrongly have assigned a Gospel to so unimportant a character" as Mark or Luke, an argument that would make the apocryphal books of Enoch and Baruch authentic. The entries on *Nazarene* and *Nazirite* fail to suggest a connection, nor is there any mention under *Nazareth* that there does not seem to have been any such place before the third or fourth century. The long article on St. Paul pays no attention to the many demonstrations by Jewish and Christian scholars that Paul's ignorance of the Hebrew Bible and of Jewish custom makes it impossible for him to have been the rabbinically trained strict Pharisee the New Testament claims. Lastly, the writers of the *Oxford Dictionary* are sometimes surprisingly credulous: Sir Leonard Woolley's excavations at Ur are taken "to indicate a historic foundation for the Babylonian tradition of a very widespread flood"; the death of Solomon is dated "c. 933 B.C." with all the boldness of Archbishop Ussher and no additional evidence.

Where the *Oxford Dictionary of the Christian Church* may prove most disturbing to readers not of its persuasion (and, one might hope, to many who are) is in its arrogance. Thus the entry on *Capital Punishment* concludes: "Its abolition in certain countries, however, and the great diminution since 1800 of the number of crimes punishable by death in others, may legitimately be ascribed to Christian enlightenment" (perhaps the author means the enlightenment *of* Christians). The entry on *Slavery* concludes: "It is now generally condemned on account of the almost inevitable abuses accompanying it and of its opposition to the spirit of the Gospel." How odd to find that the Scriptures of the Mandaeans are "a farrago of inconsistent teachings"—so unlike our own well-ordered Bible.

The dictionary tends to be particularly harsh with the aggressively evangelical Protestant sects. Of the English Ranters of the seventeenth century: "Their revolutionary and immoral doctrines made them the object of deep suspicion." Mormon history "has been marked by constant internal dissensions and strife with the Federal authorities." The Christian Science Church was founded after Mrs. Eddy's recovery from "various ailments, generally held to have been of a hysterical nature," and "Its teaching on the unreality of matter, sin, and suffering conflicts with the fundamental Biblical doctrines of the Creation, Fall, and Redemption." Jehovah's Witnesses "can hardly be regarded as a religious society, since, acc. to Rutherford's own statement, they hold that 'religion is against God.'" Their periodicals "carried on a vigorous propaganda against the British Empire as well as against all institutional religion. The RC Church, the C of E, and the Free Churches are the constant butt of abuse in these publications, which deny most of the fundamental Christian doctrines." A biographical entry on Judge Rutherford notes, "In 1918–19 he served a term of imprisonment at Atlanta (Georgia) for insubordination and disloyalty, and he was frequently accused of fraudulent practices, even by his own followers," and credits him with being the author of "innumerable pamphlets propagating his subversive views." A biographical entry on C. T. Russell, Rutherford's predecessor and the founder of the sect, notes that "In 1909 his wife obtained a divorce on the grounds of his immoral conduct with members of his 'Church' and he went abroad for a time," and concludes: "Despite the great parade of learning in his books he was unable to name in the courts the letters of the Greek alphabet."

The ODCC seems remaikably callous to cruelties committed by the Church against dissenters and heretics. The entry on *Secular Arm* explains: "The Church has not felt justified in imposing in her own tribunals penalties which involve mutilation or death, but the Church courts have had to deal with some cases, chiefly those of heresy, in which it was felt that sterner punishments were needed than they could impose. The assistance of the secular arm was therefore sought." The article on *Oxford* boasts: "The close and continuous connection with the life of the Church is shewn by the trials of T. Cranmer, N. Ridley, and H. Latimer in the University Church of St. Mary," which is surely a peculiar way of saying that three English Protestant martyrs, educated by Cambridge, were burnt by Oxford. An entry lists *The Spiritual Works of Mercy*: "There are traditionally seven: (1) converting the sinner; (2) instructing the ignorant; (3) counselling the doubtful; (4) comforting the sorrowful; (5) bearing wrongs patiently; (6) forgiving injuries; (7) praying for the living and the dead." The *Oxford Dictionary* perhaps aspires only to the first three.

The book's arrogance toward Judaism seems equally un-Christian. "Hence," says the article on *Bible*, "the OT was ordained as the possession of the Church to whom (and not to the Jews) Christians held that since the Coming of the Lord it primarily belonged." Thus Aaron is "a type of Christ," the Burning Bush is "a type of the Blessed Virgin," and so on. "Theism," says the entry on that topic, "is in various forms the view of the world common to all Christian philosophers, and, in a less perfect form, also required by the Jewish and Mohammedan religions." Jewish monotheism is elsewhere identified as "deism." Dean Milman's *History of the Jews* was distinguished by "The freedom and freshness with which he handled the OT narratives, treating the Jews as an oriental tribe." *Mixed marriage* is defined as "A marriage between Christians of different religious allegiances." The brief and inadequate entry on *Covenant* makes no mention of what Jews regard as the fundamental Old Testament covenant, the covenant of circumcision with Abraham; and the writer of the entry on the parable of the Good Samaritan in the Gospel According to St. Luke apparently has no idea that the parable is an anti-Semitic anecdote.

The dictionary describes the achievements of a long line of Jewish converts to Christianity—from Johann Pfefferkorn in the sixteenth century devoting himself to the destruction of all Jewish sacred writings, to Michael Solomon Alexander in the nineteenth translating the Book of Common Prayer into Hebrew—and praises the missionary work that "resulted in some very talented converts." The biographical entry on General William Booth of the Salvation Army notes his "partly Jewish origin" and his "shrewd commercial sense." The entry on *Ghetto* gives no hint of disapproval, and the entry on *St. William of Norwich* says, "This is the first known case of the blood accusation against the Jews; but as the authorities took no action, the account is open to much suspicion," which suggests that the writer believes in Jewish ritual murder, and would not suspect an account where the authorities took action.

The dictionary's attitude toward science can only be called cavalier. There is no entry on Charles Darwin, and one of only twelve lines on Darwinism, but there is a lengthy account of T. H. Huxley, concluding, "Huxley had few claims to be considered an exact thinker." Do the authors of the *Oxford Dictionary* really believe that they have been ordained with the power to bind and loose in the realm of exact thought? Do they mean, for example, that Huxley was an inexact thinker as compared with St. Anselm, with his doctrine that Original Sin is transmitted by our "seminal identity" with Adam, or St. Augustine, with his distinctions between *dulia*, the reverence proper to saints, *hyperdulia*, the reverence proper to the Virgin Mary, and *latria*, the reverence proper to God alone? Are they comparing Huxley with the scientists who have distinguished among Ascetical, Moral, and Mystical Theology, or among the Church Militant on earth, the Church Expectant in Purgatory, and the Church Triumphant in Heaven?

Secular philosophy is handled very respectfully in the dictionary, and there are long entries on philosophers and various philosophic terms, but the social sciences are treated quite as insolently as is evolutionary biology. The entry on *Anthropology* knowledgeably defines Sacred Anthropology, the study of man as contrasted with God or angels in regard to "his creation, elevation to supernatural status, and his fall," but is woefully inadequate on secular anthropology, mentioning only Java Man and "handicraft-work," with no book on the subject later than 1912 in the appended bibliography. Of modern psychologists we are told that they "frequently interpret sin mainly as psychological disorder, often teach that the forms of temptation rooted in the appetites are primarily natural instincts, which as such ought, at least to some extent, to be satisfied." As might be expected, Freud's "disciple" Jung is the only acceptable psychologist: "Jung's ideas have found much approval also among students of religion and led to some fruitful developments."

Occasionally a catch in the dictionary's voice suggests that the arrogant tone actually conceals anxiety. The article on *Toleration* that begins so boldly—"Christianity, which claims to be the only true religion, has always been dogmatically intolerant"—ends with a whimper: "The modern problem is not so much one of toleration for other religious convictions as that of the preservation of religion in view of the general indifference and secularization of life." The entry on *Christian* notes that in modern times the word has tended "in nominally Christian countries" to lose any creedal significance and mean only something "ethically praiseworthy" or "socially customary." Another entry sadly recognizes the difficulty of keeping all these shiny Indian clubs spinning: "Popular ideas about the Trinity, in intention orthodox, often tend to be tritheistic in expression" (as does, we might note, the Apostles' Creed, with its statement that Jesus Christ "sitteth on the right hand of the Father"). Running through the book there is a nervous attempt to blame all sorts of things on contemporary secularization, a typical example being: "In the present century the growth of unbelief and superstition has encouraged the revival of astrology in certain quarters." The entry on *Burial Services*, however, gives the show away: for the Christian, death should be an occasion for joy, but "the prevalence of merely nominal Christianity made such joy not always fitting." The date of the change from joy to grief is given as the eighth century. There is a suggestion that Hitler and the H-bomb may change it all: "More recently the recognition of demonic forces in contemporary civilisation has led to a renewed theological emphasis on the gravity of sin in the spirit of St. Augustine and the Reformers." At the same time, there is a fear that the lower-class origins of Christianity (those Jews, that cow's stall) may alienate the better people, and the article on *Jesus Christ* is quick to point out "Jesus is once called the 'carpenter,' or stone mason, but the family though manual workers were not necessarily ill-educated." (Surely St. Joseph could have named all the letters of the Greek alphabet in court.)

No double-column work of fifteen hundred pages could be quite so monolithic, and of course the *Oxford Dictionary of the Christian Church* is not. Some of the entries show a genuine Christian charity toward enemies or opponents: the great persecutor Julian the Apostate did attempt "to reform the morals and elevate the theology of paganism, himself giving (it must be allowed) a conspicuous example of austerity and purpose"; the Puritan controversialist John Owen was "always tolerant and fair" and "Many of his writings show deep spiritual insight and a firm grasp of NT Christianity"; John Wesley was beyond doubt "one of the greatest Christians of his age." Some of the tensions that assenting to the Thirty-Nine Articles accumulates are worked off on art and literature, where the entries tend to be boldly opinionated: Fra Angelico's "greatest artistic talents lay in his use of brilliant colour and his powers of decoration"; Matthew Arnold's *Empedocles on Etna* "though poorly constructed as a dramatic work, contained some fine lyrics"; and so forth. Some of the book's entries in the fields of ecclesiology, liturgeology, and the study of vestments are frankly aesthetic, so that an account of a Yorkshire abbey concludes: "To-day the abbey lies in ruins, but the greater part of the exquisite Early English cruciform church remains, with many of the altars *in situ*."

Some of the ODCC is written in a theological jargon so muddy as to be almost incomprehensible, like the remark about Leontius of Byzantium: "He was a staunch upholder of the Chalcedonian Christology which he interpreted on Cyrilline principles, introducing the notion of the Enhypostasia." There are inexplicable omissions: one misses entries on the Rcd Dean of Canterbury, Simone Weil, and the foreskins of Jesus among the relics of early Christendom; some topics of chiefly American interest are similarly slighted, among them Covenant Theology, the Universalist Church, and Father Divine. Apparently the greater part of the book was written before the Dead Sea Scrolls made their impact, and the half-dozen mentions of the scrolls are added on as afterthoughts without the revisions they require in traditional opinions. Thus the entries on *Bible, Damascus Fragments, Essenes, Gnosticism, Logos,* and *Manuscripts of the Bible* had been superseded by the time they appeared.

This reviewer noted a few errors or confusions, and scholars will surely find many more. The information that Bar-Cochba's real name was "Simeon" is credited mysteriously to "the Jews"; actually we get it, like most of our information about the Second Revolt, from his surviving coins. An entry on *E*, one of the narratives believed to be embodied in the first books of the Bible, says the Elohist writer "regularly" calls God "Elohim"; actually he does so only until God reveals his true name to Moses, after which he too calls God "Jahveh." *Bodisatva* is defined as "a title of the Buddha"; more correctly *Bodhisattva*, it is the stage of spiritual perfection just below that of the Buddha. The entry on *taurobolium* identifies it with the worship of Cybele and Attis, not Mithras. An entry on Joanna Southcott says that her sealed box of prophecies was opened in 1927 and proved to contain a woman's nightcap and a lottery ticket; that was someone's practical joke, and the real box has not yet been opened, since her conditions require an Archbishop of Canterbury willing to open it. *Theosophists* are identified as regarding "Christ as purely human," as they certainly do not.

Where it is not wrong, the dictionary is often maddeningly vague. It says of the Roman Catholic Biblical Commission, "Among its most notable decisions are those on the Mosaic authorship of the Pentateuch (1906), on the authenticity and historicity of the Fourth Gospel (1907), and on the Synoptic problem (1912)" without explaining what was decided. It refers to Emerson's "extremely unconventional views on the Eucharist" without revealing them; it says that Archbishop Lang "played an important part in public affairs in connection with the abdication of Edward VIII" without saying *what* part; it notes that Charles Péguy "had a strong faith in the Eucharist which domestic circumstances made it impossible for him to receive" without taking us beyond that teasing point; it says of St. Peter, "There are considerable historical reasons for believing that his tomb in St. Peter's in Rome is authentic" but cites none of them. Occasionally a cross-reference promises an entry that is not produced.

Where the *Oxford Dictionary* delights is in its odd and relatively useless information, the gleanings of thousands of unavailable and specialized publications (as well as of such standard works as the *Dictionary of National Biography* and the *Oxford English Dictionary*). One can learn that the theft of a book from the Ambrosian Library at Milan is a sin from which only the Pope can absolve; that there have been Binitarians as well as Trinitarians and Unitarians; that St. Catherine, martyred on a wheel, is the patron saint of wheelwrights and attorneys; that the Ethiopian Church still circumcises; that St. Francis of Assisi is thought to have made the first *crèche*; that the Eastern Church forbids fourth marriages; that "tawdry" is derived from the cheap finery sold at the fair of St. Audry or Ethelreda; that barrel organs and trumpets called "vamping horns" were widely used in eighteenth-century English churches; and that the Wandering Jew made an appearance in Salt Lake City in 1868. There are some wonderful characters, ranging from St. Alphonsus Liguori—a prominent Neapolitan lawyer who realized the transitoriness of earthly glory and renounced the world when his client lost a hundred-thousand-pound lawsuit on a technicality—to Jenny Geddes, a Scottish vegetable-seller who achieved immortality by throwing her folding stool at the head of the Bishop of Edinburgh in St. Giles' Cathedral when the hated Scottish Prayer Book was introduced.

In places, the dictionary even reveals a dry wit. We learn of *Canaan:* "Of the original inhabitants (called Canaanites) some survived, and appear to have had a reactionary influence upon the development and maintenance of Hebrew monotheism." Of St. Gemma Galgani we are told: "Apart from her conviction of occasional diabolical possession, her spiritual life was normally peaceful." An account of the Holy Sepulchre in Jerusalem remarks: "The scene on Sunday mornings, when the various rites, all with music, are proceeding simultaneously, is unique in Christendom." On *obscurantism:* "Christians have sometimes been charged with it by secular critics, and professing Christians have also sometimes made the charge against one another, but it has rarely, if ever, been admitted." On the doctrine of the early Church, based on Matthew 22:14 ("For many are called, but few are chosen"), that the number of the damned is considerably larger than the number of the saved: "The tendency of most modern theologians who have been bold enough to seek an answer to this and other such questions has been towards a more optimistic view." With such leaven to leaven the lump, perhaps even the *Oxford Dictionary of the Christian Church,* for all its black sins may yet, in later editions, be numbered among the saved.

Myth,
Ritual, and
Nonsense

The Child Ballads

1. From "The Raggle Taggle Ballads O"

[1951]

THE BOOK WE NEED on the ballads would go about things very un-
fashionably. It would begin—it *must* begin—by asking the basic
questions, what *are* the ballads, how do they originate, how and
why do they transmit? These tough questions, particularly the matter of origin, cannot be evaded, because everything else is related to
them. Origin implies structure, structure implies function. If you
believe, with Percy, that the ballads were written by minstrels, then
they take on certain formal characteristics and values of minstrel
poetry, they are aimed at the entertainment of a noble audience,
and without extensive alterations they could hardly serve a peasant
group or be preserved by it. If, on the other hand, you believe with
Louise Pound that they were written or shaped by monks for a
popular audience, then they take on other formal characteristics
and values, and have to meet the test of new didactic functions and
an even more unlikely popular preservation. If you believe, with
Gummere, that they were composed by an improvising throng
through a process centering in incremental repetition, then they
would have the stanza-unit structure of "The Old Chisholm Trail"
or the blues, rather than a central dramatic core, and would have a
spontaneous-expression function that would make composing new
ballads far preferable to handing on old ones.

It seems beyond question to this reviewer that the ballad, like
forms from counting-out rhyme to Bible myth whose origin has
already been established, is of ancient anonymous collective origin.

It derives from a ritual, of which it is the dramatic text, what Theodor Gaster has called the "libretto," presumably sung by a narrator, while the actor-dancers pantomime the action. When the ritual dies out, the dramatic song continues in oral currency, adapting new meanings to fit new times and functions. If the ballad is this, then it never derives from a historical incident, although part of the "identification" process of later singers is to tack on historical names and references. When Evelyn Kendrick Wells says in *The Ballad Tree*: " 'Mary Hamilton' (173), 'The Death of Queen Jane' (170), and 'The Bonny Earl of Murray' (181), based on actual incidents, have lost their topical allusions and developed the note of common human appeal," she is precisely reversing the actual order of events. "Mary Hamilton" and "The Death of Queen Jane" are the familiar patterns of the consort sacrificed for producing a son who will grow up to kill the king (in other variants, like "The Cruel Mother" (Child 20), it is the baby sacrificed). These patterns have been identified with, respectively, a licentious court (at which there was no Mary Hamilton and no such scandal), and a queen who died twelve days after childbirth (or soon enough to be identified with a Caesarean story). "The Bonny Earl of Murray" is the familiar pattern of the ritual contender for the queen (the ballad even suggests the ritual contests) identified with a handsome earl who had the bad luck to incur the jealousy of King James.

If the ballads originate out of rite, at a stage in antiquity we can reconstruct from survivals in the texts—a matrilineal, totemic, hunting society of great primitiveness—then no ballads can arise later, when these conditions no longer obtain, although old ones may be vastly transformed to fit new conditions (it is in this sense that folk literature is dead, that it can only be transmitted and adapted, no longer originated). If any ballads seem to center in comparatively modern historical events, they have either been entirely transformed (as a ritual seasonal combat might become a border raid) or else are what we must call "broadsides," modern poems written by individuals in the ballad form, which may or may not gain some measure of oral currency. If ballads arise in antiquity out of myth and rite, like Greek drama and epic, their perfection is not the product of "communal recreation" or any shaping in transmission, but is something they begin with, and all transmission tends toward deterioration and simplification (this seems to fit almost all the evidence, and where it does not, we have to presume that descent is not from the broadside or inferior text but from a common ancestor). Finally, if ballads arise out of basic human rituals, common to many of the cultures of the world, and fit basic human needs, equally common, diffusion becomes no likelier than polygenesis, and any ballad could have arisen independently anywhere.

The only usable classification, in the sort of book to fit our needs, would be by ritual pattern. Many ballads center around sacrificial killings—M. J. C. Hodgart in *The Ballads* notes "Sir Hugh" (Child 155) and "Lamkin" (Child 93)—while others are sacrificial escapes: the conquest of Bluebeard or the Minotaur by the virgin who breaks the sequence of sacrifices, "Lady Isabel and the Elf Knight" (Child 4) and "Babylon" (Child 14); or a ransom-rescue, "The Maid Freed From the Gallows" (Child 95). Some center in seasonal combats, like "The Gypsy Laddie" (Child 200), while others tell only part of the Persephone story, like "James Harris (The Daemon Lover)" (Child 243). Some are King of the May rites, like the Robin Hood ballads, or woodland animal combats like "Johnie Cock" (Child 114). Some are family myths of incest and murder, very similar to the Greek stories, like "Edward" (Child 13) and "Sheath and Knife" (Child 16). Others center in marriage combats, or rites of magical transformation, or initiation-rebirth, or king-killing, or sacred marriage and totem feast. Only when we can see the ballads in terms of these origins can we begin to study their development into what we presently have.

The next essential is a body of terms for the process of change, a terminology for the "folk work" analogous to Freud's for the "dream work." We need not only to recognize collective variants of such psychoanalytic processes as condensation, displacement, splitting, and secondary elaboration, but we must develop the academic concept of "folk etymology" into a broad concept of "folk rationalization" whereby ballads are rewon as meaningful by the alteration of obscurities into familiar concepts. Against this strong tendency of the material to alter to fit new conditions we must oppose an equally strong conservative tendency, and must analyze variation in terms of their interaction. What this requires, of course, is an actual literary criticism of texts, an analysis of *struc-*

ture, but where the criticism of art literature is three dimensional, dealing with a relative fixity, folk criticism must be four dimensional, treating a work in a constant process of variation in time.

Just as this structural discussion is based on a theory of origin, it must take into account a theory of function. The ballad begins in collective rite, it makes the tribe's crops grow; to the extent that it survives in a folk group however attenuated, it has comparable public functions; even sung by an individual in a recording studio, or heard by one in a night club, it produces individual symbolic actions that are our modern protestant equivalents to the public rituals. If Frazer is our authority on the function of the organic tribal rite, Malinowski's methods show us how the ballad functions for a surviving community, and Kenneth Burke points up the individual symbolic action. The dazzling equations between one end of the process and the other, between the tribe's fertility dance and the individual's sexual twitch, have been the special insight of psychoanalysis, and a line of workers from Freud to Roheim have given us usable correlations. All this, of course, assumes an essential identity of function. Where function alters, and a Robin Hood that was a scapegoat-killing ceremony (Frazer), the affirmation of a moral pattern of behavior (Malinowski), a miming of parricide (Freud), and so forth, becomes politicalized (a banner of Saxon protest against Norman tyranny), we must draw on historical knowledge and insight to treat a whole new set of functions. In this case, meanings have been reversed until what was a symbol of organic community, the spring rite of death and rebirth, becomes precisely its opposite, a symbol of alienation *from* the community, a social protest, and the old vessel bears very different contents. In "The Cutty Wren" (not in Child) we get a similar process, the development from a totem rite to a vigorous protest against the medieval barons, and the magical and incantatory style of the song becomes a cryptic talk of conspiracy.

Here it might be well to glance at the conjectural history of one ballad in more detail. "The Gypsy Laddie" is the story of a wife, identified in some texts as the Countess of Cassilis, who is charmed away from her husband by Johnie Faa, the king of the gypsies. The lord pursues her with his men, in a majority of Child's eleven versions, and recaptures her from the gypsies, who are promptly executed. In the typical American versions, like "The Gypsy Davie" or "The Raggle-Taggle Gypsies O," however, she prefers to stay with the gypsies, and sends her lord packing. As Child makes clear about his versions, the ballad as a historical record is absurd: no Countess of Cassilis apparently did or could have eloped with any Johnie Faa. "Johnie Faa" was for centuries the traditional name for the king of the gypsies, but how did the lady's name get into the ballad? A Mr. Macmath suggested very plausibly to Child that the opening line "The gypsies they came to my lord Cassilis' gate" is a folk corruption of "The gypsies they came to my lord's castle gate" and nothing more.

With history dismissed, we can begin to look for the ballad's origins. We know that the ritual combat between the forces of summer and winter was performed in many parts of the world, in many different guises, and has survived in England in such forms as Mummers Plays, Morris and Sword Dances, etc. Frazer reports a typical Manx May Day ceremony in which the two sides battled for their respective queens. All the evidence insists that the origin of "The Gypsy Laddie" was such a spring ritual battle, at which the lady, or Persephone figure, representing life and vegetation, who had been seized by the dark men of winter in the fall ceremonies and ostensibly held captive by them underground, was won back from them by the forces of summer. As the rite died out and its meaning became obscured, the libretto continued as a ballad, and by a gradual rationalizing the dark men of winter became wife-stealing gypsies, the light men of summer became the lord's loyal retainers, and, by processes suggested above, the characters gradually acquired a locality and an identity; the sequence going from rite to drama, drama to narrative song, narrative song to pseudo-historical account.

The most interesting evidence of this is the conclusion of Child's text E, taken from *The Scottish Gallovidian Encyclopaedia*, published in 1824. Having no idea what to make of these final stanzas, Child dismisses them as "entirely untraditional" and "spurious." Instead of the conventional conclusion of the A text:

> And we were fifteen well-made men,
> Altho we were nae bonny;

And we were put a' down for ane,
　A fair young wanton lady.

E concludes:

Quoth the gypsies, We're fifteen weel-made men,
　Tho the maist o us be ill bred ay,
Yet it wad be a pity we should a' hang for ane,
　Wha fashed himself wi your fair lady.

Quoth the lady, My lord, forgive them a',
　For they nae ill eer did ye,
And gie ten guineas to the chief, Jockie Faw,
　For he is a worthy laddie.

The lord he hearkened to his fair dame,
　And O the gypsies war glad ay!
They danced round and round their merry Jockie Faw,
　And roosed the gypsie laddie.

Sae the lord rade hame wi his charming spouse,
　Owre the halls and the haughs sae whunnie,
And the gypsies slade down by yon bonny burnside,
　To beek themsells there sae sunnie.

Cheesy as this is stylistically, it is no cheesier than the dialogue of many of the Mumming Plays, and there is no reason whatsoever for dismissing it as spurious. It is the authentic ending of folk drama at a late stage—nothing is serious, it was just a play, the villains take a bow and are rewarded, and everyone dances and gets drunk.

The problem of the American texts, where the lady remains with the gypsies, rejects her husband (who comes alone), and affirms the romantic advantage of true love in a plaidie over landed wealth, is a little more complicated. The likeliest conjecture is that they derive from another rite, perhaps the fall ceremonies at which the lady is taken and proves unable or unwilling to return. If, however, they come from the same source as the British texts, then they have been entirely altered in ending (all the ingredients for the refusal exist in Child's F and G, and H and I, from Shropshire and Ireland respectively, clearly suggest it) to fit new psychological function, and what once affirmed the holy regularity of the seasonal pattern now affirms, to the hard-working rural housewife, only her choice of true love and hardship rather than the life of loveless luxury no one has offered her.

Once we can handle ballads in this fashion, many of the problems that beset Miss Wells and Hodgart disappear. On a continuum from rite to song, with dance and drama in its background, the ballad can be seen going off at one point to be stitched together into epic, at another to be glamorously rewritten as romance. The broadsides and fakes, lacking this origin, have another structure and style; where they get into oral currency at all, they have another fate and function. A broadside like "Jesse James" fills some of the needs that the Robin Hood ballads did, moving in on the folk form, but it is not a ballad, and it can only partially substitute for a ballad. When we can tell ritual ballad from broadside, we can handle the latter as art work rather than folk work, equally valid but another kind of thing, and value each in its own terms. For those who, like this writer, think that the ritual ballad at its best reaches an aesthetic height shared only by the greatest products of the human imagination, the responsibilities for creating a whole new study of the ballad are enormous, but the rewards, in comprehension and deepened appreciation of the most misapprehended body of great poetry left to us, can be equally enormous.

2. Ballads for Americans

[1955]

THE ENORMOUS POPULARITY of dubious American folk song in our time has never really affected the scholarly study of the ballad, which goes on classifying its Scandinavian analogues and disputing its eighteenth-century emendations oblivious to the planging of guitars all around. MacEdward Leach's anthology *The Ballad Book* is the first real attempt to bring the two groups together, to extend Professor Francis James Child's generally accepted corpus to include American "ballads" like "The Jam on Gerry's Rock" and

"Betsy from Pike," and, presumably, to supplant Kittredge's one-volume edition of Child in classroom use with this Anglo-American medley.

My disagreement with Professor Leach regarding the origin, structure, and function of the ballad is fundamental, and a great many general statements made in his introduction seem to me demonstrably untrue on the evidence of his own texts. The communal theories of ballad origin from which my own views derive are in turn dismissed in his introduction as the fallacies of nineteenth-century scholars "led astray by lack of precise definition." At least three statements in Leach's introduction, however, I can heartily concur with and I consider to be points that badly need making: that the ballad is not the wild and irregular verse form the Romantic Movement took it to be, but is rigidly conventional and regular *in terms of its tune*; that "by and large the ballad tends to degenerate" in folk transmission, not polish gemlike; and that the finest American ballads, with "a spontaneity and a seriousness that the others lack," are the Negro ballads, such as "John Henry," "Frankie and Albert," and "Stagolee."

Leach prints about 180 of the 305 ballads to which Child gave numbers, some in as many as four variants, with an emphasis on recently collected American texts and on Danish analogues in English translation. These are intelligently selected, and except for a few copying errors (stanza 19 of "Tam Lin," stanza 14 of "The Twa Magicians") they are carefully edited. All but a handful have some headnotes, in the scholar's moderate and sensible tone, even where they hit obvious absurdity, as in the case of Phillips Barry's theory that Lamkin was a leper (Leach calls it "a rather wide speculation"). The editor tends to have a good eye, or ear, for "the nice literary hand of the 18th-century poet," and to know a broadside when he sees one. He includes at least one good early text unknown to Child (of "The Great Silkie of Sule Skerry") and adds English broadsides and a few English songs Child did not consider ballads if he knew them ("The Bitter Withy," "The Corpus Christi Carol," and "The Bold Fisherman"), where the weight of later opinion would tend to agree with Leach. For the most part, however, his additions are "American ballads by origin or adoption" and American variants of Child ballads.

Leach includes no music (except for two examples in the intro-duction), arguing that ballad tunes cannot be indicated accurately, and then admitting delicately that problems of space and expense may have had something to do with his decision. Despite his view that "ballad structure cannot be studied accurately without con-stant reference to the music," he does not even indicate (as Child did and almost everyone since has) where the tunes may be found. An appended "Selected List of Ballad Recordings" may have been assumed to make up for this lack, but it is so haphazard, incom-plete, inadequate, and uncritical as to be just about useless. The list includes recordings of songs not found in the book, and distin-guishes neither short-play records from long-play nor out-of-print records from those obtainable. Its only critical feature, an asterisk to indicate recordings "especially recommended for authenticity," seems rather arbitrary, awarding its cachet to several notorious Greenwich Village hillbillies and refusing it to, say, a Finnish recording (not authentic as what, Finnish?).

To those of us who believe that the ballad is a very ancient anon-ymous communal work originating in ritual drama, that it derives from the sung text of an acted sacrificial rite, and that its making is a closed account, Leach's insistence on individual modern author-ship seems pointless. It seems to leave him no distinction at all between ballads and broadsides, other than the author's talent, and catches him inevitably in the contradiction between such state-ments as "the originators of the traditional ballads had no literary pretensions, no literary sophistication," and "One needs only to read 'Mary Hamilton' or 'The Unquiet Grave' or 'Child Waters' or 'Sir Patrick Spens' to know that poets and skillful artificers were behind these ballads." In either theory of modern authorship, what can he mean by saying that "Sir Lionel" is "a tale that goes back perhaps to the cult of the Great Mother"?

Leach believes that many, if not most, ballads are historical ("a stirring local event occurs in a community"), but he keeps running into the absence of history: "The name of Sir Patrick Spens appears in no Scottish or English records," "Percy, said to be killed at 'Chevy Chase,' was in command of the English" fourteen years later. His insistence that the structure or form of ballads is realistic and journalistic, like the "modern newspaper story," rather than mythic and dramatic, leaves him unable to see the obvious miming in such ballads as "The Maid Freed from the Gallows," which he believes *developed* into children's game, drama, and *cante-fable* in America, and leads him flatly to base the Robin Hood dramas on the ballads, rather than the reverse. Leach's sense of the ballad's function as story-telling and reportorial, rather than magical and symbolic, leaves him constantly puzzled over what seem to him to be mysterious accidents of transmission: "The Lass of Roch Royal" is "rather rare in spite of the fact that it is a moving and tragic story"; he writes of "The Bonny Earl of Murray," "One wonders why all the dramatic story was passed by, by the ballad maker."

Insofar as the ballad is ritual in origin, dramatic in structure, and magical in function, its true affinities are not with tear-jerking English broadsides like "Young Edwin in the Lowlands Low," which Leach aspires to add to the canon, but with ancient English ritual and totemic songs like "The Cutty Wren" and "The Derby Ram," which he ignores; or with "The Lyke-Wake Dirge," which he prints in the introduction only to show the difference between its lyric character and the narrative structure of "Willie's Lyke-Wake."

Fundamentally, our judgment of Leach's ambitious attempt to revise Child's corpus must hinge on the problem of the ballad in America, and here if we do not watch our steps we are apt to sink out of sight in waving fields of corn. Variants of about a hundred Child ballads have been recovered in this country through assiduous labor, and most of them have ill repaid that labor. There are occasional touches of life and vigor, as in a Tennessee "Johnnie Scot" in which wicked King Edward asks:

> "Is this young Johnny Scot?" he said,
> "Or old Johnny Scotling's son,
> Or is it the young bastard-getter
> From Scotland has come in?"

Most of the American texts are corrupt and wretched beyond belief. A Vermont "Elfin Knight" has for refrain:

> Fluma luma lokey sloomy
> From a teaslum tasalum templum
> Fluma luma lokey sloomy.

A North Carolina "Earl Brand" turns into jumble:

> "My father is of a regis king,
> My mother's a quaker's queen."

American folk etymology seems to be so half-hearted, so disinclined to push until *some* meaning is obtained, that William's foreboding dream of slaughtered swine in "Fair Margaret and Sweet William" becomes in a Kentucky variant: "I dreamed last night of young science in my room." A Nova Scotia refrain for "The Gypsy Laddie" goes:

> Red Lady dingo, dingo day,
> Red Lady dingo, dingo Daisy;
> Red Lady dingo, dingo day,
> She's away with the Gypsy Daisy.

Where the American Child ballads are hopelessly deteriorated, corrupt and meaningless in good part, the American originals are mostly (with the exception of the Negro songs) the inept work of broadside writers and hacks, fairly described by Leach as "stiff with literary starch," or "insipid and cheaply sentimental." In a few cases (such as "Young Charlotte," written by Seba Smith) we know the poet's name and have the printed text before it went into folk dissemination. The American ballad problem is actually not a problem of origins at all but one of folk transmission, the sentimentalization and deterioration of the Child ballads, and the downward migration of the products of broadside writer or hack poet. If "Jesse James," "Casey Jones," and their like are narrative songs of considerable value, we need not call them folk ballads to appreciate them, and can fairly recognize that they are the compositions of anonymous song writers of ability, and that folk-singing no more entitles them to be folk products than it does "My Old Kentucky Home" or "Sweet Adeline."

The true English and Scottish popular ballads are something else again. At their best[1] they are an unrivaled tragic poetry with the

---

[1] In an article, "The Language of Scottish Poetry," in *Kenyon Review*, Winter, 1954, I suggested as candidates toward a classic tradition: "The Wife of Usher's Well," "The Twa Sisters," "Edward," "Clerk Saunders," "Sir Patrick Spens," "Johnie Cock," "Mary Hamilton," "The Bonny Earl of Murray," "Child Maurice," "Young Waters," "The Baron of Brackley," "Lamkin," "The Cruel Mother," "The Twa Corbies," and "The Daemon Lover."

sort of dramatic tension we are most familiar with in Attic drama. The shock we experience in Euripides' *Medea* when the infanti- cidal witch appears above the stage in a chariot drawn by dragons, in place of the *theophany* we have been expecting, is the same sort of shock (deeply disturbing and just on the edge of the ludicrous) we get at the ending of "Gil Brenton":

> Now or a month was come an gone,
> This lady bare a bonny young son.

> An it was well written on his breast-bane,
> "Gil Brenton is my father's name."

The pity and terror of Oedipus' recognition of his crimes in Sophocles' play is the same pity and terror we experience in the last line of "Edward," and we may even find it in the fourth stanza of "Lizie Wan," when Lizie replies flatly to her brother's question about her health:

> "I ail, I ail, dear brither," she said,
> "And I'll tell you a reason for why;
> There is a child between my twa sides,
> Between you, dear billy, and I."

When the innocent May Catheren will not burn in the bonfire at the end of "Young Hunting," and she is taken out and the false lady who slew Hunting is substituted, all we need be told is that the fire:

> O it took upon her cheek, her cheek,
> An it took upon her chin,
> An it took on her fair body,
> She burnt like hoky-gren.

Leach's glossary defines "hoky-gren" as "blanketed fire" (the term is somewhat disputed), but what the line says, in contrast to "her fair body," is definable in no glossary. Richard Blackmur says of Yeats's "A Deep-Sworn Vow" that "the words accumulate by the simplest means an intolerable excitement," and there could be no better description of the poetic language of the ballads, as we get it, say, in "The Hunting of the Cheviot":

> For Wetharryngton my harte was wo,
>   that euer he slayne shulde be;
> For when both his leggis wear hewyne in to,
>   yet he knyled and fought on hys kny.

It is this quality in the ballads, the language of purest incantation, that no poet has ever been able to get in his ballad imitations (with Coleridge's "Ancient Mariner" perhaps coming closest). It comes into the ballad from myth and rite, and if Yeats achieves it in poems like "A Deep-Sworn Vow," as a hymn in a private redemptive religion, it is wholly lacking in such of his imitation ballads as "Father Gilligan."

The quality of the ballads that our poets *have* been able to achieve (I think of such poems as John Crowe Ransom's "Captain Carpenter") is their irony, the underplayed contrast in "Lord Ingram and Chiel Wyet":

> Lord Ingram wood her Lady Maisery
>   Into her father's ha;
> Chiel Wyet wood her Lady Maisery
>   Amang the sheets so sma.

It is the irony of Musgrave in "Little Musgrave and Lady Barnard," caught in bed with the lady by Lord Barnard and on the edge of his doom, replying to Barnard's "Doest thou find my lady sweet?":

> "I find her sweet," quoth Little Musgrave,
>   "The more 't is to my paine;
> I would gladly give three hundred pounds
>   That I were on yonder plaine."

Perhaps the only profitable relationships of our poetry to our folk tradition (and the great English and Scottish ballads *are* our folk tradition, not "The Little Mohee") are ironic ones, are in fact gestures emphasizing our distance from a ballad folk.

I once believed that the modern poet could draw on the rhythms of ballads and blues with Auden, on the flatness of folk speech with Fearing, and I can recall writing a pronunciamento in college to that effect. I am now somewhat more skeptical. It may be that all our poets can learn from these great ballads is how to write something very different, another kind of incantation, more like negative magic, drenched with irony. Empson's "Missing Dates," that ominous, lilting anticipation of radioactive fallout, is the sort of ironic building-at-some-distance-from-the-ruins-of-balladry that I mean. Perhaps what MacEdward Leach's ambitious *Ballad Book* can do best is remind us that America is not really what the chauvinists would have her, the heir of all the ages, but only a late colony of Europe trying very hard to lay the foundations for a native culture.

3. *The Child Ballad in America: Some Aesthetic Criteria*

[1957]

MOST OF THE ATTENTION that has been paid to the words of the Child ballad in America has been scholarly; I should like to propose some critical considerations. The most comprehensive study we have had in the field, Tristram P. Coffin's critical bibliography, *The British Traditional Ballad in North America*, is an invaluable work, but it is confined by its nature to description and classification primarily in terms of plot—what John Crowe Ransom would call poetic structure rather than texture. In his introductory essay "A Description of Variation in the Traditional Ballad of America," Coffin manages to discuss most varieties of alteration, in texture as well as structure, with their causes, but as a scholar he is forced to discuss them rather neutrally and eschew conclusions, whereas as critics we may build on his work and reprehend as forcibly as we wish. Coffin lists some factors causing change (we might say degeneration) in basic plot or mood as follows:

> Such headings would include the elimination of action, development toward lyric, loss of detail through forgetting; fragmentation; convention and cliche; localization; the effect of literalness; rationalization; sentimentalization; moralization; manner of use; secondary growth; new ballads which rise from the old; and mergers.

Somewhat less neutrally, he adds later: "Squeamishness and religious scruples continually haunt the American folk singer."

I should like to consider the problem rather differently, primarily in terms of an Old World configuration we find in the Child ballads, and a New World configuration they adapt to here. For convenience, my examples will be taken wherever possible from MacEdward Leach's new anthology, *The Ballad Book*, which offers a representative American text or two for many of its Child ballads. We must first note that fewer than half of Child's 305 ballads ever got to America at all, and of those that did, most never attained much popularity here. Only a handful have been widespread in the United States. Mrs. Jane Gentry of Hot Springs, North Carolina, sang sixty-four different songs for Cecil Sharp, at least fifteen of them Child ballads. Her repertoire, although unusually full, seems fairly typical, and her fifteen traditional ballads are a good sampling of some of the more popular ones in America. She sang "The False Knight upon the Road" (Child 3), "The Twa Sisters" (Child 10), "Edward" (Child 13), "The Cherry Tree Carol" (Child 54), "Young Hunting" (Child 68), "Lord Thomas and Fair Annet" (Child 73), "The Wife of Usher's Well" (Child 79), "Little Musgrave and Lady Barnard" (Child 81), "Lamkin" (Child 93), "Johnie Scot" (Child 99), "Geordie" (Child 209), "James Harris (The Daemon Lover)" (Child 243), "The Gray Cock" (Child 248), "Our Goodman" (Child 274), and "The Sweet Trinity" (Child 286).

Among the important ballads that never got to America are some that seem too grimly supernatural, such as "Gil Brenton" (Child 5); some patently too disreputable, such as "Kempy Kaye" (Child 33); and a group in which villainy triumphs or evil goes unpunished, among them "Clerk Saunders" (Child 69), "Young Waters" (Child 94), "Johnie Armstrong" (Child 169), and "The Baron of Brackley" (Child 203). Among those of very limited appearance here, for similar reasons, are such fine ballads as "The Twa Magicians" (Child 44), "Sir Patrick Spens" (Child 58), "The Unquiet Grave" (Child 78), "Child Maurice" (Child 83), and "Johnie Cock" (Child 114).

Those ballads that do survive the ocean voyage suffer curious sea changes. Magic and the supernatural slough off readily, even where they seem the ballad's point, and demons, ghosts, elves, and mermaids rationalize and humanize. The terrible death curse of the victim in "The Twa Sisters," spoken by a harp strung with her hair, tends to disappear in the American versions, along with the harp, and in the common American "Bow Down" texts (if the girl is not actually rescued), only the miller is punished, in an absurd ending that ignores the elder sister:

> The miller was hung in his own mill-gate,
> For drowning of my sister Kate.

A Maine text of "The Cruel Mother" (Child 20) has the murdered children return, but drops their judgment and curse. None of the enormous number of American versions of "James Harris (The Daemon Lover)," so far as I know, keeps the lover convincingly demonic or retains his cloven hoof. In the American texts the wife of a house carpenter elopes with her sailor beau, the ship springs an accidental leak (in one Virginia text nothing happens to it at all), and the wife regrets her impetuousity. As against the satanic ending of Scott's version:

> He strack the tap-mast wi' his hand,
> The fore-masts wi' his knee,
> And he brake that gallant ship in twain,
> And sank her in the sea.

an American broadside concludes:

> A curse be on the sea-faring men
> Oh, cursed be their lives,
> For while they are robbing the House-Carpenter
> And coaxing away their wives.

Like magic and the supernatural, sex, incest, and kin-murder tend to disappear or diminish, in a folk process very like individual repression. In the typical American "Son Davie" or "Little Yaller Dog" variants of "Edward," the murder is of a brother rather than a father, and there is never the final revelation of the mother's instigation that gives the last line of the Percy text some of the pity and terror of the end of the *Tyrannus*. (Despite Archer Taylor's argument in *"Edward" and "Sven I*

Rosengård", I cannot for a moment accept the parricide and the mother's complicity as literary additions.) Coffin notes a characteristic American tendency to make kin-murder fratricide rather than parricide, and in a version collected by Cecil Sharp in Tennessee this has gone to the end of the line and the victim is a brother-in-law. Coffin points out that in American texts of "The Cruel Brother" (Child 11), "The Twa Brothers" (Child 49), and "Lizie Wan" (Child 51), the British suggestions or assertions of incest "have vanished or are rapidly vanishing." Examples of the toning down of the frank sexuality of the ballads in America are almost innumerable, and we might note that even the mention of the lady's nakedness in "Lady Isabel and the Elf Knight" (Child 4) seems on its way out.

Much of the starkness of tragedy diminishes as the ballads transform in our culture. The terrible ending of "Lady Maisry" (Child 65) in Jamieson's text, Lord William's announcement of his vengeance for the burning of his betrothed:

> "O I'll gar burn for you, Maisry,
> Your father an your mother;
> And I'll gar burn for you, Maisry,
> Your sister an your brother.

> "An I'll gar burn for you, Maisry,
> The chief of a' your kin;
> An the last bonfire that I come to,
> Mysel I will cast in."

is lost in all the American versions, where he kisses the corpse, writes his will, and dies. Another ending at the stake, the burning of the fair wicked lady "like hoky-gren" in Herd's text of "Young Hunting," becomes in the Kentucky "Loving Henry" an inconclusive dialogue with a little birdie. Lord Barnard's fearful punishment of his wife in "Little Musgrave and Lady Barnard" in the *Wit Restored* version:

> He cut the paps from off her brest;
> Great pitty it was to see
> That some drops of this ladie's heart's blood
> Ran trickling downe her knee.

becomes a more chivalric (and considerably less significant) splitting of her head in the Kentucky "Little Mathie Grove" and the New Hampshire "Lord Banner." Where the British texts of "The Gypsy Laddie" (Child 200) have the gypsies put down, often executed, and the lady restored to her husband, in the American "Gypsy Davy"'s the lord comes alone to appeal to his wife and is repudiated as she chooses romantic love and freedom rather than loveless wealth and security (here the opposition of the American ethos to tragedy seems very clear). In a Kentucky "Black Jack Davie" the gypsy casts the glamourie owre her by babbling, "How old are you, my pretty little Miss?" and she responds with the proud declaration of love, "I'll be sixteen next Sunday."

Many of the Child ballads in America lose not only the tragic movement that Francis Fergusson has called "from Purpose through Passion to Perception," but any narrative or dramatic movement at all. "Riddles Wisely Expounded" (Child 1) reduces itself to the riddles and answers alone in Virginia, and "The Elfin Knight" (Child 2) to a comic dialogue of tasks and countertasks in Kentucky, North Carolina, and Vermont. "Mary Hamilton" (Child 173) has dwindled down to a lyric lament in Maine and Virginia, without any of the story but the protest over the queen's ingratitude, and in one Virginia text, to three stanzas that do not mention the queen. "John of Hazelgreen" (Child 293) has become two lyric stanzas in Virginia; "The Lass of Roch Royal" (Child 76) is almost exclusively the two well-known shoe-my-foot stanzas, and finally, in Davis' U text, it comes down to what seems an irreducible single stanza.

As these ballads relinquish their Old World tragedy and ominousness, they adapt to an American configuration in which, Kenneth Burke has noted, death is held "in exceptionally bad repute." One paradoxical way they become less real is by the addition of realistic touches. The murdering brother in "The Two Brothers" goes to "some graded school" in a version Sharp collected in Virginia, and Lady Maisry's lover runs a still in a version of Child 65 he obtained in Kentucky. A Maine Lord Randall leaves his poisoner "a barrel of powder to blow her up high," and Young Hunting's murderer in South Carolina "sits out on her porch playing her piano." At the extreme of the process, ballads are trivialized to the point where they become comic songs about animals. "Sir Lionel" (Child 18) becomes "Old Bangum" (in the opinion of some scholars), a ludicrous fight with a boar, and in a Missouri version has the refrain:

> Dillum down dillum
> Dillum down
> Kibby ky cuddle down killy quo cum.

One of the grandest and most terrifying ballads in the canon, "The Twa Corbies" (Child 26), becomes the parody crow song "Billy Magee Magaw," and the new-slain knight is a butchered horse in Iowa, a pig with three cork legs in Virginia, and a poor little lamb crying "Baa, Baa, Baa" elsewhere.

Another type of acclimatization is a Christianizing at best and a vague pietizing at worst. "The Wife of Usher's Well," a nakedly pagan ballad about the ironic limits of magical power, becomes the American "Three Babes" or "Lady Gay," in which Christian prayer returns the children to Usher's Well and higher spiritual responsibility carries them back to Heaven. The ending of a Georgia text reads as though it were deliberate parody of the familiar Scott version:

> "Wake up, wake up," said the oldest one,
> "The chickens will soon crow for day,
> And yander stands our Saviour dear,
> And to Him we now must go.
>
> "Farewell, dear father, farewell, dear mother,
> Farewell to Aunt Kate and Kane,
> For yander stands our Saviour dear,
> And to Him we now must remain."

"Sir Hugh, or The Jew's Daughter" (Child 155) has lost its serious Christianity, the power of the Virgin and her holy well producing the miraculous voice of the corpse out of it, in many American versions, but it has gained a superficial Christian piety in Indiana, Connecticut, and other texts in the boy's burial with Bible and prayer book at his head and feet. Sometimes morality reverses the whole dramatic action of the ballad, as in the Missouri "Earl Brand" (Child 7) where the girl turns against her lover when he slays her father, or the Maine "Riddles Wisely Expounded" where the Devil has become a suitor captivated by the girl's wit, and the ballad concludes handsomely:

> Now maidens, pretty maidens,
> Be neither coy nor shy,
> But always, when a lover speaks,
> Look kindly and reply.

Finally, many ballads in America simply go into meaningless nonsense. The model for American refrains seems to be the demented refrain of Percy's "The Maid and the Palmer" (Child 21), happily unique in Child:

> Lillumwham, lillumwham!
> Whatt then? what then?
> Grandam boy, grandam boy, heye!
> Leg a derry, leg a merry, mett, mer, whoope, whir!
> Driuance, larumben, grandam boy, heye!

A West Virginia refrain for "The Twa Sisters" is:

> Hey oh, my Nanny!
> And the swim swom bonny.

In America, folk etymology sometimes produces not secondary meaning but no meaning at all. The refrain of "The Twa Sisters" Mrs. Gentry sang for Sharp (from the old witch charm "juniper, gentian and rosemary") was:

> Jury flower gent the roseberry
> The jury hangs over the roseberry.

When folk etymology spreads beyond the refrain, it can turn a whole ballad into a crazy jumble. The "Lamkin" that Mrs. Lena Bare Turbyfill of Elk Park, North Carolina, recorded for Herbert Halpert and the Library of Congress as "Bolakins" in 1939 gets the "false nurse" as "the foster," "much red gold" as "many marigolds," punishes the foster at "the stake of stand-by" (for "the stake a-standing by"), and hangs Bolakins "to the sea-gallows tree," whatever that may once have been. Eventually some ballads work into total idiocy, like the "Poor Anzo" version of "Lord Randall" that Reed Smith discusses in his chapter "The

Road Downhill" in *South Carolina Ballads*. Anzo is asked why he left his sweetheart and replies, "Here is a red hot iron will broil a bone brown"; asked what he would like for supper, he concludes, "Make me a little breely broth soup."

What has happened to the Child ballad in America, in sum, is that it has become inadequate narrative, aborted drama, happy-ending tragedy, corrupt and meaningless verbiage, and bad poetry in general. Some of this may be the effect of transmission in time, which seems to degenerate and deteriorate folk literature wherever we can observe its effects. Some of it, however, is certainly the effect of the American ethos, with its denial of death, its resistance to the tragic experience, its deep repression of sexuality, its over-riding pieties, and its frantic emphasis on the rationalistic, the inconsequential, and the optimistic. It almost seems that these ballad texts are bad precisely to the degree that they have become successfully American, that they reflect our dominant values and resemble other unlovely features of our popular culture. The con-clusion for folklorists to draw is not that American ballads should not continue to be vigorously collected and carefully studied, but that in the course of those worthwhile activities they need not be overvalued in aesthetic terms, that the folklorist should not pre-tend or insist that they are high art when so many of them are patently trash. Here we might note with some melancholy that if the rediscovery of the British traditional ballad inspired the Ro-mantic Movement in poetry, our rediscovery of the American ballad has for the most part inspired our poets in quest of a folk tradition to go seek it elsewhere.

NOTE [1963]: "The Child Ballad in America: Some Aesthetic Criteria" appeared in the *Journal of American Folklore*. It was soon answered by D. K. Wilgus with "Shooting Fish in a Barrel: The Child Ballad in America" (in the April–June, 1958, issue of the same journal). Wilgus showed with examples that the Child ballad had deteriorated at least as much in Great Britain as it had in the United States. What I had ascribed to the "American ethos" is clearly a much more general phenomenon, perhaps a "modern ethos." In the course of his argument, Wilgus quotes some stanzas from a text of Child 155, "Sir Hugh," collected in Somerset in 1907. They are much worse than any American example I produced, and are funny enough to warrant reprinting here. They read:

> She took him to the parlour door
>   And led him through the kitchen
> And there he saw his own mother dear,
>   She were picking of her chicken.
>
> Down on his bended knee he fell:
>   "Mother, pardon me,
> For if I live to be a man,
>   I will give thee gold in three (fee?).'
>
> She placed a prayer-book at his head
>   And a testament at his feet;
> She placed the Bible at his heart
>   And a pen-knife in so deep.
>
> She wrapped him up in a blanket warm
>   And tooked him to a well,
> Saying, "Goodbye, goodbye, my pretty little boy,
>   I hope you are quite well."

The Symbols of
Folk Culture

[1954]

LOOK AT A PEOPLE'S MONEY, it has been said ambiguously, if you want to learn what they worship. An American encountering ancient Greek coins for the first time is apt to be struck by an enormous contrast in seriousness between their symbols and ours. There is a real difference in kind between Gelas the man-headed bull and the stuffed American bison; between an ithyphallic, hooved, and tailed satyr carrying off a nymph, and Liberty seated holding a mob cap on a stick; between the *cista mystica*, or basket from which a sacred serpent emerges in the Bacchic mysteries, and Jefferson's Monticello; between Athena's owl and the American eagle clutching decorative arrows: between Alexander of Macedon horned as Zeus Ammon and Franklin's kindly old head.

The Greek symbols seem never conventional or allegorical, but always the literal picturings of objects full of *mana*, magical power. The owl *is* Athena, pop-eyed and stern. Alexander does not wear his horns as a king might wear a laurel wreath or a crown, as a token of honor or rank; he *is* Zeus Ammon, and the horns sprout from his head as a visible emanation of his godhood. Our eagles and vacuous Liberty belles, on the other hand, represent qualities and personify abstractions precisely because as a culture we worship nothing in common, and are able to endow no objects with *mana*. If, as our critics at home and abroad never tire of repeating, we worship money itself, the actual metal tokens, it is because we know it to represent more tangible power than any of the symbols pictured on it. A dollar bill, we know, can get certain things done—increasingly few, it must be admitted—but the Masonic pyramid culminating in a human eye pictured on its reverse can get nothing done. Send not to ask for whom the eye watches; it watches for none of us.

The absence of a folk culture in America seems to be precisely the absence of these *mana* experiences. If we were to define a folk culture it might include some such categories as these: the hero, ritual communion, the cycle of the year as a pattern of life related to the earth, the symbols of worship, and the dignity of occupation. Any examination of our civilization along these lines would tend to show that not only do we lack the authentic culture trait but that at every point we possess shoddy and commercialized substitutes. We are thus haplessly neither a folk culture nor a dignified anything else, but rather a pseudo-folk culture.

The hero is the individual embodiment of the community's power, the vanquisher of its dragons and minotaurs, its champion in battle or its fount of cunning, its Crucified Savior or its Sincere Man at One With Nature. He may have five beautiful pupils in each eye like Cuchulain or be as ordinary-looking as the third son who triumphs in fairy tales; he may be a coyote or a spider, a brotherly rabbit or a puss in boots; he may be a magician who commands like Moses or a magician who tricks like Maui. Whatever he is, he is distinguished by power, by the possession of *mana*; in some great struggle his power is triumphant, although he may have to pay for it—immediately with Samson or later with Prometheus.

Our spurious folk heroes, whether manufactured by the dilution of European legends and endocannibalism, like Paul Bunyan, Pecos Bill, and Febold Feboldson, or distorted from real men, like Davy Crockett, Mike Fink, and Johnny Appleseed, are the heroes of anecdote and bluster, with no powers, no struggle, and no triumph or failure. We are taught the real heroes of American history in our schools and the real heroes of Hebraic-Christian mythology in our Sunday schools, but if as adults we remember that Marion the Swamp Fox fed a British officer on potatoes, or how Jael did in Sisera, they are still no more heroes of our own culture than the elder Brutus or William Tell. As for our movie stars, our war aces and transatlantic fliers, our sports champions and public enemies, it would be hard to read even an invocation by the light of their brief candles.

The experience of ritual communion, whether we think of it in terms of the primitive nature rite, the Athenian drama, the revival meeting, or the Plains Indian sun dance, is a true collective act, a temporary merger of individual identity in a collective whole that is larger than the sum of its parts and at its conclusion releases its individual units purged and fulfilled, as though they had been cast up from the belly of the fish. Our football classics and baseball World Series tend to assemble us into two collectives of rival partisans, introducing the principle of division as well as merger, and little catharsis is possible where one group of two must to the end challenge the identification of hero and villain.

At least one critic has classified the mass experience in a darkened cinema temple with ritual communion. Surely this is too passive an experience to constitute an action at all, and for every patron who walks out of the movie theater purged and fulfilled, there must be a dozen who stagger home with no sensation beyond that of being too long in a warm bath. Our public ceremonials on the order of ticker-tape parades and political rallies are collective without being cathartic, as our barroom brawls are cathartic without being collective. The only culture trait we possess which might fairly be called a full ritual communion—collective, purgative, and overwhelming—is the lynch mob, and it is not one we should care to encourage.

The cycle of the year, with its rhythm of birth, growth, death, decay, rebirth, its sequence of natural festivals in intimate association with these life processes, at once celebrating them and spurring them on—"a time to plant, and a time to pluck up that which is planted"—is the feature of folk culture perhaps most cruelly parodied in our urban life. Our year of the earth's cycle is marked off by a green tie on St. Patrick's Day, a new hat on Easter, a carnation on Mother's Day, a loud popping noise on the Fourth of July, a heavy meal and a long nap on Thanksgiving, a plastic tree covered with artificial snow on Christmas, and a funny hat on New Year's Eve. If these names cause us vague disquiet, suggesting that we are somehow involved with a giving of thanks or a sacred birth (perhaps of Santa Claus) we can gain some sort of relief by letting our joyous two weeks on Cape Cod be planned for us by a magazine calling itself Holy Day. With the development of frozen foods, the urban American no longer notices the seasons, as he once did, by the changing fruits and vegetables in the market, and the day someone produces an oyster that can be eaten in the R-less months, our year will become a series of unvarying days differentiated only by periodic and mysterious occasions for the presentation of gift-wrapped candy boxes.

Our symbols of worship, the objects full of *mana*, have suffered a similar debasement. Nations in the past, perhaps, lived by no more than a Cross and a Crown, but in forswearing both in Colonial days we left ourselves with only a cracked Liberty bell and a balding eagle. The confederate army fought for a cause many of us feel to be an unjust and degrading one—the preservation of a culture based on human slavery—but we must nevertheless grant its soldiers the dignity of their principles and their colors. To the misguided adolescents who wear its cap and flaunt its banner on automobiles and bicycles, we need grant neither principle nor dignity, only a recognition of the hunger for some meaningful symbol that fills their lives. If, as has been reported, the display of an ear of wheat was the crowning revelation of the Eleusinian mysteries, why do we so resolutely identify size with importance, and chisel our statesmen on cliffsides, with moles the size of boulders? The magic symbol of the Trinity seems to appear in our culture chiefly in the form of pawnshop balls and Three-in-One oil, but crowds stand reverently before Babe Ruth's old number 3 uniform in the baseball museum at Cooperstown, as though the number itself contained his power, as the egg contains the ogre's life. Even graven idols, if we really did bow down to them, would be better than the symbolic vacuum of our culture.

We are no better off in regard to the dignity of occupation. An organic society is legitimately differentiated within itself in the division of labor, the specialization that every historical culture we know has had to at least some degree. If the mature men hunt and the mature women hoe, if the baron seizes vineyards and the cooper makes barrels, one activity is as necessary and as dignified as the other. But in our culture many occupations are degrading, undignified, and wholly lacking in human value. Thus we get a spurious commercial glamorization of certain of the more romantic sorts of nineteenth-century manual labor, and a whole category of pseudo-folk song about the buffalo skinner, the cow puncher, the sailing-ship seaman, even the illicit distiller. As our whalers increasingly become factory workers afloat, our whaling shanties fill the airwaves.

In making up any fair balance sheet, it would be necessary to note pockets of genuine folk culture surviving among certain groups in this country, although their survival for much longer is questionable. Our children at play have a true folk culture, age-old and magical, in their games and songs, their skip-rope and counting-out rhymes, their ritual combats and pacifications. Whether it can long withstand the hearty and overenthusiastic teaching, from books, of children's folklore in the schools, is another question, and even now much of its special regional character has been lopped away. If there is no native American folk culture except the Indian, there is certainly an American folk culture, brought over by the English and still surviving in pockets in the Appalachians and elsewhere, brought over by the Negroes and modified almost out of recognition, and brought over by many other immigrant groups. Although such forces for homogeneity as the radio and the movies constantly threaten these survivals, and although immigrant folk culture tends to be shamefaced in the first generation, half-forgotten and ignored in the second generation, and welcomed by the third generation in exactly the proportion that it is lost to them, these little clusters of authentic folk material are national assets as real as so many sequoias. It is our debt to numberless workers in the field of folklore that they have preserved and disseminated this material, and if along with it they have preserved and disseminated, as equally authentic and valuable, mock ballads of back-country rapine, we can readily enough excuse them and rely on time's winnowing.

If America is a country without a true folk culture, there are worse conditions. Nazi Germany had, if not a folk, at least a *volkisch* culture of blood and soil, with a Hero, hysterical rallies that were something really like ritual communion, a symbol—the swastika—full of *mana* and black bile, and other features that have been identified as values above. Its example would perhaps suggest that the purposeful restoration of these lost elements may be infinitely less preferable than their absence. We would not want the *volkisch* culture of the Nazis any more than we would want a folk culture like that of a feudal peasantry—brutal, super-stition-ridden, and bleak—or like the Aztec, where the cancerous development of ritual stifles all other activities, and in its con-tempt for human life wipes out the values its rituals ostensibly seek to promote and sustain.

We can never, of course, return to the past. The nostalgic re-vival of moribund languages like Gaelic in Ireland and Hebrew in Israel, although it seems to be succeeding at least physically in the latter case, will not bring back Finn or Solomon, and will not even solve the traffic problem or wipe out the rural slums. The Israeli farmer may sell his land every seven years to a legendary Arab named, I think, Mahmoud, because his putative ancestors thought it would please the Lord more to keep land fallow on the sabbati-cal year, but he would nevertheless do well to harvest it with a better combine than those putative ancestors had. Like him, we are inextricably caught up in a civilized condition, and rather than yearning after a return to the past with its meaningful symbols, we must project our real sentimental nostalgia for them into some viable approach to our own time.

Here the techniques of the artist would seem most useful to us. Painters like Klee, Picasso, and Chagall; musicians like Bartók and Britten; dancers like Graham; poets like Yeats, Lorca, Thomas, and Auden are not creating in a folk or primitive tradition, but are using the myth and legend, the magic and ritual, of these cultures with some degree of ironic adaptation to their own needs. Klee's painting "Around the Fish" is not the Australian bark drawing it resembles, but an ironic comment on his own sophisticated in-ability to see inside the fish as the primitive artist can; Auden's "Epilogue" is not the ancient English totemic song "The Cutty Wren" but a sophisticated variant, turning the ominous magic of the original to his own metaphoric purposes. If we are to have a folk culture it will be along these lines, within our most sophisticated formal arts rather than in our popular arts, and its characteristic feature will be irony. That is not the happy, unself-conscious condition of Herakles slaying the Cretan bull on a Greek coin, but it is approximately the condition in which Sophocles or Euripides found themselves when they inherited a bull-slaying rite transformed into Athenian tragedy, and it is not too unpromising a condition. Our arts may not rival the flowering of Greece any more than our coins do, but to the extent that they can furnish us with meaningful and moving symbols they can bring *mana* back into a culture sadly deficient in it, and may yet save us where eagle and bison failed.

The Ritual View
of Myth and
the Mythic

[1955]

T HE RITUAL APPROACH comes directly out of Darwin, and thus,
I suppose, ultimately from Heraclitus, whose *"panta rei"* seems
to be the ancestor of every dynamic approach. When Darwin concluded *The Origin of Species* (1859) with a call for evolutionary
treatment in the sciences of man, he opened the door to a variety
of genetic studies of culture, and when he showed in *The Descent
of Man* (1871) that human evolution was insignificant organically
although vastly speeded up culturally (we might not be so quick
to say "ethically" as he was), he made cultural studies the legitimate heirs of evolutionary biology. The same year as *The Descent*,
in response to *The Origin*, E. B. Tylor's *Primitive Culture* appeared, drawing an immediate fan letter from Darwin. It staked
off quite a broad claim to cultural studies in its subtitle "Researches into the Development of Mythology, Philosophy, Religion, Language, Art, and Custom." Tylor's general principle,
almost his Law, is that survivals are significant because they em-
body, sometimes in trivial or playful form, the serious usages of
earlier stages. In material culture, it meant that such important
tools as the bow and arrow, the mask, and the magician's rattle
evolved into the toys of children; in nonmaterial culture, it meant

278

that myths were based on rites, although, like many rationalists before him, Tylor believed that they had been consciously devised as explanations.

Tylor's evolutionary anthropology, carried on by such successors as R. R. Marett and A. C. Haddon, became the central tradition of British anthropology, but the emphasis gradually shifted from Tylor's concern with belief and custom to the more tangible areas of social organization, economics and material culture. Meanwhile, at Cambridge, a classicist named James G. Frazer had found *Primitive Culture* a revelation, and his interest in ancient survivals was broadened and extended by his friend William Robertson Smith's studies of religion, in which Smith made use of the comparative method, invented by Montesquieu and developed by German philology. Weaving together the two main strands of Tylor's evolutionary survivals and Smith's comparative method, in 1885 Frazer began publishing a series of periodical articles on custom. When one of them, on a curious priesthood at Nemi in Italy, tied in with Smith's ideas about the slain god and outgrew article size, he kept working on it and in 1890 published it as the first edition of *The Golden Bough* in two volumes, dedicated to Smith. For Frazer in *The Golden Bough*, myth is still Tylor's rationalist "a fiction devised to explain an old custom, of which the real meaning and origin had been forgotten," and the evolution of custom is still Tylor's "to dwindle from solemn ritual into mere pageant and pastime," but Frazer constantly approaches, without ever quite stating, a synthesis of the two, with myths not consciously devised rational explanations but the actual dwindling or later form of the rite. Long before 1915, when the third and final edition of *The Golden Bough* appeared, that synthesis had been arrived at.

Since 1882, Jane Ellen Harrison, Frazer's contemporary at Cambridge, had been writing on Greek mythology and art, and in 1903, after she had seen a clay seal at Cnossos with its sudden revelation that the Minotaur was the king of Crete in a bull mask, she published *Prolegomena to the Study of Greek Religion*, which clearly stated the priority of ritual over myth or theology. Her book acknowledged the co-operation of Gilbert Murray at Tylor's Oxford, and Frazer, F. M. Cornford, and A. B. Cook at Cambridge. Cook, whose *Zeus* did not begin to appear in book form for another decade, started publishing material toward it in periodicals about that time. His important series "Zeus, Jupiter, and the Oak" in the *Classical Review* (1903) took an approach similar to Harrison's. By the time Murray published *The Rise of the Greek Epic* (1907), reading such mythic figures as Helen and Achilles as ritual concretizations, he was able to draw on some of the Cambridge work his earlier writings had influenced. By 1908, when the Committee for Anthropology at Oxford sponsored six lectures, published under Marett's editorship later that year as *Anthropology and the Classics*, with the aim of interesting students of the humanities in "the lower culture," students of the humanities at the sister university had been turning their attention to the lower cultures for two decades, and the seed Tylor planted had flowered elsewhere.

The watershed year was 1912, when Harrison published *Themis*, a full and brilliant exposition of the chthonic origins of Greek mythology, including an excursus on the ritual forms underlying Greek tragedy by Murray (to whom the book is dedicated), a chapter on the ritual origin of the Olympic Games by Cornford, and copious material from Cook's forthcoming work. (Like the *Prolegomena*, this book had been inspired by a visit to Crete, where Harrison encountered the "Hymn of the Kouretes," which suggested that ritual magic, specifically the rite of a year-daimon, was the central element in early Greek religion.) In *Themis*, Harrison made three important points with great clarity: that myth arises out of rite, rather than the reverse; that it is "the spoken correlative of the acted rite, the thing done; it is *to lego-menon* as contrasted with or rather as related to *to dromenon*" (a Greek definition of myth is "*ta legomena epi tois dromenois*," "the things said over a ritual act"); and that it is not anything else nor of any other origin.

Basic to this view, as Harrison makes clear, is a dynamic or evolutionary conception of process, in which rites die out, and myths continue in religion, literature, art, and various symbolic forms with increased misunderstanding of the ancient rite, and a compensatory transformation for intelligibility in new terms. Thus myths are never the record of historical events or people, but freed from their ritual origins they may attach to historical events or people (as Alexander was believed to be, or claimed to be, a god and the son of a snake, because mythic Greek kings like Cecrops had been ritual snake gods); they never originate as scientific or etiological explanations of nature, but freed from their ritual origins may be so used (as stars have their positions in the sky because the mythic hero threw them there, but *his* origin is in rite, not primitive astronomy).

The ritual approach to mythology, or any form based on myth, thus cannot limit itself to genetic considerations. In the artificial division I have found most useful, it must deal with the three related problems of *origin*, *structure*, and *function*. If the origin is the ancient anonymous collective one of ritual, the structure is intrinsically dramatic, the *dromenon* or thing done, but that form ceaselessly evolves in time in the chain of folk transmission. Here the considerations are neither historic nor anthropological, but formal in terms of literary structure, principles of *Gestalt* organization, and dynamic criteria. In folk transmission, the "folk work" involves operations comparable to those Freud found in the "dream work"—splitting, displacement, multiplication, projection, rationalization, secondary elaboration, and interpretation —as well as such more characteristically aesthetic dynamics as Kenneth Burke's principle of "completion" or the fulfillment of expectations, in the work as well as in the audience. In regard to function, as the myth or text alters, there is at once a changing social function, as the work satisfies varying specific needs in the society along Malinowskian lines, and an unchanging, built-in function best described by Aristotle's *Poetics* and Freudian psychology, carrying with it its own context, taking us through its structural rites. In other words, the book of Jonah in the reading satisfies our need to be reborn in the belly of the great fish as efficiently as the initiatory rites from which it presumably derived satisfied the same need in the initiates. If these are now as then "fantasy gratifications," they are the charismatic experiences of great art now, as they were the charismatic experiences of organic religion then.

In a relatively short time, the ritual approach to folk study has met with remarkable success. There had of course been individual ritual studies in various areas long before 1912. Most of them were in the field of children's lore, where ritual survivals, after Tylor had called attention to them, were readily apparent. Some of the earliest studies were William Wells Newell's *Games and Songs of American Children* (1883), Henry Carrington Bolton's *The Counting-Out Rhymes of Children* (1888), Alice Gomme's *The Traditional Games of England, Scotland and Ireland* (1894), and Lina Eckenstein's *Comparative Studies in Nursery Rhymes* (1906). Much of this work has never been superseded, and similarly, the most impressive ritual studies we have of the Bible appeared at the turn of the century: for the Old Testament, William Simpson's *The Jonah Legend* (1899), and for the New, John M. Robertson's series of books on the mythic Jesus, beginning with *Christianity and Mythology* (1900). All of these people seem to have operated in relative isolation, independently working through to conclusions about their own material without knowing what was going on in other areas or recognizing the general application of their conclusions.

With the appearance of *Themis*, a powerful general statement of the theory buttressed by a prodigy of scholarship in several complicated areas of Greek culture, a "Cambridge" or "ritual" approach became generally available. Within a few years, its application to Greek studies had been enormously widened: Cornford's *From Religion to Philosophy* (1912), traced the ritual origins of some basic philosophic ideas; Harrison's *Ancient Art and Ritual* (1913) turned her theory on Greek plastic and pictorial arts; Murray tested his ritual forms on one tragic dramatist in *Euripides and His Age* (1913) (both it and *Ancient Art and Ritual* as popularizations for the Home University Library); Cornford tested the same forms on Greek comedy in *The Origin of Attic Comedy* (1914); and the first volume of Cook's enormous storehouse of ritual interpretation, *Zeus*, appeared (1914).

The first application of the theory outside Greek studies was Murray's 1914 Shakespeare Lecture, "Hamlet and Orestes," a brilliant comparative study on the common ritual origins of Shakespeare and Greek drama. In 1920 appeared Jessie Weston's *From Ritual to Romance*, treating the Grail romances as the "misinterpreted" record of a fertility rite, and Bertha Phillpotts' *The Elder*

Edda and Ancient Scandinavian Drama, tracing the ritual sources of northern epic poetry. The next year Margaret Murray's *The Witch-Cult in Western Europe* appeared, claiming a real "Dianic cult," the survival of the old pagan religion, persecuted by Christianity as witchcraft, the book constituting the first substantial excursion of the theory into history. In 1923, the widening ripples took in fairy tales, in P. Saintyves' *Les Contes de Perrault et les Récits Parallèles;* folk drama, in R. J. E. Tiddy's editing *The Mummers' Play;* and law, in H. Goitein's *Primitive Ordeal and Modern Law.* In 1927, A. M. Hocart's *Kingship* appeared, tracing a great variety of material to a basic royal initiatory ceremony, and in 1929 Scott Buchanan's *Poetry and Mathematics* (the first American work along these lines in the third of a century since Bolton) boldly proposed a treatment of experimental science in ritual terms, and imaginatively worked some of it out.

In the thirties, S. H. Hooke edited two important symposia, *Myth and Ritual* (1933) and *The Labyrinth* (1935), in which a number of prominent scholars studied the relationships of myth and ritual in the ancient Near East; Lord Raglan published *Jocasta's Crime,* a ritual theory of taboo (1933), and his enormously influential *The Hero* (1937), which broadly generalized the ritual origins of all myth, as against the historical; Enid Welsford investigated the sources of an archetypal figure in *The Fool* (1935); Allen, Halliday, and Sikes published their scholarly edition of *The Homeric Hymns* (1936), extending previous considerations of Greek epic and dramatic poetry into sacred lyric; and in the late thirties William Troy began publishing his as yet uncollected ritual studies of such writers as Lawrence, Mann, and Fitzgerald.

By the forties, old subjects could be gone back over with greatly augmented information. George Thomson combined a ritual and Marxist approach in *Aeschylus and Athens* (1941) and *Studies in Ancient Greek Society* (the first volume of which appeared in 1949), Rhys Carpenter amplified Murray's earlier treatment of Homer in *Folk Tale, Fiction and Saga in the Homeric Epics* (1946), Lewis Spence brought Newell, Bolton, and Lady Gomme somewhat up to date in *Myth and Ritual in Dance, Game, and Rhyme* (1947), and Hugh Ross Williamson expanded Margaret Murray's brief account (in *The God of the Witches,* undated) of the deaths of Thomas à Becket and William Rufus as Dianic cult sacrifices in *The Arrow and the Sword* (1947). Venturing into fresh fields, Gertrude Rachel Levy in *The Gate of Horn* (1948), traced some ritual sources of culture down from the Stone Age, paying considerable attention to plastic and pictorial art, and in 1949 there were two important literary applications, Francis Fergusson's *The Idea of a Theatre*, a reading of modern drama in terms of the ritual patterns exemplified in Sophocles' *Oedipus the King*, and John Speirs's "Sir Gawain and the Green Knight," in *Scrutiny*, Winter, 1949, the first of an important series of ritual studies of medieval English literature.[1]

So far in the fifties half a dozen new territories have been explored and to some extent colonized. Theodor H. Gaster's *Thespis* (1950) generalized a ritual origin for the whole body of Near East sacred literature; Gertrude Kurath's articles on dance in the Funk and Wagnalls' *Dictionary of Folklore* the same year embraced a body of primitive and folk dance forms in the same approach; Cornford's luminous "A Ritual Basis for Hesiod's *Theogony*" was published posthumously in *The Unwritten Philosophy* (1950) (although it had been written in 1941); and C. L. Barber published an ambitious exploration of Shakespeare in "The Saturnalian Pattern in Shakespeare's Comedy" in *The Sewanee Review*, Autumn, 1951.[2] Since then we have had the publication of Levy's second volume, *The Sword from the Stone* (1953), a ritual genesis of epic; Herbert Weisinger's *Tragedy and the Paradox of the Fortunate Fall* (1953), a similar treatment of tragedy; and Margaret Murray's third book on the Dianic cult, *The Divine King in England* (1954). In this listing I have made no attempt at completeness, confining it to those writers with whose work I am most familiar, and only one or two titles by each (Murray, Cornford, and Harrison have written about a dozen books each), but the breadth and variety of even this truncated list should make it obvious that the "Cambridge" view has gone far beyond the confines of Greek mythology, and that it is apparently here to stay.

[1] Since published as *Medieval English Poetry* (1957). [1963]
[2] This was later expanded into a book, *Shakespeare's Festive Comedy* (1959). [1963]

Since the ritual approach to myth and literature does not claim to be a theory of ultimate significance, but a method of study in terms of specific significances, it can cohabit happily with a great many other approaches. If its anthropology has historically been Frazerian, the comparative generalization across many cultures, many of its most successful works, from *Themis* to Speirs on Gawain, have stayed narrowly within one area, and where it deals with social function, its anthropology is most profitably Malinowskian (if an unusually historical Malinowskian). The Boas tradition in American anthropology, with its bias against crosscultural generalization and evolutionary theory, in favor of empirical cultural studies and known diffusion, has often seemed inimical to the ritual approach at those key points. Many of the Boas rigidities, however, seem to have softened in the decade since his death. The new culture and personality anthropology from Ruth Benedict's *Patterns of Culture* (1934) to E. Adamson Hoebel's *The Law of Primitive Man* (1954) seems as cheerfully comparative as *The Golden Bough*. Neo-evolutionism is again fashionable. *Primitive Heritage* (1953), Margaret Mead's anthology with Nicholas Calas, calls for "the restoration of wonder," and means, apparently, let us take Frazer and Crawley more seriously. If out of this comes a neo-Frazerian generalizing anthropology, based not on dubious material wrenched out of its configuration but on detailed and accurate field studies done with Boasian rigor, no one would welcome it more than the ritualists.

In regard to psychology, the ritual approach can draw centrally on Freudian psychoanalysis, informed by new knowledge and less circumscribed by ethnocentric patterns. This requires modernization without the loss of Freud's central vision, which is tragic where such rebels as Adler and Jung and such revisionists as Fromm and Horney are cheery faith-healers, unshrinking where they bowdlerize, stubbornly materialist where they are idealist and mystic, and dynamic, concerned with process, where they are static and concerned with one or another variety of timeless *élan vital*. After we have brought the Frazerian anthropology of *Totem and Taboo* up to date and restored Freud's "vision" of the Primal Horde, in Burke's terms, to its place as "essence" rather than "origin," the book remains our most useful and seminal equation of primitive rite with neurotic behavior, and thus the bridge to Burke's own "symbolic action," the private, individual symbolic equivalent for the ancient collective ritual. In the form of "symbolic action," psychoanalytic theory gives us the other dimension of function, the wish fulfillment or fantasy gratification, and can thus answer some of our questions about the origins of origins.

As Jung's work increasingly seems to move toward mystic religion and away from analytic psychology, it appears to be of increasingly little use to a comparative and genetic approach. Strong as Jungian psychology has been in insisting on the universal archetypal identity of myth and symbol, its explanation of this identity in terms of the collective unconscious and innate awareness militates directly against any attempt to study the specific forms by which these traits are carried and transmitted in the culture (as does Freud's own "memory traces"). As Jung is used in the work of Maud Bodkin or Joseph Campbell, as a source of suggestive insights, it seems far more to our purposes, and we can readily utilize Campbell's universal "great myth" or "monomyth," a concept itself derived from Van Gennep's *rites de passage*: "a separation from the world, a penetration to some source of power, and a life-enhancing return." We must first, however, restore the Jungian myth to its roots, either a specific myth and text (literary study) or a specific culture and rite (anthropology). The ritual approach is certainly compatible with varieties of mysticism, as the conclusions of Weston's *From Ritual to Romance* or Harrison's *Epilegomena to the Study of Greek Religion* (1921) make clear, and Harrison was herself strongly drawn to Jung as well as to Bergson. Despite their examples, and the opinions of even so impressive a ritual poet as William Butler Yeats, the job of mythic analysis would seem to require a basic rational materialism, and a constant pressure in the direction of science and scholarship, away from mysticism and the occult. Within these limits of naturalism, and on the frame of this central concern with ritual, all possible knowledge and all approaches to myth—from the most meticulous motif-classification to the most speculative reconstruction of an ur-text—can be useful, with pluralism certainly the desirable condition.

There are only two varieties of approach, I think, with which the ritual view cannot usefully coexist. One is the euhemerist, the idea that myths are based on historic persons or events. This theory has been driven back from rampart to rampart over the years, but it stubbornly holds to each new defensive position: if it is forced to give up a historic William Tell, it retreats to a historic Robin Hood; if the historic Orpheus even Harrison's *Prolegomena* accepted in 1903 seems no longer tenable, perhaps Moses is; if there was no Leda and no egg, could there not have been a real Helen? By now, in regard to the great myths, we know that none of these is possible, even at those key points the Trojan War and the figure of Jesus. With stories unquestionably made up about real people, whether fictions about Napoleon or Eleanor Roosevelt jokes, it becomes a simple matter of definition, and if the euhemerists of our various schools want to call those stories myths, they are welcome to them. We find it more useful to apply some other term, insofar as the distinction between myth and history is a real and a basic one.[2]

The other approach to mythology that seems to offer no point of juncture with the ritual view is the cognitionist idea that myths derive from a quest for knowledge. In nineteenth-century forms— the theories that myths were personifications of nature, or of the weather, or of the sun and moon—cognitionism seems substantially to have died out. In various insidious twentieth-century forms—the theories that myths are designed to answer etiological questions about how death came into the world or how the bunny got his little furry tail, or that taboo is primitive hygiene or primitive genetics—cognitionism is still pervasive. Again, all one can say is that myths do not originate in this fashion, that primitive peoples are speculative and proto-scientific, surely, but that the lore primitives transmit is another order of knowledge. If they knew that the tabooed food carried trichinosis or that the tabooed incestuous marriage deteriorated the stock, they would not save the first for their sacred feasts and the second for their rulers. Once more, if our various cognitionists want to call myth what is unquestionably primitive proto-science—techniques for keeping a pot from cracking in the firing or seasonal lore for planting and harvesting—that is their

[2] Myth must also be distinguished from all the other things we loosely call by its name: legend, tale, fantasy, mass delusion, popular belief and illusion, and plain lie.

privilege. The Alaskan Eskimos who took the Russian explorers for cuttlefish "on account of the buttons on their clothes," as Frazer reports, obviously had speculative minds and a sense of continuity between the animal and human orders not unlike that informing Darwin's theory, but the difference between their myth of The Great Cuttlefish That Walks Like a Man (if they had one) and *The Origin of Species* is nevertheless substantial.

If we keep clearly in mind that myth tells a story sanctioning a rite, that it is the spoken correlative of that rite, then it is obvious that it is not science but a form of independent experience, analogous to literature. The pursuit of cognition in myth or folk literature has led to all the worst excesses of speculative research, whether the political slogans and events Katherine Elwes Thomas found hermetically concealed in nursery rhymes in *The Real Personages of Mother Goose* (1930), the wisdom messages, deliberately coded and jumbled, that Robert Graves uncoded in *The White Goddess* (1948), or, most recently, the secret fire worship Flavia Anderson discovered hidden behind every myth in *The Ancient Secret* (1953).

Among the important problems facing the ritual view at present is an adequate working-out of the relationship between ritual, the anonymous regular recurrence of an action, and history, the unique identifiable experience in time. The problem is raised dramatically in the latest book by Margaret Murray, one of the pioneers of ritual studies. Called *The Divine King in England*, it is the third in her series on the Dianic cult and easily her wildest. Where *The Witch-Cult in Western Europe* named two historical figures, Joan of Arc and Gilles de Rais, as voluntary sacrificial figures in the cult, and her second book, *The God of the Witches*, added two more, Thomas à Becket and William Rufus, the new book makes the bold claim on English history that "at least once in every reign from William the Conqueror to James I the sacrifice of the Incarnate God was consummated either in the person of the king or in that of his substitute," generally in a regular seven-year cycle. Since I have already reviewed the book at length in the Fall, 1955, issue of *Midwest Folklore*, I can here only briefly summarize the problem. Murray's historical excursion is not only dubious history (as reviewers have pointed out, showing the errors of dates and durations by which she gets her seven-year victims, the number jugglery by which she gets her covens of thirteen), it is totally unnecessary history. She is certainly right about survivals of the Old Religion into modern times, but she seems to be basically in error about the manner in which it survives, to be confusing origins with events. As the ancient rites die out in literal practice, their misunderstood and transformed record passes into myth and symbol, and that is the form in which they survive and color history, without being themselves the events of history. In English history, assuming as she does that the primitive divine king was once slain every seven years, the monarch and his subjects might very well feel an ominousness about each seventh anniversary, and might welcome the death of the king or some high personage, but the step from that to the idea that the dead man was therefore the voluntary victim of a sacrificial cult is the unwarranted one. Murray's witch cult was a genuine worship of the old gods, surviving into modern times in a distorted form, but her Royal Covens are only the travesty of historical scholarship.

If the fallacy of historicity is still with us, the fallacy of etiology may finally be on its way out. In *Themis*, as far back as 1912, Harrison wrote:

> The myth is not at first aetiological, it does not arise to give a reason; it is representative, another form of utterance, of expression. When the emotion that started the ritual has died down and the ritual though hallowed by tradition seems unmeaning, a reason is sought in the myth and it is regarded as aetiological.

In his recent posthumous volume edited by Lord Raglan, *The Life-Giving Myth* (1952), A. M. Hocart finally shows the process whereby myth goes beyond explaining the ritual to explaining other phenomena in nature, thus functioning as general etiology. In Fiji, he reports, the physical peculiarities of an island with only one small patch of fertile soil are explained by a myth telling how Mberewalaki, a culture hero, flew into a passion at the misbehavior of the people of the island and hurled all the soil he was bringing them in a heap, instead of laying it out properly. Hocart points out that the myth is used etiologically to explain the nature of the island, but did not originate in that attempt. The adventures of Mberewalaki originated, like all mythology, in ritual performance, and most of the lore of Hocart's Fijian informants consisted of such ritual myths. When they get interested in the topography of the island or are asked about it, Hocart argues, they do precisely what we would do, which is ransack their lore for an answer. Our lore might include a body of geological process, and we would search through it for an explanation; theirs has no geology but tells the acts and passions of Mberewalaki, and they search through it similarly and come up with an explanation. It should take no more than this one pointed example, I think, to puncture that last survival of the cosmological origin theories, the etiological myth, except as a category of function.

After the relationship to history and to science or cognition, we are left with the relationship of ritual theory to belief. For Harrison, as for Frazer, ritual studies were part of comparative religion, and a hoped-for result, if not the ultimate aim, was finding a pattern in which a person of sense or sensibility could believe. Harrison concludes her essay in the Darwin centenary volume: "It is, I venture to think, towards the apprehension of such mysteries, not by reason only, but by man's whole personality, that the religious spirit in the course of its evolution through ancient magic and modern mysticism is ever blindly yet persistently moving." In the course of his researches, Darwin himself lost most of his faith, but for Asa Gray, as for some Darwinians since, the doctrine of evolution celebrated God's powers and strengthened Christian faith. For John M. Robertson, the demolition of the historicity of Jesus was a blow against Christianity on behalf of free thought; for W. B. Smith and Arthur Drews it was a way of purifying Christianity by purging it of legendary accretions. William Simpson seems to have hit on the idea of Jonah as an initiation ritual because he was preoccupied with such matters as a Freemason. There is apparently no necessary correlation between knowledge and belief; to know all is to believe all, or some, or none.

Most contemporary ritual students of myth, I should imagine, are like myself unbelievers, and it would seem to get progressively more difficult to acknowledge the essential identity of religious myths, and their genesis from the act of worship itself, the god out of the machinery, while continuing to believe in the "truth" of any one of them (or of all of them, except in the woolliest and most Jungian fashion). On the other hand, in *Cults and Creeds in Graeco-Roman Egypt* (1953), we saw Sir Harold Idris Bell, a professional papyrologist, produce a learned and impressive study of the pragmatic competition of religions in Hellenistic Egypt, with the constant proviso that one of those systems, Christianity, was not only morally superior to the others, but was the divinely inspired true faith. So perhaps to know all *is* to believe all.

Finally, then, a number of technical problems remain. In its brief history, the ritual view has illuminated almost the whole of Greek culture, including religion, philosophy, art, many of the forms of literature, and much else. It has done the same for the games, songs, and rhymes of children; the Old and New Testaments, epic and romance, Edda and saga, folk drama and dance, folk tale and legend, Near East religion, modern drama and literature, even problems in history, law, and science. A few forms of folk literature have not yet been explored in ritual terms, prominent among them the English and Scottish popular ballads (the present writer has made a tentative foray in that direction) and the American Negro blues. A ritual origin for the ballads presumes a body of antecedent folk drama, from which ballads evolve as narrative songs (as the drama in turn derived from ritual sacrifice), which hardly exists except in a few late poor fragments such as Robin Hood plays, and which must consequently be conjectured. Such conjecture is not impossible, but it is a hard job involving heavy reliance on that frail reed analogy, and it still awaits its analogist. The blues raise serious problems. If they are a true folk song of ancient anonymous collective ritual origin, rather than a folk-transmitted song of modern composition, then they precede any American conditions experienced by the Negro and must have an African source. There would be no trouble here, except that nothing like them has ever been found in Africa, perhaps because it does not exist, perhaps because it would look so different before its sea change that no one has yet identified it. In any case, a ritual origin for the blues constitutes a fascinating problem, although not a critical issue (too much obviously convincing ritual interpretation has been produced for the theory to stand or fall on any single form). A ritual account of the ballads and the blues would close two large chinks, and might keep out drafts even in the coldest climate of opinion.

The relationship of ritual and ritual myth to formal literature has hardly yet been touched. The brilliant work that should have inaugurated such a movement in criticism was Gilbert Murray's 1914 Shakespeare Lecture, "Hamlet and Orestes." In it he showed the essential identity of the two dramatic heroes, not because of any direct linkage between the two, but because Shakespeare's Hamlet, through a long northern line of Amlethus, Amlothi, and Ambales, derived from precisely the same myth and rite of the Winter King—cold, mad, death-centered, bitter, and filthy—that Orestes derived from in his warmer clime. The plays are neither myth nor rite, Murray insists, they are literature, but myth and rite underlie their forms, their plots, and their characters. (Greek drama itself represents a fusion of two separate derivations from ritual: the forms of Attic tragedy arise out of the sacrificial rites of tauriform or aegiform Dionysus, the plots of Attic tragedy come mostly from Homer; and the bloody plots fit the ritual form so well, as Rhys Carpenter shows most fully, because the Homeric stories themselves derive from similar sacrificial rites far from Mount Olympus.) In the four decades since Murray's lecture, literary criticism has scarcely noticed it. A student of Murray's, Janet Spens, published a ritual treatment of Shakespeare, *An Essay on Shakespeare's Relation to Tradition* (1916), which I have never seen, but which Barber describes with serious reservations. Until Barber's own essay almost nothing had been done with Shakespeare along ritual lines. Troy and Fergusson have dealt with a handful of novels and plays in ritual terms, Carvel Collins has written extensively on Faulkner, and the present writer has similarly tackled Thoreau and a few others, but there has been very little else.

The chief difficulty seems to lie in the need to recognize the relationship of literature to folk tradition, while at the same time drawing Murray's sharp line between them. Literature is analogous to myth, we have to insist, but is not itself myth. There has been a great deal of confusion on this point, best exemplified by Richard Chase's *Quest for Myth* and *Herman Melville* (both in 1949). Chase simply equates the two, defining myth in the former as "the aesthetic activity of a man's mind," turning Melville's works in the latter into so many myths or mythic organizations. Here we ought to keep in mind a number of basic distinctions. Myth and literature are separate and independent entities, although myth can never be considered in isolation, and any specific written text of the protean myth, or even fixed oral text, can fairly be called folk literature. For literary purposes, all myths are not one, however much they may be one, the monomyth or ur-myth, in essence or origin. What such modern writers as Melville or Kafka create is not myth but an individual fantasy expressing a symbolic action, equivalent to and related to the myth's expression of a public rite. No one, not even Melville (let alone Moritz Jagendorf), can invent myths or write folk literature.

The writer can use traditional myths with varying degrees of consciousness (with Joyce and Mann perhaps most fully conscious in our time), and he often does so with no premeditated intention, working from symbolic equivalents in his own unconscious. Here other arts closer to origins, such as the dance, where the ritual or symbolic action is physically mimed, can be profoundly instructive. Just as there are varying degrees of consciousness, so are there varying degrees of fruitfulness in these uses of traditional patterns, ranging from dishonest fakery at one extreme to some of the subtlest ironic and imaginative organizations in our poetry at the other. The aim of a ritual literary criticism would be the exploration of all these relations, along with missionary activity on behalf of some of the more rewarding ones.

What begins as a modest genetic theory for the origin of a few myths thus eventually comes to make rather large claims on the essential forms of the whole culture. If, as Schroedinger's *Nature and the Greeks* (1954) shows, the patterns of Greek myth and rite have been built into all our physics until the last few decades, perhaps ritual is a matter of some importance. Raglan and Hocart argue that the forms of social organization arise out of it, Goitein throws in the processes of law, Cornford and Buchanan add the forms of philosophic and scientific thinking (perhaps all our thinking follows the ritual pattern of *agon* or contest, *sparagmos* or tearing apart, then *anagnorisis* or discovery and *epiphany* or showing-forth of the new idea). Even language itself suggests at many points a ritual origin. From rites come the structures, even the plots and characters, of literature; the magical organizations of painting; the arousing and fulfilling of expectation in music; perhaps the common origin of all the arts. If ritual is to be a general theory of culture, however, our operations must get more tentative and precise in proportion as our claims become more grandiose. We then have to keep distinctions even clearer, know so much more, and use every scrap of fact or theory that can be used. Having begun so easily by explaining the myth of the Sphinx, we may yet, working humbly in co-operation with anyone who will and can co-operate, end by reading her difficult riddle.

American Negro Literature and the Folk Tradition

[1958]

BY "AMERICAN NEGRO LITERATURE" I do not mean any special body of writing, like Petrarchan sonnets, but only that varied American literature produced by Negroes. It is my contention that it has, or that some of it has, a relation to a living folk tradition that is rare in American writing, and very much worth our study. At the same time, I would insist that this special criterion of analysis does not involve any special criteria of evaluation, and that the writing of Negro authors must be judged by the same standards we use to judge the writing of any other authors. Such standards have not always been the case. One Negro critic has charged that white reviewers discriminate against Negro writing. This is obviously so in isolated instances, although even here it would probably be more accurate to say that white reviewers are often deaf to many of the resonances of Negro writing. I am sure that for the most part, however, the bias has gone the other way, and that there has been almost a concerted leaning-over-backward to welcome as masterworks one ultimately unimpressive Negro book after another. Some of this is the unconscious guilt of white Americans, some of it is an odd sort of romantic primitivism, and some of it surely is the general shape of our marketing culture, which heralds masterworks everywhere, daily. In any case, it is an insult to every serious Negro writer, as to every serious writer of any complexion.

In discussing Negro writing in relation to a folk tradition, I do not mean a folksy tradition. I have in mind the dependence of writers like Yeats and Synge on Irish folk culture, not of James Whitcomb Riley or Edgar Guest on Hoosier corn. There is a whole spectrum of possible relations to a folk tradition, ranging from such unpromising connections as simple imitation and fakery, archaism or sentimentalizing, to a number of complicated, ironic, and richly rewarding connections. I propose as much as possible to confine myself to some of the latter.

Without attempting any sort of historical survey of Negro writing, I would suggest that several obviously different strains are visible. One is a body of writing largely indistinguishable from white writing, with no specifically Negro character at all, which exists in an unbroken line from the poems of Phillis Wheatley, an eighteenth-century slave and apologist for slavery, to the historical novels of Frank Yerby. A second strain has a specifically Negro character, or at least subject matter. It is the naturalism of the social protest or documentary, the account of lynching, passing, discrimination, or varieties of resistance, and its examples are legion. A third is the naturalism of the regional or folksy, which was once about watermelon eating on the old plantation, and now seems to be mostly about hair straightening and razor fighting in Harlem. It is my intention to bypass these populous avenues, and to discuss the half-dozen or so Negro writers who seem to me largely to have gone beyond any sort of mimicry or naturalism, and to have joined the mainstream of modern literature in its symbolist and ironical flowing, who use literary form as an act of the moral imagination with Melville and Dostoevsky, Kafka and Joyce, Eliot and Baudelaire. These Negro writers, although not all of them are from the South, clearly relate to the renaissance of white Southern writing we have seen in our day, particularly in fiction, from Faulkner to Flannery O'Connor. I intend to discuss this small band of Negro writers, and to mention a few others, in relation to three forms of Negro folk literature: the folk tale, the blues, and the sermon. Other forms, among them spirituals and ballads, rhymes and games, have comparable literary extensions, but three should suffice to show some of the possibilities.

To talk about the folk tale, oddly enough, we have to begin with the familiar figure of the "darky" entertainer: Stepin Fetchit, Rochester, the Kingfish of the Amos 'n' Andy program. His role is to parody the familiar stereotype of the Negro: stupid, ignorant, lazy, fraudulent, cowardly, submoral, and boundlessly good-natured. The comic point of the act is that the performer is not really this subhuman grotesque, but a person of intelligence and skill, in other words, a performer. Assuming this role, a smart man playing dumb, is a characteristic behavior pattern of Negroes in the South (and often in the North) in a variety of conflict situations. *No Day of Triumph*, the reporting by a brilliant and sensitive Negro, J. Saunders Redding, of a trip through the South in 1940, gives us a typical example. He was driving into Kentucky with a Negro hitchhiker he had picked up, when they were stopped in a strikebound mining town by a guard with an automatic rifle. Before Redding could say anything, the hitchhiker shifted automatically into just such a "coon" act:

> "Cap'n, we'se goin' to Kentucky. See all dat stuff back dere, Cap'n? Well, dat stuff 'longs ter Mista Rob French, an' he sho' will raise hell ef we don' git it to him," Bill lied convincingly.
>
> "That gittar too?" the guard questioned, already softened to a joke.
>
> Bill grinned. "No, suh, Cap'n. Dis yere box is mine. Dis yere's ma sweetheart! If we-all hed time an' you hed time, I'd beat one out fer you," Bill said.
>
> "G'on. But don' stop nowheres. Don' even breathe hard," the guard said, grinning.
>
> "No, suh, Cap'n. I ain't much of a breever noway. Jus' 'nough ter live on. No, suh. I don' want no mo' o' white folks' air den I just got ter have."

One of the memorable characters in Richard Wright's autobiography *Black Boy* is a Memphis elevator operator called Shorty, who specializes in playing what Wright calls "the role of a clown of the most debased and degraded type." Shorty gets quarters

from white passengers by an obsequious clown act that culminates
in his inviting the white man to kick his rump. When Wright,
full of "disgust and loathing," asks him, "How in God's name can
you do that?" Shorty answers simply, "Listen, nigger, my ass is
tough and quarters is scarce." Wright's fictional use of the stereotype constitutes something like Shorty's revenge. In Wright's
latest novel, *The Outsider*, the hero, Cross Damon, is a Negro
intellectual and existentialist criminal of terrifying literacy and
paranoia. At one point in his criminal career he needs a false birth
certificate, and gets it by the same "darky" act. Cross thinks: "He
would have to present to the officials a Negro so scared and
ignorant that no white American would ever dream that he was
up to anything deceptive." He does so, batting his eyes stupidly,
asking for "the paper that say I was born," explaining in answer to
every question only that his white boss said he had better have it
right away. Of course he gets it immediately. The novel explains:

> And as he stood there manipulating their responses, Cross knew
> exactly what kind of man he would pretend to be to kill suspicion
> if he ever got into trouble. In his role of an ignorant, frightened
> Negro, each white man—except those few who were free from
> the race bias of their group—would leap to supply him with a
> background and an identity; each white man would project out
> on him his own conception of the Negro and he could safely hide
> behind it. . . . He knew that deep in their hearts those two white
> clerks knew that no human being on earth was as dense as he had
> made himself out to be, but they wanted, needed to believe it of
> Negroes and it helped them to feel racially superior. They were
> pretending, just as he had been pretending.

A comically related use of the "darky" act appears in Rudolph
Fisher's *The Conjure-Man Dies*, which so far as I know is the
only Negro detective story. Here there are no whites at all: victim,
murderer, detective, police, and all the other characters are
Negroes. The "darky" act is thus directed not at a character in
the book, but at the white reader. Shortly after the murder, an
uncouth kinky-haired buffoon appears, exclaiming:

> "Great day in the mornin'! What all you polices doin' in this
> place? Policeman outside d' front door, policeman in d' hall,
> policeman on d' stairs, and hyer's another one. 'Deed I mus' be in

d' wrong house! Is this Frimbo the conjure-man's house, or is it the jail?"

He turns out, of course (and I hope the reader will forgive me for giving away the plot of a twenty-five-year-old mystery), to be the murderer, an intelligent and literate man, disguised in a wig and a "coon" act. The point here seems to be that for a Negro reader, no Negro ever talked like that to his fellows, and the character is immediately suspicious. To a white reader, Fisher apparently assumes (and probably with justice), the disguise would be impenetrable because it fits white stereotypes. Writing a mystery that would mystify whites but convey essential hints to Negro readers seems an odd burlesque equivalent to Cross Damon's power manipulations.

The fullest development I know of the darky act in fiction is Ralph Ellison's *Invisible Man*, where on investigation every important character turns out to be engaged in some facet of the smart-man-playing-dumb routine. The narrator's grandfather, who was "the meekest of men," confesses on his deathbed:

> "Son, after I'm gone I want you to keep up the good fight. I never told you, but our life is a war and I have been a traitor all my born days, a spy in the enemy's country ever since I give up my gun back in the Reconstruction. Live with your head in the lion's mouth. I want you to overcome 'em with yeses, undermine 'em with grins, agree 'em to death and destruction, let 'em swoller you till they vomit or bust wide open."

Dr. Bledsoe, the president of the college, a tough and unscrupulous autocrat, pretends to be a simple pious Negro for the school's white trustees, explaining to the narrator: "I had to be strong and purposeful to get where I am. I had to wait and plan and lick around. . . . Yes, I had to act the nigger!" Tod Clifton, a young intellectual in the Brotherhood, perversely turns to peddling black Sambo dolls on the street, singing and making them dance, and is thus himself a kind of Sambo doll when he is shot down. Rinehart, like his prototype, Melville's Confidence-Man, has so many disguises—from the Reverend B. P. Rinehart, Spiritual Technologist, to Rine, the sweet man and numbers runner—that we see only comic masks, and have to conjecture the master illus-

ionist behind them. And so on, from character to character, with
the narrator himself the ultimate darky act, an invisible blackness
that conceals a sentient human being.

The origins of this figure in clown make-up are many. He comes
immediately from vaudeville, burlesque, and the minstrel show,
but behind those sources he is an authentic figure of folk tale, in
fact the major figure of Negro folk tale. In one form, he is Brer
Rabbit (more accurately, "Ber" or "Buh" Rabbit), who appears
an innocent but can outwit fox and wolf; in another form he is
John, who appears an ignorant slave but can always outwit Ole
Massa. When Richard M. Dorson was collecting folk tales in
Michigan, an informant told him, "Rabbit always the schemey
one," and an informant in Florida similarly told Zora Neale
Hurston, "John was too smart for Ole Massa. He never got no
beatin'!" Behind both figures in American Negro tales there is
the prototype of the West African trickster hero of so many
cycles: Spider on the Gold Coast, Legba the creator god's son in
Dahomey, Rabbit or Tortoise elsewhere. Like other trickster heroes
in other folklores, he is not quite animal, man, or god, but par-
takes of all three natures.

If Wright, Fisher, and Ellison get the darky act from the
realities (and travesties) of Negro life in America, from folk tales
of Buh Rabbit and John, and ultimately from West African mythology, those are still not the only sources. The same mocking
figure dances through Western literature from the *Eiron* in Greek
old comedy and the Fool in *Lear* down to Holden Caulfield in
J. D. Salinger's *The Catcher in the Rye* and Kingsley Amis' Jim
in *Lucky Jim*. We see a related figure called into being by the
hard doctrine of 1 Corinthians 3:19, "For the wisdom of this
world is foolishness with God," and 4:10, "We are fools for
Christ's sake."

In other words, when the Negro writer retreats furthest from
white models and deepest into Negro folk tradition, back in fact
to African myth, he is paradoxically not furthest from Western
literature but finds himself sharing a timeless archetype with
Aristophanes, Shakespeare, and St. Paul, who in turn derived it
from *their* folk sources in myth and ritual. High Western culture
and the Negro folk tradition thus do not appear to pull the

writer in opposite directions, but to say the same thing in their different vocabularies, to come together and reinforce insight with insight. Prince Myshkin in *The Idiot* derives identically from the *Eiron* and Fool of drama, the Fool in Christ, and a folk figure of wisdom-in-stupidity out of Russian peasant life and lore instead of Negro life and lore.

The relationship of Negro writing to the blues is, if anything, even more immediately visible than its relationship to the folk tale, although it is much harder to describe, since the blues is an extraordinarily complicated and subtle form, much of it depending on the music, which I shall have to ignore here. Most blues songs seem to divide readily into two types, a slow lament and a faster and gayer form. The slow lament says, with Ma Rainey:

> C.C. rider, see what you done done, Lord Lord Lord,
> Made me love you, now your gal done come,
> You made me love you, now your gal done come.

or with Bessie Smith:

> I was with you, baby, when you didn't have a dime,
> I was with you, baby, when you didn't have a dime;
> Now since you got plenty money you have throwed your
>   good gal down.

The fast blues says, with Joe Turner:

> You so beautiful, but you gotta die someday,
> Oh, you so beautiful, but you gotta die someday;
> All I want's a little lovin', baby, before you pass away.

or with Jabo Williams:

> Please, fat mama, keep them great big legs off of me,
> Please, fat mama, keep them great big legs off of me. . . .
> Them great big legs gonna keep me away,
> Them big legs keep me away.

or with Rosetta Crawford:

> I'm gonna get me a razor and a gun,
> Cut him if he stand still, shoot him if he run;
> 'Cause that man jumped salty on me.

Superficially, the choice seems to be the impossible pair of alternatives Freud gave us in *Beyond the Pleasure Principle*, destroy others or turn the destruction inward. Yet beyond it in the memorable blues performance there seems always to be some resolution, transcendence, even catharsis and cure.

The themes of the blues appear everywhere in Negro literature. One of the most predominant is the theme of leaving, travel, journey: "I'm gonna move to Kansas City"; "Some day, some day, I'll shake your hand goodbye"; "Well, babe, goin' away and leave you by yourself"; "Pick up that suitcase, man, and travel on." Walter Lehrman, in an unpublished study of the blues (to which I am considerably indebted), finds some sort of movement away from "here" in eighty-three out of one hundred lyrics. This sort of aimless horizontal mobility is a constant in American Negro life, substituting for frustrated possibilities of vertical mobility: if a Negro cannot rise in a job, he can change jobs; if he cannot live well here, he can try elsewhere. The major theme of Wright's *Native Son* is Bigger's aimless running; in *The Outsider* it is the journey from Chicago to New York to start a new life that proves the impossibility of any such rebirth. In Ellison's *Invisible Man* the movement is first the great Exodus out of the South, north to the Promised Land. Then, when that fails its promises, it is a random skittering up and down Manhattan, between Harlem and "downtown," until the narrator achieves his only possible vertical mobility, significantly *downward*, into a sewer (an ironic verticality already anticipated in Wright's story "The Man Who Lived Underground").

The dramatic self-pity of the blues, as we hear it in Billie Holiday's:

> My man don't love me, treats me oh so mean,
> My man he don't love me, treats me awful mean;
> He's the lowest man that I've ever seen.

or Pine Top Smith's:

> Now my woman's got a heart like a rock cast down in the sea,
> Now my woman's got a heart like a rock cast down in the sea;
> Seems like she can love everybody and mistreat poor me.

is the constant note in the work of such a writer as James Baldwin. In *Go Tell It on the Mountain*, the adolescent hero, John, is ugly, friendless, and always the smallest boy in each class. When he encounters *Of Human Bondage* he identifies (almost inconceivably) with Mildred. In Baldwin's "Autobiographical Notes" in *Notes of a Native Son*, the author identifies himself with Caliban, and says to white Prospero, "You taught me language, and my profit on't is I know how to curse." In *Giovanni's Room*, the book's most contemptible-pathetic character, Jacques, retires "into that strong self-pity which was, perhaps, the only thing he had which really belonged to him."

Accompanying the self-pity is a compensatory grandiose fantasy. In the blues, Bessie Smith sings:

> Say, I wisht I had me a heaven of my own,
> Say, I wisht I had me a heaven of my own;
> I'd give all the poor girls a long lost happy home.

In Negro writing, the grandiose fantasy is often upward, but rarely so otherwordly as a private heaven. The nameless Negro protagonist of "The Man Who Lived Underground," after a casual and pointless robbery, papers the walls of his sewer cavern with hundred-dollar bills, hangs gold watches and rings from nails all around him, and makes the dirt floor a mosaic of diamonds. The narrator of *Invisible Man* wires *his* hole in the ground with 1,369 light bulbs covering every inch of the ceiling, and plans on five phonographs simultaneously playing Louis Armstrong's record of "Black and Blue" while he eats pink and white—vanilla ice cream covered with sloe gin. In *Go Tell It on the Mountain*, John lives in a fantasy world where he is "beautiful, tall, and popular." In his daydreams he feels "like a giant who might crumble this city with his anger; he felt like a tyrant who might crush this city beneath his heel; he felt like a long-awaited conqueror at whose feet flowers would be strewn and before whom multitudes cried, Hosanna!" Sometimes John fancies, in the direct imagery of the blues, that he has "a closet full of whisky and wine," at other times, in his family's imagery, that he is the John of Revelation, or St. Paul. His identification with Maugham's

Mildred is not only self-pity but power fantasy. Baldwin writes: "He wanted to be like her, only more powerful, more thorough, and more cruel; to make those around him, all who hurt him, suffer as she made the student suffer, and laugh in their faces when they asked pity for their pain."

The long monologue by "Flap" Conroy in Redding's *No Day of Triumph,* in its combination of bitter misery with high-spirited defiance, is almost an extended blues. Flap opposes reality to blues fantasy, "*White folks* got the world in a jug an' the stopper in their hand," and then immediately denies it, "That's what *they* think." Bigger and his friend Gus in *Native Son* daydream of flying planes and dropping bombs on the white world. In *The Outsider,* this has become a vision, by a Negro in a bar, of flying saucers landing from Mars and disembarking *colored* men, come to put the white overlords of earth in their place. In Langston Hughes's *Simple Speaks His Mind,* Simple, who alternates between feeling "like I got the world in a jug and the stopper in my hand" and varieties of depression, also alternates between fury that Negroes are not allowed to run trains and fly planes, and fantasies of space flight:

> Why, man, I would rock so far away from this color line in the U. S. A., till it wouldn't be funny. I might even build me a garage on Mars and a mansion on Venus. On summer nights I would scoot down the Milky Way just to cool myself off. I would not have no old-time jet-propelled plane either. My plane would run on atom power. This earth I would not bother with no more. No, buddy-o! The sky would be my roadway and the stars my stopping place. Man, if I had a rocket plane, I would rock off into space and be solid gone. Gone. Real gone! I mean *gone!*"

Balancing this complex of misery and compensation in the slow blues, we have the abuse and bawdry of the fast blues. Georgia White sings:

> When we married, we promised to stick through thick and thin,
> When we married, we promised to stick through thick and thin;
> But the way you thinnin' out is a lowdown dirty sin.

"Speckled Red" sings:

> Now you're a dirty mistreater, a robber and a cheater,
> I slip you in the dozen, your pappy is your cousin,
> Your mama do the Lordy-Lord.

(The reference is to "the dozens," a formalized Negro game, particularly common among children, creating what John Dollard calls "a pattern of interactive insult" by chanting slurs on the cleanliness, odor, legitimacy, fidelity, and heterosexuality of the opponent's immediate family, particularly his mother.) Simple and Hughes's narrator slip each other repeatedly in the dozens, as do the college boys in Redding's novel *Stranger and Alone*, along with the characters in many other Negro works. There is a particularly interesting example in *Invisible Man*. The nameless protagonist, brought up on charges before a committee of the Brotherhood, is asked indignantly where he got the "personal responsibility" he claims, and automatically answers, "From your ma," before he corrects himself.

Related to the theme of obscenity and abuse in the blues is a pervasive cynicism, the cynicism of "If you don't like my peaches, don't shake my tree; I ain't after your woman, she's after me," or "Papa, papa, you in a good man's way; I can get one better than you any time of day." The Negro poet who has made this note uniquely his own is Fenton Johnson. I quote part of his poem "Tired," which catches the fast blues' mingled tones of despair and mean comedy:

> I am tired of work; I am tired of building up somebody
>   else's civilization.
> Let us take a rest, M'Lissy Jane.
> I will go down to the Last Chance Saloon, drink a gallon
>   or two of gin, shoot a game or two of dice and
>   sleep the rest of the night on one of Mike's barrels.
> You will let the old shanty go to rot, the white people's
>   clothes turn to dust, and the Calvary Baptist Church
>   sink to the bottomless pit.
> You will spend your days forgetting you married me and
>   your nights hunting the warm gin Mike serves the
>   ladies in the rear of the Last Chance Saloon.
> Throw the children into the river; civilization has given
>   us too many.

Along with the themes and attitudes of the blues, their techniques and diction are equally pervasive in Negro writing. In the
folk blues, the formal unit is not the song but the individual
stanza (what in ballad study is called the "commonplace"),
and the composer or singer strings traditional stanzas together to
produce his own composition. The formal organization of the
blues is "Little Brother's Blues," recorded by the Lomaxes, for the
and associative, like a good deal of modern poetry. A typical folk
blues is "Little Brother's Blues," recorded by the Lomaxes, for the
Library of Congress, at Texas State Penitentiary in 1934 (I will
not bother repeating the first lines of each stanza):

> Lord, you light weight skinners, you better learn to skin,
> Old Mister Bud Russell, I tell you, he wants to starve the men.
>
> O my mama, she called me, I'm gonna answer "Mam?"
> "Lord, ain't you tired of rollin' for that big-hat man?"
>
> She's got nine gold teeth, long black curly hair,
> Lord, if you get on the Santa Fe, find your baby there.
>
> I been prayin' Our Father, Lord, Thy kingdom come,
> Lord, I been prayin' Our Father, let Your will be done.
>
> One, two, three, four, five, six, seven, eight, nine,
> I'm gonna count these blues she's got on her mind.

Here motifs of work, compulsion and hunger, mother and rebellion, nine gold teeth and long black curly hair, train journey and
baby, God's will and counting the digits, all associate thematically
with doing time in a prison camp and the contrasted pole of freedom and gratifications, as T. S. Eliot associates garlic and sap-
phires in the mud.

The Negro poet most obviously identified with this sort of
thematic and associative organization is Melvin B. Tolson, in his
remarkable long poem *Libretto for the Republic of Liberia*. Allen
Tate in a preface places the poem "in the direct succession" from
Hart Crane's *The Bridge*, and other critics have identified its
techniques with those of Eliot's *Waste Land* or Pound's *Cantos*.
Reinforcing rather than denying these analogies, I would insist on
its kinship to the associative organization of the blues. In any

case, it is an intricate and sophisticated work, and the advance in complexity it represents can best be shown by comparing a stanza with one from its obvious predecessor, Paul Laurence Dunbar's "Ode to Ethiopia." Dunbar writes:

> On every hand in this fair land,
> Proud Ethiope's swarthy children stand
>   Beside their fairer neighbor;
> The forests flee before their stroke,
> Their hammers ring, their forges smoke,—
>   They stir in honest labor.

Tolson writes:

> And now the hyenas whine among the barren bones
> Of the seventeen sun sultans of Songhai,
> And hooded cobras, hoodless mambas, hiss
> In the gold caverns of Falémé and Bambuk,
> And puff adders, hook scorpions, whisper
> In the weedy corridors of Sankoré. *Lia! Lia!*

The language of the blues is rich in the sort of irony and ambiguity to which the modern criticism of poetry has heightened our consciousness. Pine Top Smith sings:

> Now I combed her hair, even manicured her fingernails,
> Now I combed her hair, even manicured her fingernails;
> Every time I get in trouble, she let me go to jail.

Robert Johnson sings:

> She's a kind-hearted mama, studies evil all the time.

The poetry of Gwendolyn Brooks shows something of this range of irony, from the mockery of a folk tradition in "The Ballad of Late Annie" to the poignant Dickinsonian cadences of poem IV of "The Womanhood" in *Annie Allen,* which I must quote entire:

> A light and diplomatic bird
> Is lenient in my window tree.
> A quick dilemma of the leaves
> Discloses twist and tact to me.
>
> Who strangles his extremest need
> For pity of my imminence

On utmost ache and lacquered cold
Is prosperous in proper sense:

He can abash his barmecides;
The fantoccini of his range
Pass over. Vast and secular
And apt and admirably strange.

Augmented by incorrigible
Conviction of his symmetry
He can afford his sine die.
He can afford to pity me

Whose hours at best are wheats or beiges
Lashed with riot-red and black.
Tabasco at the lapping wave.
Search-light in the secret crack.

Oh open, apostolic height!
And tell my humbug how to start
Bid balance, bleach: make miniature
Valhalla of my heart.

Negro writers have ceaselessly attempted to define the emotional ambivalence of the blues: "grief-gaiety," "melancholy-comic," "wistfulness-laughter," "making light of what actually is grave," or the blues line itself, "I'm laughing just to keep from crying." In his *Libretto*, that treasure ship of plunder from the world's cultures and languages, Tolson uses a Yiddish phrase for this ambivalence, "*lachen mit yastchekes*," which he translates in the notes as " 'laughing with needles being stuck in you'; ghetto laughter." "As for the laughter," a character in Redding's *Stranger and Alone* thinks, "unless one had experienced it, he cannot imagine how it rips and tears you with pain." In an interview in the *New York Times*, Baldwin stated what are clearly his intentions as a writer: "I have always wondered why there has never, or almost never, appeared in fiction any of the joy of Louis Armstrong or the really bottomless, ironic and mocking sadness of Billie Holiday." His own books display a comparable ambivalence everywhere. Florence in *Go Tell It on the Mountain* "did not want his touch, and yet she did: she burned with longing and froze with rage." Gabriel "hated his sins—even as he ran towards sin," and "prayed, as his mother had taught him to pray, for loving kindness; yet he dreamed of the feel of a white man's forehead against his shoe." John, the young protagonist, is ambivalent toward his stepfather, his mother, his aunt, his idol Elisha, even to God. In *Notes of a Native Son*, Baldwin generalizes from the irony of his father's death on the day the father had a child: "Life and death so close together, and love and hatred, and right and wrong, said something to me which I did not want to hear concerning man, concerning the life of man." *Giovanni's Room*, as befits a novel about sexual ambivalence, shows both sides of every coin: the narrator yields to Giovanni, "With everything in me screaming *No!* yet the sum of me sighed *Yes*"; he later feels "a hatred for Giovanni which was as powerful as my love and which was nourished by the same roots"; when he intends to desert him for a girl, "I really felt at that moment that Judas and the Saviour had met in me"; when he has his final battle with Giovanni, "He grasped me by the collar, wrestling and caressing at once, fluid and iron at once: saliva spraying from his lips and his eyes full of tears."

Ellison made the first critical attempt I know to relate the blues to specific Negro literature in an article on *Black Boy* entitled "Richard Wright's Blues" in *The Antioch Review*, Summer, 1945. He began by defining the form as a symbolic action:

> The Blues is an impulse to keep the painful details and episodes of a brutal experience alive in one's aching consciousness, to finger its jagged grain, and to transcend it, not by the consolation of philosophy, but by squeezing from it a near-tragic, near-comic lyricism.

and concluded:

> Let us close with one final word about the Blues: Their attraction lies in this, that they at once express both the agony of life and the possibility of conquering it through sheer toughness of spirit. They fall short of tragedy only in that they provide no solution, offer no scapegoat but the self.

This conception did not really fit Wright's *Black Boy* very well (it would apply much more aptly to "The Man Who Lived Underground"), but it turned out to be a remarkably accurate manifesto for Ellison's own novel, *Invisible Man*, published seven years later. If we want "a near-tragic, near-comic lyricism" in a fictional image we need go no further than its final tableau of the Harlem riot of 1943. Here Ras the Exhorter, a bitter Negro nationalist, arrays himself as an Abyssinian chieftain, armed with spear and shield, and rides out against the police guns. We see the scene through the eyes of an anonymous Harlem citizen:

> "Hell, yes, man, he had him a big black hoss and a fur cap and some kind of old lion skin or something over his shoulders and he was raising hell. Goddam if it wasn't a *sight*, riding up and down on this ole hoss, you know, one of the kind that pulls vegetable wagons, and he got him a cowboy saddle and some big spurs."
>
> "Aw naw, man!"
>
> "Hell, yes! Riding up and down the block yelling, 'Destroy 'em! Drive 'em out! Burn 'em out! I, Ras, commands you.' You get that, man," he said, " 'I *Ras*, commands you—to destroy them to the last piece of rotten fish!' And 'bout that time some joker with a big ole Georgia voice sticks his head out the window and yells, 'Ride 'em, cowboy. Give 'em hell and bananas.' "

Finally, "riding like Earl Sande in the fifth at Jamaica," Ras charges to his death.

If the blues is the ancestor of the low rhetoric in Negro writing, the sermon is the ancestor of the high. Oratory has a surprisingly prominent place in American Negro life: Redding notes that the children in his family "were all trained at home in the declining art of oratory and were regular contestants for prizes at school"; Baldwin was a preacher in a Harlem store-front church for several years in his teens; when Ellison decided not to make his protagonist a writer, making him a speaker was the obvious choice. Their books are inevitably full of oratorical set pieces: *No Day of Triumph* reproduces a Negro funeral sermon and *Stranger and Alone* a Southern governor's campaign speech; the effective end of *Native Son* is Max's impassioned defense of Bigger in court; a whole chapter of *Invisible Man* is devoted to blind Barbee's sermon on the Founder of the school, and the narrator makes several eloquent political speeches; *Go Tell It on the Mountain* includes two of Gabriel's remarkable sermons. Listen to such an example of the Negro folk sermon as "The Man of Calvary," by "Sin-Killer" Griffin, which John Lomax recorded in 1934 during an Easter Sunday service at a Texas penitentiary, and which the Library of Congress issues on a record. The three principal ingredients seem to be: a Biblical violence of acting and suffering ("Roman soldiers came riding in full speed and splunged Him in the side"); apocalyptic, almost surrealist imagery like that of the Book of Revelation (the sun "clothed itself in sack cloth-ing and went down," the moon sank in blood and "done bled away," "each little star leaped out of its silver orbit" and became a funeral torch); and a contrasting tone of concentrated wisdom, like that of the Book of Proverbs.

All three of these tones are markedly evident in Negro writing. The violence, like so much else, is overdetermined: it comes not only from the Bible, but from all the harsh realities of American Negro life, and it relates to the mock-violence of the blues ("Cut him if he stand still, shoot him if he run"). Our most extreme example is Richard Wright, whose writings are almost indescribably violent: Native Son from the beating of the rat to death in the first pages to the imminent electrocution of Bigger in the last; the innumerable whippings, bone-smashings, rapes, murders, and burnings in the stories. The tone of Black Boy is set in the first pages when Wright is almost beaten to death by his mother; the poems are a dreadful tissue of mobs "battering my teeth into my throat till I swallowed my own blood" and "the tall flames that cooked and charred the black flesh." This overreaches itself to the point of Grand Guignol horror in The Outsider. Cross frees himself in a subway wreck, to give one moderate example, by smashing a corpse's head to a bloody pulp. He then escapes out the window by standing on the chest of a dead woman, "feeling his shoes sinking into the lifeless flesh and seeing blood bubbling from the woman's mouth as his weight bore down on her breast." And so on for four hundred pages.

The apocalyptic imagery of the sermon appears in Negro writing at least as far back as the fantasies of W. E. B. DuBois, particularly Darkwater in 1919, with its black Christ born in Georgia and the destruction of Manhattan by a comet. Jean Toomer's Cane, published in 1923, displays a lower-keyed, rather whimsical surrealism: "Her mind is a pink mesh-bag filled with baby toes." In our time, two principal examplars of these juxtapositions have been Ellison and Baldwin. Open *Invisible Man* at any page: here is a stag smoker entertained by a combination of Negro boys fighting a battle royal, a graduation address, and a naked white dancer with a small American flag tattooed on her belly; there, an artificial eye in a glass of water staring intently at the narrator everyone else finds invisible. *Go Tell It on the Mountain* is full of the same wild imagery: John hears the sounds of his parents in bed together "over the sound of rat feet, and rat screams"; after his conversion at the end he sees the Devil on the streets of Harlem, disguised as a lean cat eying him from behind a garbage can, or a gray bird perched on the metal cornice of a roof.

Baldwin talks of "something ironic and violent and perpetually understated in Negro speech," and complains that despite the "force and precision" of the spoken language, Negro writing "has been generally speaking so pallid and harsh." This force and precision is the third strain of the sermon, its gnarly eloquence. The same quality is common to the Bible, West African speech forms (Tolson quotes a number of remarkable African proverbs), and American Negro folklore. Zora Neale Hurston was told, "Hard work in de hot sun done called many a man to preach." "You ain't the only frog done fattened hisself for snakes," says a character in *No Day of Triumph*. "Any time a nigger with white folks," remarks a figure in Redding's novel, "he alone." "Reach and draw back a nub," taunts the narrator in *Invisible Man*. "Me and the Lord," Florence's husband remarks in *Go Tell It on the Mountain*, "don't always get along so well. He running the world like He thinks I ain't got good sense."

Negro writing, because of the special vulnerabilities and resources of Negro writers, is in a position to deal with certain ironies and ambivalences of the American condition as most white writers (at least outside the South) are not. Negro writers are, as it were, a special kind of radar to extend our vision. Wright in "The Ethics of Living Jim Crow" and *Black Boy*, Tolson in the *Libretto*, Ellison in the Prologue and Epilogue to *Invisible Man*, Baldwin in *Notes of a Native Son*, have all tirelessly articulated this peculiar role, with its consequent responsibilities. The social and racial relations of America are changing radically. In 1900 almost three-quarters of the Negroes in America had lived in the rural South; by 1950, fewer than one-fifth of them did. Where one out of three Negroes over sixty-five is illiterate, fewer than one out of twenty is, in the younger generation. The seventeen million Negroes in the United States now earn a sum about equal to the national income of Canada. Not long ago the Cotton Club in Harlem would not admit Negroes unless they were celebrities, now Broadway and 52nd Street night clubs advertise eagerly for the Negro trade. One has only to read Toomer's 1923 portrait of Negro life in the South in *Cane*, and its 1942 equivalent, Redding's *No Day of Triumph*, to see the changes wrought by two decades, and a comparable 1957 book would show changes about again as great. Nor does this process go on only in the United States. Any daily paper will show the varieties of ferment of the world's Negro peoples, and we can see its articulate consciousness in such fiction as *In the Castle of My Skin* by George Lamming of the Barbados, or *The Palm-Wine Drinkard* and *My Life in the Bush of Ghosts* by the Nigerian writer Amos Tutuola.

"The artist must lose such lesser identities [as Negro] in the great well of life," Waldo Frank says in his foreword to *Cane*. That has not been the view of many Negro artists of our time. In Paris, Baldwin reports, the American Negro "finds himself involved, in another language, in the same old battle: the battle for his own identity," and this turns out to be part of a larger American quest: "The American in Europe is everywhere confronted with the question of his identity." There is a Negro character in Claude McKay's *Home to Harlem* for whom identity is largely a matter of cuisine: "He would not eat watermelon, because white people called it 'the niggers' ice-cream.' Pork chops he fancied not. Nor corn pone. And the idea of eating chicken gave him a spasm." Ellison has written exhaustively on the identity problem in "Richard Wright's Blues" and elsewhere, but his most graphic account of it is a similarly culinary identification in *Invisible Man*. The narrator had always scorned Negro food, along with other backward "darky" trappings, in his effort to rise in the white world, until a moment in the middle of the book when on impulse he buys a yam from a peddler and eats it on the street. At that moment, in the magical equation of "yam" with "I am," he comes to terms with his Negro identity and folk tradition, while maintaining his quest for a fully developed human consciousness. In other words, he wants yams, but he wants to be a twentieth-century Western man eating them. It is in just this fashion that the blues, say, develop in significance; starting with the specific lament for lost love, calamity, or hard times, and ending with these events metaphoric for the most universal human condition.

The folk tradition, for the Negro writer, is like Ellison's yams, not the regression or reversion it appears to be, but another path to the most ironic and sophisticated consciousness. Tate's preface to *Libretto for the Republic of Liberia* finds that full utilization of the resources of modern poetry and language has made Tolson "not less but more intensely *Negro*." There is an almost unavoidable unconscious pun in dealing with Negro culture. A silly white Negrophile in Fisher's *The Walls of Jericho* says she prefers Negroes to whites because "You see, they have so much color." Margaret Just Butcher, the Negro author of *The Negro in American Culture*, makes the pun continually in what I am sure is entire innocence: "The Negro observably colored the general temper and folkways of the American south"; Negro comedy "richly colored Southern local and regional culture, and eventually that of the whole nation"; a work typifies "the well-meaning, somewhat colorless accounts by white authors"; *Uncle Tom's Cabin* is written in "sharp blacks and whites, no shadings." The reality behind the pun is that Negro life in America, Negro folk literature, and some Negro writing does have color in every sense; not only skin pigment, but all the rich pigmentation of the fullest possible awareness. The best Negro literature and folk literature extends our perception to a far wider range. "Who knows," the narrator of *Invisible Man* asks in the book's last line, "but that, on the lower frequencies, I speak for you?" Perhaps, we can add, on the very highest, the almost inaudible frequencies as well?

NOTE [1963]: This was originally written as the first Ludwig Lewisohn Lecture at Brandeis. When I finished the manuscript I sent it to my friend Ralph Ellison for an opinion. He replied with a long eloquent letter arguing the other half of the truth, the indebtedness of American Negro literature to the European literary tradition. As a result we produced a rather contrived debate in *Partisan Review*, Spring, 1958. A shortened version of my lecture was followed by his rejoinder, "Change the Joke and Slip the Yoke"; the two constituting "The Negro Writer in America: an Exchange." Ellison's article is particularly interesting for its statements about the influences on his own work.

Literature
and the
Culture

The Problem
of Jewish Identity

1. Identities of Isaac Babel

[1956]

Now THAT Frank O'Connor has been awarded "some claim to greatness" by Arthur Mizener, and Wyndham Lewis is celebrated as "the greatest prose master of style of my generation" by T. S. Eliot, perhaps it is time we heard more of Isaac Babel. In his lifetime this Soviet Jewish writer published three books of short stories: *Red Cavalry*, based on his experiences fighting in Poland in 1920 with Budenny's First Cavalry Army, in 1923; *Odessa Tales*, based on his boyhood, in 1924; and a collected volume with additional stories in 1932. Since 1938, when Babel published some reminiscences of Gorky, his name is said not to have appeared in a Soviet publication, and he is believed to have died in a penal camp in 1939 or 1940, with several conflicting accounts of his arrest and death available. *Red Cavalry* was brought out here by Knopf in 1929, in a graceless translation by Nadia Helstein, woefully bowdlerized and cut; and a small group of Babel's Jewish stories from all three books was published as *Benya Krik, the Gangster and Other Stories* by Schocken Books in 1948, beautifully translated by Avrahm Yarmolinsky. (Unfortunately, out of their context in *Red Cavalry* and with their chronology reversed, the Jewish stories alone give a distorted impression of Babel's work.)

With the publication for the first time in any language of the body of Babel's short stories, in *The Collected Stories*, ably edited

319

and translated by Walter Morison, with an introduction by Lionel Trilling, we finally have an adequate English text, and Criterion Books deserves fairly handsome congratulations. If Trilling's intelligent and sensitive introduction is not the last word, it is at least a good word, and his currently fashionable voice may succeed in introducing Babel to the thousands of readers the book deserves instead of the hundreds it might otherwise get. Morison's translation may be, for all I know, more faithful to the Russian than Yarmolinsky's, but it seems to me to weaken some of the comic effect and to be less eloquent at key rhetorical points. In Morison's version, a rich Odessa merchant is called "Jew-and-a-Half" because "no single Jew could have had so much dash and so much cash"; in Yarmolinsky's translation, he is "Yid-and-a-Half" because "no one Jew could contain so much insolence and so much money." In the story "The Rabbi's Son" in *Red Cavalry*, the dying body of Elijah, the Communist son of Rabbi Motale Bratslavsky, the last of the Chernobyl dynasty, is carried into Babel's railroad car by two sturdy female typists. As Morison has it, the girls "stared dully at his sexual organs, the stunted, curly-covered virility of a wasted Semite." In Yarmolinsky, the girls "stared drily at his private parts, the tender curly maleness of a spent Semite." (The Helstein text simply has "and stared at him." In addition, by ending the book on this penultimate story, with its noble climax of Jewish and Communist idealism, and chopping off the last story, in which the narrator achieves his "dream" of riding a horse like a Cossack and being accepted, she does Babel a substantial injustice.)

Reading *The Collected Stories*, one's first impression is likely to be that whereas any given story seems clear and sharp, as a group they become much more ambiguous and evasive. We are forced to come to terms very quickly with Babel's ambivalences: he is a Soviet writer for whom the welcomed Revolution is mostly an image of the mindless animal brutality of Cossacks, a Jewish writer whose essence of Jewish life is "a violent smell of rotten herrings," a traditional Russian writer who identified so strongly with Maupassant that for a while he tried to write in French. (This identification, characteristically, was not with the triumphant "lion in the path," but with the insane dying Maupassant, regressively crawling on all fours and eating his excrement.)

Trilling describes one of Babel's major themes as "the test and the initiation," but I would prefer to characterize it more generally as changes of identity through rituals of rebirth. To my reading, there are not one but two narrators in *Red Cavalry* (besides the illiterate Cossacks who tell their stories in the first person): one a gentile intellectual addressed as Lyutov, who refers to "the occult crockery the Jews use only once a year, at Eastertime," and sees the Polish Jews as living in filth and meaningless suffering, like animals; the other a Jewish intellectual, Babel himself, who gets away from the Red Army in Zhitomir on the eve of the Sabbath, "oppressed by the dense melancholy of memories," to search for "a Jewish glass of tea, and a little of that pensioned-off God in a glass of tea." One of the Odessa stories of Benya Krik, the Jewish gangster who "can spend the night with a Russian woman and satisfy her," is told, not by Babel, but *to* Babel by Reb Arye-Leib, an old man from the poorhouse, so that he can reproach Babel with being everything Benya is not, a coward "with spectacles on your nose and autumn in your heart." Arye-Leib says:

> What would you have done in Benya Krik's place? You would have done nothing. But *he* did something. That's why he's the King, while you thumb your nose in the privy.

Thus in *Red Cavalry* Babel is reborn as Lyutov, without his Jewishness; still scorned as "you guys in specs" and "four-eyes," he is reborn again without his crippling intellectualism in the last story and accepted on terms of something like equality. That this ersatz Cossack is in turn an inadequate *persona* only comes clear in the stories after *Red Cavalry*, where it is succeeded by even more ambiguous personalities and culminates in the image of the little child Karl-Yankel, who is to receive the Soviet Kingdom. The physical horrors of *Red Cavalry*—a young Polish prisoner is shot with a carbine at close range "and bits of his brain dripped over my hands"; the narrator inadvertently urinates on a Polish corpse in the dark, and when he lights a lantern sees the urine "pouring out of his mouth, bubbling between his teeth, gathered in his empty eye sockets"—are a catharsis by violence, the agency of these rebirths. The narrators are never participants in the violence: Lyutov goes into action with no cartridges in his revolver, cannot bring himself

to shoot a dying friend to keep him from Polish torture, and ironically implores fate "to grant me the simplest of proficiencies—the
ability to kill my fellow-men." Out of the bloodshed and fury, as
Babel saw it, would come the Revolutionary redemption he hoped
for, but when Gedali, the Jewish proprietor of a junkshop in Zhitomir, tells him his dream of a Revolution of joy, an International
of good people, Babel answers harshly that Gedali's impossible
International "is eaten with gunpowder and spiced with best-
quality blood."

The book's dichotomy is not simply between "the way of violence and the way of peace," as Trilling says, or between "the Cossack ethos" and "the Jewish ethos," as Raymond Rosenthal
suggested in his seminal article, "The Fate of Isaak Babel," in *Commentary*, February, 1947. "Violence" and "peace" are both ambivalent terms: going into action with an unloaded gun is neither one,
surely, but a kind of pacific violence; the narrator's refusal to shoot
his friend Dolgushov, thus letting him die slowly, "entrails hung
over his knees," or suffer torture by the Poles, seems a very violent
peacefulness indeed. Within the image of the Cossack there is a
similar duality: the aloof Cossack officer riding through Babel's
childhood Odessa "as though through a mountain pass," his hands
in lemon-colored chamois gloves, is not the subhuman Cossack
troopers Babel knew in Poland, wearing bast shoes. The category
"Jew" similarly includes the narrow-chested Polish Jews, "these
long bony backs, these tragic yellow beards," as well as "the stout
and jovial Jews of the south, bubbling like cheap wine." Babel
writes in one of his autobiographical stories: "Like all Jews I was
short, weakly, and had headaches from studying." However, he
simultaneously knows of "that unexpected breed of Jews, the tough
fighting men, raiders, and partisans," and in his own family there
is Uncle Leo who died in a brothel in Los Angeles, the narrator's
grandfather who lost his pulpit for blasphemy and forgery, and a
considerable number of drunkards and seducers neither short,
weakly, nor studious. If Elijah Bratslavsky's virility is wasted or
spent, Benya Krik's is not, and even that least likely erotic image,
Benya's sister Deborah, a forty-year-old goitrous virgin, concludes
her wedding festivities

urging her fainthearted husband toward the door of their nuptial chamber, glaring at him carnivorously. Like a cat she was, that holding a mouse in her jaws tests it gently with her teeth.

The true dichotomy in Babel's writing is between culture and nature, or art and the life of action, or freedom and necessity, or any philosophic phrasing of the Darwinian conflict between life in a moral order alienated from nature and natural law, and life in a natural order antecedent to morality. Babel's true quest is not to *be* a Cossack, but to form an organic unit, a horse-man, with a horse (as a Cossack does), instead of riding (as Babel had) so that the horse's back was covered with festering sores. In the stories of Babel's boyhood this ambition was preceded by earlier passions for keeping pigeons and learning to swim, and here the Jewish tradition of a life outside nature is the enemy. "The hydrophobia of my ancestors—Spanish rabbis and Frankfurt money-changers—dragged me to the bottom," Babel writes, and the conflict of "rabbis versus Neptune" is only resolved when "the local water god," a gentile athlete, teaches him to swim and earns his love, "the love that only a lad suffering from hysteria and headaches can feel for a real man." This is a neat enough Christian baptism, but the story ends with the boy studying nature and the names of trees and birds with the same desperate monomania (culturally inherited from Spanish rabbis and Frankfurt money-changers) with which he had previously studied Talmud and Gemara.

In one of the finest comic stories in the book, "In the Basement," the young Babel tries to drown out the sound of his eccentric relatives disgracing him before a respectable school friend by reciting Antony's speech over Caesar's corpse louder and louder. This effort to use art to deny life is inevitably doomed when the art, as the rhetoric of filial loyalty and disloyalty, only brings him closer to his problem. At the end of the story, when the boy determines to end his ruined career by drowning himself in the household water barrel, his crazy grandfather (the defrocked rabbi, the blasphemer, the forger) pulls him out and has the last word on behalf of life. "Grandson," he says, "I am going to take a dose of castor oil, so as to have something to lay on your grave."

In this complicated conflict of nature and culture, the Jews represent the heirs of all the world's culture. Babel characteristically never puts this in terms of large statements about the Judaeo-Christian tradition or the inheritance of Western humanism. Instead, Gedali's junkshop contains "gilt slippers, ship's cables, an ancient compass, a stuffed eagle, a Winchester with the date 1810 engraved upon it, a broken saucepan." To the beggars of Odessa at Jewish weddings come "fat-bellied jars of Jamaica rum, oily Madeira, cigars from the plantations of Pierpont Morgan, and oranges from the environs of Jerusalem." In a Jewish shop in Odessa are "olives that had come from Greece, olive oil from Marseille, coffee in beans, Malaga from Lisbon, 'Philippe and Canot' brand sardines, and Cayenne pepper." To the inn of Lyubka, nicknamed "the Cossack," a Jewish procuress and smuggler, come "cigars and fine silks, cocaine and files, unbonded tobacco from the State of Virginia, and dark wine from the Island of Chios." If the world's goods also include the sacred books of "that pensioned-off God" and Guy de Maupassant, the payment for them starts with the inability to swim or ride, and ends with what the young Babel foresees in Maupassant's tragic end: "My heart contracted as the foreboding of some essential truth touched me with light fingers."

The sun that hangs over Babel's fictional world is bloody and violent: "the orange sun rolled down the sky like a lopped-off head," "the young Sabbath crept along the sunset, crushing the stars beneath her little red heel," "the purple eye of the sunset, groping over the earth," the sun "climbed to the middle of the sky and hung there quivering like a fly overcome by the heat," "the sun lolled from the sky like the pink tongue of a thirsty dog," in the "flames of the setting sun" the scenery is "swollen with crimson blood," "in the sky the walls of the sunset caved in." There is real gore on the Cossacks and Poles in *Red Cavalry*, but even the peaceful Jews of Odessa are covered with symbolic blood. The ritual circumciser in "Karl-Yankel" is like one great clot: "When he was doing his snipping he didn't drain the blood off through a little glass tube but sucked it away with his splayed lips, and his tangled beard got all blood-smeared"; as a consequence he is redheaded, "like the first redheaded man on earth," and his head is "a little red walnut," "a clotted little walnut." The old Jewish women of Odessa are distinguished by "sweat with the pinkness of fresh blood, sweat as pink as the slaver of a mad dog."

The Cossack men, as might be expected, are stallions, so literally that a girl who has just been raped by six of them walks "with the awkward gait of a cavalryman when he puts his numbed legs on the ground after a long ride." Women are invariably seen as the baby sees them, with the nourishing breast looming large in the foreground. The mistress of a Cossack officer walks "bearing her bosom on her high heels, a bosom that stirred like an animal in a bag"; the regiment's "nurse" Sasha rides with "her enormous breasts swung around to her back," or walks "with her wobbling breasts"; a woman in one of Babel's wartime dreams "freed her breast from the black lace of her bodice and raised it to me, carefully, like a nurse proffering food"; the Moldavanka, the Odessa ghetto, is "our deep-bosomed mother"; and "Guy de Maupassant" focuses on Maupassant's story "Idyll," in which an adult "sucked the breast of the stout nursing mother to relieve her of the milk with which she was overladen." Often this breast imagery becomes perverse and disconcerting: the Polish roads flow "like streams of milk spurting from many breasts," the hips of girls smell of "the odors of the sea and of milk." Women are often identified with cows, full of "bovine juices" or filling up "with juice as a cow's udder fills on the pastures with the pink milk of spring." The identification is just as likely to be with butchered cows, "soaked in milk and stinking of it like a sliced udder," so that Sasha's body is "fresh and strong-smelling as the meat of a cow that has only just been slaughtered." The most powerful maternal image in the book, the nursing mother Lyubka "the Cossack" has enormous breasts, freely handled by everyone in the story, and she sees the fact that her milk has dried up, leaving her baby to howl, as the Oedipal child might see it, as a punishment for this erotic misuse.

Much of Babel's imagery aims at the deliberate shock effect of surrealism: Christ's wounds are "oozing seed, a fragrant poison to intoxicate virgins"; in the Heavenly wings there is a "dismal electrician" with a "moon-extinguisher"; the great Rabbi Motale Bratslavsky greets the narrator piously, "surrounded by the liars and the possessed" (here again I prefer Yarmolinsky's "surrounded by liars and madmen"); fawning officers "fished for roast chicken in the Army Commander's smiles"; the Babel house is "impregnated with the smell of leeks and Jewish destiny." Very little of the terrestrial imagery is pictorial, with the consistent exception of the Moldavanka gangsters, who look as though they were in a child's painting: they wear raspberry waistcoats, russet jackets, and azure shoes; Benya himself wears a chocolate jacket, cream pants, and raspberry boots; they all dress like "birds of paradise" and drive "lacquered carriages."

If the touch occasionally falters, and the imagery turns cute ("An orange star which had slid to the very brim of the horizon gazed wide-eyed at them"), for the most part Babel's effects are meticulously successful. Presumably the narrator of "Guy de Maupassant" reflects the author's concept of craft when he writes: "A phrase is born into the world both good and bad at the same time. The secret lies in a slight, an almost invisible twist. The lever should rest in your hand, getting warm, and you can only turn it once, not twice. . . . No iron can stab the heart with such force as a period put just at the right place." The story that to my taste is Babel's finest, "The Story of My Dovecot," is a triumph of delicate indirection and craft. It tells the narrator's experience during the 1905 pogroms without ever using the word "pogrom" until the very last sentence, summoning up all the violence and horror of the events with two "objective correlative" images: the boy's beloved pigeon crushed against his head, so that the warm guts trickle down his face, and his granduncle Shoyl, a fish peddler, lying murdered with a live pike perch still flapping in a rip in his trousers.

The progress of the stories is the traditional tragic or ritual one "from Purpose through Passion to Perception." If the boy aspired to vengeance on Shoyl's murderers and eventual despoiling of the despoilers who looted his father's store during the pogrom, *Red Cavalry* is the purgation of those purposes. Both are "Cossack" ideals eloquently achieved in the book. Matthew Pavlichenko, slapped and insulted by his master, comes back with the Red Army and stamps the *barin* to death: "trampled on him for an hour or maybe more. And in that time I got to know life through and through." Prishchepa, whose parents have been killed by the Whites and their property seized by the neighbors, comes back when the Whites have been driven out and goes around the village collecting the family belongings: "In the huts where he found gear that had belonged to his mother, a pipe that had been his father's, he left old women stabbed through and through, dogs hung above the wells, icons defiled with excrement." But Pavlichenko has in reality gotten to know life no better, and Prishchepa has not really restored his despoiled home but only ravaged others, and now has nothing to do but put the furniture back into the empty house, set fire to it, kill all the farm animals, and ride wildly off.

When Babel returns to Odessa after the Revolution all impulse for revenge and recovery has been burned out of him, and he aspires only to recreate the image of the events in art, to win through to perception, and: "remembering those sorrowful years, I find in them the beginning of the ills that torment me, the cause of my early fading." The narrator of the story "The Kiss," quartered in the home of a Polish schoolmaster during the fighting, and recognizing by the barricaded door and the trembling of his hosts that *he* has become the image of the persecutor, spends the night sleepless, "tormented and muddled." The next morning he says to the daughter of the family, "You must know that I have a law degree, and am reckoned a highbrow"—desperately flaunting a personality he has been at such pains to suppress.

If the synthesis of Jew and Cossack (as Rosenthal first pointed out) is Benya Krik the Jewish "Cossack," Benya too is ultimately unsatisfactory in that his fine comic play-acting and his masterful extortion letters have real consequences in the murder of an innocent Jew by one of his drunken gangsters. Babel is with the victim's employer, shouting at Benya in fury, "A fine trick you've thought up, killing live people." Lyubka Shneiveis "the Cossack," a maternal ogress who beats up peasants with her fists, fails as a synthesis similarly (as her mother's milk fails). The old Turk lying in her courtyard on the way back from Mecca, refusing a doctor to die in sanctity, turns out to be stronger in the integrity of his principles than she is in hers. If the narrator's ambition as a boy was to be like Benya and have a "Cossack" father like Benya's father Mendel, the drunken and violent drayman, and a "Cossack" mother like Lyubka, the symbolic parents he finally achieves in "Di Grasso," the last story in the book, are Jews as absurd, ineffectual, and ironically "good" as his own parents. They are the impresario Nick Schwarz, with whom Babel has pawned his father's gold watch, and his wife Madam Schwarz, who is so moved by the acting of an Italian company that she makes Nick give the watch back to the boy (accompanied by "a vicious pinch"), leaving young Babel suddenly able to see the living realities of Odessa around him "as they really were: frozen in silence and ineffably beautiful."

The last sentences of Babel's stories tend to carry a great amount of weight, as though eloquence could only burst through the taut style at the very last moment. Thus, "My First Goose," which recounts the narrator's only personal act of violence in *Red Cavalry*, his brutal killing of the landlady's goose to ingratiate himself with his fellow soldiers, ends: "But my heart, stained with bloodshed, grated and brimmed over." In "The Rabbi's Son," the dead Elijah Bratslavsky is revealed to have been an ambiguous blending of religious Jew and Communist, and his spilled pack reveals

> mandates of the propagandist and notebooks of the Jewish poet, the portraits of Lenin and Maimonides lay side by side, the knotted iron of Lenin's skull beside the dull silk of the portraits of Maimonides. A lock of woman's hair lay in a book, the Resolutions of the Party's Sixth Congress, and the margins of Communist leaflets were crowded with crooked lines of ancient Hebrew verse.

The story concludes: "And I, who can scarce contain the tempests of my imagination within this age-old body of mine, I was there beside my brother when he breathed his last." "Karl-Yankel," the comic story of an Odessa baby after the Revolution who is hotly contested by orthodox Jewry and Communist atheism (his grandmother is on trial for having him secretly circumcised in contempt of the Revolution) concludes:

> I had grown up on these streets, and now it was Karl-Yankel's turn. But they hadn't fought for me as now they were fighting for him: few were those to whom I had been of any concern.
> "It's not possible," I whispered to myself, "it's not possible that you won't be happy, Karl-Yankel. It's not possible that you won't be happier than I."

Ultimately, Babel's irony overwhelms everything, and Karl-Yankel is no more satisfactory a synthesis of warring opposites than Elijah the Rabbi's son; Benya and Lyubka the Jewish Cossacks are no more adequate than Jew or Cossack alone. When old Rabbi Motale had asked the narrator, "What is the Jew's occupation?" the answer was, "I am putting into verse the adventures of Hersch of Ostropol," when his actual occupation at the moment was writing propaganda articles for *Red Trooper*. This identification with the Jewish folk hero Herschel Ostropolier, a trickster and jester who is never what he seems to be, manages to undercut both the Rabbi's values and *Red Trooper*'s. The sleepy old defense lawyer in "Karl-Yankel," covered with tobacco ash, would be, we are assured, the head of the Sanhedrin, the Jewish high council, "if the Sanhedrin existed in our days." Is this a joke at Jewish tradition, Soviet jurisprudence, the modern world, or no joke at all?

In the last analysis, Babel evades all his categories, and our own. As Trilling writes, Babel's ambiguous art "was not a dialectic that his Russia could permit," and it seems clear that by the thirties Babel's fiction was unpublishable in the Soviet Union. Yet the signs of inner collapse and regression, the failure of any synthesis or resolution to sustain his vision, are so substantial that we need not look to external censorship to explain his silence. Ultimately Babel was neither so tough as Maupassant nor so shifty as Herschel Ostropolier. Not even his age-old body could contain the tempests of his imagination, let alone any combination of nature and culture, the Jewish community or the Soviet state. In the dozen first-rate stories he left us we have short fictions to rank with any in our time, and in his brief life and work we have perhaps the cautionary tale he saw in Maupassant's, the foreboding of some essential truth.

2. *David Daiches' Two Worlds*

[1956]

DAVID DAICHES' ESSAY in autobiography, *Two Worlds*, comes subtitled "A Jewish Childhood in Edinburgh," and its assurance that those two worlds combine picturesquely has convinced at least the jacket designer, who stencils a menorah against a colored background that looks suspiciously like a tartan. "The two worlds, in my childhood, were not really separate," Daiches informs us. Scottish Presbyterian orthodoxy accepted Daiches' Jewish orthodoxy with respect and interest, and his Scripture teacher would ask, "What does the Hebrew say, Daiches?" whenever they came to "some obscure incident." Linguistically, Daiches notes, "Scots preserves many Germanic words lost in standard English and found, in a similar or even identical form, in Yiddish"; in one comic chapter, which appeared in *The New Yorker*, he explores the vagaries of the Scots-Yiddish spoken by the Jewish immigrants in Edinburgh. Coexistence has occurred on many levels: for his doctorate at Oxford, Daiches studied English translations of the Hebrew Bible; as a poet, he translated Judah Halevi into Lallans Scots; as an ethnolinguist, he noted how the whisky slogan "Take a peg of John Begg" transforms into *"Nem a schmeck fun Dzon Beck."*

As a child, Daiches reports, he responded loyally to pulls in both directions. He carried a pocket history of the Jews to school, to refer proudly to facts and figures, while "In my secret heart I wanted to wear a kilt"; he found "the sound of bagpipes deeply rousing" and was moved equally by "the plaintive melodies of Jewish liturgy"; he was driven to win a university scholarship to "vindicate the character of the Jew in Scotland." The important difference Daiches felt, which he returns to again and again in the book, was in relation to time: the secular year seemed to be outside time, while the Jewish world was cyclic and time-bound. "The streets and meadows and hills of Edinburgh represented the timeless world," as though "the sun stood still in the sky and time was arrested forever," while "my religion, with its fixed times and seasons, its recurring sabbaths and feasts and fasts, each with its own synagogue and domestic ritual, was a world strictly divided into temporal units." The Jewish pressure toward a life wholly within culture and outside nature, which Isaac Babel anatomizes in the stories of his childhood, was not Daiches' experience: young Davie was thought to be as legitimately occupied going tadpoling in Dunsappie Loch as in his daily practice of piano and fiddle; if his father thought rugger and cricket essentially absurd, he approved of, and himself participated in, walking and climbing, swimming and golf.

Ah, "his father." It has hardly been possible to write this much about the book without mentioning Daiches' father. He was Dr. Salis Daiches, rabbi of the Edinburgh Hebrew Congregation and "virtual spiritual head of the Jews in Scotland." *Two Worlds* is actually less a reminiscence of Daiches' childhood than a memoir of Daiches' father, who died in 1945, "one day after Hitler and three weeks after Roosevelt." Rabbi Daiches brilliantly interpreted the niceties of rabbinic law for his congregation and visitors; "he was a great preacher," Daiches says, whose eloquence "I have rarely heard equalled"; he did his Ph.D. thesis on Hume and was a profound student of Kant; he wrote scholarly essays, collected in the book *Aspects of Judaism,* as well as frequent letters to the daily *Scotsman,* resonant with the voice of Scottish Jewry, which "did an immense amount to create a pro-Jewish public opinion in the country." Rabbi Daiches was an odd but not unprecedented combination of progressivism and orthodoxy: he ruled that switching electricity on and off was not "kindling a fire" on the Sabbath; he disliked Yiddish, his native tongue, and was rather snobbish about those "only half emerged from the ghetto"; he was optimistic about "the emergence of Judaism as a proud and respected part of a pluralistic European culture"; his religion was a "humanist utilitarianism." Yet, Daiches says, "he had a profound religious sensibility" beneath that surface; and he abhorred the liberal and reform Judaism with which his ideas had so much in common.

Daiches describes his father as naive and unworldly, even childlike, yet "in many respects remarkably tough-minded." The senior Daiches was "a fine figure of a man" and something of a dandy; in his later years he relaxed enough to stop waxing his mustache, and on vacations to discard his stiff collar and silk hat for gray flannels and a blue blazer; he learned to swim at forty and took up a pipe. Rabbi Daiches never felt entirely free with his children, Daiches says, but he eventually got so he could drink a glass of beer in a bar with his sons. (Daiches' paternal grandfather, also a famous rabbi and scholar, the world's leading authority on the Jerusalem Talmud, had no such difficulty, and annoyed his earnest grandson by never talking to him about anything but girls and such vulgar matters.) Daiches writes of his father in a tone of respect and love, yet many of his reminiscences speak eloquently of strain and difficulty, and the relationship seems to have involved an extreme of dominance and subordination. In one remarkably interesting anecdote, Daiches says his reaction as a child to a legal victory of his father's over a rabbinic rival was to think, "So perish all the King's enemies!" "These chapters from my autobiography turn out to be a tribute to him," Daiches writes. "He is the hero, not I." Yet it is a tribute of an oddly ambivalent sort, and at times the hero is indistinguishable from a villain.

As a venture in autobiography, *Two Worlds* is hardly a major work. Where it deliberately invites comparison with Proust—"Even now, the taste of seed cake, like Proust's *madeleine*, brings back . . ." —the comparison can only be demolishing. If one thinks of another recent memoir of a Jewish childhood, Alfred Kazin's *A Walker in the City* (which Daiches reviewed appreciatively in *Commentary*, December, 1951), one is immediately struck by the far greater lyricism and beauty of the Kazin book.

Daiches seems unsure of the audience he is writing for, shifting continually between the assumption of a shared culture and explanation of the simplest matters. Evasion is fatal to autobiography, which must lay the heart bare in a fashion not even required of lyric poetry. Daiches either has little psychological insight into his own motivations, or is often disingenuous. He begins a long disquisition on his relations with his older brother: "There is, in Jewish tradition as in many other traditions, a peculiar *mystique* attached to the eldest son." Every incident of his account shows envy, rivalry, and preferential treatment, even to "more and fancier cakes at his *bar mitzvah* party than at mine." The tone is typically, "I found myself, inexplicably, bursting into tears," or, "my mother's remark, which I have never forgotten." Yet Daiches concludes:

> How difficult it is to tell the truth and not be misleading! It might be imagined from what I have written above that I had a grievance against Lionel for being the eldest son and against my parents for treating him as such. But I had no shadow of such a grievance (in spite of individual instances such as that of the

chessmen) nor did I ever really believe that Lionel got preferential treatment from my parents.

Daiches simply refuses to make the connections. For example, he tells two oddly parallel anecdotes in *Two Worlds*. In the first, he explains that when he stayed with his paternal grandfather at Leeds his grandfather used to have pickled herring and dark bread served to himself privately every night before dinner. When the boy, fascinated by the mysterious ceremony, finally nerved himself to tell the old man that he too liked pickled herring, he was handed it generously and ate "rather more than I really wanted." In the second, Daiches tells the story of an old fierce-looking Edinburgh peddler named Moishe Pinkinsky, who was moved to share his sandwich of dark bread and chopped herring with a gentile stranger in his train compartment. "I ate for dear life," the gentile later told his friends, from whom the story got to Daiches, "and, you know, it tasted damn good. Some kind of caviar." Daiches never notices the parallel, nor that he too is in the role of the uncomprehending stranger, the *goy*.

The true drama of *Two Worlds* is thus found mostly below the surface, in hints, fragmentary revelations, and unconscious weightings. It is of course the story of Daiches' break with his father, primarily over his marrying a gentile classmate. This was followed by his flight to America in 1937 to save his father's face (his father had threatened to resign his position as rabbi); then a variety of appeasing gestures on both sides, including the young couple's orthodox Jewish wedding in America and a "Yom Kippur blessings" cable from Daiches' parents; finally some sort of partial reconciliation when Daiches and his wife returned to Scotland for a visit in 1939, with a grandson. The next time Daiches came back, just before his father's death, the old man preached a sermon about Jacob's sending Joseph out into the world, which Daiches took as addressed to him, "offering full understanding and reconciliation."

The last paragraph of the book identifies his father's adjustment to Daiches' break with his tradition as "rueful rather than either complacent or tragic." Daiches' own final adjustment in the book is, curiously, none of those things, merely the literary critic's neutral discovery that Robert Louis Stevenson is an analogue: "Stevenson's problems as a young man in Edinburgh were startlingly like my own; his relations with his father were like mine; we both went to America for similar reasons; we both achieved the same kind of ultimate reconciliation with our families." That the book is ultimately self-justification is made clear by its dedication to Daiches' mother ("hoping that this new perspective on familiar scenes will explain rather than disturb"). Yet it never fairly rises to the height of its own story, to the full perception that would warrant all that purpose and passion.

What gives Daiches' book its exceptional interest and importance is not, in other words, his literary or imaginative power, but his typicality. In some fashion Daiches appears to be a representative Jewish figure for our time, and what we have in common with him seems central where the differences seem peripheral. Edinburgh is not that different from Binghamton. Daiches is an aristocrat, as *Two Worlds* makes clear, with an ancestry of "rabbinical scholars and Talmudists of considerable eminence," going back to Rashi in the eleventh century, and beyond that, Daiches had from family tradition, to King David. (One convinced classmate proclaimed, "If Daiches' father had his right, he would be King of the Jews," and the young prince used to lie awake at night wondering whether he might not be the Messiah.) True, our ancestry is less distinguished, but is not every Jew a king, and do we not all claim descent from Father Abraham, and most of us from the Vilna Gaon in addition?

Daiches claims that he never encountered anti-Semitism until he came to America at twenty-five, but it seems unlikely; some of us grew up in the Jewish majority culture of Flatbush and Borough Park, and hardly knew a gentile until we went away to college, but we knew anti-Semitism nevertheless. Orthodoxy and being a rabbi's son shut Daiches off from a lot—he was deprived of the school literary society, which met on Friday nights, and the cricket matches, which were held on Saturday afternoons; he felt a barrier between himself and his brother, and other Jewish boys, because "We were the rabbi's sons; people must watch their step in front of us"; for many years he never tasted fish and chips, because they were fried in animal fat, or bakeshop pastries, lest they be made of lard; he could not take girls to dances at the university (perhaps they too were made of lard?). Yet precisely what he could not be shut off from, the gentile culture that came to him through books, turned Daiches in the literary direction so compatible with his Talmudic training and habits of mind, and so characteristic of many with similar backgrounds. At the age of fifteen Daiches wrote an epic poem in the style of *Marmion* on the subject of the Chanukah story, a *Maccabead*; in his last year of secondary school, he was translating the *Odyssey* into limerick verse; at the University of Edinburgh he was senior president of the English Literature society, literary editor of the magazine, and so forth.

Now, like so many skewed Talmudists, Daiches is a specialist in the rabbinic niceties of literary criticism, a teacher of Milton and Burns, the author of a dozen volumes on literary subjects. Daiches remembers the characteristic form of discourse in his household to have been argument, with parents, visitors, anyone; as he recalls, "it seems to me that we talked pretty nearly all the time." Now, of course, it is the lecture and the seminar. As befits a rabbi's son, Daiches has a far better command of Hebrew than any of us, if less of a secular Yiddish culture than such comparable American figures as Alfred Kazin or Irving Howe. (A few of us, luckless, fought Hebrew school too thoroughly to have much Hebrew training, and if our parents were Yiddish-speaking they preserved it as a private language in which to keep things from the children, as Dylan Thomas' parents did with Welsh, and as Cleopatra's parents, for all we know, did with Greek.)

Daiches' religious experience seems fairly typical, even to the intermarriage and the children raised on Jewish tradition filleted like a shad, with all the tiny irritating bones of religion picked out and thrown away. Unlike him, many of us would call ourselves "atheist" rather than "agnostic," not out of preference for the harsher and more provocative word, but because "godless" seems a more honest descriptive term than "unknowing." The first major doctrinal break with Jewish faith that Daiches recalls was over that key point the *Akedah*, the sacrifice of Isaac, which has so strongly appealed to religious sensibilities from Kierkegaard to Dr. Wellisch. Daiches found it revolting then, and says he is still horrified by it. In his last year at the university, he began "to doubt profoundly" the authority of Judaism in the divine Revelation of the Torah to Moses, and within two or three years all faith had departed. When Daiches revisits Edinburgh now he still attends the synagogue, as a sentimental exercise, but the old *"frisson"* (the French word is characteristic) that used to go down his spine at the climax of the Yom Kippur service is apparently gone for good. Others of us would record an essentially similar progress, mostly earlier, with different stimuli. One renegade of my acquaintance dates his break with Jewish religion to agonized childhood broodings on the custom of the *shabbos goy* (which Daiches recalls in *Two Worlds* with fond nostalgia), on the theory that a religion unconcerned with the soul of the Polish "super," encouraging *him* to violate God's commandment, was no religion he could accept.

In personal and dramatic terms, David Daiches thus raises the whole problem of Jewish identity and identification. In February, 1951, he published in *Commentary* a thoroughly provocative statement, "American Judaism: A Personal View," which many readers (among them this one) found spoke quite eloquently to their condition. In it he explained that having been raised in Jewish orthodoxy he had become an agnostic and broken with the synagogue, but that orthodoxy with its rituals and liturgies had a satisfaction and consistency, even a beauty, that made any modernized or reformed Judaism seem irrelevant and absurd. The choice was thus "Rabbinical Judaism" entire, or nothing, and Daiches chose nothing. (In *Two Worlds*, Daiches explains that it was his father's arguments against the illogicalities of Liberal Judaism that destroyed it as a "line of defense to which I might retreat," and thus paradoxically drove him to agnosticism.) Daiches' own solution, he said, is to teach his children "the Hebrew tradition," which he defines as Jewish history and the Hebrew language, not religion. They are to read the Bible and Talmud, in Hebrew, as secular works.

The response to Daiches' statement was rather remarkable. In a formal rejoinder, "The Task of Being an American Jew," Rabbi Leo S. Baeck thanked Daiches for his graphic raising of the issues, strongly denied the existence of any Jewish Creed requiring belief or disbelief, and devoted most of his space to a historical defense of reform, claiming that in a larger perspective, even those Jews who had formally renounced their Jewish identity—Heine, Marx, Disraeli—were nevertheless within Judaism. The reaction of a number of other rabbis, in the letter columns, ranged from ironic praise for the article as one of *Commentary*'s rare defenses of orthodoxy, to a strong denunciation by a rabbi in North Dakota of the "*chutzpah*" of Daiches' uncommitted, hence unexistentialist, view. Letters from laymen ranged similarly from one who went some distance beyond Daiches to deny that Judaism was any part of "Western civilization" and to characterize the Talmud as "largely pointless rubbish," to one who noted that God "chose an agnostic to voice His Call in the wilderness." One correspondent, Miss Carolyn A. Lisberger of San Francisco, revealed that like Daiches she was a Jew and an agnostic, that like him she also went occasionally to the synagogue; and she explained that she kept her "identity as a Jew," defining it as "an identification with a group that has a common heritage, a historical culture, an ethics that are rooted in a Jewish humanistic concern down the ages." What is visible most clearly in Miss Lisberger's letter, but is the peculiar feature of all the letters, is that no one equates Jewish identity with belief in, or practice of, the Jewish religion. Thus no correspondent, however indignant, denied that Daiches the agnostic was a Jew, although a number denied his typicality, authority to speak on the issue, or intellectual honesty.

A writer I know well had been stamping around in fury outside the Jewish religion for many years, because he could not believe in the reality of God or the afterlife, before he discovered in a colloquy with a pious uncle that he had left under a misapprehension, that none of his pious relations believed in those things, except, it was explained to him, one crazy great-aunt who had believed that when she died she would sit in Moses' capacious lap. His relatives believed in right religion, in Torah, in faithful ritual performance, in ancestral tradition; as Rabbi Baeck says, Judaism is not a credal religion. But is a religion without faith any religion at all, and were not my friend's pious relatives *shul*-going atheists, Chinese ancestor-worshipers?

These days the fashion seems to run to making Jewish identity a matter of some rigorous pair of alternatives. Defining Judaism as

revealed religion, Daiches says we must hold to traditional orthodoxy or assimilate; and casting a regretful eye back on the Sabbath
service, he chooses to assimilate. Arthur Koestler, in an even more
emphatic essay, "Judah at the Crossroads," in *The Trail of the
Dinosaur*, defines Jewish identity as historic nationhood and makes
the choice one of becoming a citizen of Israel or assimilating. He
too, with a shrug of regret, decides for assimilation.

Daiches' all-or-nothing attitude toward religion, with orthodoxy
impossible but reform absurd, is not unfamiliar in those who have
deserted any rigorous communion; it is a fairly common attitude of
lapsed Catholics toward Protestantism, and is, for example, precisely the attitude of Stephen Dedalus in Joyce's novels. Sometimes, for a variety of reasons, the "all" is chosen after a dabble in
"nothing"—in the saintly old Gandhi, spinning in his loin cloth,
it is hard to remember the young London dandy who wore evening
clothes and wickedly ate beef. The Daiches family were amateur
students of what the anthropologists call acculturation; Daiches
writes, in an unusually patronizing sentence, of the same Moishe
Pinkinsky who broke his bread with a stranger:

> Moishe and his like were regarded in our family with affectionate
> indulgence as interesting examples of a transitional stage in the
> emancipation from the ghetto.

In a review of Nathan Ausubel's *Treasury of Jewish Humor* in
Commentary, January, 1952, Daiches defines what we think of as
characteristic Jewish humor, ironic and wry, as similarly a transi-
tional stage in Jewish history, existing neither before nor long after
the ghetto. Yet while he watches acculturation with an ethnol-
ogist's eye, Daiches is himself acculturation in action, as much the
product of a stage in culture contact as any drunken and demoral-
ized Ojibway. When he says in the article on American Judaism,
"Let those of us with a Jewish background . . . teach our children
Hebrew and Jewish history," does he think that he can transmit
his Jewish background, without the sanctions of religion, to his
half-gentile children and to their children? If he does manage to
transmit historical and linguistic loyalties to his children and grand-
children, will they then be Jews, or only the sort of gentile pro-

Semites Daiches cheerfully describes in *Two Worlds* as "lunatic" and "embarrassing"?

Is Daiches himself in fact a Jew, and to whom, and what does being a Jew mean? To the historic Jewish community, Daiches is a Jew if he never goes to the synagogue, ignores the Law, and believes nothing; he was circumcised in the covenant at eight days as a *ben b'rith*, confirmed in the covenant at thirteen as a *bar mitzvah*, and nothing can cancel those things out, I should imagine, but excommunication (which has gone out of fashion) or the formal renunciation in Christian baptism (and not even that for Rabbi Baeck). Daiches might be thought a bad Jew, an agnostic Jew, but a Jew nevertheless, as the letters to *Commentary* make clear. To the gentile community, he and his children and probably their children are Jews because they have "Jewish blood." But is Daiches a Jew in his own mind? The covenant in which he was circumcised and confirmed is a contract with God, periodically renegotiated in the Old Testament, in which in return for certain behavior God promises the seed of Abraham, among other things, the land of Canaan for an everlasting possession. But if Daiches, like Koestler, does not want the land of Canaan, does not obey the requirements of his share of the deal, and in fact does not believe in the historicity of the contract or the existence of the other contracting party—could we not fairly say that the covenant is canceled for him, as for many of us? And will his children, or our children, be circumcised and confirmed in it?

"Whether the Jews are a race or a nation or a religious community has long ceased to bother me," Daiches writes in "American Judaism: A Personal View." But it might well bother him. If we know more modern anthropology than Alfred Rosenberg or Julius Streicher did, we know that the Jews are not a race, and that "race" is a term of very limited application. If the Jews are a nation, as Koestler maintains, it is the nation of Israel and some dispersed stragglers who hope to be there in time for the next Passover, but Daiches is not one of those. With some melancholy, he writes in *Two Worlds*:

> And I remember during my first year at Edinburgh University thinking that the summit of my academic ambitions would be to

become professor of English at the newly founded Hebrew University in Jerusalem. It is perhaps a sad and certainly an ironic comment on human affairs that when I was offered that position at the end of the war I declined it.

He does not even think much of Israel's language, Hebrew in "the unmusical and inflexible Sephardic pronunciation," loyal as he is to the arguments in his father's book in favor of "a modified form of the Ashkenazic pronunciation." If the Jews are a religious community, Daiches stands outside it, but no one seems to think that they are, and if they were, which religious community would it be?

In what then does Daiches' Jewishness inhere? If it is not racial, national, or religious, it must be a cultural identity, either internal (language, history, habits) or external (the world's judgment from a name, a gesture, the jut of a nose). Culturally, then, this learned disciple of those wonder-working rabbis I. A. Richards and Kenneth Burke is a Jew, as are all of us like him; and, as his book makes clear, proud to be one, along with the excommunicated Spinoza, the baptised Marx, the atheist Freud, the assimilated Proust, the heaven-storming Einstein. Ultimately, perhaps, more than historical and linguistic identification, Jewish identity is habits of mind, patterns of taste. Daiches was never so much his father's son as when disobeying his father's order against fraternizing with gentile girls at the university, thinking:

> Presumably it was all right if I got into conversation with a girl after a lecture or after a society meeting. Was it all right to walk a few steps while talking with her? If so, how many?

But these habits of mind are not inherited, they were trained in Daiches by the study of Talmud and Torah. Will his children have them? Will their children? Some of us now, proud in Jewish cultural identity, have not much more to transmit than a few words of mispronounced Yiddish, a midnight longing for a pastrami sandwich, a sardonic anecdote. We, and David Daiches, may yet find that with the best will in the world, timeless Jewish cultural identity without time-bound Jewish ritual, "with its fixed times and seasons, its recurring sabbaths and feasts and fasts," diminishes and attenuates over the years and the generations, until finally it is only the memory of a memory, the dim recollection that once there was a glorious city where now only the bleak undifferentiated waves roll.

NOTE [1963]: All these anonymous friends who broke with the Jewish religion are of course myself; since my father's death I am free to say so without causing pain. I probably owe Daiches an apology for using his book as a vessel for my own problems. I should also be clearer about what motivated the fellow on page 337, who broke with Judaism because he lost his faith, taking Judaism to be a credal religion. He had been reading too many English novels about young men who had fatal doubts and left the Church, and he was so bemused by literature that he couldn't tell Orthodox Judaism from the Church of England.

Since writing the review I have learned that Judaism understands religion to inherit through the mother. Thus, to the Jews, Daiches' children are Jewish only if their mother converted. My children are not Jews to the Jews, however much they may be Jews to the world.

Some Trends in
the Novel

[1958]

THE CONCEPT OF TRENDS in the novel, or trends in any literary form, is of course artificial, a retrospective abstraction, but it is sometimes a convenience. No writer writes anything as part of a trend, but that annoyingly articulate reader we call the critic sometimes follows after the writer, at a safe distance, picking up work already done and trending it. Never very rewarding at any time, this park-custodian activity would seem particularly luckless at present, when the novel appears to be in a curious period of stagnation, with all the old trends somewhat played out, and no new developments yet very tangible. Naturalism, which has been the main line of our fiction at least since Dreiser, seems now to consist of no more than Caroline Slade's gentle documentaries on the theme of 'Tis Pity She's a Whore, or vast pointless excursions into the slums with such writers as Willard Motley and Leonard Bishop. In its more lyrical form, as such a writer as Sherwood Anderson represents it, naturalism can now claim only earnest, decent, and essentially talentless writers like Albert Halper or England's Alexander Baron. That flood of naturalism so overpowering in the thirties, the left-wing or proletarian novel, seems to have dried up almost without a trace, leaving only a few stagnant puddles. Naturalism as ironic melodrama, as we knew it in such books as Cain's *The Postman Always Rings Twice* and McCoy's *They Shoot Horses, Don't*

342

They?, seems to have persuaded a whole generation of young European writers, under Gide's leadership, that the American novel is virile and significant, but by the time Europe learned about it, this tradition was already as stone-cold dead as the marathon-dancing and flagpole-sitting it celebrated and so much resembled.

Three somewhat unattractive trends in the novel seem clearly visible at present, although perhaps they have always been clearly visible, and represent no more than the statistical tendency of most novels at any given time to be bad ones. In any case, they are undeniable trends, and before peering about under rocks for more hopeful signs, we might pause to note them. The first is a tendency of our established and most famous writers to parody their own earlier work or rewrite it downward. We might regard this as the Louis Napoleon principle, following Marx's engaging suggestion, made when he was a political journalist and before he took his own historical laws quite so seriously, that every historical event is shortly afterward followed by its parody, adducing Louis Bonaparte's revolution a generation after Napoleon's as his typical example. Our leading novelists seem to be devoting themselves to the demonstration of this principle with a unanimity that is one of the most depressing features of the current stagnation in our fiction. Thus Hemingway rescued himself from the critical obituaries that followed *Across the River and Into the Trees* by writing a compact and moving work, *The Old Man and the Sea*, that turns out, on examination, to be his fine short story "The Undefeated," done over again with less power. Where the aging bullfighter was heroic in failure and tragic in stature by his stubborn refusal to admit defeat and incompetence, the aged fisherman is sentimentalized to be somehow victorious in principle, his fish skeleton a more worthwhile capture than any amount of merchandise for the market, by means of the author's change of the rules in the course of the game. Where the form of "The Undefeated" was heroic tragedy, the form of *The Old Man and the Sea* might be called Christian comedy, in which faith and grace automatically redeem from worldly failure.

In *Requiem for a Nun* Faulkner has similarly written a sequel to an earlier work, *Sanctuary*, to give its protagonist (one can hardly say heroine) some of the doom-ridden grandeur of the Sartoris family. Whereas *Sanctuary* had a symbolic rightness in that Temple's innocent natural evil allowed her to pass unscathed through the wildest Jacobean melodrama and artificial evil, more sinning than sinned against, the Aeschylean framework of retribution and redemption Temple is made to bear in *Requiem for a Nun* serves only to take her out of her corncob sanctuary into a dimension where she and the characters around her simply become ridiculous. Similarly, the story of the Passion, so subtly underlying *Light in August* and pervading it with meaning, is rewritten overtly as the ponderous and ham-handed allegory of *A Fable*.

In the same fashion, Steinbeck's carefree fantasy world of *Tortilla Flat* has become the self-conscious moral slum of *Cannery Row*, and O'Hara has rewritten *Appointment in Samarra* with a female hero as *A Rage to Live*, demonstrating that where Julian English's speedy doom could achieve a kind of meteoric brilliance, prolonged over Grace Caldwell Tate's long lifetime it possesses only a seeping dullness. When we add to these the law of entropy in Farrell's trilogies and tetralogies slowly running down, each with measurably less life in it than the last, and Dos Passos's later novels that read like some cruel satire on *USA*, we have not much left to boast of in the recent work of our important novelists.

A second trend might be called "the disguises of love," taking its title from Robie Macauley's novel. One of the oddest of these disguises is the writing of stories about homosexual love in the imagery of heterosexual love. I have elsewhere discussed this Albertine strategy—for Proust's Albert-made-Albertine is surely the godfather of all such operations—and here would only note the nature of the strategy and a few examples. At its simplest, it is simply metamorphosizing a boy with whom the male protagonist is involved into a girl, as in Corvo's *The Desire and Pursuit of the Whole,* with its boyish girl gondolier Zildo, or the mannish Mexican girl Amada who moves in with the writer in Tennessee Williams' short story "Rubio y Morena." We see its more complicated form in Robin Maugham's novelette *The Servant,* where a wicked manservant corrupts a weak-willed young English gentleman by means of a preposterous adolescent nymphomaniac he sneaks into the house, eventually estranging him from his noble

fiancée, and on examination both girls turn out to be only symbolic vehicles for homosexual love of the young gent, the nymphomaniac for the servant's nasty love, and the fiancée for the male
narrator's pure love, leaving our original polygon a rather odd
triangle.

I would submit that this Albertine strategy underlies such fiction
as Paul Bowles's, Frederick Buechner's, and Williams' own more
complicated *The Roman Spring of Mrs. Stone* (as it underlies
such plays as "A Streetcar Named Desire" and all derivatives,
like William Inge's "Picnic," where a Kowalski-like natural male
animal breaks through the defenses of a conventional-seeming
young woman). Macauley's *The Disguises of Love*, on its appearance, was reviewed in *The New Yorker* by Anthony West, with
considerable attention to the fact that in it the usual relations
between the sexes in our culture seemed to be curiously reversed.
West observed that in essence the frail pushover of a hero, Professor Graeme, was villainously seduced and his life ruined by a
heartless young female student, Frances, who determined "to
have her will of him," to the extent of reserving a double room
with bath for their first date. I would argue that all the book's
absurdity disappears when it is regarded as a sophisticated example
of the Albertine strategy, with Frances simply a male student
named Francis and enough clues in the book's title, constant preoccupation with the theme of gender reversal, and imagery, to
suggest that here we may have the strategy's conscious parody,
that Macauley may not only have anticipated our investigations
but even assisted them by pointing up the evidence.

Other current varieties of love's disguises can be dealt with in a
more perfunctory fashion. One of the most widespread is a kind
of infantile regression, where happiness is equated with a pre-
sexual or pre-genital attachment to an older woman or women.
Perhaps the best example of this is the fiction of Capote, particularly *The Grass Harp*, that rather touching fairy tale about an
adolescent boy who finds refuge from the complex responsibility
of maturity by living in a tree house with two old women and
several other eccentrics. Carson McCullers's *The Member of the
Wedding* is a similar exercise in regression (it is worth noting
parenthetically how readily these infantile fantasies seem to adapt

for the stage), as is the entire literary output of Saroyan. The child-centered world of Salinger's fiction, where ambiguous attachments to girl children are the constant refuge from a distressing adult life, shows a similar tendency, but Salinger seems to me a writer of far too much talent and seriousness to remain permanently fixed on this level. With other variants of the sexual impulse—the sadistic nastiness in Steinbeck's *East of Eden*, the novels of Edgar Mittel-holzer, and recent Erskine Caldwell; the kiss-and-tell tradition as it diminishes in interest from Henry Miller to Maude Hutchins—we need have no particular concern.

A third, and most widespread trend, consists of those books that appear to be novels and are not. They might be called "pseudo-fictions," on the analogy of I. A. Richards' "pseudo-questions" and "pseudo-statements," which would not only name them accurately—they are false-fictions rather than non-fictions—but might lend our activities some of the optimistic semantics-will-save-us tone of a quarter of a century ago, as though all these complicated matters could readily be put in order. We must insist, not on a definition, but on certain minimal requirements: that fiction be an exercise of the moral imagination; that it organize experience into a form with a beginning, middle, and end; and that it center around a dramatic action. A pseudo-fiction may be quite a good work of its sort, although most of them are not; what must be recognized is that its sort is not the form we have traditionally called the novel. The appreciation that pseudo-fiction aims at is "Yes, that is just what it must be like"; the inescapable sense any work of the fictive imagination, from *Don Quixote* to *The Weaver's Grave*, gives is "Life is surely nothing like this anywhere. This is art."

We can readily see what pseudo-fictions are by contrasting the moving and effective reporting of Hersey's *Hiroshima* with the pretentious disguised reporting of the same writer's *The Wall*; or, even more clearly, by contrasting Schulberg's pseudo-fiction about F. Scott Fitzgerald, *The Disenchanted*, in one direction with Mizener's brilliant biography of Fitzgerald, *The Far Side of Paradise*, and in the other direction with Fitzgerald's own truly fictive rendering of the same pathetic story, *Tender Is the Night*. In recent years we have had the political or current events pseudo-fiction of Trilling's *The Middle of the Journey* and Irwin Shaw's *The Troubled Air* (the former enormously better than the latter but absolutely comparable in kind); the pseudo-fiction about the war in such wordy best-sellers as *From Here to Eternity*, *The Naked and the Dead*, and *The Caine Mutiny*; biographical and autobiographical pseudo-fictions by Angus Wilson and Mary McCarthy; and some particularly uninteresting pseudo-fictions about a fake new generation, the "beat" generation, by such beat generators as Calder Willingham, Chandler Brossard, and Jack Kerouac.

Particularly saddening are the examples of several English novelists who seem to fall into pseudo-fiction when they are tired, as our own established novelists fall into self-parody. Thus Koestler and Orwell, who created truly imagined political fiction and semifiction in *Darkness at Noon* and *Down and Out in Paris and London*, failed to do anything of the sort in the journalism of *Thieves in the Night* and *1984*; Huxley and Waugh have continued to grind out works of satiric intent long after the imaginative grasp that made their earlier works novels was exhausted. Diaries, journals, familiar essays, war experiences, newspaper columns, sociology, religious parables, everything from an account of making a movie in Africa with John Huston to the inside dope on the Jelke ring is given a thin veneer of "fictionalizing" these days and published as a novel, while the few works of actual fiction brought out each year wither on the *New York Times*'s "And Bear in Mind" list. (Now that the novel no longer sells as it did, in comparison with nonfiction, it will be interesting to see whether the next decade reverses the process, and gets us our *Moby-Dicks* as *The Whales Around Us*.)

Before we take a look at some trends in the novel that seem more hopeful, one reservation suggested above needs re-emphasis. Put most simply, it is that bad works can share the preoccupations of good. Insofar as discussion focuses on problems of theme and value, as this one has, it should be obvious that a very poor book can share its theme and values with a masterpiece without acquiring any of the masterpiece's virtues. These categories of hopeful trends are thus no guarantee of quality, and in fact each category includes a very mixed bag of works, not at all meant to be exhaustive. A novel can be deliberately produced with every feature of major fiction and still somehow fail to come alive, which is my impression of the novels of Robert Penn Warren, although I am defensively aware how much my view is a minority one.

With that out of the way, let me say that the most hopeful direction fiction seems to me to be taking at present is toward the conscious use of myth and ritual as an organizing principle. The tendency in literary discussion is to speak of myth alone, but since in actual terms the two are inseparable, the myth being nothing more or less than the "story" or spoken correlative of the rite, we would do well to consider them together whenever we can. A work of fiction that emphasizes myth and slights the physical reality of ritual tends to be thin and heady, in my opinion the trouble with Mann's *Joseph* novels, whereas a work of fiction centered on both, like Mann's shorter *Death in Venice* or *Mario and the Magician*, has a depth and resonance that is one of the sure signs of major art.

A recent work that seems to me resonant in its use of myth and ritual in precisely this fashion is Ralph Ellison's *Invisible Man*, organized around a theme that has been basic to American fiction from *Moby-Dick* to *The Great Gatsby*: the ancient ritual myth of the Quest. Ellison's nameless hero pursues the secret of visibility, his own fully human identity, as the knight of Romance pursued Grail Castle, and breaking through the enchanted wood of the "Keep this nigger boy running" practical joke that is the book's key metaphor (an *act as scene* in Kenneth Burke's terminology), he achieves at the end, if not the goal of fully conscious humanity, at least a sure footing on the spiral stairway to it. Another recent work organized on the framework of the Quest, *The Palm-Wine Drinkard*, by a young Nigerian named Amos Tutuola, makes an instructive comparison with *Invisible Man*. Tutuola's story, the drinkard's pursuit of his dead palm-wine tapster into the town of the deads, is a complicated ritual of the Quest without any kind of mythic or intellectual structure to give it focus or coherence. It is without, in short, the tradition of picaresque novel behind it, and ultimately the book becomes only a series of fantastic adventures, projecting such attitudes of Tutuola's culture as the weird money economy and the terrified loathing of children the way a Rorschach test might.

Similarly, we could note the *Huckleberry Finn* framework of the rites of passage, the series of ceremonial initiations leading to maturity, in Shirley Jackson's *Hangsaman,* a book I am in no position to discuss, or, in a more fragmentary form, in Salinger's *The Catcher in the Rye.* Salinger's book suffers technically from its reduction to the limited vision and vocabulary of a sixteen-year-old boy; with the addition of an adult narrator's perspective to the novel, capable of adding a myth adequate to its rites, it might have been, not the engaging tour de force we were given, but the substantial imaginative work for which Salinger so clearly shows the potentiality. The theme of the sacrificial victim or expiatory ritual, embracing such diverse works as Kafka's *The Trial,* West's *Miss Lonelyhearts,* and Cozzens' *Castaway,* takes on a brooding topicality in Jocelyn Brooke's *The Scapegoat.* Where even a work we tend to call nonfiction, like Thoreau's *Walden,* centers around a year's cycle of death and rebirth and identifies its form with a quest for a horse, a hound, and a turtle dove, it is not hard to see that these rituals or symbolic actions of initiation, rebirth, and redemption lie very close to the center of aesthetic experience, and their conscious use by the novelist would seem about as artificial as his conscious use of human life for his subject matter.

A second hopeful trend in our fiction seems to me something we probably have to call, despite the term's pomposity, "pre-existentialism." In his book *Existentialism From Within,* E. L. Allen writes that "existentialism is an attempt at philosophising from the standpoint of the actor instead of, as has been customary, from that of the spectator." I have to take Dr. Allen's word on that, since I am as innocent of philosophy as Emerson's cutworm, but if we accept the definition, its immediate relevance to a certain kind of novel is obvious. I would call "pre-existentialist" that fiction that comes to the view independently, as a discovery in the novelist's craft, rather than formally, pushing a wheelbarrowful of speculative thought. Wright's *Native Son* and particularly his novelette "The Man Who Lived Underground" seem to me examples of the first; his recent *The Outsider,* deliberately patterned on French existentialist fiction, an example of the second.

Kenneth Burke's novel as a series of declamations, *Towards a Better Life,* would be almost the proto-existentialist work of fiction in our time, its rhetorical form a brilliant device for the self-exposure of motives. Novels we once thought were primarily political, like Malraux's *Man's Fate* and Silone's earlier work, now seem obviously "pre-existentialist" in their reduction of all our large vacant generalities to the crises of individual human action.

As the example of Wright ironically suggests, Negro experience in America would seem to predispose a novelist to this approach more than any length of time spent in Paris, and Ralph Ellison has discussed the break in American sensibility typified by Hemingway's dismissal of the freeing of Jim in *Huck Finn* as a false note, and the consequent renunciation of a whole depth of insight into the nature of American experience that our nineteenth-century fiction had possessed. "Pre-existentialism" may in fact be a characteristically Negro-centered note in our fiction, and, as we might expect, it is a major aspect of Faulkner's work, although I do not find it much in evidence in the work of such white Southern writers as Eudora Welty and Carson McCullers. Several underated American novelists seem to me characteristically pre-existentialist along these lines, among them William March, John Sanford, and the Robert M. Coates of that fine and almost unknown book, *Yesterday's Burdens.*

Finally, for our third encouraging trend, there is a miscellaneous body of real fictions distinguishable from pseudo-fictions by form, by a core of resolved action, and above all by the presence of moral imagination. It is a quality we can identify in the brilliant short fictions of Katherine Anne Porter as unmistakably as in those of Hawthorne. One symptom of genuine fiction is the presence of that faintly disreputable word "love" undisguised, rather than in the varieties of concealment noted above. Virginia Woolf, Elizabeth Bowen, and Joyce Cary have in their various ways created traditions for dealing with the reality of human love, Cary a particularly virile and robust one, and in this country we can note with pride such recent work as Peter Taylor's *A Woman of Means,* Brendan Gill's *The Trouble of One House,* James Agee's *A Death in the Family,* and John Cheever's *The Wapshot Chronicle.*

H. J. Kaplan's *The Plenipotentiaries* is that amazing conception, a rewriting of Henry James and a characteristically Jamesian
situation in contemporary terms, and Jean Stafford did something
similar with the Proustian tradition in *Boston Adventure*, before
going on to create her own specialized fictional structures in *The
Mountain Lion* and *The Catherine Wheel*. Algren's *The Man
With the Golden Arm* is an equally rare bird, a work in the line
of slum naturalism, familiar from Algren's previous books, but
this time somehow suffused with poetry and rich with symbolism.
Saul Bellow's *The Adventures of Augie March* is another such.
These true fictions are as unmistakable when they are concerned
with sin and the darker places of the human heart, as in the work
of Bernanos, Mauriac, and Graham Greene, as when sin has become bad taste and the human heart is no darker than a well-
kept front parlor, as in the novels of E. M. Forster, Ivy Compton-
Burnett, and Henry Green.

The special case of the British young Angries seems to me to
have been more completely misunderstood than any other recent
trend in the novel. Reading these books by Kingsley Amis, John
Wain, Iris Murdoch, Thomas Hinde, John Braine, and others,
critics have been so obsessed with their superficial revolution in
manners that they have failed entirely to notice their real revolution (or counter-revolution) in form. Here suddenly was the new
protagonist of the Welfare State, the lower-class hero upgraded
by a state-supported education at a red-brick university: despising
the values of his new class even more than his old, always a cad
or bounder, sometimes a teddy boy or spiv. A characteristic reaction was Somerset Maugham's in the London *Times*, commenting on the first of these novels to create a sensation, Kingsley
Amis's *Lucky Jim:*

> *Lucky Jim* is a remarkable novel. It has been greatly praised and
> widely read, but I have not noticed that any of the reviewers have
> remarked on its ominous significance. I am told that today rather
> more than sixty per cent of the men who go to the universities go
> on a Government grant. This is a new class that has entered upon
> the scene. It is the white-collar proletariat. Mr. Kingsley Amis is
> so talented, his observation is so keen, that you cannot fail to

be convinced that the young men he so brilliantly describes truly represent the class with which his novel is concerned.

They do not go to the university to acquire culture, but to get a job, and when they have got one, scamp it. They have no manners, and are woefully unable to deal with any social predicaments. Their idea of a celebration is to go to a public house and drink six beers. They are mean, malicious and envious. They will write anonymous letters to harass a fellow undergraduate and listen in to a telephone conversation that is no business of theirs. Charity, kindliness, generosity are qualities which they hold in contempt. They are scum. They will in due course leave the university. Some will doubtless sink back, perhaps with relief, into the modest class from which they emerged; some will take to drink, some to crime and go to prison. Others will become schoolmasters and form the young, or journalists and mould public opinion. A few will go into Parliament, become Cabinet Ministers and rule the country. I look upon myself as fortunate that I shall not live to see it.

Blinded by beer foam and scum, Maugham like others failed to notice that *Lucky Jim* itself was a mannered and traditionalist return to the conventions of the eighteenth-century comic novel, those of *Roderick Random* or *Tom Jones*. The true rebellion the young Angries are leading is against the modern novel of sensibility and consciousness, with its priesthood of James and Proust, Joyce and Virginia Woolf. They revive for us the novel of comic incident, harking back to Dickens and Trollope, Fielding and Smollett, ultimately to *Moll Flanders* and the origins of English fiction. The one of this group who seems to me (on the basis of an incomplete reading of their works) possessed of the richest comic talent is Iris Murdoch, and her first novel, *Under the Net*, came as a remarkable demonstration that the English picaresque tradition, the ironic mock-Quest, is still extraordinarily viable in the twentieth century.

The relationship between the contemporary novel in English (which seems a more usable unit than "the American novel") and the European is a complicated matter, and perhaps there are more relationships than one. The Italian novel, like the Italian film, has seemed in the last decade to have attained tremendous vitality and power. Recently we have been able to get a better perspective on it by the publication in America, many years delayed, of an early novel written under Mussolini by one of the most impressive of the Italian novelists, Alberto Moravia. Published here as *The Time of Indifference*, it is a depressing yet oddly moving paean of despair, very unlike Moravia's later work. *The Time of Indifference* opposes the melancholy, almost impotent, nostalgic values of an upper-class Italian family to those of an unattractive go-getter, the lover first of the mother and then of the daughter, while the family's son, who is not Prince Hamlet nor was meant to be, articulates the book's philosophy of indifference and sinks through ineffectual gestures of revenge into total apathy.

This opposition between older humane values that can only be celebrated as dying, and new efficient values that are accepted as the wave of the future but portrayed in all their unloveliness, is a thoroughly familiar motif. It is the constant theme of all serious Soviet fiction, from the marvelous stories of Isaac Babel in the 1920s, in *Red Cavalry* and *Benya Krik*, where the older values are typified by Jewish *shtetl* culture, opposed to the new revolutionary dynamism; through such works as Olesha's *Envy*, where Ivan Babichev and his crazy machine "Ophelia"—the symbol of all of Western humane culture—refuse to be vanquished by his brother Andrey, the forward-looking sausage-maker who is himself a kind of horrible synthetic sausage; right down to Leonov's ambiguous *Road to the Ocean* in the 1940s.

Seeing this drama of the old Quixotic man going down to defeat before the new efficient man under Fascism and Communism, we might be tempted to call it the reaction of the novelist to a totalitarian culture, but how can we miss it in Shakespeare, with his wonderful all-for-love Antonies losing to the beardless new bureaucratic Octaviuses, his Falstaffs cast off by the young dynamic Prince Hals? It is, in fact, the protest of the artist against the death and decay of the old values in any society; it was a major Russian preoccupation long before the Revolution, and was James Fenimore Cooper's theme some time before Moravia got around to it. Hemingway's Robert Cohn is as much the new man as Andrey Babichev or King Henry the Fifth; Sartoris and

Snopes are Antony and Octavius for us. Moravia's role in recent Italian fiction suggests that a backward-looking and nostalgic protest is not opposed to a literature of hope and faith so much as it is an essential precursor of it, and an ambiguous ingredient within it.

If we can thus learn neither hope nor despair from Europe, we can certainly not export any hard-boiled ersatz substitutes for either. The cult of Hammett, Cain, and McCoy is absurd in a France already possessed of a Céline and a Genet who have gone to the end of that line, and a Malraux transmuting contemporary melodrama into authentic tragedy. Our problem in the last analysis is formal, not thematic. We have had writers like Rex Warner and Ruthven Todd using Kafka's tradition to write political fables, and writers like Isaac Rosenfeld and William Sansom mining it for moral or religious fables, but whom have we able to write like Kafka in a concentration of myth and ritual so intense that no single level of interpretation can contain it, in a short work like "The Metamorphosis" that is simultaneously an allegory of the artist, an appeal against the social order, and an odyssey of the human soul? Where our fables are thin, and our documentations of life are ultimately unsatisfying, the dichotomy suggests that we need a synthesis of the two separated traditions. Dostoevsky, we might note, has all the richness of observed life in Dickens, *plus* a deeper moral or symbolic dimension. *Moby-Dick* is another such work, with humane and hopeful values perhaps more congenial to our needs; *Ulysses* and *Finnegans Wake* clothe our own paltry experience with all the ancient grandeur of myth and magic. Where such a novelist as Cozzens can write, in *By Love Possessed,* a triumph of dispassionate observation, and in *Castaway* a little masterpiece of passionate fantasy, we need the union of both, the work at once large in detail *and* significance. All our current trends in the last analysis come down to this: the plea for the wedding, full of richness and ceremony, of black Othello and delicate Desdemona, which John Peale Bishop described so movingly in his poem "Speaking of Poetry." This ritual marriage is the formula for a major art of the novel, as it is the formula for any great art, and we can do no more at present than hope for its consummation in our time.

NOTE [1963]: Part of this general survey is based on an earlier article, "The Albertine Strategy," not included here. It appeared in the Autumn, 1953, issue of *The Hudson Review*. The following number (Winter, 1954) contains a witty letter by Robie Macauley, disputing my contentions in detail, along with a churlish reply by myself, reading in part: "I am not prepared to be scared out of a critical reading of a novel by the author's waspish insistence that it is not *his* reading." My reply was later quoted in the *Times Literary Supplement* issue on American literature as an example of the insolence and arrogance of American literary critics. I suppose that it is.

In the five years since writing "Some Trends," my opinions about some of these novelists have changed; or, rather, some of my swans have turned out to be geese. It does not seem necessary to name them. Since I have had occasion to read a lot of current fiction for my *New Leader* column, I have discovered that things are much worse than I thought, and that the flood of trash is exceeded only by the flood of puffery expended on it by well-known writers and critics.

The Tragic Vision

[1959]

A GREAT FINANCIER sits in the Chicago courtroom, his face haggard. He is bankrupt, and worse, exposed to the world as a criminal. A short while ago he stepped out of his limousine like a king emerging from the royal coach; soon he will be doing all his stepping in the prison yard. In Hollywood, an old actor, the matinee idol and foremost lecher of his time, now hopelessly alcoholic, ends his days friendless in a shabby rooming house. A few blocks from Madison Square Garden in New York, a punch-drunk fighter, once the most arrogant of champions, begs from saloon to saloon.

These falls from great heights engage our emotions peculiarly. More than fifteen hundred years ago, St. Augustine raised the ques-of that peculiarity. "What is the reason," he asks in his *Confessions*, "that a spectator desires to be made sad when he beholds doleful and tragical passages, which he himself could not suffer to endure?" That is still the important question about tragedy: why do we enjoy the portrayal of suffering? Trying to answer it, we have to look back at the history of tragic drama, watch tragedy spread into other forms, then take note of whatever special sorts of tragedy we might have today, in a best-selling novel or a political downfall. Our values and literary styles are as far from those of ancient Athens and Elizabethan England as neckties are from Spanish ruffs or atom bombs from Greek fire. Our tragedies, however, would be as understandable to them as their Oedipus and Hamlet are to us. There seems to be something about the tragic vision, some essential affirmation of the human spirit, that remains timeless and universal however much its superficial appearance changes.

The ancient Greeks might be said to have invented tragedy, as they invented so much of our culture, although there are anticipations of it in the earlier literature of the ancient Near East. The story of Saul in the books of Samuel in the Bible looks very like tragic drama, as do the fates of David's descendants in the books of Kings. Even earlier, in the Babylonian epic of Gilgamesh, we hear the authentic voice of tragedy in Gilgamesh's awful mourning for his dead companion Enkidu (as moving in its way as the lament of David for Absalom). Behind that there are still earlier Sumerian and Akkadian related epics taking us back almost to the beginnings of history.

Nevertheless, the earliest tragic drama we have, whatever its sources, flowers suddenly in Athens in the fifth century B.C., in the marvelous plays of Aeschylus, Sophocles, and Euripides. A century later Aristotle codified its principles in his *Poetics*, and that fragmentary treatise may still be the best insight we have into the art. Aristotle defined tragedy as the imitation or representation of an action, serious, complete in itself, and of an adequate magnitude, written in embellished language. In that action a man like ourselves, neither wholly good nor wholly bad, is brought low through some shortcoming or tragic flaw in him. Its function is the arousing of the audience's pity for him and terror of his fate, and the purging of these emotions in the tragic resolution.

Aristotle based his definitions principally on Sophocles' *Oedipus the King*, which he thought the greatest and most successful of Greek tragedies, as many others have since. Unfortunately, Aristotle's definitions do not fit other Athenian tragedies as neatly. The protagonist of Euripides' *Medea* is not a flawed man like ourselves, but a remorseless semidivine witch, and she is not brought low at the end but appears in glory in the sky. The protagonist of Sophocles' *Antigone* does not bring on her tragic fate through any shortcoming but because of her pious determination to give her brother proper burial, although the tyrant Creon had forbidden it; and Orestes in the *Oresteia* of Aeschylus kills his mother not because he has a tragic flaw but because the god Apollo had commanded him to avenge her murder of his father. We can only accept *Medea* as a tragedy in the later concepts of Longinus' treatise *On the Sublime*, written in the first or second century A.D., which puts a new emphasis on such features of the tragic experience as "nobility," "grandeur," "transport," "inspired and vehement passion." Only in the nineteenth century, with Hegel's concept of tragedy as brought about through inability to obey two contradictory imperatives, does the tragic nature of the *Antigone* and *Oresteia* begin to make sense.

From the work of classical scholars like Gilbert Murray at Oxford and Jane Harrison at Cambridge, we have learned that the form of Greek tragedy, which began as the sacrificial rites of the god Dionysus, preserves the stages of the annual sacrifice of the year-spirit: his contest with his enemy, his suffering, death, and tearing-apart; the lamentation for him, then the discovery of his body and its resurrection as the new year. These rites mimic, and thus magically produce, the annual cycle of vegetation: birth, growth, flourishing, decay, death, rebirth. Its culmination in nature is the joy of spring. The comparable affirmation in Greek drama heralds the Reliving Dionysus, who will spring up again from his dismembered fragments, and the final mood of Greek tragedy thus goes beyond pity and terror to exultation and joy.

The Greeks saw this tragic pattern, some higher end implicit in human suffering, not only on the stage but everywhere in their experience. Homeric epic is full of it. In the *Iliad*, Homer gets the whole of tragic acceptance into Achilles' fierce speech to the young Trojan Lycaon, who has begged him for mercy, just before he kills him. I quote from W. H. D. Rouse's translation:

> Come, my friend, die too; why do you cry like that? Patroclus died too, and he was a much better man than you. Don't you see me too, a fine big man? My father is a brave man, my mother is a goddess; yet I too have death and fate fast upon me. The day shall come, morning or evening or midday, when someone shall take my life too in battle, with a thrust of the spear or an arrow from the bow.

In the *Odyssey*, perhaps the finest tragedy of all (it is one of Longinus' examples of the "sublime"), is the disdainful silence of the ghost of Ajax when Odysseus meets him in Hades, and finds him still implacable over the wrong Odysseus did him in life. Here, in Ajax's simple gesture of turning away in bitter silence, we learn more powerfully than any words could tell us that the human spirit is stronger than death.

There is always a danger in quoting what Matthew Arnold called "touchstones" out of context, since the whole of a work is what produces its effect, not a moving scene, speech, or line. The *Iliad* and the *Odyssey* are not tragic dramas, but the tragic vision, that man must go down into the depths of the human condition, that he must fall before he can rise, is strong within them.

The same vision runs through Greek lyric poetry—we need look no further than Simonides' great (and not fully translatable) epitaph on the Spartan dead at Thermopylae:

> O passer by, tell the Lacedaemonians that we lie here obeying their orders.

We find it in Greek philosophy, most dramatically in the death of Socrates in Plato's *Phaedo*. In Greek history, we have the Athenian historian Thucydides showing bitterly in his "Melian Dialogue" that when Athens, arrogant in its power, destroyed the weak and inoffensive little city of Melos, killing the men and enslaving the women and children, its subsequent fall was divine punishment for pride and transgression just like that of a tragic hero, and it could only arise again humbled and transformed. Some modern thinkers have even found the pattern of tragedy underlying the origin of scientific thought among the Greeks. Alfred North Whitehead says that the basic scientific assumption of an order of nature comes from Greek tragedy, so that "The laws of physics are the decrees of fate." In his brilliant and little-known book *Poetry and Mathematics*, Scott Buchanan suggests that the experimental method itself, perhaps even the basic patterns of our thinking, come from the rites of contest, tearing-apart, and apotheosis that underlie Greek tragedy.

Modern tragic drama begins properly with Christopher Marlowe's *Doctor Faustus*. In the last scene, as Lucifer and Mephistophilis come to get him, Faustus cries out:

Oh, I'll leap up to my God! Who pulls me down?
See, see where Christ's blood streams in the firmament!
One drop would save my soul—half a drop: ah, my Christ!

With this cry from the heart as damnation closes in on him, Faustus suddenly becomes not a cardboard necromancer but a man like ourselves, and the vigor of the emotion pulls apart Marlowe's singsong blank-verse line and makes Shakespearean tragedy possible. Marlowe himself, killed young in a tavern brawl, is a sacrificial figure like his Faustus, and out of his ashes arise the glories of the Elizabethan theater.

Shakespeare extends all Marlowe's possibilities further (perhaps to their limits), and without knowing Aristotle's writing succeeds in producing tragedies that fit the formula of the *Poetics* better than most Greek drama. Macbeth and Othello, Hamlet and Lear, are precisely men like ourselves, neither wholly good nor bad, brought low by a tragic shortcoming: Macbeth's ambition, Othello's credulity, Hamlet's indecision, and Lear's blind inability to tell love from its counterfeit. Shakespeare increases our ability to identify with the tragic action by weakening or discarding the supernatural motivation so strong in *Doctor Faustus*: the witches in *Macbeth* and the ghost in *Hamlet* are only trappings, the external forms of inner voices; and Othello and Lear battle not supernatural beings but malign human antagonists, Iago and the wicked daughters.

After Shakespeare, tragic drama in English runs downhill, turning into wilder and wilder bloody melodrama in the seventeenth century, becoming neoclassical and rather stiff in the joints in the eighteenth century, and leaving the theater entirely in the nineteenth century to become the unperformable closet dramas of poets. When tragedy is revived in our theater, the impetus comes from abroad, from Henrik Ibsen in Norway and Anton Chekhov in Russia. Here we have the new realistic tragedy of the middle class, with scenes in parlors rather than on battlements or blasted heaths. Again (as with the Greeks) we have no villains, only the protagonists' own crippling failures of insight, will, and love. Sometimes, in Chekhov, there is no crack of doom at all, only a fog of gloom and inertia settling over a household, as oxidation is sometimes the vivid flash of fire and sometimes the slow corruption of rust. Whatever rebirth is promised here will not spring up like Dionysus from the dismembered flesh, but will be a new growth, a better cherry orchard perhaps, out of decay.

With the Irish theater of John M. Synge and Sean O'Casey, we are back to something like Greek drama, with destiny again working its remorseless ways. Now, however, instead of a Greek chorus we have two vulgar old women, a fruit peddler and a charlady, foretelling the fates in *The Plough and the Stars*; we must accept as "men like ourselves" not Prince Hamlet or King Lear but those sodden frauds "Joxer" Daly and Captain Boyle in *Juno and the Paycock*; and in *Riders to the Sea*, instead of proud Queen Hecuba of Troy, we have the peasant woman Maurya (whose name sounds so much like the Greek *Moira*, Fate) giving us the ultimate Greek tragic acceptance after her last son has been drowned:

No man at all can be living for ever, and we must be satisfied.

In the tragic drama of our own time, the playwrights seem to be still consolidating the revolution of Ibsen, Chekhov, and the Irish playwrights; reshaping the tragic vision to fit a world of new classes and values, a world with neither villains nor heroes, a world that has lost much of its faith and most of its hope. Perhaps least typical of our time is T. S. Eliot's *Murder in the Cathedral*, a frankly religious work written to be performed in church, yet a tragic drama all the same. Here, telling the story of the martyrdom of St. Thomas à Beckett in the twelfth century, Eliot finds tragedy in the vision of man as a flawed agency of divine purpose.

Eugene O'Neill's *The Iceman Cometh* is a much more characteristic tragedy of our time in that it denies the existence of divine purpose, or any purpose, and shatters its characters, the derelicts of Harry Hope's saloon, with the discovery that all faith is a lying "pipe dream." Theodore Hickman, the salesman who sells them this discovery, is the "Iceman" of the title, a salesman of death, and when he is taken away by the police at the end, their shabby and pathetic hopes spring up again like some kind of unkillable life.

Tennessee Williams' *A Streetcar Named Desire* takes a highborn lady with the passions of Queen Phaedra in Euripides' *Hippolytus* on that streetcar ride into the slums of New Orleans, and through them into disgrace and madness. Like the inhabitants of Harry

Hope's saloon, Blanche DuBois has her "pipe dreams" (the plantation she grew up in is called "Belle Rêve," beautiful dream). When
she and her dreams are smashed at the end, in a scene of magnificent theatrical hokum, the hope may be for her sister's child by the
coarse animal Stanley Kowalski, growing up free of all such dreams.

If Blanche DuBois is like Queen Phaedra, driven by the arrows of
the love goddess Aphrodite to disgrace and madness, Willy Loman,
the salesman of Arthur Miller's *Death of a Salesman*, is King Oedipus with a sample case, pursuing his own identity and responsibility
("Was it my fault?") to his doom. Here too are the phony "pipe
dreams," but Willy has a true vision of a better sort of life, a life
where "a man is not a piece of fruit," to be nibbled and thrown
away. In his wife's big speech, the ultimate value of the human
personality is passionately if somewhat inelegantly affirmed:

> I don't say he's a great man. Willy Loman never made a lot of
> money. His name was never in the paper. He's not the finest char-
> acter that ever lived. But he's a human being, and a terrible
> thing is happening to him. So attention must be paid. He's not
> to be allowed to fall into his grave like an old dog. Attention,
> attention must be finally paid to such a person.

When they bury Willy at the end, that vision of human mean-
ingfulness survives.

Beyond a slut Phaedra and a slob Oedipus, the end of the line
would seem to be Samuel Beckett's *Waiting for Godot*, where the
very bottom of the social order, two ragged and half-crazed bums,
speak for us, and affirm the ultimate misery of the human condition, yet its deathless hope. Even Blanche DuBois tried to freshen
up the Kowalskis' upholstery, and Willy Loman saw buyers long
after they had stopped buying, but Vladimir and Estragon do not
act at all, they merely wait. What they wait for, Mr. "Godot," may
not exist, and it may not matter if he does or does not. Francis Fergusson, in *The Idea of a Theater*, has phrased the tragic rhythm of
action as "from Purpose through Passion to Perception." Here is an
authentic tragedy in which purpose, passion, and perception all
coalesce in one timeless static "waiting." Vladimir, the more intellectual of the two bums, affirms their sad pride in waiting in
words surprisingly reminiscent of Simonides' epitaph:

We have kept our appointment and that's an end to that. We are not saints, but we have kept our appointment. How many people can boast as much?

For us, as for the Greeks, tragedy has escaped the confines of drama, and we find it everywhere in our literature. One theme of lyric poetry that seems authentically tragic (as it was for Phaedra) is overpowering physical passion, fleshly love as tragic fate. It develops in Provençal poetry, and reaches its high point in Dante's *Divine Comedy*, when Francesca in Hell tells Dante, while Paolo weeps, of the moment when she and he sinned. Modern poetry has made us thoroughly familiar with this tragic and devastating passion. Sometimes it is all implied, as in the marvelous economy of William Butler Yeats's six-line poem "A Deep-Sworn Vow":

> Others because you did not keep
> That deep-sworn vow have been friends of mine;
> Yet always when I look death in the face,
> When I clamber to the heights of sleep,
> Or when I grow excited with wine,
> Suddenly I meet your face.

At other times it is defined so physically that we are reminded of Dante, as in John Crowe Ransom's "The Equilibrists," from which I quote a stanza that may take us even further back, to the Reliving Dionysus:

> Great lovers lie in Hell, the stubborn ones
> Infatuate of the flesh upon the bones;
> Stuprate, they rend each other when they kiss,
> The pieces kiss again, no end to this.

Some of the same tragic passion appears in Negro blues songs, understated in the words but overwhelming in the music, as when Jimmy Rushing, accompanied by Sam Price at the piano, sings Leroy Carr's "How Long":

> If I could holler like a mountain jack,
> Go up on the mountain, and call my baby back.
> Baby, how long? Baby, how long? Baby, how long?

In our fiction, we have the old tragic pattern of pride and fall, but with strange new varieties of prides and falls. Captain Ahab in Melville's *Moby-Dick* is like the mad infatuate Shakespeare heroes,

Lear or the later Othello. He has a new sort of heroic antagonist, however, no longer a malignant villain, but blind wild nature embodied in the great white whale. In Ahab's frenzied desire to "Strike through the mask!" and get at the ultimate evil of the universe, he is carried down to death lashed to the great whale. Only a transformed Ishmael, riding on a coffin, survives to tell the tale. The bitter intellectual protagonists of Dostoevsky all in their different fashions believe that they are above or beyond society, like King Oedipus. Then like him they are smashed down below it, with some possibility of beginning their regeneration there.

In stories like Mann's *Death in Venice* and Kafka's "The Judgment," we get a kind of Freudian tragedy of repression. It is, however, a kind of tragedy that Euripides knew all about in *The Bacchae*, where puritanic King Pentheus represses his sensual nature until the god Dionysus, disguised as a handsome stranger, releases all that he has kept hidden and leads him to disgrace and death. Mann's Gustave Aschenbach similarly represses his sensual nature and presents an image of stiff rectitude to the world, until the appearance of the beautiful Polish boy Tadzio similarly breaks down his defenses and destroys him. Kafka's Georg Bendemann despised his old father in his dirty underwear, as Pentheus at first despised the effeminate stranger. Suddenly the old father, like Euripides' stranger, turns out to conceal a divine omnipotence; he cries out, "I sentence you to death by drowning," and Georg dashes out and hurls himself off a bridge.

In other modern fiction the only transgression is the aspiration of the poor to rise to a degree of freedom and happiness. Perhaps the most tragic moment in James Joyce's *Ulysses* is the scene where Stephen Dedalus sees his ragged younger sister Dilly at a bookstall buying a coverless French Primer for a penny, and realizes that she has the same aspirations he has, but that he can only save himself by letting her sink.

> She is drowning. Agenbite. Save her. Agenbite. All against us. She will drown me with her, eyes and hair. Lank coils of seaweed hair around me, my heart, my soul. Salt green death.
> We.
> Agenbite of inwit. Inwit's agenbite.
> Misery! Misery!

Suffering the "agenbite of inwit" (an Anglo-Saxon equivalent for "remorse of conscience"), in one tragic moment Stephen both accepts his common humanity and denies it out of desperate necessity. In Dylan Thomas' beautiful story "One Warm Saturday," the poor young man finds his true love in a wild drunken evening and then loses her in a nightmarish tenement house. The story ends:

> The light of the one weak lamp in a rusty circle fell across the brickheaps and the broken wood and the dust that had been houses once, where the small and hardly known and never-to-be-forgotten people of the dirty town had lived and loved and died and, always, lost.

Nor are the rich without their tragedies. In Shirley Jackson's *The Sundial*, a fantasy about the end of the world, the matriarch Mrs. Halloran brings on her death by donning a golden crown, precisely as King Agamemnon in the *Oresteia* of Aeschylus incurs the wrath of the gods and his own death by treading on the carpet of royal purple. In James Gould Cozzens' *By Love Possessed*, the upright and wealthy lawyer Arthur Winner is brought through suffering to feel something of the love and charity of the poor and dispossessed, a "winner" only of insight through humiliation.

The same tragic patterns confront us everywhere in our newspapers. We see the fated love of great princes in the British royal family (as though it existed to remind us of that lost Shakespearean world), first in the heartbreaking abdication broadcast of Edward VIII, then in the silent smoldering tragedy of Princess Margaret. Our own great tragic princes include the ruined financier, the fallen theatrical star, the washed-out sports champion with whom we began this inquiry. The next shattered Hollywood romance may be for our time as grand a doomed passion as that of Paolo and Francesca. The tragic movement is as visible in life as in art, since it comes into art from life. If Orson Welles's film *Citizen Kane* was tragic, so was the life of William Randolph Hearst that inspired it; if O'Neill's autobiographical plays and F. Scott Fitzgerald's autobiographical novels are tragic, so, visibly, were their lives. Below these famous figures there are the sordid tragedies and nameless sufferers of the tabloids: a daily creation of grimy Clytemnestras, Orestes, Electras, and Phaedras.

When King Farouk of Egypt is driven from his throne we feel only the poetic justice that a wicked and dissolute wastrel has at last been humbled, a sense of relief and restoration of faith rather than any tragic exultation. But when Sherman Adams, a man like ourselves, neither wholly good nor wholly bad, an image of rectitude concealing a tragic shortcoming, is toppled from his high seat of power, we have true Aristotelian tragedy, and can feel pity and a kind of terror. When the people of Athens got bored with hearing Aristides called "the Just" and sentenced him to banishment, it was not simply spite and envy of an upright man. It was the same tragic sense they had of Pentheus and Hippolytus, and we of Adams, that too great a display of perfection challenges the gods, that pride goeth before a fall.

We return then, finally, to the mysterious satisfaction of tragedy, the question St. Augustine raised so many centuries ago. For Aristotle, as we have seen, it lay in catharsis, the arousing and purging of pity and terror. For Hegel it was a sheer intellectual pleasure in the unfolding of the dialectic. Some, like Lucretius, have argued cynically that it is no more than a kind of sadistic pleasure we take in the sufferings of others. Schopenhauer believed with ultimate pessimism that the hero of tragedy atones for "the crime of existence itself." In Freud's view, the satisfaction of tragedy is that the lower impulses he calls id find symbolic gratification in the hero's misdeeds, while the higher part of the personality he calls superego finds *its* symbolic gratification in seeing the hero punished (and through him, the personality's own id). Other psychological theory has talked similarly of our "empathy" or "projection" onto the protagonist's crime and punishment.

Kenneth Burke, in *The Philosophy of Literary Form*, has defined all art as the arousing and fulfilling of expectations. If we accept that basic conception of form, tragedy must always have a kind of inevitability. The Elizabethans seem sometimes to have conceived of it as merely a story that ended in death. There is similarly a tendency in our own time to see it as merely a sad ending, and perhaps to complain that there is so much misery in real life that art should be cheerful. Not everything ending unhappily, however, is tragedy; it must satisfy the expectations it has aroused. An example of a work that sets out deliberately to violate these expectations is a remarkable French movie of a few years back called *Forbidden Games*. The audience is led to believe, by all sorts of suggestions, that the rustic Romeo-and-Juliet youths of two feuding families will marry, reconcile the families, and bring happiness to a homeless child. The young people in fact do not marry, the families are not reconciled, and the child returns to misery. The audience is left at the end horribly wrenched and moved, but feeling only a terrible pathos, none of the inevitability, rightness, and grandeur of tragedy.

The awful deaths of children in the news are pathetic in this fashion rather than tragic. The grisly kidnaping and murder of the Lindbergh baby bore no relationship to anything the poor infant had done, nor was the horrible Chicago parochial school fire a moral judgment of any sort. These frightful accidents move us deeply, even to tears, but they are essentially meaningless and ugly where tragic death is meaningful and even beautiful.

The best explanation I know of the nature of tragedy is Herbert Weisinger's *Tragedy and the Paradox of the Fortunate Fall*, a book to which my own understanding of the subject is considerably indebted. Weisinger insists that "the tragic protagonist must be made to achieve victory at the moment of his deepest despair." Tragedy, he reminds us, is "man's most vehement protest against meaninglessness"; it gives us "the sense of assurance, achieved through suffering, of rational order"; it proclaims that "man is free, but he is free within the limits set for us by his condition as man."

It is in terms of some such affirmations as these, I think, that the tragic vision is ultimately so rewarding. If it teaches us human limitation, it also teaches us human possibility. Hobbes reminds us that the life of man has been characteristically "solitary, poor, nasty, brutish, and short." Tragedy answers that it has frequently been all of that, but that it is never ludicrous or meaningless. How far this tragic vision of man is, despite its recognition of all the outer degradation and the inner evil, from views of man in some contemporary literature as "Angry" or "Beat." Tragedy reaffirms a nobility and grandeur in the human condition, even Longinus' sublimity. If it is man's fate to go down inevitably into suffering and death, some exultation nevertheless rises to the skies.

Stances Toward
Mass Culture

[1960]

IN THE FRANTIC burgeoning of mass culture in our time, what can we define as its ideals, dangers, and limitations? In my opinion, the most important ideal is pluralism, making a wide variety of aesthetic goods available, rather than lifting us all half an inch by the great collective bootstrap. That is why paperbacks and long-playing records seem so hopeful a tendency despite their defects; *Marjorie Morningstar* and *Babysittin' Boogie* are available in their millions, but *The Philosophy of Literary Form* and *Don Giovanni* (not to speak of *Fat Mama Blues*) are available in their thousands. Even the magazine situation is dreary and discouraging but still triumphantly pluralist; there is a magazine, however tiny, subsidized, or absurd, to publish every kind of writing, to furnish any sort of reading or looking (within the limits of the law) that any few readers or lookers want. One has only to compare the situation with England, which has one little magazine to every fifty of ours, or with Russia, which has not had one since Mayakovsky's day, to see the virtues of pluralism. It is only when the expenses of production become prohibitive, with a newspaper or film company, a radio or television station, that a wide variety of aesthetic goods becomes impossible, and only ventures that will satisfy many thousands or millions are feasible. Then it is necessary to talk of improving standards, raising levels, educating public taste, taking the initiative for better quality, and such functions more proper to a benign tyranny than to our anarchic cultural democracy.

The second ideal, about which I am somewhat more dubious but still hopeful, is the natural evolution of taste, given a variety of possibilities. (In other words, *it* depends on pluralism, although pluralism, as a good in itself, would make sense even if taste were known to be static). This is the assumption that a certain number of those who read and enjoy *The Deer Park* will go on to read, and prefer, *The Possessed*; that some will comparably graduate from rock 'n' roll to traditional blues. This happens naturally at school age (although not in every case) and the ideal assumes its happening at every age. Here the evidence is rather mixed. William Phillips, in an article in *Partisan Review*, describes the question as "the old senseless argument about whether a man who listens to popular tunes has taken the first step to Schoenberg." This may, however, be a very important question for the future of our culture.

Some years ago the Book-of-the-Month Club sent around a circular listing its selections from the year of its founding, 1926, to 1949. The circular clearly made the point (which I do not think it was designed to make) that these had worsened annually, from books like Sylvia Townsend Warner's *Lolly Willowes* and Elinor Wylie's *Orphan Angel* in 1926, to Frances Gaither's *Double Muscadine* and the Gilbreths' *Cheaper by the Dozen* in 1949. Over the years since, despite (or because of) the presence of such learned fellows as Gilbert Highet on the profit-sharing board of judges, the selections seem to have continued to deteriorate. If someone had subscribed and taken the selections over the past thirty years, *his* taste would not have evolved onward and upward. But the turnover is very high; how could we find out about those who learned to read books for pleasure as subscribers, then resigned from the club to read better books on their own?

The B.B.C. radio, with its three programs designed for three levels of taste, would seem a perfect device for encouraging this sort of cultural mobility. Yet I wonder what percentage of listeners of mature years graduated from family comedy on the Light to sea shanties on the Home to translations of Bulgarian poetry on the Third? How many slid slowly downward? Now, unfortunately, the Third has been curtailed, and with the increased cost of television production and a competing commercial channel, it has not been possible for the B.B.C. to set up anything of the sort for television. Here for the first time some planned range of availability was created in a mass medium, but we know too little about its cultural results.

The third ideal of mass culture I take from a letter Patrick D. Hazard wrote to me some time ago, in connection with remarks I had published about the ironic mode. He wrote: "Now it seems to me that a great many intellectuals in America have achieved a viable irony, but I wonder how the great mass who are no longer folk and not yet people can find a footing for their ironic stance. Do any of the following seem to you footholds?" He then proceeded to list such newer comic performers as Mort Sahl and Jonathan Winters, such older comic performers as Groucho Marx and Fred Allen, and such miscellaneous phenomena as Al Capp, *The Threepenny Opera*, and *Humbug* magazine. His comment on the list was: "These things seem to question in one way or another some aspect of flatulence in popular culture, its sentimentality, fake elegance, phoney egalitarianism, or its perennial playpen atmosphere."

I did not know the answer to the question then and do not know it now, but I present Hazard's question and comment to raise the possibility of a third ideal. This is that mass culture throws up its own criticism, in performers of insight, wit, and talent, and in forms of irony and satire, to enable some of the audience to break through mass culture itself into a broader or deeper set of aesthetic values. Again, I much prefer this sort of evolutionary possibility to types of patronizing enlightenment. We do well to be wary when a former *Time* editor like Thomas Griffith writes *The Waist-High Culture* to ask whether we haven't sold our souls "for a mess of pottage that goes snap, crackle and pop," or television producer David Susskind tells *Life*:

> I'm an intellectual who cares about television. There are some good things on it, tiny atolls in the oceans of junk. . . . You get mad at what you really care about—like your wife. I'm mad at TV because I really love it and it's lousy. It's a very beautiful

woman who looks abominable. The only way to fix it is to clean
out the pack who are running it and put in some brainy guys.

We assume that if Griffith ran *Time* it would crackle less, that
Susskind is the sort of brainy lover TV needs. I would sooner rest
my hopes in Groucho Marx, who does not describe himself as an
intellectual, or the late Fred Allen, who had a cleansing bitterness and despair about the media themselves, and wasn't cam-
paigning for Frank Stanton's job. If there are such footings as
Hazard suggests for an ironic stance in mass culture, let them
not crusade under our feet.

The dangers of mass culture are much easier to define than the
ideals. The foremost one, which may negate all the ideals, is an
overpowering narcotic effect, relaxing the tired mind and tran-
quilizing the anxious. Genuine art is demanding and difficult,
often unpleasant, nagging at the mind and stretching the nerves
taut. So much of mass culture envelops the audience in a warm
bath, making no demands except that we all glow with pleasure
and comfort. It is this that may negate the range of possibility
(the bath is warmer at the shallow end), keep taste static or even
deteriorate it a little, muffle the few critical and ironic sounds
being made. That premature cultural critic Homer knew all about
this effect, at various times calling it Lotus Eaters, Calypso, Circe,
and the Sirens, and he just barely got our hero through intact.

An obvious source of danger is the cults. In one direction we
have the cult of the folk. Just ten years ago, I published an article
called "The American Folksy" in *Theatre Arts*, protesting that
we were being overwhelmed by an avalanche of pseudo-folk corn.
I turn out not to have been very prophetic. What I then took
to be the height of something like the great tulip craze can now
be seen to have been only the first tentative beginnings of something so vast and offensive that it dwarfs historical parallels. I
named a half-dozen folksy singers of the time, but could not have
guessed that a decade later there would be hundreds if not
thousands, that magazines would be devoted to guitar and banjo
styles, that the production of washtub basses would be an American industry. I certainly could not have predicted Elvis Presley. I
mention this failure of imagination now only to explain why the

ramifying vertical combine that lives by falsifying America's cultural past seems to me a major deterrent to any of the hopes for mass culture.

Opposed to the cult of the folk, which identifies (however falsely) with a tradition, and blows hot, or passionate, is the cult of the hip, which denies (however falsely) having any tradition, and blows cool. At the juvenile end it tells sick jokes, glorying in in the impassivity of:

> "Mrs. Brown, can Johnny come out and play ball?"
> "But you children know he has no arms or legs."
> "That's O.K. We want to use him for second base."

At higher levels it admits wryly to Jules Feiffer's truths, professes Zen, or joins Norman Mailer in glorifying the Negro orgasm, making what he called in *Dissent* "the imaginative journey into the tortured marijuana-racked mind and genitalia of a hipster daring to live on the edge of the most dangerous of the Negro worlds." At this point, obviously, cool has become pretty hot, an outlaw folk tradition has been established, and perhaps both these polar cults are recognizable as the same sort of fantasy identification. To the extent that mass culture permits, encourages, and thrives on these adolescent gratifications, it is as spurious and mendacious as its harshest critics claim.

One more danger inherent in mass culture, and perhaps the most menacing one, is the existence of a captive audience with no escape. In regard to art, it is not much of a problem; many will sit through worse than they expected, and a few will sit through better than they desire. As a machinery for selling us consumer goods, using all the resources of a prostituted psychology and sociology, mass culture becomes more menacing, although here too it seems to throw up its counterstatements. Against a million voices stridently shouting "Buy!" the tiny neo-Thoreauvian voice of J. K. Galbraith whispers "Reduce your wants," and is immediately amplified by a book club and blurbs from a number of magazines that would not last a week if his advice were heeded. It is when the same technique is used to sell us politics that our status as a captive audience to mass media becomes menacing;

a Barry Goldwater today but a Big Brother or a Big Daddy tomorrow.

At this point we are informed that the fashionable cult of New Conservatism, with its scorn for our worship of the mob and the mob's brittle toys, will save us, if only we elect to follow Edmund Burke and Calhoun instead of those demagogues Jefferson and Paine. The corrective here is reading the tribute to Roy Campbell that Russell Kirk published in *The Sewanee Review,* and discovering that Kirk's heart's vision is not Edmund Burke orating nobly in the House of Commons, but Roy Campbell spanking a small effeminate Marxist poet on a public lecture platform. In short, New Conservatism yearns masochistically for its fantasy storm troopers, and Kirk and his fellows are less the doctor than the disease.

Some of the limitations of mass culture have already been suggested. One absolute limitation is the Law of Raspberry Jam, that the wider you spread it the thinner it is. Another is the nature of art itself. Advancing sensibility, stretching the limits of form, purifying the language of the tribe, genuine art is always for an elite of education (which does not mean formal education), sensibility, and taste. When art's freshness has grown somewhat stale, diluted by imitators and popularizers, its audience widens, although true art will always continue to demand more than a mass audience cares to give it.

A special limitation, not inevitable and not universal, is the timidity of those in positions of authority in the mass media. Jerry Lewis, of all people, wrote in the *New York Times Magazine:*

> Unfortunately, TV fell into the well-manicured hands of the Madison Avenue bully boys, who, awed by the enormousness of the monster, began to "run scared." They were easy prey for the new American weapon—the pressure group.

Steve Allen's reply in the same symposium suggests that we confront no simple matter of pressure or censorship, that here horses break themselves with alacrity and great civic responsibility. Allen writes:

There are, frankly, a few things I joke about in private that I do not touch upon on the air, but this implies no feeling of frustration. I realize that some tenets of my personal philosophy would antagonize the majority without educating them; hence, no good could come of experimenting with such subjects.

Matching the timidity of the producers is the ignorance of the consumers. Who knows what they might want if they knew what there was to want, if they knew what they didn't know? This again is a special and perhaps transistory limitation. As education spreads and leisure increases, some of our mass audiences may acquire, if not what we call "taste," at least a wider knowledge of cultural possibility. The well-poisoner is an unlovely figure, but the responsibility of those poisoning *these* reservoirs from which millions drink is comparably greater. What defense has an ignorant and eager reader, buying *The Origin of Species* in the Everyman edition, against its introductory assurance that authoritative scientists no longer believe these things? He has scarcely heard of Darwin, how is he to know that W. R. Thompson is not the voice of modern science? If he happens to read T. H. Robsjohn-Gibbings' book attacking modern architecture and design, it is the confession of a contemporary designer to what the reader has always rather suspected; he is not apt to have encountered Mr. Robsjohn-Gibbings' hi-fi unit with Doric columns in a decorator's studio. Because it knows no better, in short, the mass audience is condemned to the fate of never knowing any better.

The final limitation of mass culture I would suggest is its tendency to sanctify the old, safe, and official. In his eighties, Robert Frost becomes the bard of Washington and all America throbs to his absurd views about American painting and other matters. In his eighties, Carl Sandburg enthralls a joint session of Congress with a slushy eulogy to Lincoln. I quote what I take to be an innocent irony in the *Times* correspondent's account of the latter event:

> In its kindest of moods, Congress has little patience for poets, and normally it can scarcely sit still for Presidents or heads of foreign states. Mr. Sandburg, however, held them as they have not been held since General of the Army Douglas MacArthur's address to a joint session.

Any serious young American artist who could pack his audience into a closet (like young Robert Frost, who could not get his first book of verse published in this country) has the consolation of knowing that if he has the good fortune to live long enough he can become a Grand Old Man, and just at the time when he has nothing left to say a thicket of microphones and cameras will enable him to say it to the world.

We come, finally, to the matter of taking a stance or stances. Each of us confronts mass culture in a number of roles. My own include customer, parent, journalist, critic, teacher of literature. The role of teacher seems the best one from which to tackle the problem, since the college teacher of literature is not only assumed to be a custodian of traditional values, but must deal with the new values in his day-to-day contact with what students read and write. He cannot entirely ignore them or wash his hands of them. I would propose that there are at least six different things he must do about mass culture, varying with the quality and promise of the specimen involved, the differing needs of students, and his own needs and perhaps moods. I list them by the operative verbs, using literary examples as much as possible.

Reject. This is a traditional function of the critic of mass culture, and it can be performed in a variety of moods, from the high good fun of H. L. Mencken whacking one or another fatuosity of the booboisie to the owlish pomposity of recent *American Mercury* pundits. The best current example of rejection is Leslie Fiedler, who has written that the writer's proper role is a nay-saying and destructive one, that he should not hesitate to bite the hand that feeds him. Fiedler's slogan for Hollywood and TV is "We must destroy their destructiveness." As a teacher, I would reserve this rejection for the real junk, Mickey Spillane and *Peyton Place.* Here, it seems to me, any sort of undercutting or resistance is legitimate, short of actually snatching the book out of the student's hands and pitching it into the garbage. Let the teacher rant and rave, appeal to his authority, the student's shame, or the ghost of Henry James. Let him expose and deride this pernicious trash in every way possible. The really hopeless is only a small percentage of the total output of mass culture, however, which allows the teacher to save some of his energy for other operations, and to contribute a small sum to a subscription to replace Leslie Fiedler's teeth when they wear out.

Embrace. This too is a traditional function, and we have had intellectual cults of the popular arts, of Chaplin or Keaton, Krazy Kat or Donald Duck, since there were popular arts. Reuel Denney's article on Pogo, reprinted in his book *The Astonished Muse,* is a fine example of the passionate professorial embrace. Denney shows learnedly that the strip is "a study in the disintegration of the New Deal phase of the Democratic party," that "if the political stance of the strip is Democratic and Steffens-like, the literary stance is post-Joycean, and the psychological stance is post-Freudian." Poor Albert Alligator becomes a parataxis of oral aggression, although at this point I begin to suspect that Denney is having a pull at the reader's leg. It was very shrewd of George P. Elliott to make his impossible sociologist in *Parktilden Village* the creator, as the result of his researches, of a cartoon strip that appealed to every cultural level. George Orwell was in something of this position, studying boys' books with loving attention, then himself writing a superior boys' book in 1984, which sold its million copies in paperback. The products of mass culture one can wholeheartedly welcome and embrace are probably as small a percentage as those one ought wholeheartedly to reject. I would suggest such rare best-sellers as *The Catcher in the Rye,* hovering on the edge of serious literature, such sparkling musical comedies as *Guys and Dolls* and *Pajama Game,* and comedians and comic strips to taste.

Ignore. This is perhaps more a teacher's dodge than any other. Several years ago at Bennington, David Riesman made some remarks (which I daresay he has since published) about the tyranny of the curricular. When he was an undergraduate, he said, his intellectual solace was that he could read Marx and Freud, which *they* (his teachers) didn't know about or didn't approve, and thus have an area of his mind and life that Harvard could not regiment. At a place like Bennington, he said, Marx and Freud would immediately be made the subject of courses, as would anything else in which the students showed interest. I sat in the audience trying to get the arrow out of my throat, since that year I was teaching a course in Marx and Freud (along with Darwin and Frazer), and I had just organized a lively faculty seminar on rock 'n' roll, at which we told the students what it was all about. The only comfort I had was that however tyrannous the curricular, there was always *something* the students could block off privately; if they were being taught Marx and "Fats" Domino, perhaps they were pursuing Racine and Mozart on the sly. In any case, they had *some* underground culture the faculty would do best not to know about. I find this tactic of ignoring very useful in regard to West Coast poetry (I suspect that that book of verse called *Howl* circulates surreptitiously at Bennington, but I have never made any attempt to find out), in regard to the intricacies of modern cool jazz ("He doesn't dig *Mulligan!*"), and most particularly in regard to any combination of the two. Probably I would be better off, we would all be better off, ignoring more, letting them keep private whatever current work speaks to their condition, letting education grow up without daily watering and all those infernal sun lamps.

Improve. Here we have the traditional pedagogic tactic of using what the student likes as a guidepost to something better. Ah, one can sigh in relief, at last some *constructive* criticism, not that irresponsible ignoring. It is this attitude of exploring mass culture for signs of hope and maturity that has distinguished *Commentary* over the years. I think of such articles as Robert Warshow's "Paul, the Horror Comics, and Dr. Wertham," reprinted in Rosenberg and White's *Mass Culture*, and Norman Podhoretz's "Our Changing Ideals, as Seen on TV," reprinted in Brossard's *The Scene Before You*. A sign of the awareness of the problem by a group of English teachers is the recent organization of a new section of the Modern Language Association, dealing with Literature and General Culture. An organizing statement that was circulated before the meeting expressed the hope that by studying mass culture, "We may come to learn what clearly separates the best-seller from the work of distinction and, if our aims become in part educational, offer our students the necessary exercises in discrimination." Again, I am wary of the big battalions. Teaching this sort of discrimination has always been the teacher's function, as it has always been the critic's. The works that call for it are those mixed bundles that cannot be rejected or embraced and should not be ignored, works of genuine imagination flawed by crassness, hokum, or sheer want of craft. I think of the novels of Norman Mailer and the plays of Tennessee Williams. What attracts the student or reader to them is better available in Dostoevsky and Chekhov, in Fielding and Shakespeare, but they may be precisely the bridges to get there, and in any case are worth study in their own terms.

Replace. Beyond all this, the college teacher of literature as a custodian of traditional value has to remember what he has in his custody. John Crowe Ransom, in his 1958 Phi Beta Kappa address "Our Age Among the Ages," reprinted in *Kenyon Review,* came to a civilized and pluralist but deeply pessimistic conclusion. He wrote:

> At any rate, the old ways of life have been disappearing much too rapidly for comfort, and we are in a great cultural confusion. Many millions of underprivileged persons now have income and leisure which they did not have before. They have the means to achieve the best properties of a culture, if they know how to spend their money wisely. And it is a fact that they spend handsomely on education. Now, I am in the education business, and I can report my observations on that. It is as if a sudden invasion of barbarians had overrun the educational institution; except that the barbarians in this case are our neighbors and friends, and sometimes they are our own children, or they are ourselves, they are some of us gathered here on this very fine occasion. We should not fear them; they are not foreigners, nor our enemies. But in the last resort education is a democratic process, in which the courses are subject to the election of the applicants, and a course even when it has been elected can never rise above the intellectual passion of its pupils, or their comparative indifference. So, with the new generation of students, Milton declines in the curriculum; even Shakespeare has lost heavily; Homer and Virgil are practically gone. The literary interest of the students today is ninety per cent in the literature of their own age; more often than not it is found in books which do not find entry into the curriculum, and are beneath the standard which your humble servants, the teachers of literature, are trying to maintain. Chaucer and Spenser and Milton, with their respective contemporaries, will have their secure existence henceforth in the library, and of course in the love and intimate acquaintaince of a certain academic

community, and there they will stay except for possible periods
when there is a revival of the literature of our own antiquity. Our
literary culture for a long time is going to exist in a sprawling
fashion, with minority pockets of old-style culture, and some sort
of majority culture of a new and indeterminate style. It is a free
society, and I should expect that the rights of minorities will be
as secure as the rights of individuals.

Ransom's prediction may be exactly accurate, yet the teacher cannot reconcile himself to a minority status for his values in his own
classroom, however reconciled he is to it everywhere else. He must
ceaselessly bring to the attention of his students the greatest literature he knows. It is not easy for an ill-educated man to teach Homer
and Virgil, Greek drama and the Bible, Milton and Shakespeare,
as I can testify, but it is essential, and in our curricula Darwin and
Marx, ballads and blues, must have a place but not the primary
place. "The best that has been thought and known," as Arnold
somewhat pompously put it, is even more vital for college students
these days when they seem to come already knowing all the worst.

Warn. Here the teacher as critic of mass culture needs a good
stout voice, along with the prescience of Ortega y Gasset and the
bitterness of Randolph Bourne. The evidence, from Q. D. Leavis'
Fiction and the Reading Public in 1939 to Margaret Dalziel's *Popular Fiction 100 Years Ago* in 1959, suggests that in some significant
respects the standards of mass culture are deteriorating over the
centuries, and that instead of flying the kites of our hopes for evolution and awakening, we had better dig in and try to keep things
from getting worse than the Victorian penny-dreadful. The notable
voice here is Randall Jarrell's, and in "The Appalling Taste of the
Age" in the *Saturday Evening Post*'s Adventures of the Mind series,
he warned us in the most violent terms that the digest and the
revised simplified version menace not only high literary culture but
the art of reading itself, the use of the written word. In the most
terrifying chapter of *Capital*, "The Working Day," Marx told us
of English laboring children so brutalized and degraded by working
twelve and sixteen hours a day in the mills that they did not know
the name of the Queen, or the story of Noah, or where London was.
Now Jarrell tells us of our own children, raised in comfort and love,
getting the most expensive education in the world, who do not

know who Charlemagne was, or the story of Jonah, or what comes before E in the alphabet. Warn? One should bellow and curse and call down doom like the prophet Jeremiah.

Yes, but of course also reject and embrace, ignore, improve, and replace. The teacher and the critic of mass culture cannot simply reduce himself to one attitude, but must keep varying the attack, like a young pitcher learning to supplement his high school fast ball with a curve and a change of pace. Among the dangers of mass culture is the danger to the critic of atrophy, not to call it *rigor mortis*: of hardening in one fixed position. The comparable danger to the writer or artist is being squeezed dry too fast, like a television comedian, or brought up into the big time too soon, like a young fighter. The defense in both cases is wariness, and periodic rites of withdrawal. The ultimate ideal of mass culture is the ideal of the whole culture (to return to the anthropologists' term), something nearer the good life for all mankind. Here Homer and the Athenian tragic dramatists are useful in reminding us of basic limitation, of men's flawed, blind, and mortal nature, and of the ironies of hope and expectation. We are not the good society, but we do have a vision of it, and that vision is a pluralist one, in which many different forms of satisfaction, including clearly spurious ones, can coexist peacefully. Mass culture is here to stay, but so, I hope, are those of us who want another sort of culture for ourselves and for anyone else who wants it, or who can be educated, led, or cajoled into wanting it. Insofar as all of mass culture represents someone's organization of experience into what he intends as meaningful and pleasurable patterns, it is all a kind of shabby poetry, but we dare not forget that there are other kinds of poetry too.

About the Author

STANLEY EDGAR HYMAN was born in New York City in 1919. He took a degree at Syracuse University in 1940 and in the same year joined *The New Yorker* as a staff writer, a position he still holds. In 1945 he became a member of the literature faculty of Bennington College. Since 1961 Mr. Hyman has contributed regular lead reviews to *The New Leader*. He edited *The Critical Performance* (1956), a collection of essays by various writers; his own earlier books are *The Armed Vision* (1948), *Poetry and Criticism* (1961), *The Tangled Bank* (1962), and *Nathanael West* (1962). Mr. Hyman and his wife, the novelist Shirley Jackson, live in North Bennington, Vermont. They have two sons and two daughters.

STANLEY EDGAR HYMAN was born in New York City in 1919. He took a degree at Syracuse University in 1940 and in the same year joined *The New Yorker* as a staff writer, a position he still holds. In 1945 he became a member of the literature faculty of Bennington College. Since 1961 Mr. Hyman has contributed regular book reviews to *The New Leader*. He edited *The Critical Performance* (1956), a collection of essays by various writers; his own other books are *The Armed Vision* (1948), *Poetry and Criticism* (1961), *The Tangled Bank* (1962), and *Nathanael West* (1962). Mr. Hyman and his wife, the novelist Shirley Jackson, live in North Bennington, Vermont. They have two sons and two daughters.